SO-AIU-666

BUSINESS ETHICS
94/95

Sixth Edition

Editor

John E. Richardson
Pepperdine University

Dr. John E. Richardson is Associate Professor of Management in the School of Business and Management at Pepperdine University. He is president of his own consulting firm and has consulted with organizations such as Bell and Howell, Dayton-Hudson, Epson, and the U.S. Navy, as well as with various service, nonprofit, and franchise organizations. Dr. Richardson is a member of the American Management Association, the American Marketing Association, the Society for Business Ethics, and Beta Gamma Sigma honorary business fraternity.

A Annual Editions
A Library of Information from the Public Press

Cover illustration by Mike Eagle

The Dushkin Publishing Group, Inc.
Sluice Dock, Guilford, Connecticut 06437

The Annual Editions Series

Annual Editions is a series of over 60 volumes designed to provide the reader with convenient, low-cost access to a wide range of current, carefully selected articles from some of the most important magazines, newspapers, and journals published today. Annual Editions are updated on an annual basis through a continuous monitoring of over 300 periodical sources. All Annual Editions have a number of features designed to make them particularly useful, including topic guides, annotated tables of contents, unit overviews, and indexes. For the teacher using Annual Editions in the classroom, an Instructor's Resource Guide with test questions is available for each volume.

VOLUMES AVAILABLE

Africa
Aging
American Foreign Policy
American Government
American History, Pre-Civil War
American History, Post-Civil War
Anthropology
Biology
Business Ethics
Canadian Politics
Child Growth and Development
China
Comparative Politics
Computers in Education
Computers in Business
Computers in Society
Criminal Justice
Drugs, Society, and Behavior
Dying, Death, and Bereavement
Early Childhood Education
Economics
Educating Exceptional Children
Education
Educational Psychology
Environment
Geography
Global Issues
Health
Human Development
Human Resources
Human Sexuality
India and South Asia
International Business
Japan and the Pacific Rim

Latin America
Life Management
Macroeconomics
Management
Marketing
Marriage and Family
Mass Media
Microeconomics
Middle East and the Islamic World
Money and Banking
Multicultural Education
Nutrition
Personal Growth and Behavior
Physical Anthropology
Psychology
Public Administration
Race and Ethnic Relations
Russia, Eurasia, and Central/Eastern
    Europe
Social Problems
Sociology
State and Local Government
Third World
Urban Society
Violence and Terrorism
Western Civilization,
    Pre-Reformation
Western Civilization,
    Post-Reformation
Western Europe
World History, Pre-Modern
World History, Modern
World Politics

Library of Congress Cataloging in Publication Data
Main entry under title: Annual Editions: Business ethics. 1994/95.
        1. Business ethics—Periodicals. I. Richardson, John E., comp. II. Title: Business ethics.
ISBN 1–56134–266–1   658.408

© 1994 by The Dushkin Publishing Group, Inc., Guilford, CT 06437

Copyright law prohibits the reproduction, storage, or transmission in any form by any means of any portion of this publication without the express written permission of The Dushkin Publishing Group, Inc., and of the copyright holder (if different) of the part of the publication to be reproduced. The Guidelines for Classroom Copying endorsed by Congress explicitly state that unauthorized copying may not be used to create, to replace, or to substitute for anthologies, compilations, or collective works.

Annual Editions® is a Registered Trademark of The Dushkin Publishing Group, Inc.

Sixth Edition

Printed in the United States of America

Printed on Recycled Paper

Editors/Advisory Board

EDITOR

John E. Richardson
Pepperdine University

ADVISORY BOARD

Members of the Advisory Board are instrumental in the final selection of articles for each edition of Annual Editions. Their review of articles for content, level, currentness, and appropriateness provides critical direction to the editor and staff. We think you'll find their careful consideration well reflected in this volume.

Cameron Bailey
Middlesex Community College

Donald J. Beelick
Wright State University

John Bunch
Kansas State University

Archie B. Carroll
University of Georgia

James G. Coe
Taylor University

Clifford Darden
Pepperdine University

Gerald R. Ferrera
Bentley College

Nancie Fimbel
San Jose State University

David J. Fritzsche
Florida International University

William J. Kehoe
University of Virginia

Robert A. Larmer
University of New Brunswick

Timothy C. Mazur
Santa Clara University

Thomas Mulligan
Brock University

Patrick E. Murphy
University of Notre Dame

Lisa H. Newton
Fairfield University

Donald P. Robin
University of Southern Mississippi

Gary-Lou Upton
University of Richmond

Michael Van Breda
Southern Methodist University

David Vogel
University of California, Berkeley

Jon West
University of Miami

STAFF

Ian A. Nielsen, Publisher
Brenda S. Filley, Production Manager
Roberta Monaco, Editor
Addie Raucci, Administrative Editor
Cheryl Greenleaf, Permissions Editor
Diane Barker, Editorial Assistant
Lisa Holmes-Doebrick, Administrative Coordinator
Charles Vitelli, Designer
Shawn Callahan, Graphics
Steve Shumaker, Graphics
Lara M. Johnson, Graphics
Libra A. Cusack, Typesetting Supervisor
Juliana Arbo, Typesetter

To the Reader

In publishing ANNUAL EDITIONS we recognize the enormous role played by the magazines, newspapers, and journals of the *public press* in providing current, first-rate educational information in a broad spectrum of interest areas. Within the articles, the best scientists, practitioners, researchers, and commentators draw issues into new perspective as accepted theories and viewpoints are called into account by new events, recent discoveries change old facts, and fresh debate breaks out over important controversies.

Many of the articles resulting from this enormous editorial effort are appropriate for students, researchers, and professionals seeking accurate, current material to help bridge the gap between principles and theories and the real world. These articles, however, become more useful for study when those of lasting value are carefully *collected, organized, indexed,* and *reproduced* in a *low-cost format,* which provides easy and permanent access when the material is needed. That is the role played by *Annual Editions.* Under the direction of each volume's *Editor,* who is an expert in the subject area, and with the guidance of an *Advisory Board,* we seek each year to provide in each *ANNUAL EDITION* a current, well-balanced, carefully selected collection of the best of the public press for your study and enjoyment. We think you'll find this volume useful, and we hope you'll take a moment to let us know what you think.

Recent events have brought ethics to the forefront as a topic of discussion throughout our nation. And, undoubtedly, the area of society that is getting the closest scrutiny regarding its ethical practices is the business sector. Both the print and broadcast media have offered a constant stream of facts and opinions concerning recent unethical goings-on in the business world. Insider trading scandals on Wall Street, the marketing of unsafe products, money laundering, and questionable contracting practices are just a few examples of events that have recently tarnished the image of business.

As corporate America struggles to find its ethical identity in a business environment that grows increasingly complex, managers are confronted with some poignant questions that have definite ethical ramifications. Does a company have any obligation to help solve social problems such as poverty, pollution, and urban decay? What ethical responsibilities should a multinational corporation assume in foreign countries? What obligation does a manufacturer have to the consumer with respect to product defects and safety?

These are just a few of the issues that make the study of business ethics important and challenging. A significant goal of *Annual Editions: Business Ethics 94/95* is to present some different perspectives on understanding basic concepts and concerns of business ethics and to provide ideas on how to incorporate these concepts into the policies and decision-making processes of businesses. The articles reprinted in this publication have been carefully chosen from a variety of public press sources to furnish current information on business ethics.

This volume contains a number of features designed to make it useful for students, researchers, and professionals. These include a *topic guide* for locating articles on specific subjects related to business ethics, the *table of contents abstracts* with summaries of each article and key concepts in bold italics, and a comprehensive *index.*

The articles are organized into five units. Selections that focus on similar issues are concentrated into subsections within the broader units. Each unit is preceded by an overview that provides background for informed reading of the articles, emphasizes critical issues, and presents *challenge questions* focusing on major themes running through the selections.

Your comments, opinions, and recommendations about *Annual Editions: Business Ethics 94/95* will be greatly appreciated and will help shape future editions. Please take a moment to complete and return the article rating form on the last page of this book. Any book can be improved, and with your help this one will continue to be.

John E. Richardson
Editor

Contents

Unit 1

Ethics, Values, and Social Responsibility in Business

Eight selections provide an introduction to business ethics and social responsibility.

To the Reader   iv
Topic Guide   2
Overview   4

1. **Business Ethics: A Manager's Primer,** Gene Laczniak, *Business,* January–March 1983.   6

   Gene Laczniak offers some solid and pragmatic advice for managers facing **ethical dilemmas.** He also discusses how the process of ethical behavior in an organization stems from the diverse and sometimes **conflicting determinants of personal values, organizational pressure, and societal values.**

2. **Principles of Business Ethics: Their Role in Decision Making and an Initial Consensus,** Archie B. Carroll, *Management Decisions,* Volume 28, Number 8, 1990.   13

   Archie Carroll lucidly delineates how such approaches as the **Golden Rule,** intuition, and **utilitarianism,** as well as other ethical principles, are used in business decision making.

3. **Integrity: An Essential Executive Quality,** Donald G. Zauderer, *Business Forum,* Fall 1992.   18

   The author believes that **managers** who lack integrity place themselves and their organizations at risk. He identifies several traits of managers that compromise integrity and suggests some specific actions that can help build a **culture** where integrity can be regularly practiced.

4. **Ethics in Practice,** Kenneth R. Andrews, *Harvard Business Review,* September/October 1989.   23

   The author believes that **management's values** are evident in every strategic decision made. He also feels that when management focuses its total loyalty on **the maximization of profit,** it becomes the principal obstacle to achieving higher standards of ethical practice.

5. **State Your Values, Hold the Hot Air,** Alan Farnham, *Fortune,* April 19, 1993.   29

   Although the author feels that many **corporate value statements** are empty rhetoric, he still believes that a well-thought-out and carefully written value statement can assist **marketing** and help capture a company's elusive essence.

6. **Understanding Pressures That Cause Unethical Behavior in Business,** O. C. Ferrell and John Fraedrich, *Business Insights,* Spring/Summer 1990.   32

   The article delineates how **personal values,** the **competitive environment,** and organizational pressures and opportunities combine to determine ethical decisions in business. The authors discuss how an ethically sensitive **corporate culture, code of ethics,** and enforced ethical policies improve ethical behavior in companies.

7. **To Pose a Question of Ethics,** Robert McGarvey, *Kiwanis Magazine,* February 1993.   36

   The author believes that mere knowledge of an **ethical or a legal code** does not guarantee a sufficient framework to resolve complex **ethical dilemmas.**

8. **The Corporate Ethics Test,** Ronald E. Berenbeim, *Business and Society Review,* Spring 1992.   40

   The reader is given a chance to compare his or her ethical choices in three hypothetical cases with those of top CEOs. The cases concern **whistle-blowing, insider information, conflicts of interest,** and **acquisitions and layoffs.**

The concepts in bold italics are developed in the article. For further expansion please refer to the Topic Guide and the Index.

Unit 2

Employees and the Workplace: Ethical Issues and Dilemmas

Twenty selections organized within seven subsections examine crucial employee-related issues and their ethical implications for management's decision-making practices and policies.

Overview   44

A.   *EMPLOYEE RIGHTS AND DUTIES*

9.   **Balanced Protection Policies,** Benson Rosen and Cath-   46
     erine Schwoerer, *HR Magazine,* February 1990.
     The need for employers to reexamine the balance between
     employee and employer rights in order to maintain a competi-
     tive work force in the next century is addressed.

10. **What the Boss Knows about You,** Lee Smith, *Fortune,*   51
     August 9, 1993.
     An **employee's right to privacy** in the workplace, according to
     the author, is increasingly under fire. What companies demand to
     know and what employees insist on keeping private seem to be on
     a collision course.

11. **A Reluctant Invasion,** Doug Wallace, *Business Ethics,*   56
     January/February 1993.
     The article presents a situation where a manager—after laying off
     an employee—learns that the employee is **HIV positive.** How can
     a manager help an employee without invading his or her **privacy**?

B.   *EMPLOYEE CRIME*

12. **In-House Hackers: Rigging Computers for Fraud or**   59
     Malice Is Often an Inside Job, William M. Carley, *Wall*
     Street Journal, August 27, 1992.
     Rigging computers for fraud or malice, according to the author, is
     often an inside job. This article describes how **employees** are
     becoming increasingly ingenious in finding ways to **misuse or**
     sabotage their companies' computer systems.

13. **Ethics and Employee Theft,** William J. Kehoe, from *Re-*   62
     ducing Employee Theft: A Guide to Financial and Organiza-
     tional Controls, Quorum Books, 1991.
     William Kehoe delineates how **employee theft** is a problem for
     both **managers** and their **employees.** He believes that when
     ethics are instilled within the organization—and the **culture** be-
     comes one of pride and honesty—employee theft will be deterred.

C.   *SEXUAL TREATMENT OF EMPLOYEES*

14. **Six Myths of Sexual Harassment,** Jan Bohren,   66
     Management Review, May 1993.
     The author explores some of the myths surrounding **sexual**
     harassment. He also suggests preventive steps for **manage-**
     ment to take to deal with sexual harassment in the workplace.

15. **Sexual Harassment: What to Do,** Anne B. Fisher, *Fortune,*   70
     August 23, 1993.
     In this article, the author explains why **sexual harassment** is not
     really about sex—but about the abuse of power. She also dis-
     cusses ways companies are using **workshops** to help stamp out
     this form of abuse.

16. **Three Decades after the Equal Pay Act, Women's**   73
     Wages Remain Far from Parity, Joan E. Rigdon, *Wall*
     Street Journal, June 9, 1993.
     A recent survey reveals that "**women's earnings** have [only]
     gained on men's by a ratio of one-third of one percent a year over
     the past three decades."

The concepts in bold italics are developed in the article. For further expansion please refer to the Topic Guide and the Index.

D. DISCRIMINATORY AND PREJUDICIAL EMPLOYMENT PRACTICES

17. **The Americans with Disabilities Act: The Cutting Edge of Managing Diversity,** Robert Ledman and Darrel Brown, *SAM Advanced Management Journal,* Spring 1993.   **75**

    The authors provide practical suggestions to help **management** implement **the Americans with Disabilities Act** smoothly and to take advantage of the increased workforce diversity it represents.

18. **Denny's: The Stain That Isn't Coming Out,** Chuck Hawkins, *Business Week,* June 28, 1993.   **79**

    Denny's restaurants have been barraged by **lawsuits** and accusations alleging a pattern of **racial discrimination.**

19. **Torn between Halo and Horns,** David R. Altany, *Industry Week,* March 15, 1993.   **81**

    An *Industry Week* survey revealed that when "industry **managers** are confronted with clear-cut issues, they agree with near unanimity to abide by and enforce the **corporate code.** When the ethical waters grow murky, however, consensus on acceptable behavior breaks down."

E. DOWNSIZING OF THE WORK FORCE

20. **After the Layoff: Closing the Barn Door before All the Horses Are Gone,** Robert C. Ford and Pamela L. Perrewé, *Business Horizons,* July/August 1993.   **84**

    The authors describe how "financial aspects are not the only criteria **management** needs to pay attention to during **layoffs, restructurings, and mergers.**"

21. **Companies Discover That Some Firings Backfire into Costly Defamation Suits,** Gabriella Stern, *Wall Street Journal,* May 5, 1993.   **91**

    The author underscores why management cannot be too careful in the approach surrounding the **firing of an employee.** A list of some important "do's" and "don'ts" of firing is provided.

22. **"You're Fired,"** Doug Wallace, *Business Ethics,* January/February 1992.   **93**

    This article describes an actual case where an employee is **fired unfairly** for what he suspects is a result of an ethical stance he had once taken. The reader is given the opportunity to interact with the case and to decide what action the employee should take.

F. WHISTLE-BLOWING IN THE ORGANIZATION

23. **Changing Unethical Organizational Behavior,** Richard P. Nielsen, *The Executive,* May 1989.   **95**

    Richard Nielsen depicts some intervention strategies that can be used to change unethical behavior (secret and public **whistle-blowing,** for example), provides some cases of how each strategy can be implemented, and describes some important limitations of the strategies.

24. **Why *Your* Company Should Have a Whistle-blowing Policy,** Tim Barnett, *SAM Advanced Management Journal,* Autumn 1992.   **103**

    Tim Barnett delineates why certain "**legal,** practical, and ethical imperatives" make developing **whistle-blowing policies** advisable.

The concepts in bold italics are developed in the article. For further expansion please refer to the Topic Guide and the Index.

G. *HANDLING ETHICAL DILEMMAS AT WORK*

25. **Implementing Business Ethics,** Patrick E. Murphy,   **109**
Journal of Business Ethics, (7) 1988.
A pragmatic approach to implementing business ethics is presented. For a successful implementation of ethics, there must be
top management support and a ***corporate culture*** that is
supportive of ***codes of ethics, conferences and training programs,*** and an ethical audit.

26. **Ethical Judgment,** Sherry Baker, *Executive Excellence,*   **118**
March 1992.
In facing **ethical dilemmas,** the author offers some thoughtful
questions that can stimulate and sharpen moral reasoning and
ethical judgment.

27. **Pepsi Faces Problem in Trying to Contain Syringe**   **120**
Scare, Michael J. McCarthy, *Wall Street Journal,* June 17,
1993.
The author describes how Pepsi's ***management*** is really on the
horns of an ***ethical dilemma*** in regard to the widespread reports
of tampering with its soft drinks.

28. **Promises to Keep,** Doug Wallace, *Business Ethics,* July/   **122**
August 1993.
An ***ethical dilemma*** is presented where a manager in the human
relations department of a company was asked to allow promised
employee bonuses to be diverted to company executives.

Overview   **124**

A. *CHANGING PERSPECTIVES IN BUSINESS AND
SOCIETY*

29. **The Moral Audit,** S. Andrew Ostapski, *Business and Eco-*   **126**
nomic Review, January–March 1992.
Corporations maintain a favorable public image through public
relations and, in some cases, philanthropic acts. These methods,
however, do not fulfill a ***corporation's moral obligations.*** A
company must identify any harm their products may inflict on
society, and it must correct that potential harm.

30. **The New Crisis in Business Ethics,** Kenneth Labich,   **130**
Fortune, April 20, 1992.
During these tough ***economic*** times, according to the author, more
managers are cutting ethical corners and putting more heat on
subordinates. The result has been an eruption of questionable and
sometimes ***criminal behavior*** throughout corporate America.

31. **Work and Family,** *Business Week,* June 28, 1993.   **133**
Flexible schedules, day care, job sharing, telecommuting are all
ways some organizations have responded to an older, more
diverse work force. The article reveals why those organizations
that have helped ***employees*** balance work and family have been
given a powerful competitive edge.

Unit
3

Business and Society: Contemporary Ethical, Social, and Environmental Issues

Eleven articles organized within three subsections
provide an analysis of important ethical, social, and
environmental issues affecting both domestic and
multinational business operations.

32. **The (R)Evolution of the American Woman,** Catherine M.   **139**
Daily, *Business Horizons,* March/April 1993.
Catherine Daily believes that "a cultural revolution must occur for
women to achieve **equality** within the workplace."

33. **Business Rethinks, Refines, Recycles, and Recoups,**   **144**
Ted J. Rakstis, *Kiwanis Magazine,* August 1993.
Ted Rakstis explores how "**the green movement**" is branching
"further into offices, shops, and factories as the working world
learns that recycling makes both dollars and sense."

B.   *MAJOR CONTEMPORARY DILEMMAS*

34. **Combating Drugs in the Workplace,** Minda Zetlin,   **148**
Management Review, August 1991.
Some **drug-abuse incidents** are not clear-cut, presenting problems not only of good **management,** but also of good ethics. The
author presents five dilemmas relating to drug-related issues
drawn from real-life **workplace** situations.

35. **AIDS in the Workplace: The Pandemic Firms Want to**   **155**
Ignore, Rose Knotts and J. Lynn Johnson, *Business Horizons,* July/August 1993.
The authors are convinced that corporations can no longer "sidestep the problems generated by the AIDS pandemic." They make
constructive suggestions on how a company can formulate an
AIDS policy statement and prepare for an AIDS crisis program.

36. **Social Responsibility and Need for Low Cost Clash at**   **160**
Stride Rite, Joseph Pereira, *Wall Street Journal,* May 28,
1993.
Stride Rite is viewed as a company that has been **socially
responsible** and one which has done many good deeds. But
closing its facilities in depressed inner cities has raised some
difficult questions: What makes a company socially responsible?
How far can social responsibility be expected to go?

C.   *GLOBAL ETHICS*

37. **Is U.S. Business Obsessed with Ethics?** David Vogel,   **163**
Across the Board, November/December 1993.
David Vogel elucidates how the norms of ethical behavior tend to
vary widely in different capitalistic nations and why some **foreign
managers** resent the distinctive American **ethical practices**
being forced on them.

38. **Companies Clean Up,** Jane Sasseen, *International Management,* October 1993.   **167**
"**European businesses** are trying to put corruption scandals
behind them and adopting new **codes of ethics.** They hope to
see virtue" gain its own reward—"in the bottom line."

39. **Ethics: Are Standards Lower Overseas?** Andrew W.   **170**
Singer, *Across the Board,* September 1991.
The author scrutinizes the common perception that U.S. standards and **values** are higher than those **overseas.** Is this accurate?

Unit 4

Ethics and Social Responsibility in the Marketplace

Eight selections organized within two subsections describe the practice of incorporating ethics into the marketplace.

Overview   174

A. MARKETING STRATEGY AND ETHICS

40. **Marketing by Professionals: Some Ethical Issues and Prescriptions,** Patrick E. Murphy and Gene R. Laczniak, *Business Insights,* Spring/Summer 1990.   176

Some of the critical **ethical issues** faced by professionals in their **marketing and advertising practices** are addressed. Specific suggestions that can help advertising and marketing by professionals to remain on a high ethical plane are provided.

41. **Marketers Exploit People's Fears of Everything,** Kathleen Deveny, *Wall Street Journal,* November 15, 1993.   182

According to the author, "**marketers** nowadays seem increasingly willing to sell their **products** by playing on **consumers'** anxieties, and their advertising has become scarier and more graphic."

42. **Strategic Green Marketing,** Stephen W. McDaniel and David H. Rylander, *Journal of Consumer Marketing,* Volume 10, Number 3, 1993.   184

This article points out the critical nature of **environmental concerns** and provides a **strategic marketing planning process** for dealing with these rising concerns.

43. **Pinto Redux?** Andrew W. Singer, *Ethikos,* January/February 1993.   191

As with Ford's Pinto, according to the author, there is evidence that General Motors was aware of the problem with its pickup trucks' "side-saddle" gas tanks. It appears that economics and **marketing** drove the design decision just as they did the decision not to recall the Pinto.

B. ETHICAL PRACTICES IN THE MARKETPLACE

44. **The Ethics of Bootstrapping,** Scott Cook, *Inc.,* September 1992.   194

Scott Cook founded Intuit, maker of the check-writing software product Quicken, with $151,000 in 1984. Cook freely shares his experience as a little, struggling, start-up venture that faced **ethical questions** almost every day.

45. **Practical Applications of Healthcare Marketing Ethics,** Robert L. Goldman, *Healthcare Financial Management,* March 1993.   197

Robert Goldman discusses "four ethical principles that can be applied to help" hospital marketers "ensure that **marketing decisions** conform to the highest ethical standards."

46. **America's Hamburger Helper,** Edwin M. Reingold, *Time,* June 29, 1992.   200

McDonald's stands out not only as one of the more **socially responsible** companies in America but also as one of the nation's few truly effective social engineers.

47. **Who Scores Best on the Environment,** Faye Rice, *Fortune,* July 26, 1993.   202

A recent *Fortune* study reveals which companies are in the vanguard of the **green revolution**—and which ones are lagging behind.

The concepts in bold italics are developed in the article. For further expansion please refer to the Topic Guide and the Index.

Unit 5

Developing the Future Ethos and Social Responsibility of Business

Six selections consider guidelines and principles for developing the future ethos and social responsibility of business.

Overview   206

48. **The Challenge of Ethical Behavior in Organizations,** Ronald R. Sims, *Journal of Business Ethics,* July 1992.   208

The author lays out some of the challenges that **ethical organizations** will face in the future: **international competition,** new technologies, increased **quality, employee motivation and commitment,** and managing a diverse work force. Also, the author presents some suggestions for creating and maintaining an ethically oriented culture.

49. **Creating Ethical Corporate Structures,** Patrick E. Murphy, *Sloan Management Review,* Winter 1989.   217

The author believes that "**ethical business practices** stem from ethical **corporate cultures.**" He discusses several companies' experiences with three types of ethics-enhancing structures: corporate credos, **ethics training programs and workshops,** and tailored corporate **codes of ethics.**

50. **How to Be Ethical, and Still Come Top,** *The Economist,* June 5, 1993.   224

The article describes the importance of business ethicists "getting their hands dirty" and becoming more attuned to the real **ethical dilemmas** and issues that managers face. They should also be careful to use language that is not "foreign to **managers** schooled in the lexicon of finance and economics."

51. **The Pyramid of Corporate Social Responsibility: Toward the Moral Management of Organizational Stakeholders,** Archie B. Carroll, *Business Horizons,* July/August 1991.   225

Archie Carroll says total **corporate social responsibility** entails the simultaneous fulfillment of a firm's economic, **legal, ethical,** and philanthropic responsibilities. He feels that social responsibility can only become a reality if more **managers** become moral instead of amoral or immoral.

52. **Another View of the Golden Rule,** Joseph L. Mancusi, *HRMagazine,* April 1991.   236

In a **culturally diverse** setting, the author recommends modifying the **Golden Rule** to the Mancusi Platinum Rule: "Do unto others as they would like to have it done unto themselves."

53. **Is Business Waking Up?** Craig Cox, *Business Ethics,* January/February 1992.   238

The article prognosticates 10 trends that will carry **socially responsible** businesses through the 1990s and beyond.

Index   241
Article Review Form   244
Article Rating Form   245

The concepts in bold italics are developed in the article. For further expansion please refer to the Topic Guide and the Index.

Topic Guide

This topic guide suggests how the selections in this book relate to topics of traditional concern to students and professionals in the field of business ethics. It is useful for locating articles that relate to each other for reading and research. The guide is arranged alphabetically according to topic. Articles may, of course, treat topics that do not appear in the topic guide. In turn, entries in the topic guide do not necessarily constitute a comprehensive listing of all the contents of each selection.

TOPIC AREA	TREATED IN:	TOPIC AREA	TREATED IN:
AIDS	7. Pose a Question of Ethics 10. What the Boss Knows about You 11. Reluctant Invasion 35. AIDS in the Workplace	Downsizing (cont'd)	30. New Crisis in Business Ethics 36. Social Responsibility and Need for Low Cost Clash 38. Companies Clean Up
Codes of Ethics (Codes of Conduct)	1. Business Ethics: A Manager's Primer 3. Integrity 4. Ethics in Practice 5. State Your Values 6. Understanding Pressures 7. Pose a Question of Ethics 8. Corporate Ethics Test 13. Ethics and Employee Theft 19. Torn between Halo and Horns 25. Implementing Business Ethics 26. Ethical Judgment 37. Is U.S. Business Obsessed with Ethics? 38. Companies Clean Up 40. Marketing by Professionals 48. Challenge of Ethical Behavior in Organizations 49. Creating Ethical Corporate Structures 50. How to Be Ethical, and Still Come Top	Employee Conduct and Responsibility	7. Pose a Question of Ethics 10. What the Boss Knows about You 13. Ethics and Employee Theft 14. Six Myths of Sexual Harassment 19. Torn between Halo and Horns 37. Is U.S. Business Obsessed with Ethics?
		Employee Health and Safety	14. Six Myths of Sexual Harassment 17. Americans with Disabilities Act 24. Why *Your* Company Should Have a Whistle-blowing Policy 47. Who Scores Best on the Environment
		Employee Rights	2. Principles of Business Ethics 3. Integrity 9. Balanced Protection Policies 10. What the Boss Knows about You 11. Reluctant Invasion 13. Ethics and Employee Theft 17. Americans with Disabilities Act 20. After the Layoff 21. Companies Discover That Some Firings Backfire 24. Why *Your* Company Should Have a Whistle-blowing Policy 28. Promises to Keep 31. Work and Family 32. R(Evolution) of the American Woman 34. Combating Drugs in the Workplace 49. Creating Ethical Corporate Structures 51. Pyramid of Corporate Social Responsibility 52. Another View of the Golden Rule 53. Is Business Waking Up?
Conflicts of Interest	2. Principles of Business Ethics 20. After the Layoff 22. "You're Fired" 27. Pepsi Faces Problem 28. Promises to Keep 44. Ethics of Bootstrapping 49. Creating Ethical Corporate Sturctures 51. Pyramid of Corporate Social Responsibility		
Consumer Protection	27. Pepsi Faces Problem 29. Moral Audit 40. Marketing by Professionals 41. Marketers Exploit People's Fears 43. Pinto Redux? 44. Ethics of Bootstrapping	Environmental Disregard and Pollution	2. Principles of Business Ethics 33. Business Rethinks, Refines, Recycles, and Recoups 38. Companies Clean Up 42. Strategic Green Marketing 46. America's Hamburger Helper 47. Who Scores Best on the Environment 48. Challenge of Ethical Behavior in Organizations 53. Is Business Waking Up?
Discrimination	3. Integrity 10. What the Boss Knows about You 11. Reluctant Invasion 16. Three Decades after the Equal Pay Act 17. Americans with Disabilities Act 18. Denny's: The Stain That Isn't Coming Out 19. Torn between Halo and Horns 21. Companies Discover That Some Firings Backfire 22. "You're Fired" 32. R(Evolution) of the American Woman 35. AIDS in the Workplace 48. Challenge of Ethical Behavior in Organizations 52. Another View of the Golden Rule	Equal Employment Opportunities	16. Three Decades after the Equal Pay Act 34. Combating Drugs in the Workplace 46. America's Hamburger Helper
		Ethical Dilemmas	2. Principles of Business Ethics 7. Pose a Question of Ethics 19. Torn between Halo and Horns 20. After the Layoff 27. Pepsi Faces Problem 28. Promises to Keep 36. Social Responsibility and Need for Low Cost Clash
Downsizing	9. Balanced Protection Policies 20. After the Layoff 21. Companies Discover That Some Firings Backfire 22. "You're Fired"		

TOPIC AREA	TREATED IN:	TOPIC AREA	TREATED IN:
Ethical Dilemmas (cont'd)	50. How to Be Ethical, and Still Come Top	**Multinational Corporations and Global Business Ethics**	8. Corporate Ethics Test 25. Implementing Business Ethics 36. Social Responsibility and Need for Low Cost Clash 37. Is U.S. Business Obsessed with Ethics? 38. Companies Clean Up 39. Ethics: Are Standards Lower Overseas? 48. Challenge of Ethical Behavior in Organizations 50. How to Be Ethical, and Still Come Top 52. Another View of the Golden Rule
Ethics Training	8. Corporate Ethics Test 13. Ethics and Employee Theft 14. Six Myths of Sexual Harassment 15. Sexual Harassment: What to Do 25. Implementing Business Ethics 30. New Crisis in Business Ethics 35. AIDS in the Workplace 48. Challenge of Ethical Behavior in Organizations 52. Another View of the Golden Rule		
Insider Information	4. Ethics in Practice 48. Challenge of Ethical Behavior in Organizations 49. Creating Ethical Corporate Structures	**Product Safety and Quality**	5. State Your Values 24. Why *Your* Company Should Have a Whistle-blowing Policy 27. Pepsi Faces Problem 30. New Crisis in Business Ethics 41. Marketers Exploit People's Fears 43. Pinto Redux? 44. Ethics of Bootstrapping 47. Who Scores Best on the Environment 48. Challenge of Ethical Behavior in Organizations
Insider Trading	6. Understanding Pressures 13. Ethics and Employee Theft 48. Challenge of Ethical Behavior in Organizations		
Legal and Legislative Environment	1. Business Ethics: A Manager's Primer 4. Ethics in Practice 7. Pose a Question of Ethics 9. Balanced Protection Policies 10. What the Boss Knows about You 16. Three Decades after the Equal Pay Act 17. Americans with Disabilities Act 18. Denny's: The Stain That Isn't Coming Out 21. Companies Discover That Some Firings Backfire 24. Why *Your* Company Should Have a Whistle-blowing Policy 25. Implementing Business Ethics 30. New Crisis in Business Ethics 34. Combating Drugs in the Workplace 35. AIDS in the Workplace 39. Ethics: Are Standards Lower Overseas? 42. Strategic Green Marketing 51. Pyramid of Corporate Social Responsibility 52. Another View of the Golden Rule 53. Is Business Waking Up?	**Sexual Harassment and Discrimination**	2. Principles of Business Ethics 3. Integrity 14. Six Myths of Sexual Harassment 15. Sexual Harassment: What to Do 32. R(Evolution) of the American Woman 35. AIDS in the Workplace
		Social Responsibility	27. Pepsi Faces Problem 31. Work and Family 33. Business Rethinks, Refines, Recycles, and Recoups 36. Social Responsibility and Need for Low Cost Clash 38. Companies Clean Up 42. Strategic Green Marketing 43. Pinto Redux? 45. Practical Applications of Healthcare Marketing Ethics 47. Who Scores Best on the Environment
		Whistle-blowing	1. Business Ethics: A Manager's Primer 23. Changing Unethical Organizational Behavior 24. Why *Your* Company Should Have a Whistle-blowing Policy 30. New Crisis in Business Ethics 37. Is U.S. Business Obsessed with Ethics? 48. Challenge of Ethical Behavior in Organizations
Marketing Practices	1. Business Ethics: A Manager's Primer 4. Ethics in Practice 5. State Your Values 22. "You're Fired" 25. Implementing Business Ethics 27. Pepsi Faces Problem 29. Moral Audit 33. Business Rethinks, Refines, Recycles, and Recoups 36. Social Responsibility and Need for Low Cost Clash 38. Companies Clean Up 41. Marketers Exploit People's Fears 42. Strategic Green Marketing 43. Pinto Redux? 44. Ethics of Bootstrapping 45. Practical Applications of Healthcare Marketing Ethics 46. America's Hamburger Helper 47. Who Scores Best on the Environment 53. Is Business Waking Up?	**White-Collar Crimes**	4. Ethics in Practice 9. Balanced Protection Policies 10. What the Boss Knows about You 12. In-House Hackers 13. Ethics and Employee Theft 30. New Crisis in Business Ethics

Ethics, Values, and Social Responsibility in Business

Ethical decision making in an organization does not occur in a vacuum. As individuals and as managers, we formulate our ethics (that is, the standards of "right" and "wrong" behavior that we set for ourselves) based upon family, peer, and religious influences, our past experiences, and our own unique value systems. When we make ethical decisions within the organizational context, many times there are situational factors and potential conflicts of interest that further complicate the process.

Decisions do not only have personal ramifications—they also have social consequences. Social responsibility is really ethics at the organizational level, since it refers to the obligation that an organization has to make choices and to take actions that will contribute to the good of society, as well as the good of the organization. Authentic social responsibility is not initiated because of forced compliance to specific laws and regulations. In contrast to legal responsibility, social responsibility involves a voluntary response from an organization that is above and beyond what is specified by the law.

The eight selections in this unit provide an overview of the interrelationships of ethics, values, and social responsibility in business. The lead article, "Business Ethics: A Manager's Primer," offers practical and insightful suggestions to managers, enabling them to approach the subject of business ethics with more confidence. The next three articles discuss the significance of ethical principles and values in personal and organizational decision making. "State Your Values, Hold the Hot Air" describes how a well thought-out and carefully written value statement can be helpful in capturing a company's elusive essence.

The sixth article delineates how a code of ethics, personal values, and ethical instruction are some of the critical ingredients necessary to take into the competitive environment as management endeavors to deal with employees, stockholders, and consumers in an ethical manner. The article, "To Pose a Question of Ethics" reveals that resolving ethical dilemmas is not a simple undertaking. "The Corporate Ethics Test," the final article, allows the reader to compare his or her ethical choices in four hypothetical cases to those of top executives.

Looking Ahead: Challenge Questions

Do you believe that corporations are more socially responsible today than they were 10 years ago? Why or why not?

In what specific ways do you see companies practicing social responsibility? Do you think most companies are overt or covert in their social responsibility activities?

React to your reading of "Integrity: An Essential Executive Quality." Do you agree with the author's analysis of the traits that can compromise a manager's integrity? Why?

What are the economic and social implications of "management accountability" as part of the decision-making process? Does a company have any obligation to help remedy social problems, such as poverty, urban decay, and pollution? Explain your response.

From an organizational perspective, what do you think are the major arguments for and against social responsibility?

Business Ethics: A Manager's Primer

The application of different ethical maxims to a given situation may produce divergent ethical judgments. The 14 propositions given here should enable management to deal with the subject of business ethics with confidence.

Gene Laczniak

Dr. Laczniak *is Associate Professor of Business and Chairman of the Department of Marketing at Marquette University, Milwaukee, Wisconsin. The author would like to acknowledge the helpful comments of Professors T.R. Martin and Patrick E. Murphy of Marquette University in the development of this article.*

Too many business managers have been shortchanged in their business education. They have been cheated because during their college years their business professors failed to integrate ethical issues into management education. While some practicing managers have taken courses in "business ethics" or "social responsibility," they typically have not learned to appreciate fully the crucial role that ethics plays in business decision making. To a large degree this has happened because many business educators shy away from integrating ethics into mainstream business classes such as marketing, finance, and production.

Why do educators find it so difficult to teach business ethics or, for that matter, to address ethical issues when dealing with other topics of business strategy? Largely for the following three reasons. First, many business educators pride themselves on their analytical approach; in contrast, addressing ethics is associated with a softer type of analysis, and occasionally with a preachy mentality. This might be deemed the *soapbox* factor. A second closely related cause is that the foundation for meaningful remedies in the area of business ethics is perceived as subjective and unscientific. In other words, many business professors feel that ethics is too elusive a subject for extended lecture treatment. This constitutes the *soft* factor. Third, some business educators believe that dealing with business ethics in the classroom will have little or no lasting effect upon the morality of their students; this might be labeled the *superfluous* factor. Consequently, a great many business educators have not given business ethics its proper due in the classroom because of their perceptions that the subject is soapboxish, soft, and superfluous.

This article compiles and analyzes some propositions that are useful for understanding business ethics. These propositions are grouped into three categories: (1) propositions that serve as useful foundations; (2) descriptive propositions; and (3) proscriptive propositions.

Propositions That Serve as Useful Foundations

Proposition 1: Ethical conflicts and choices are inherent in business decison making. This proposition is a logical springboard for appreciating the importance of business ethics because it legitimates the inseparability of business decisions and moral consequences. Substantial support for this postulation is available. One classic study of business ethics reported that at some point in their careers 75% of the responding managers felt a conflict between profit considerations and being ethical.[1] Later studies noted that the majority of managers questioned also felt this pressure to be unethical.[2] Similarly, another widely publicized study indicated that 65% of the managers surveyed sometimes felt pressure to compromise their personal ethical standards.[3]

More importantly, this proposition can provide the business manager with the motivation to discover and analyze the numerous ethical implications of current business practices. For example:

• Is it ethical for pharmaceutical companies to market infant formula in developing countries as an alternative to breast feeding when it is common knowledge that sanitary containers and unpolluted water are frequently not available and that babies will be deprived of the immunological benefits inherent in breast milk?

• Is it proper for a public relations firm to attempt to bolster the worldwide image of a country accused of numerous human rights violations?

• Is it moral for a firm to ship a product designated unsafe

"Business Ethics: A Manager's Primer," Gene Laczniak, *Business*, January-February-March, 1983, pp. 23-29. Reprinted by permission of Georgia State University, Atlanta.

in one market, such as the United States, to another market where the regulations do not apply?

Every business manager can add examples to the ones just noted. The point is that this proposition emphasizes that the ethical implications of business practices are legion.

"...a high organizational ethic could induce a manager with low integrity to behave more properly."

Proposition 2: Proper ethical behavior exists on a plane above the law. The law merely specifies the lowest common denominator of acceptable behavior. This proposition undercuts the argument that legality is the only criterion for judging acceptable behavior. If this proposition does *not* hold, the study of ethics is extraneous. While some members of the legal profession may challege this postulate, the entire field of moral philosophy rests on its inherent truth. This proposition provides a rationale for examining the compelling argument that ethical propriety and legality do not necessarily coincide. For example, it is not *illegal* to exhort children to ask their parents to buy a product promoted *via* a commercial on a children's television show. Whether such a practice is *unethical*, because it exploits the gullibility of children, can be vigorously debated.

In addition, this proposition provides an opportunity to explore some fundamental differences between legal and ethical perspectives. For instance, the law is a *reactive* institution that applies to situations only after they have occurred. Ethics is usually more *proactive*, attempting to provide guidance prior to a situation's occurrence. Similarly, within the law, a transgression must be proven beyond a reasonable doubt, whereas from an ethical perspective, an action is morally wrong independent of conclusive proof that it in fact took place. For example, suppose the quality control manager of an electrical supply house knowingly sends out Christmas tree lights that could potentially short out because of a design defect and thereby cause a fire. The lights, however, do not malfunction. Legally, the manager is not culpable because no harm occurred; ethically, a violation of trust has clearly occurred. Thus this proposition embodies the concept that the realm of ethics provides guidance for managerial actions and supplements the requirements provided by law.

Proposition 3: There is no single satisfactory standard of ethical action agreeable to everyone that a manager can use to make specific operational decisions. Few business executives would question this generalization. This proposition establishes that advocating a particular moral doctrine is not the point of examining the issue of ethics. Rather, while there are many ethical perspectives of great worth, the issue of morality *in general* is at question. In other words, the power and impact implicit in managerial decisions demands an examination of the responsibility for those actions. Thus, ethical considerations are properly examined in reference to the managerial process.

Proposition 4: Managers should be familiar with a wide variety of ethical standards. Several ethical maxims are used as the theoretical foundation for a variety of industry statements on ethics. Typical of the more simplistic maxims are:

The utilitarian principle—Act in a way that results in the greatest good for the greatest number.

The professional ethic—Take only actions that would be viewed as proper by a disinterested panel of professional colleagues.

The golden rule—Act in the way you would expect others to act toward you.

Kant's categorical imperative—Act in such a way that the action taken under the circumstances could be a universal law or rule of behavior.

The TV test—A manager should always ask, "Would I feel comfortable explaining to a national TV audience why I took this action?"

Obviously, these maxims are difficult to apply to specific situations and can sometimes lead to conflicting resolutions, particularly if analyzed in the context of a *case situation*. For example, consider the case of a sales representative who, against stated company policy, routinely pads his expense account vouchers 10% to 15%. However, he does this with the knowledge that his fellow sales representatives and his supervisor do the same thing and tacitly approve of this action. In this circumstance, does the golden rule justify the behavior? Wouldn't the professional ethic imply that the practice should cease? This is a rudimentary illustration, but it underscores the fact that various modes of moral reasoning exist and that the application of different ethical maxims to a given situation may produce divergent ethical judgments.

Proposition 5: The discussion of business cases or of situations having ethical implications can make managers more ethically sensitive. Perhaps this is the most debatable of the five propositions ventured thus far because a certain substantial segment of business educators and managers would question its truth. The position of this group is that academic course work cannot instill integrity in a future manager. They believe that students come into the classroom with a relatively intransigent morality. Therefore, classroom efforts directed at personal values are an exercise in futility.[4]

Notice, however, that the proposition as stated promises only the *potential* for increased sensitivity to ethical concerns, not wholesale changes in morality. One expert provides some limited support for this proposition when he reports that a sample of MBA graduates who took a course in business ethics seemed to develop ethical sensitivity over a period of time.[5] Furthermore, other researchers have contended that the academic community has the reponsibility to provide courses in business ethics regardless of their effect.[6] In the view of these experts, such offerings will not transform personalities overnight but will stimulate thinking about ethical issues. In short, sufficient justification exists for encouraging discussion among managers about business ethics, and for the expectation that the effort will have some moral payoff in the business world.

In summary, the five foundation propositions provide a rationale for business ethics as (1) an area of significant managerial concern, (2) distinct from the realm of law, (3) an area, like many areas of management, that has few pat answers but (4) worth exploring because of its relevance to effective and responsible management decision making.

Descriptive Propositions

With these five foundation propositions, the business manager is now ready to address the specific process of ethical behavior as it occurs in the organization. Unfortunately, little can be definitively stated about how ethical or unethical behavior evolves in a business firm. In part, this is why business ethics are considered subjective or soft—a dimension that was referred to earlier. Nevertheless, a few useful, general propositions can be established for ethics in the organization.

Proposition 6: There are diverse and sometimes conflicting determinants of ethical action. These stem primarily from the individual, from the organization, from professional norms, and from the values of society. This proposition underscores the multiple influences that characterize the business environment and shape ethical actions; it also highlights the complexity of pressures that can be part of resolving an ethical question. Consider, for example, the following sample situation:

Smith University holds as part of its endowment portfolio a large block of stock in the multinational Jones Company. The stock was donated to Smith University by the founder of the Jones Company. The Jones Company is heavily involved in apartheid-ruled South Africa. Members of the university community, especially students and faculty, are pressuring the university to immediately sell all its Jones Company stock. Some members of the community where Smith University is located have even threatened to picket Smith classes. Mr. Courtney, vice president of Finance at Smith and a former diplomat, knows Jones Company to be a model corporate citizen in South Africa, treating black and white employees alike. However, the management of Jones Company supports the existing South African government. Furthermore, Courtney believes the Jones Company stock is extremely depressed at this time and that its sale would not be in the best interest of the endowment fund, the major source of student scholarships. Should Courtney and Smith University sell the stock immediately?

Notice the multiple pressures that may be present in a situation such as this: *Societal* pressures dictate selling the securities. Moreover, Courtney's *personal* beliefs, stemming from his religion and philosophy, make him shudder at the inflexibility of the South African government. On the other hand, *organizational* pressures dictate restraint, since Courtney and other officers of the university feel the Jones securities will soon appreciate in value. Similarly, from a *professional* viewpoint, Courtney knows that the sale of the Jones stock would be a symbolic act at best and at worst a slap in the face to a company that has been a Good Samaritan in South Africa and a close friend to the university. How does Courtney resolve these conflicting pressures? No precise answer exists. Somehow he takes the various viewpoints into consideration and recommends an action with which he is comfortable. It is even possible that his recommendation, whatever it is, will be overruled at a higher level of the organization.

The foregoing examination of Proposition 6 suggests another proposition. In the last analysis, Courtney must make a decision that will have ethical consequences. Ultimately, the factors and subfactors to which ethics are attributable—influences such as religion, professional norms, societal expectations, and organizational pressures—somehow combine to shape an *individual* decision that is associated with Courtney and according to which Courtney could be morally judged. This leads to the next proposition.

Proposition 7: Individual values are the final standard, although not necessarily the determining reason for ethical behavior. The upshot of Proposition 7 is that multifaceted influences affecting the likelihood of ethical action by the decision maker will ultimately be reflected in an individual decision. The action taken will be perceived by others as embodying the ethical values of the decision maker. Introduction of this proposition helps businesspeople realize the individual responsibility inherent in managerial decision making. In other words, no matter what factors lead a manager to make a particular decision, there is a measure of individual responsibility that cannot be denied because in the last analysis the decision was made by a given manager. For example, the product manager who knowingly sends a shipment of unsafe products to retail stores cannot avoid individual culpability by claiming that economic pressures in the organization necessitated the action.

One major organizational implication of Proposition 7 is that management should strive to maintain a laudatory *organizational* ethic because this dimension is somewhat controllable by the organization. This lessens the likelihood that organizational considerations will pressure the individual manager to compromise his or her personal beliefs and behave unethically. Conversely, a high organizational ethic could induce a manager with low integrity to behave more properly. For example, the American Telephone and Telegraph Corporation (AT & T) provides all employees with a copy of a booklet that states that if employees report to outside sources the improper behavior of AT & T management or employees, no disciplinary or retaliatory action will ever be taken.

Proposition 8: Consensus regarding what constitutes proper ethical behavior in a decision-making situation diminishes as the level of analysis proceeds from abstract to specific. Put another way, it is easy to get a group of managers to agree *in general* that a practice is improper; however, casting that practice in a specific set of circumstances usually reduces consensus. For example, almost all

---

"...younger, middle managers feel greater pressures to compromise their personal ethics."

---

businesspeople will agree that stealing by employees is wrong. But consider the following specific question: Is it alright for a manager to unwittingly take a few pens and pads of paper home for personal use? What about a stapler? A calculator? A typewriter? What if the pens will be used by orphans to play games at a charity picnic? Where does one draw the line?

Even a simplistic example like this can cause debate. The difficulty is compounded as the circumstances become more involved. In any event, Proposition 8 emphasizes the uncertain environment in which managers necessarily function as they attempt to make the ethically proper decision. Consider the following ethical precepts—with which all businesspeople would agree—along with the complication introduced by some hypothetical situation-specific examples.

• *Business has the obligation to honestly report financial progress and potential to holders of company debt and equity. Situation:* The annual report of the Columbia Railroad Co. reports that the firm has financially outperformed all its competitors. This was largely due to the sale of some highly appreciated Manhattan real estate. The income from this transaction is noted with only a footnote in the financial statement. Columbia avoided having the income classified as a special treatment "extraordinary item" because of some complex legal maneuvers and

because it has other real estate assets that might provide similar profits in the future. Should the income from the real estate be highlighted more clearly in the annual report?

• *Business has the obligation to treat potential, current, and past employees fairly. Situation:* Employee Harry Harris is apprehended stealing tools and equipment valued at $500 from the company. Company policy calls for dismissal in such instances. However, Harris is 63 years old—two years from pension—and has had a clean slate until this incident. Is it ethical for the company to fire him at this point in his career?

• *Business has the obligation to provide consumers with facts relevant to the informed purchase of a product or service. Situation:* The Doe Co. manufactures Clean & Gleem, an all-purpose cleaning concentrate that consumers mix with four parts water. Clean & Gleem has been sold this way for 25 years. A recent issue of *Consumer Reports* indicates that Clean & Gleem will clean just as effectively if mixed with eight parts water. Thus, consumers need only use half as much concentrate. Should the Doe Co. inform customers of this fact? Would it be unethical not to do so?

In summary, Proposition 8 and these examples of some specific "tough choice" cases provide some insight into the difficulty of steering an ethically proper course.

Proposition 9: The moral tone of an organization is set by top management. Stated another way, the organization is but a lengthened shadow of the morality of persons in charge. For instance, one study found that managers ranked the behavior of superiors as the strongest single factor in deterring unethical behavior.[7] Similar results are reported in more recent studies.[8]

The organizational implications of this proposition are clear. If employees take their cues concerning ethical behavior from top management, then the first line of responsibility for setting high ethical standards falls to these corporate executives. The following example partially embodies the proposition:

An employee embezzled $20,000 over several years. When confronted with the incriminating evidence, the employee was not contrite and expressed the belief that he was just as entitled to the company's money as any member of top management. He pointed out that upper management dipped into petty cash for lunch money, used company stamps to mail Christmas cards, and had company personnel help with yard work at their personal residences.

Numerous other real-world examples of this proposition abound. The J.C. Penney Co. is a classic illustration of a company with a reputation for high ethical standards along with a record unblemished by any major scandal. Much of the credit must go to the founder, who was so convinced that ethics and profit were compatible that the company's outlets were originally called the "Golden

Rule" stores. In contrast, many of the so-called "dirty tricks" and the political whip cracking of the Nixon administration can be explained by the win-at-all-costs philosophy of the men at the top.

Proposition 10: The lower the organizational level of a manager, the greater the perceived pressure to act unethically. At first glance, this proposition might seem contradictory to Proposition 9. After all, if the moral tone of an organization resides in top management, why the concern with the subsidiary levels of management? The answer lies in the fact that while a *general ethical climate* is established by an organization's superiors, many of the operational decisions that have ethical implications will actually be made at levels other than top management. Thus because the frequency of decision making is greater, the lower-level manager may simply have more opportunities to behave ethically or unethically. Furthermore, it may be that the areas of responsibility of middle management are treated as profit centers for purposes of evaluation. Consequently, anything that takes away from profit—including ethical behavior—is perceived by lower-level management as an impediment to organizational advancement and recognition.

Surveys of managers seem to confirm that ethical conflict is felt most strongly by lower-level managers.[9] Thus, top management's exhortations and policy regarding ethics will be a factor in ethical behavior at these levels of management, but only *one* factor. If organizational advancement and salary adjustments are made primarily by the rule of bottom-line unit performance, pressure will exist on middle managers to compromise ethical standards if profit can be served. In this sense, the "ethical buck" stops at the bottom rather than the top of the organization.

Top management should recognize that ethical pressure points will exist at all levels of the organization. Therefore, a sanctimonious statement of a manager's standards does not discharge a firm's duty to foster high ethical standards. Efforts should be made to communicate to all levels of management that ethical behavior will be monitored and will be rewarded accordingly. This proposition reminds business managers that they will be involved in potential ethical conflicts when they enter the organization. The proposition also implies that mechanisms, such as codes or policy statements, that could be used by top management to communicate an ethical commitment "down the line" should be examined for their usefulness to middle management.

Within the context of Proposition 10, it is interesting to note that some analysts have speculated that managers behave more ethically as they grow older—a kind of "mellowing" factor. Since managers in top management are usually older than those at the lower level, this might partially explain why the younger, middle managers feel greater pressures to compromise their personal ethics. Similarly, one can reason that top-level managers have attained career success already; thus they have the luxury

of subscribing to high ethical norms, while lower-level managers must still prove themselves, which perhaps requires a more aggressive (and likely less ethical) posture. This "mellowing" hypothesis is controversial and does not yet merit the status of a proposition.

"...ethical propriety and legality do not necessarily coincide."

Proposition 11: Individual managers perceive themselves as more ethical than their colleagues. This postulate is the product of many studies of ethics in management. Typically, it evolves because of the following situation: An individual manager is interviewed by a researcher or reporter about a specific questionable practice, such as the use of invisible ink to track questionnaires after respondents have been promised confidentiality. The manager responds that X% of his colleagues would participate in such a practice but, of course, he or she would not. Thus, more than anything else, this proposition emphasizes the human tendency of managers to discuss ethics in a manner that will protect themselves from incrimination or to rationalize their own uprightness.

One implication of this proposition is that the actual ethical norms of businesspeople are probably more accurately reported in what they say their typical colleague would do in a situation than in what they report they themselves would do. The introduction of this proposition serves to remind the business manager of the difficulty of maintaining one's objectivity when one is involved in analyzing ethical questions that hold personal ramifications.   Propositions 6 through 11 are limited in number but in fact establish some fundamental insights into the realm of business ethics. Namely:

• Multiple factors influence ethical decision making. Some are controllable, some are not. Ultimately, the final decision regarding an ethical question is strongly motivated by the manager's individual values.

• Consensus regarding ethical propriety is difficult to achieve when evaluating many specific situations; moreover, managers have a tendency to overstate their own ethical sensitivity.

• Ethical pressures are felt most acutely by lower- and middle-level managers who look to top management for behavioral cues but are themselves confronted with many difficult decisions.

Proscriptive Propositions Concerning Ethics

Propositions regarding business ethics, while easy to postulate, are difficult to propose with the confidence that they will have a significant impact on the organization. One is reminded of the quip by Mark Twain, "To be good is noble. To tell people to be good is even nobler and much less trouble." Nevertheless, organizations with a reputation for impeccable ethical conduct have cultivated and enhanced their outstanding moral demeanor with organizational adjustments that have had an impact on ethical performance. The following propositions focus on such organizational strategies.

Proposition 12: Effective codes of ethics should contain meaningful and clearly stated provisions along with enforced sanctions for noncompliance. A code of ethics or some other formal statement of ethical concern is the minimum commitment to organizational social responsibility all firms should be expected to make. Unfortunately, the vast majority of executives have little confidence in the effectiveness of codes in improving morality because of their vagueness and the difficulty of enforcing them.[10] All too often such codes have become meaningless public relations gimmicks. Still, codes are not without value. They represent a public commitment regarding the prohibition of practices and can diffuse potential ethical problems. For example, consider the purchasing agent who wonders whether it is proper to accept a bottle of 12-year-old Scotch whiskey at Christmastime from a sales representative. He may reason that there is no explicit quid pro quo expected and that since the gift is given at holiday time, the practice is acceptable. Nevertheless, the manager makes this assessment half-heartedly, because he knows the sales representative's firm has several contracts pending and the practice looks suspicious. A specific code statement that prohibits the giving or receiving of gifts with a value of more than $5 would have eliminated the ethical question concerning the gift.

Successful codes tend to be those that are specific *and* enforced. To anticipate every ethical contingency that can arise in a business situation and to hope to include it in a code is both naive and unrealistic. However, certain specific ethical problems tend to arise in particular industries, and these problems require the special scrutiny of management. For instance:

• Producers of heavily sugared products must face the question of how ethical it is to advertise to children, given both the persuasibility of this group and their susceptibility to tooth decay.

• Companies selling whole life insurance must question the ethics of promoting a financial institution that can lock an individual into a low return on investment in perpetuity.

Almost every business environment suggests some relatively unique ethical questions.

The question of code enforcement is a matter of behavioral psychology. Unless members of the organization see a code of ethics monitored and subsequently enforced with visible sanctions, they will ascribe little organizational importance to the code. The implication of

Proposition 12 is that a code of ethics that is not enforced is a code of ethics without teeth, and it will be treated as such by personnel at all levels in an organization.

Proposition 13: Employees must have a nonpunitive, failsafe mechanism for reporting ethical abuses in the organization. This postulate raises the issue of "whistle blowing" and its role in the firm. On one hand, no corporation likes to have its dirty linen aired in public without an opportunity to examine internally its own transgressions. On the other hand, a real commitment to ethical propriety demands that clear abuses of organiza-

---

"Successful codes tend to be those that are specific *and* enforced."

---

tional morality will be condemned and dealt with accordingly, no matter how they come to light. In recent years, too many corporate Serpicos have gone public with substantial abuses, only to be hounded by their own organizations. Organizations dedicated to high ethical standards should provide mechanisms that will assure channels of communication and subsequent protection for whistle blowers. Operationally, this sort of program requires the explicit support of high-level administrators. If top management might be involved in the transgressions, employees should be made aware of an audit committee of the board (chaired by a member independent of management, such as an outside director) to whom information can be given.

Admittedly, such a program can be difficult for management to accept. The possibility of undue negative publicity caused by an overzealous or alarmist employee is a risk. Some issues are difficult to resolve. For example, a financial auditor discovers a foreign payoff that was made several years ago by the now retired chief executive officer. Should this skeleton be allowed to leave the corporate closet? Yet, such dilemmas are the price of developing a climate of ethical responsibility in the organization.

Proposition 14: Every organization should appoint a top-level manager or director to be responsible for acting as an ethical advocate in the organization. In an organization committed to high moral standards, ethical responsibility falls into everyone's domain. But as with many things, unless someone is appointed to direct the effort the responsibility dissolves among the many. One researcher has insightfully proposed the concept of the ethics advocate—a top manager or director whose responsibility would be to elucidate the ethical implications of management's decisions.[11] For example, if a corporation is planning to shut down a plant in a particular community, the ethical advocate would seek to clarify what, if any, moral responsibility the company had to the community where the plant was located. Similarly, the representative would outline what ethical responsibilities the company has to the employees who might be discharged because of the plant shutdown. In short, the ethical advocate would serve as the verbal conscience of the corporation. Both Cummins Engine Co. and the Monsanto Corp. have introduced such positions into their organizations.

Notice that these three propositions—Propositions 12, 13, and 14—provide the business manager with a battery of questions that can be used to initially evaluate the ethical posture of an organization:

• Does the organization have a code of ethics? Is it specific? Is it enforced?

• Has the organization attempted to identify ethical concerns unique to its industry and operations?

• What is the organization's policy toward whistle blowers? What mechanisms are available to report ethical abuses? Internal channels? External channels?

• Has top management communicated its concern for a commitment to high ethical standards? How has this been practically demonstrated?

• Is there someone in the organization who serves as an ethical advocate or ombudsman? What are this person's specific responsibilities?

Conclusion

Certainly, it can be said that there is not a great deal of definitive knowledge regarding the process that leads managers to behave ethically. It is also conceded that the precise philosophical perspective managers ought to use to make ethical decisions is open to debate. Whether it be moral intuition, a particular theory of distributive justice, utilitarianism, or some other framework, reasonable people can disagree on whether a particular decision is ethically proper or not. A few will also continue to maintain that such discussions and frameworks will never have a pragmatic influence on managerial behavior. In this sense the study of business ethics remains somewhat soft, relatively subjective, arguably superfluous, and prone to a soapbox mentality.

Nevertheless, the strength of such arguments is overstated. While business ethics may be an area that is relatively soft, certain solid propositions that are supported in multiple research studies and in the practices of progressive companies can be transmitted to current and future business managers. Rather than embodying a soapbox mentality, the purpose of these propositions is to sensitize the manager to some of the realities of ethics in the organization. The fact that ethical questions are unavoidable, that subordinates look to top management for behavioral cues, and so on, are bits of managerial acumen that should be well-ingrained in the future business executive. These propositions also describe some pragmatic mechanisms that have been utilized by organizations to develop a progressive ethical climate. Numerous executives testify to the worth of these propositions as an aide to moral responsibility. Thus one may realistically view business ethics as an area consisting of a limited number of solid, successfully adapted propositions that can sensitize managers to their ethical responsibility as organizational decision makers. On these propositions business practitioners can begin to build, supplement, and amplify the necessary discussion of ethics that must take place in the boardroom and beyond.

1. Raymond C. Baumhart, "How Ethical Are Businessmen?" *Harvard Business Review* (July-August 1961): 6.

2. Steven N. Brenner and Earl A. Molander, "Is the Ethics of Business Changing?" *Harvard Business Review* (January-February 1977): 52-71.

3. Archie B. Carroll, "A Survey of Managerial Ethics: Is Business Morality Watergate Morality?" *Business and Society Review* (Spring 1975).

4. Mary Susan Miller and Edward A. Miller, "It's Too Late for Ethics Courses in Business Schools," *Business and Society Review* (Spring 1976): 39-43.

5. Theodore V. Purcell, "Do Courses in Ethics Pay Off?" *California Management Review* (Summer 1977).

6. Richard A. Konrad, "Are Business Ethics Worth Studying?" *Business and Society Review* (Fall 1978): 54-57.

7. Baumhart, "How Ethical are Businessmen?" 6.

8. John W. Newstrom and William A. Ruch, "The Ethics of Management and the Management of Ethics," *MSU Business Topics* (Winter 1975): 29-37.

9. Carroll, "A Survey of Managerial Ethics"; Brenner and Molander, "Is the Ethics of Business Changing?" 52-71.

10. Brenner and Molander, "Is the Ethics of Business Changing?" 52-71.

11. Theodore V. Purcell, "A Practical Guide to Ethics in Business," *Business and Society Review* (Spring 1975): 43-50; "Electing an 'Angels Advocate' to the Board," *Management Review* (May 1976): 4-11.

Principles of Business Ethics:

Their Role in Decision Making and an Initial Consensus

Do as you would be done by? Don't get found out? Follow your intuition? What ethical principles do managers really use in business decisions?

Archie B. Carroll

Dr Archie B. Carroll is Professor of Management and holder of the Robert W. Scherer Chair of Management and Corporate Public Affairs at the University of Georgia, USA.

> Our principles are the springs of our actions; our actions, the springs of our happiness or misery. Too much care, therefore, cannot be taken in forming our principles.
>
> Skelton

One clear conclusion that has emerged from society's and businesses' preoccupation with business ethics over the last decade is that managers at all levels need help in making ethical decisions in the workplace. It has long been established that decision making is at the heart of management. Managers need to make many decisions in their everyday working lives in which reside questions of right or wrong, fairness, justice, or, as some business ethicists say, the allocation of harms and benefits.

There are dozens of workplace issues in which ethical questions are now coming to the forefront. A recent survey conducted by Ronald Berenbeim, for The Conference Board, identified seven key issues on which at least 80 per cent of his 300 respondents agreed represented ethical issues in business today. These seven issues comprised employee conflicts of interest, inappropriate gifts to corporate personnel, sexual harassment, unauthorised payments, affirmative action, employee privacy, and environmental issues[1].

The purpose of the current discussion is to describe briefly how principles of business ethics are used in a decision-making process, and to report on a survey that was conducted among a group of managers and prospective managers. The survey was designed to present the respondents with a number of alternative business ethical principles, and then to ascertain the usefulness or power of these principles to the respondents. The respondents then ranked the principles in terms of usefulness to them in their work. Finally, we describe the consensus that seems to emerge from the findings of the study.

The Principles Approach

There are several different ways in which managers may go about improving the ethics of their decision making. One popular approach, which we shall call The Principles Approach, is based upon the idea that managers need to compare their proposed actions, decisions or behaviours with certain principles of ethics. This raises the question

From *Management Decisions*, Vol. 28, No. 8, 1990, pp. 20-24. © 1990 by MCB University Press Limited. Reprinted by permission.

of *what is* a principle of business ethics and *how* might it be applied?

A principle of business ethics is a guideline or rule which, if applied when you are faced with an ethical dilemma, will assist you in making an ethical decision. Examples of principles which have been articulated and discussed by business philosophers and ethicists include the utilitarian principle, the justice principle and the rights principle. These principles, along with others, have been described in detail elsewhere; and our purpose here is not to add to that body of thought[2].

In addition to a comparison of personal or corporate behaviour with an ethical principle is the notion of standards or norms of acceptability. These norms might be personal, organisational or societal in terms of their origin. The process of ethical decision making entails, therefore, a consideration of (1) the action, behaviour or decision being considered, (2) standards or norms against which a comparison might be made, and (3) a principle of business ethics which provides guidance as to what is most important in the decision being made: e.g. utilitarianism, justice, rights. Often, decision making is made based upon comparisons of (1) and (2) or (1) and (3).

Such a principles approach might yield a process of ethical decision making similar to that shown in Figure 1. Note here that the term "ethics screen" is used to imply a filtering process wherein actions, behaviours or decisions are compared with standards or norms, and ethical principles or guides with decision making. The proposed decision, action or behaviour then "passes" or "fails" the ethics screen, and results in the course of action being deemed acceptable or unacceptable.

The Survey

The purpose of the survey described here was to see if prospective managers (senior level business students) and actual practising managers would reach any kind of consensus on what principles of business ethics they found useful. On separate occasions, the two groups were presented with the same set of descriptions of ethical principles which were adapted from earlier work by T.K. Das and Steiner and Steiner[3]. Thirty-four business students and 88 middle managers ranked the principles presented in Figure 2. The eleven principles listed were extracted from 14 principles studied earlier by Das.

Figure 3 presents the ethical principles that were considered most important by the 88 managers. Included in the ranking is a brief statement as to what each means. These are reported here first because they come from

Figure 1. *A Process of Ethical Decision Making*

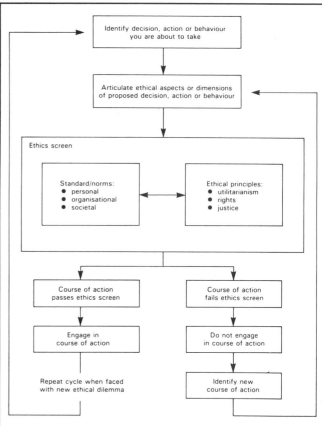

Source: Adapted from Archie B. Carroll *Business & Society: Ethics & Stakeholder Management* (South-Western Publishing Co., 1989), p. 128. Used with permission

actual practising managers and must therefore be deemed most credible.

Figure 4 summarises the ranking done by the managers, along with the ranking done by a sample of business students from a large Southeastern university. Also included is the ranking which was done in the T.K. Das study among a large group of Southwestern business students. The researcher regrets that the surveys of managers and Southeastern students did not include all of the principles listed by Das, but most of them (11 out of 14) were on the survey and this provides some useful comparisons.

Some Consensus Emerges

Several interesting findings emerge from these three surveys. Most notable is the fact that there is consensus among the three groups on the Golden Rule and the Disclosure Rule as the top two ranking ethical principles among those considered. Further, the Intuition Ethic and Categorical Imperative were ranked third and fourth by the managerial group and drew strong support from both

Figure 2. *Ranking Ethical Principles*

Below are listed 11 different ethical principles that may be used in business decision making. Rank them in terms of how powerful or useful they would be for you.

Principle	*Name of Principle**
1. You should not adopt principles of action unless they can, without inconsistency, be adopted by everyone else.	Categorical Imperative
2. Individuals should act to further their self-interests so long as they do not violate the law.	Conventionalist Ethic
3. Do unto others as you would have them do unto you;	Golden Rule
4. If it feels good, do it.	Hedonistic Ethic
5. If you are comfortable with an action or decision after asking yourself whether you would mind if all your associates, friends, and family were aware of it, then you should act or decide.	Disclosure Rule
6. You do what your "gut feeling" tells you to do.	Intuition Ethic
7. If the end justifies the means, then you should act.	Means-Ends Ethic
8. You should take whatever advantage you are strong enough and powerful enough to take without respect for ordinary social conventions and laws.	Might-Equals-Right Ethic
9. This is an age of large-scale organisations — be loyal to the organisation.	Organisation Ethic
10. You should do only that which can be explained before a committee of your professional peers.	Professional Ethic
11. You should follow the principle of "the greatest good for the greatest number".	Utilitarian Principle

* The names of these principles were not included on the survey sheet. They are supplied here just for purposes of explanation.

Figure 3. *Ethical Principles Ranked According to Value by Practising Managers. N=88*

1. The Golden Rule

   Do unto others as you would have them do unto you.

2. Disclosure Rule

   If you are comfortable with an action or decision after asking yourself whether you would mind if all your associations, friends, and family were aware of it, then you should act or decide.

3. The Intuition Ethic

   You do what your "gut feeling" tells you to do.

4. The Categorical Imperative

   You should not adopt principles of action unless they can, without inconsistency, be adopted by everyone else.

(tie) 5. The Professional Ethic

   You should do only that which can be explained before a committee of your professional peers.

(tie) 6. The Utilitarian Principle

   You should follow the principle of "the greatest good for the greatest number."

Figure 4. *Ranking of Ethical Principles by Three Groups*

Principle	Managers $n=88$	SE Students $n=34$	SW Students $n=265$
Golden Rule	1	1	1
Disclosure Rule	2	2	2
Intuition Ethic	3	5	6
Categorical Imperative	4	6	8
Professional Ethic	5(tie)	4	7
Utilitarian Ethic	5(tie)	3	3
Proportionality Ethic	*	*	4
Organisation Ethic	*	*	5

* Not on Managers or SE survey

student groups. Likewise the Professional Ethic and Utilitarian Ethic, which tied for fifth by the Managers, were strongly supported by the SE student group and partially supported by the SW group. The SW group placed two principles in the fourth and fifth position which were not on the survey of the other two groups.

It is worth noting that the *Golden Rule* — "Do unto others [as] you would have them do unto you"–is a fairly straightforward, easy to understand principle. Further, it guides the individual decision maker to behaviour, actions or decisions which he or she should be able to assess as acceptable or not based upon some direct comparisons with what he or she would consider ethical or fair. There is nothing esoteric about this. All it requires — and this is sometimes seen by some as difficult — is that the decision maker affords others the same kind and degree of consideration that he or she would think is right in similar personal circumstances.

The Golden Rule is among the oldest of the principles of living □

The Golden Rule simply argues that, if you want to be treated fairly, treat others fairly; if you want to be told the truth, tell others the truth; if you want your privacy protected, respect the privacy of others. The key is impartiality. According to this principle we are not to make an exception of ourselves. In essence, then, the Golden Rule personalises business relations and brings the ideal of fairness into business deliberations[4].

Perhaps the reason the Golden Rule is so popular is that it is rooted in history and is among the oldest of the principles of living. Further, it is universal in the sense that it requires no specific religious beliefs or faith. Almost since time began, religious leaders and philosophers have advocated the Golden Rule in one form or another. The following is illustrative[5]:

— The Hindu *Mahabharata* professes: ''Men gifted with intelligence and purified souls should always treat others as they themselves wish to be treated''.

— Confucius summed up the rules of life as follows: ''What you do not want done to yourself, do not do to others''.

— In the *Bible* Jesus taught in the book of Matthew: ''So in every thing, do to others what you would have them do to you''.

— Rabbi Hillel, when asked by a supplicant to be taught the Law, answered: ''What thou thyself hatest, do not to thy neighbour. That is the whole Law. The rest is commentary. Go and learn it.''

It is easy to see, therefore, why Martin Luther could say that the Golden Rule is part of the ''natural law'', because

it is a moral rule which anyone can recognise without any particular religious teaching. That this thousands-of-years-old wisdom should surface as the number one ethical principle is indeed suggestive of the enduring understanding of how humanity should treat humanity. Some things just never change, it is said.

Intuition is the immediate thought we have before rational thought or inference □

The *Disclosure Rule,* which could be seen as complementary to the Golden Rule, moves the focus of attention to how others whose opinions you respect would regard your decision, action or behaviour. According to the Disclosure Rule, you are probably on a sound ethical footing if you are still comfortable with a proposed action or decision after asking yourself whether you would mind if all your associates, friends, and family were aware of it. The concept of public exposure is a powerful tool; and, though it does not provide ironclad assurance that you are acting ethically, it does provide some strong indication of how the action is likely to be viewed.

The third-ranked principle by the managers studied was the *Intuition Ethic.* Whereas the previous two principles required some degree of rational thought about how the decision maker would like to be treated and how others might regard the proposed action, the intuition ethic is driven by one's quick and ready insight. Intuition, sometimes thought of as ''gut feeling'', is the immediate thought we have before engaging in rational thought or inference.

A person should not adopt principles unless they can be adopted by everyone else □

Intuition is probably the result of an endowment of moral consciousness we each have, combined with experience and wisdom gained over time. It is a kind of awareness that might be the sum total of all that the decision maker is or has experienced. It is very possible that the intuition ethic might yield an evaluation of a proposed action that embodies considerations of the Golden Rule and the Disclosure Rule as well as other principles. Managers are often driven to make quick decisions, and it is tempting to believe that they go on their own "gut feeling" when time does not permit a more careful assessment based upon other principles or guidelines.

Technically, Immanuel Kant stated the *Categorical Imperative* as follows: "Act only according to that maxim by which you can at the same time will that it should become a universal law." Stated in another way, this principle argues that a person should not adopt principles of action or behaviour unless they can, without inconsistency, be adopted by everyone else. This principle is useful in terms of the manager searching for universal guidelines of consistency, but it really does not provide pointed guidance in a decision making situation. In a sense the categorical imperative is an abstract guideline that could be imposed upon other, more useful, principles.

The *Professional Ethic* holds that you should do only that which can be explained before a committee of your professional peers. In a sense this is a more restricted version of the disclosure rule and, though useful, is not as rigorous because of the possibility that those in similar areas of work might be more understanding of ethical lapses than the general public. In other words, you could more easily find someone in your own profession or line of work to agree with your proposed action than perhaps among your friends or family who are not immediately familiar with the constraints you are up against.

Finally the *Utilitarian Principle*, which argues for the greatest good for the greatest number, is idealistic, somewhat abstract, but quite difficult to apply. How is one ever able to determine what decision or course of action reflects the greatest good for the greatest number? This principle is extremely attractive on first thought, but is very difficult to apply and use.

Summing Up

There are a number of useful ethical principles around should managers wish to use them. First, managers must *wish* to use them. All the principles in existence will not suffice if the individual leader or decision maker is not interested in being ethical. An underlying assumption to the use of the ethical principles is, then, that the manager wishes to do the right thing.

A process of ethical decision making was presented, and this entailed the manager subjecting his or her proposed action to an ethics screen composed of an assortment of ethical principles and standards of acceptability. The process should help the manager to think through or "model" what the decision making process should look like when ethical considerations are included. There is no guarantee that the ethics screen will filter out all proposed actions that may be poorly formulated. It does,

however, add a measure of ethical process to decision making. It requires the manager to "think ethically" when making decisions.

Finally, a small set of ethical principles rose to the surface as most valuable when considered by a group of practising managers and soon-to-be-managers. The three principles which were ranked highest were quite straightforward and easily understood — treat others as you want to be treated, do only what you would feel comfortable with if those whom you care most about knew it, and follow your intuition. We should add in closing, however, that the modern concern for principles of ethical decision making that are neatly wrapped in a ready-to-use package cannot really be met. Though we desire to have such precision and closure, with no loose ends or puzzling leftovers, we simply cannot identify or agree upon rules, slogans, proverbs or principles that will eliminate all thought and deep introspection.

There are ethical principles that managers can agree upon as useful for management decision making. The real challenge seems to be in their use. As Herman Nelson once said ". . .it is in the application of principles which anyone can understand that management proves itself good or bad". This quite certainly applies here. As so often is the case with successful managers or organisations, the acid test is with implementation.

References

1. Berenbeim, R.E., *Corporate Ethics*, The Conference Board, New York, 1987, p. 3.
2. De George, R.T., *Business Ethics*, 2nd Ed., Macmillan, New York, 1986.
3. Steiner, G.A. and Steiner, J.F., *Business, Government and Society: A Managerial Perspective*, Random House, New York, 1980, pp. 383-9; Das, T.K., "Ethical Preferences among Business Students: A Comparative Study of Fourteen Ethical Principles", *Southern Management Association Proceedings*, 13-16 November, 1985, pp. 11-12.
4. Barry, V., *Moral Issues in Business*, Wadsworth, Belmont, California, 1979, pp. 50-51.
5. Shinn, R.L., *The Sermon on the Mount*, United Church Press, Philadelphia, 1962, pp. 76-7.
6. *The Forbes Scrapbook of Thoughts on the Business of Life*, Forbes, New York, 1976, p. 356.

Application Questions

(1) Complete the ranking of ethical principles exercise (Figure 2 in the article). Do these principles vary according to the situation?
(2) Outline your personal ethical standpoint on privacy, environmental issues and unauthorised payments. Do they always coincide with practice in your organisation?
(3) Should principles ever be compromised?

INTEGRITY

AN ESSENTIAL EXECUTIVE QUALITY

Donald G. Zauderer

DONALD G. ZAUDERER, Ph.D., is director of the Key Executive Program at The American University in Washington, D.C. He thanks Lisa Levy, Tim Evanson, Jeff Fishel, Carol Blum, Pete Phillips, Morley Segal, and Rabbi Bruce Lustig for their contributions and comments during the preparation of this article.

What has happened to the notion of "integrity" in our nation? This author identifies 13 traits of business managers which compromise integrity and he presents specific actions that can help build a culture where integrity is practiced on a constant basis.

Stories about the absence of managerial integrity are dominating the mass media. We are reading about corruption in the Savings and Loan industry, insider trading on Wall Street, manipulative and harmful leveraged buy outs in American industry. In the political world, we are reading about negative campaigning, unlawful surveillance among political rivals, congressmen bouncing checks and failing to pay House restaurant charges. Many CEOs are being criticized for taking excessive bonuses while at the same time laying off large numbers of mid-level managers and production workers due to recessionary pressures. Even universities are under attack for raising tuition costs, charging the government for entertainment and decorating projects, approving sweetheart severance and retirement packages for administrators, and failing to emphasize quality education.

Philip Cushman, commenting in the *American Psychologist* on the breakdown in integrity claims that Americans have become emotionally and spiritually disoriented—preoccupied with how an issue affects the individual rather than how it affects the community or society.[1] Donald M. Wolfe, in yet a stronger statement contends in his article on integrity that, "The exploitative mentality has become so pervasive, and the impact of organizational practices so potent, that organizations cannot be trusted to ensure the commonweal—to protect the environment, to provide fair and human treatment for employees, to protect the safety and security of clients and customers, to refrain from misappropriation of public funds, and the like."[2] Both Cushman and Wolfe are arguing that there has been a serious erosion, accentuated in the last ten years, in the moral fabric of managers and leaders in the private and public sectors.

An Ancient Theme

Concerns such as these are not new—or unique to contemporary America. It is a pervasive theme going back to ancient times. In the book of Genesis, we learn that God formed humans with two inclinations—one good and one evil. Some Old Testament scholars see these inclinations as biological drives woven into the psychological fabric of every human being.[3]

In making decisions, managers are often faced with opposite and compelling inclinations, an internal struggle between modern versions of good and evil. Greed drove some Savings and Loan chieftains to misappropriate the savings of depositors. From all indications, they were not concerned about protecting their depositors, preserving the credibility of the banking system, or protecting the public trust that is essential to effective financial management. The concern for private gain prevailed over any concern for the public good.

Integrity is often overlooked or assumed in corporate life. There are few training programs focusing on ethical responsibility. Performance appraisal systems, corporate codes, and orientation programs often say little about principles of conduct in dealing with others. Often, a person's integrity is given little attention when compared to other characteristics in selecting candidates for positions. Corporations provide little guidance and, thus, many managers are operating without a solid infrastructure of principles guiding their behavior. If good and evil are pervasive themes in our personal and organizational lives, then corporations should consider doing more to help their managers make choices that reflect the "good"—thus preserving the good name of both the individual and the corporation.

This is a tall order. How does one get started? The logical first step is to get some understanding of what integrity means in broad terms, and then move toward clarifying those principles of conduct which might guide behavior in corporate life. In essence, corporations need to declare that certain principles define the nature of a manager's responsibility with respect to how he or she deals with others. Clarifying relational obligations is the first step in building an environment where a culture of integrity prevails over a culture of excessive and amoral self-interest.

The ideas put forth here are not intended as complete or definitive. Rather, they can provide a basis for initiating a dialogue about what set of principles might guide behavior in your organization.

From *Business Forum*, Fall 1992, pp. 12-16. © 1992 by The School of Business and Economics, California State University, Los Angeles. Reprinted by permission.

What is Integrity?

The word integrity is derived from the latin word *integri*, meaning wholeness. It is defined as a "state of being whole or undiminished." It is also defined as a state of "soundness of and adherence to moral principle."[4] Since integrity is an aspect of one's character and behavior, the definitions are highly related. It has been argued that one's character cannot become whole and integrated unless it is grounded in a solid infrastructure of moral values.[5]

What are these values? While there is no universal agreement on what moral principles should guide our behavior, we can gain perspective by integrating ancient classical ideas with modern thought. The Old Testament, recounting a thousand years of events, focuses on the struggle between good and evil. Confucius, writing in the years 551-479 BC proclaimed, "What you do not want done to yourself, do not do to others." Saint Matthew is quoted in the New Testament with an admonition that today is translated into what we call The Golden Rule: Do unto others as you would have them do unto you. Aristotle, writing over 2000 years ago, placed considerable emphasis on his conception of "happiness." In Aristotelian terms, happiness is described as a "kind of virtuous activity of the soul."[6] The term "activity" is particularly important because of its emphasis on moral action in a social environment. The major function of virtue, according to Aristotle, is to influence others to perform noble actions, and to create a society where people can develop to their full potential.[7] To achieve this end, he recommended that citizens become fully engaged in both study and the political life of the community. Wealth and the possession of goods were not considered an appropriate end, but simply served as instruments to achieve "happiness."[8]

While Aristotle focused on learning, political and social involvement, and good deeds, Immanuel Kant, writing in the 18th century, emphasized moral duties and obligations in our relationship with others. In his view, the first duty of individuals is to treat others as ends and not as means. Implicit in his statement is the belief that "no person's rights should be subordinated to anyone else."[9] If executives see workers simply as means to their own accumulation of wealth, it is quite natural to minimize their share of increased profits; to mini-mize developmental opportunities unless it is of immediate benefit to them; or to invest as little as possible in the safety and security of the worker. Alternatively, seeing the employee as an end induces one to think of him or her as a partner, whose interests you attempt to fully integrate with the interests of the organization.

One of IBMs core values, "Respect for the individual," has its roots in Kantian logic. Kant introduces a set of moral duties and obligations that should guide our relationships with each other. Principles such as honesty, generosity, and keeping one's word, are some ways in which we treat people as an end rather than a means.

Contemporary philosopher Mark Halfin further emphasizes the importance of intention in defining integrity. He defines integrity as reflected in one who "maintains a consistent commitment to do what is best—especially under conditions of adversity."[10] In attempting to do what is best, people of integrity intend to embrace noble ideals and just principles; and acknowledge and confront all relevant moral considerations when faced with a dilemma. Halfin adds two important dimensions to the conversation: It is the *intention* to do what is best based on personal analysis and reflection that matters; and it involves *doing* what is perceived to be best—even under conditions of adversity. Naturally, integrity is most severely tested under adverse conditions. One, then, does not have to be morally pure or perfect in judgment to have integrity. Rather, one's integrity is determined by the intention to do what is right.

Halfin's notion of holding onto principle under adversity, is further emphasized by authors Nancy Adler and Frederick Bird who indicated that "Individuals demonstrate integrity when they withstand pressure from others while taking risks in defense of behavior they conscientiously consider to be best."[11] Integrity is risky business. Should an employee tell government inspectors about transgressions of environmental law even though it might threaten his or her job? Should a boss spend time on employee development despite the criticisms of peers who believe it is a waste of time? Should a male confront other males about sexual harassment, and risk the criticism of peers? Integrity implies the disposition to take risks in defense of relational duties and obligations; having the courage to stand up, to maintain a course of principled action, even under attack or severe criticism.

Each of the sources adds a distinct and unique element to the emerging definition of integrity. The following summarizes their contributions:

The Old Testament: Consciously struggle to subdue the evil inclination.

The New Testament: Live according to the principal of The Golden Rule.

Aristotle: Maintain concern for the community; engage in political and social life to improve the community; inspire others to do good deeds.

Kant: Establish, affirm, and exemplify moral duties and obligations toward others; treat others as ends and not as a means.

Halfin: Maintain a consistent commitment to do what is right, especially under conditions of adversity; confront all moral considerations before taking action.

Adler and Bird: Take risks to defend just principles and ideals.

Specific Behaviors

The preceding discussion has focused on general guidelines. But how does one move from guidelines to specific behaviors? What specific behaviors reflect high integrity? How does one's integrity affect the trust of others and the strength of the commonweal?

In attempting to identify specific behaviors, a far reaching search of literature that included religion, philosophy, biographies of great leaders, psychology, and business and government ethics was conducted. Cross-cutting moral themes and principles were identified and are described in the following list: (The behaviors are expressed in a negative form—the opposite behavior follows in italics.) A manager's integrity is compromised when he or she:

Displays Arrogance by becoming puffed up with their own importance, exaggerating their worth to the organization, and speaking only with people at same or higher level. (*Posess humility*)

Promotes Self-Interest by exploiting the organization for own purpose and focusing on "what's in it for me" when considering actions. (*Maintain concern for the greater good*)

Practices Deception by making untrue statements, taking credit for the work of others, and using misleading facts to defend positions. (*Be truthful*)

Breaches Agreements by delivering

services late, or failing to follow an agreed upon decision process. (*Fulfill commitments*)

Deals Unfairly by making judgments without researching facts, discriminating in hiring and promotion, and assigning the most interesting projects to a favored few. (*Strive for fairness*)

Shifts Blame by declining to acknowledge personal responsibility, falsely accusing others, and denigrating the reputation of colleagues. (*Take responsibility*)

Diminishes Dignity by withholding recognition, declining to invite or accept input, exhibiting discourteous and impolite behavior. (*Have respect for the individual*)

Retains Envy by begrudging other's success, and competing at every opportunity. (*Celebrate the good fortune of others*)

Neglects Employee Development by providing superficial performance appraisals and failing to coach or train staff. (*Develop others*)

Avoids Risks by refusing to confront unjust actions, or declining to stand up for principle. (*Reproach unjust acts*)

Holds Grudges by failing to let go of hard feelings, and finding ways to get even. (*Be forgiving*)

Declines to Extend Self by withholding help and assistance in times that matter, and being ungenerous in rewards. (*Extend self for others*)

Displays Arrogance

Arrogant managers nourish their ego at every opportunity. They focus on the size of their offices, the quality of their furniture, the location of their parking place, and other symbols of status. They take advice from superiors, but spurn the counsel of peers and subordinates. Arrogant managers may try to intimidate subordinates with hard questions, taking delight in catching flaws in facts or logic. Their agenda is simple: to puff up their own importance. The effect is predictable. It diminishes the dignity and self-esteem of subordinates, and limits the real potential contribution of the manager.

Subordinates resent arrogant bosses, and may even retaliate. A relationship that starts with trust, loyalty, and commitment will degenerate into one characterized by suspicion, betrayal, and lack of dedication.

Promotes Self-Interest

Some people pursue their self-interest to the detriment of the organization. As an

example, financier Charles Keating bolstered his financial position by recklessly using his savings and loan money to finance risky ventures. The cost to the public was immense—notably in dollars and confidence in the entire savings and loan system.

There are many ways to exploit the system for personal gain. Doctors might order unnecessary tests to increase their income. Lawyers might complicate divorce proceedings to increase billable hours. Managers may grossly underreward subordinates to enhance their reputations for efficiency. Professors may devote little time preparing for their classes in order to pursue the larger rewards of publication. And corporate CEOs may curtail research and development to improve short-term profits and be rewarded with a generous year-end bonus. In the long term, these actions erode public trust and confidence in our institutions.

"Managers who lack integrity place themselves and their organizations at risk."

Practices Deception

Some managers regularly deceive colleagues, vendors, and clients. This deception takes many forms. They assign projects without revealing obstacles and potential risks; provide staff with false information on why management promoted someone else; or promise services to clients without any intention to deliver. Similarly, they provide subcontractors with false information on the real scope of work; provide employees with misleading information on their career potential; or promise and rescind offers to participate in important decisions. A manager who builds a career on deception will eventually stand alone.

Breaches Agreements

Managers who are unable to meet commitments lose a precious asset, their reputations. Some renege on promises to grant subordinates specialized training, career guidance or developmental assignments. Managers who regularly fail to follow through on agreements such as

these will lose credibility, trust, and effectiveness in the organization. These managers will find that peers and subordinates will no longer be inclined to respond to their needs in a timely manner.

Deals Unfairly

Some managers deal unfairly with associates. They may provide access to a favored few, base salaries and bonuses on general perception instead of concrete results, promote staff with the "right" cultural, educational, and religious background, and reward those who tell them what they want to hear. In such situations, some subordinates flourish while others feel rejected and alienated. When managers treat some staff unfairly, they inadvertently demotivate part of their staff and reduce total team effectiveness.

Shifts Blame

Some managers blame others for every problem. They furnish plausible explanations about how someone else's actions contributed to declining profits, high overhead or client dissatisfaction. They rarely acknowledge their role in the problem and expect others to accept the blame. Subordinates will resent the finger pointing, and the loyalty they once brought to the job will be replaced by alienation and distrust.

Diminishes Dignity

Some managers specialize in diminishing others. They take credit for the work of employees, make decisions without meaningful participation, decline to return phone calls of their subordinates, and insist on reviewing all decisions. These actions diminish the self-esteem of subordinates.

In some cases managers practice discrimination. They stereotype African Americans, Hispanics, Asians, American Indians, women, or anyone else with a different color, gender, or cultural background. They may stereotype minority staff as lazy, indecisive, ungenerous, fragile, or ineffective. Armed with these discriminatory assumptions, managers disregard the special talents of subordinates. This practice diminishes the self worth of employees, and by becoming a self-fulfilling prophesy, limits opportunities for advancement. To make matters worse, the organization will fail to get the maximum value of each employee.

Retains Envy

Managers inevitably try to compare the

salaries, perquisites and resources with those of their colleagues who have similar rank. They may find that someone else has a larger staff, bigger office or more generous expense account. Some will become consumed with envy and look for ways to redress the inequity. They may press the boss for better conditions, refrain from cooperating with peers, or withhold their best effort on important projects. As a consequence, their relationships will deteriorate up and down the organization.

The wise Solomon said that "envy is the rottenest of bones," implying that unrestrained feelings of envy always damage relationships. Managers who cannot transform these feelings will be unable to build a loyal following.

Neglects Employee Development
Some managers neglect to develop subordinates. For example, they rarely clarify job expectations, provide subordinates with well grounded feedback on performance, or discuss career aspirations within the context of organizational needs and opportunities.

Employees soon understand that they are at a dead-end. They may conclude that if the manager is not concerned about them, they will care less about him or her. Managers who invest little time in people will get little back from them.

Avoids Risks
It takes courage to speak the truth, especially when it may bring reprisals. For example, a manager of environmental affairs at a major oil company was fired for failing to remove documents from a plastics facility in order to conceal facts in an investigation. His superiors had forced him to choose between losing his job and taking the ethically correct action.

While confronting every action of injustice would be foolhardy, some managers damage the organization by staying silent in the face of an unjust or unethical act. Their silence, in effect, creates a precedent for similar acts of questionable integrity. Peers and subordinates with lax standards can then operate freely, increasing the risk that decisions will embarrass or weaken the organization. In the case of the oil company, for example, the fired employee went to court and was awarded $1.375 million in damages.

Holds Grudges
Life in organizations is sometimes like a hockey game. Players bash one another in attempting to gain a competitive edge. Managers are wounded when senior executives pass them over for promotion, criticize them in public, withhold information, or second guess decisions. Managers can also be angered when subordinates embarrass them by bungling a presentation with senior management. In addition, peers can wound colleagues by raising embarrassing questions in high-level meetings.

Some managers respond to these events by "getting even." They may strike back by withholding information from the boss, being inaccessible to a

"Organizations can do a great deal to build a climate where considerations of integrity are taken into account in decision-making."

subordinate; or providing a peer with half-hearted cooperation. Managers who want to get even can always find a way—usually at a cost to their reputations.

Such acts will lead superiors to doubt the manager's ability to remain cool under pressure. Subordinates will play it safe to guard against retribution. These outcomes can damage a manager's reputation as a mature professional who can be trusted to exercise good judgment.

Declines to Extend Self
Some managers rarely extend themselves for others. They focus attention on their personal objectives, and feel no sense of responsibility for assisting subordinates. For example, the regional vice president of a restaurant chain heard about a newly appointed high potential manager who was facing a serious turnover problem. With some coaching, the manager could have identified the problem. The regional V.P. never provided the needed assistance, and the manager left the business out of frustration.

People in organizations need all types of help. They may need special mentoring on how to transition into a new job, get along with a difficult boss, or balance the responsibilities of work and home. A manager who declines to extend assistance relinquishes an opportunity to empower employees and gain their loyalty.

Summing Up
Managers who lack integrity place themselves and their organizations at risk. When they transgress norms of integrity, they risk losing the trust, loyalty, and commitment of employees, suppliers and customers. The best preventative is for organizations to define the moral standards expected of everyone and to develop programs that reinforce these standards.

Many companies understand that integrity is a key element in building strategic advantage. John F. Akers, Chairman of IBM, contends that IBM has built its business on a basis of trust and confidence."[12] IBM has always understood that integrity has helped the organization build strategic advantage, avoid adverse publicity, and maintain an identity as competent, successful, and ethical.

Organizations can do a great deal to build a climate where considerations of integrity are taken into account in decision-making. The following are some actions that help build a culture where integrity is practiced on a consistent basis:

Communicate the Message from Senior Management. The words and actions of senior leaders have an enormous impact in building a culture of integrity. If senior managers are models of integrity, they will earn the right to emphasize it in speeches, memos, and policy statements. Their actions and words will be the single most important factor in determining the ethical climate of the organization.

Develop Codes of Ethical Conduct. Many corporations have established core value statements or codes of ethical conduct to communicate their expectations. Digital Corporation, for example, in its statement of philosophy emphasizes "fair personnel practices, meeting commitments to customers and employees, developing people, honest and straight forward communication with customers, being honest, fair and open with suppliers, never criticizing the competition publicly, and striving to do what is right in every situation."[13]

Develop Procedures for Discussing/ Reporting Incidents. Statements of corporate policies and procedures are another means of reinforcing ethical codes of business conduct. Boeing Corporation has an elaborate statement of business conduct, and has established a channel that enables employees to report infractions or concerns. IBM Corporation has a wide ranging set of guidelines for business conduct, and each employee must certify in writing every year that he or she has read it. The IBM Speak Up and Open Door Programs also allow employees to pursue a complaint with any higher level of management. All complaints are investigated and threats of retribution are not tolerated. Employees who transgress corporate standards face disciplinary action—even the potential for dismissal.

Establish Integrity as an Assessment Criteria. When employees understand that integrity is an evaluative criteria, they will pay more attention to this aspect of their performance.

Build Ethical Considerations into Long-Range Planning. Corporations can benefit from considering ethical issues when discussing alternatives for future action. Researcher Susan Harrison writes that corporations should "identify ethical issues in which the company is or may be involved, how each issue may impact the company, the probability of occurrence, and an appropriate response to the ethical issue."[14] This analysis can legiti-

mate ethics as a consideration in corporate decision-making; and can prepare the corporation for defending its actions on moral grounds.

Include Ethics and Business Conduct in Corporate Training. Training is often the only action that corporations take to reinforce their business conduct guidelines. By itself, it will not be effective in raising the standards of ethical conduct. Together with other actions discussed above, it can contribute to improving the ethical climate in the corporation. Such training programs can introduce corporate values and beliefs. Through the use of videos, case studies, simulations, and other methods, training can provide employees with a heightened awareness of the ethical implications of their actions, and provide them with guidance on how to exercise ethical judgment.

All of these actions will reinforce the message that employees at every level are expected to bring integrity to their jobs, and to their relationships with fellow workers, suppliers, customers, and the community. In the long run, the corporate strategic advantage will be enhanced by its reputation for integrity.

It's time to reconsider the words of John Gardner in *On Leadership*:

We must hope too that our leaders will help us keep alive traditional values that are not so easy to embrace in laws—our feeling about individual moral responsibility, about caring for others, about honor and integrity, and tolerance and mutual respect, and about individual fulfillment within a framework of shared values.

Notes

1 Cushman, Philip, "Why the Self is Empty: Toward a Historically Situated Psychology," *American Psychologist,* May 1990, 604.
2 Wolfe, Donald M., "Is There Integrity in the Bottom Line: Managing Obstacles to Executive Integrity," Suresh Srivastva and Associates, *Executive Integrity: The Search for High Human Values in Organizational Life,* San Francisco, Jossey-Bass, Inc, 1988, 152.
3 Goldman, Norman Saul, *An Investigation Into a Rabbinic Understanding of Yetzer Hara and the Unconscious,* Eastern Baptist Theological Seminar, 1980, 35.
4 Stein, Jess, (ed.), *The Random House Dictionary of the English Language,* New York, New York, Random House, 1967.
5 Taylor, Gabriele, "Integrity," *Proceedings of the Aristotelian Society,* 55 (1981), 143-159.
6 Aristotle, *The Nichomachean Ethics,* London, Penguin Books, 1975, 81.
7 Ibid, 339.
8 Ibid, 69.
9 Kant, Immanual, *The Groundwork of the Metaphysic of Morals,* trans. H.J. Paton, New York, Harper & Row, 1964, 63-67.
10 Halfin, Mark S., Integrity: *A Philosophical Inquiry,* Philadelphia, PA, Temple University Press, 36.
11 Adler, Nancy J., Bird, Frederick B., "International Dimensions of Executive Integrity: Who Is Responsible for the World?," Srivastva, Suresh and Associates, *Executive Integrity: The Search for High Human Values in Organizational Life,* San Francisco, Jossey-Bass, 1988, 252.
12 IBM Corporation, *Business Conduct Guidelines,* September 1990, 5.
13 Digital Corporation, *Personnel Policies and Procedures Manual,* 1990.
14 Harrison, Susan J., "What Corporate America is Teaching About Ethics," *Academy of Management Executive,* 1981, Vol. 5, No. 1, 29.

Ethics in Practice

*The values of a company's leaders are evident
in every strategic decision they make.*

Kenneth R. Andrews

*Kenneth R. Andrews is the Donald K. David Professor of
Business Administration, Emeritus, at the Harvard Busi-
ness School. He was editor of HBR from 1979 to 1985. This
article is adapted from his introduction to* Ethics in
Practice: Managing the Moral Corporation *(Harvard
Business School Press, 1989).*

As the 1990s overtake us, public interest in ethics is at
a historic high. While the press calls attention to
blatant derelictions on Wall Street, in the defense
industry, and in the Pentagon, and to questionable
activities in the White House, in the attorney general's office, and in Congress, observers wonder
whether our society is sicker than usual. Probably
not. The standards applied to corporate behavior
have risen over time, and that has raised the average
rectitude of businesspersons and politicians both. It
has been a long time since we could say with Mark
Twain that we have the best Senate money can buy or
agree with muckrakers like Upton Sinclair that our
large companies are the fiefdoms of robber barons.
But illegal and unethical behavior persists, even as
efforts to expose it often succeed in making its rewards short-lived.

Why is business ethics a problem that snares not
just a few mature criminals or crooks in the making
but a host of apparently good people who lead exemplary private lives while concealing information
about dangerous products or systematically falsifying costs? My observation suggests that the problem
of corporate ethics has three aspects: the development of the executive as a moral person; the influence
of the corporation as a moral environment; and the
actions needed to map a high road to economic and
ethical performance—and to mount guardrails to
keep corporate wayfarers on track.

Sometimes it is said that wrongdoing in business is an individual failure: a person of the
proper moral fiber, properly brought up, simply
would not cheat. Because of poor selection, a
few bad apples are bound to appear in any big barrel. But these corporate misfits can subsequently

be scooped out. Chief executive officers, we used to
think, have a right to rely on the character of individual employees without being distracted from business objectives. Moral character is shaped by family,
church, and education long before an individual joins
a company to make a living.

In an ideal world, we might end here. In the real
world, moral development is an unsolved problem at
home, at school, at church—and at work. Two-career
families, television, and the virtual disappearance of
the dinner table as a forum for discussing moral issues have clearly outmoded instruction in basic principles at Mother's knee—if that fabled tutorial was
ever as effective as folklore would have it. We cannot
expect our battered school systems to take over the
moral role of the family. Even religion is less help
than it once might have been when membership in a
distinct community promoted—or coerced—conventional moral behavior. Society's increasing secular-
ization, the profusion of sects, the conservative
church's divergence from new lifestyles, pervasive
distrust of the religious right—all these mean that we
cannot depend on uniform religious instruction to
armor business recruits against temptation.

Nor does higher education take up the slack, even
in disciplines in which moral indoctrination once
flourished. Great literature can be a self-evident

▌ Why do so many good people get caught falsifying costs?

source of ethical instruction, for it informs the mind
and heart together about the complexities of moral
choice. Emotionally engaged with fictional or historic characters who must choose between death and
dishonor, integrity and personal advancement, power
and responsibility, self and others, we expand our
own moral imaginations as well. Yet professors of literature rarely offer guidance in ethical interpretation, preferring instead to stress technical, aesthetic,
or historical analysis.

Reprinted by permission of *Harvard Business Review.* "Ethics in Practice," by Kenneth R. Andrews, September/October
1989, pp. 99-104. © 1989 by the President and Fellows of Harvard College. All rights reserved.

Moral philosophy, which is the proper academic home for ethical instruction, is even more remote, with few professors choosing to teach applied ethics. When you add to that the discipline's studied disengagement from the world of practical affairs, it is not surprising that most students (or managers) find little in the subject to attract them.

What does attract students—in large numbers—is economics, with its theory of human behavior that relates all motivation to personal pleasure, satisfaction, and self-interest. And since self-interest is more easily served than not by muscling aside the self-interest of others, the Darwinian implications of conventional economic theory are essentially immoral. Competition produces and requires the will to win. Careerism focuses attention on advantage. Immature individuals of all ages are prey to the moral flabbiness that William James said attends exclusive service to the bitch goddess Success.

Spurred in part by recent notorious examples of such flabbiness, many business schools are making determined efforts to reintroduce ethics in elective and required courses. But even if these efforts were further along than they are, boards of directors and senior managers would be unwise to assume that recruits could enter the corporate environment without need for additional education. The role of any school is to prepare its graduates for a lifetime of learning from experience that will go better and faster than it would have done without formal education. No matter how much colleges and business schools expand their investment in moral instruction, most education in business ethics (as in all other aspects of business acumen) will occur in the organizations in which people spend their lives.

Making ethical decisions is easy when the facts are clear and the choices black and white. But it is a different story when the situation is clouded by ambiguity, incomplete information, multiple points of view, and conflicting responsibilities. In such situations—which managers experience all the time—ethical decisions depend on both the decision-making process itself and on the experience, intelligence, and integrity of the decision maker.

Responsible moral judgment cannot be transferred to decision makers ready-made. Developing it in business turns out to be partly an administrative process involving: recognition of a decision's ethical implications; discussion to expose different points of view; and testing the tentative decision's adequacy in balancing self-interest and consideration of others, its import for future policy, and its consonance with the company's traditional values. But after all this, if a clear consensus has not emerged, then the executive in charge must decide, drawing on his or her in-

tuition and conviction. This being so, the caliber of the decision maker is decisive—especially when an immediate decision must arise from instinct rather than from discussion.

This existential resolution requires the would-be moral individual to be the final authority in a situation where conflicting ethical principles are joined. It does not rule out prior consultation with others or recognition that, in a hierarchical organization, you might be overruled.

Ethical decisions therefore require of individuals three qualities that can be identified and developed. The first is competence to recognize ethical issues and to think through the consequences of alternative resolutions. The second is self-confidence to seek out different points of view and then to decide what is right at a given time and place, in a particular set of relationships and circumstances. The third is what William James called tough-mindedness, which in management is the willingness to make decisions when all that needs to be known cannot be known and when the questions that press for answers have no established and incontrovertible solutions.

Unfortunately, moral individuals in the modern corporation are too often on their own. But these individuals cannot be expected to remain autonomous, no matter how well endowed they are, without positive organized support. The stubborn persistence of ethical problems obscures the simplicity of the solution—once the leaders of a company decide to do something about their ethical standards. Ethical dereliction, sleaziness, or inertia is not merely an individual failure but a management problem as well.

When they first come to work, individuals whose moral judgment may ultimately determine their company's ethical character enter a community whose values will influence their own. The economic function of the corporation is necessarily one of those values. But if it is the only value, ethical inquiry cannot flourish. If management believes that the invisible hand of the market adequately moderates the injury done by the pursuit of self-interest, ethical policy can be dismissed as irrelevant. And if what people see (while they are hearing about maximizing shareholder wealth) are managers dedicated to their own survival and compensation, they will naturally be more concerned about rewards than about fairness.

For the individual, the impact of the need to succeed is doubtless more direct than the influence of neoclassical economic theory. But just as the corporation itself is saddled with the need to establish competitive advantage over time (after reinvestment of what could otherwise be the immediate profit by which the financial community and many shareholders judge its performance), aspiring managers will also be influenced by the way they are judged. A highly moral and humane chief executive can preside over an amoral organization because the incentive system focuses attention on short-term quantifiable results.

Under pressures to get ahead, the individual (of whose native integrity we are hopeful) is tempted to pursue advancement at the expense of others, to cut corners, to seek to win at all cost, to make things seem better than they are–to take advantage, in sum, of a myopic evaluation of performance. People will do what they are rewarded for doing. The quantifiable results of managerial activity are always much more visible than the quality and future consequences of the means by which they are attained.

By contrast, when the corporation is defined as a socioeconomic institution with responsibilities to other constituencies (employees, customers, and communities, for example), policy can be established to regulate the single-minded pursuit of maximum immediate profit. The leaders of such a company speak of social responsibility, promulgate ethical policy, and make their personal values available for emulation by their juniors. They are respectful of neoclassical economic theory, but find it only partially useful as a management guide.

As the corporation grows beyond its leader's daily direct influence, the ethical consequences of size and geographical deployment come into play. Control and enforcement of all policy becomes more difficult, but this is especially true with regard to policy established for corporate ethics. Layers of responsibility bring communication problems. The possibility of penalty engenders a lack of candor. Distance from headquarters complicates the evaluation of performance, driving it to numbers. When operations are dispersed among different cultures and countries in which corruption assumes exotic guises, a consensus about moral values is hard to achieve and maintain.

Moreover, decentralization in and of itself has ethical consequences, not least because it absolutely requires trust and latitude for error. The inability to monitor the performance of executives assigned to tasks their superiors cannot know in detail results inexorably in delegation. Corporate leaders are accustomed to relying on the business acumen of profit-center managers, whose results the leaders watch with a practiced eye. Those concerned with maintaining their companies' ethical standards are just as dependent on the judgment and moral character of the managers to whom authority is delegated. Beyond keeping your fingers crossed, what can you do?

Fortunately for the future of the corporation, this microcosm of society can be, within limits, what its leadership and membership make it. The corporation is an organization in which people influence one another to establish accepted values and ways of doing things. It is not a democracy, but to be fully effective, the authority of its leaders must be supported by their followers. Its leadership has more power than elected officials do to choose who will join or remain in the association. Its members expect direction to be proposed even as they threaten resistance to change. Careless or lazy managements let their organizations drift, continuing their economic performance along lines previously established and leaving their ethics to chance. Resolute managements find they can surmount the problems I have dwelt on–once they have separated these problems from their camouflage.

It is possible to carve out of our pluralistic, multicultured society a coherent community with a strategy that defines both its economic purposes and the standards of competence, quality, and humanity that govern its activities. The character of a corporation may well be more malleable than an individual's. Certainly its culture can be shaped. Intractable persons can be replaced or retired. Those committed to the company's goals can generate formal and informal sanctions to constrain and alienate those who are not.

Shaping such a community begins with the personal influence of the chief executive and that of the managers who are heads of business units, staff departments, or any other suborganizations to which authority is delegated. The determination of explicit ethical policy comes next, followed by the same management procedures that are used to execute any body of policy in effective organizations.

How can you tell whether managers merit your trust?

The way the chief executive exercises moral judgment is universally acknowledged to be more influential than written policy. The CEO who orders the immediate recall of a product, at the cost of millions of dollars in sales because of a quality defect affecting a limited number of untraceable shipments, sends one kind of message. The executive who suppresses information about a producer's actual or potential ill effects or, knowingly or not, condones overcharging, sends another.

Policy is implicit in behavior. The ethical aspects of product quality, personnel, advertising, and marketing decisions are immediately plain. CEOs say much more than they know in the most casual contacts with those who watch their every move. Pretense is futile. "Do not *say* things," Emerson once wrote. "What you *are* stands over you the while, and thunders so that I can not hear what you say to the contrary." It follows that "if you would not be known to do anything, never do it."

1. ETHICS, VALUES, AND SOCIAL RESPONSIBILITY

The modest person might respond to this attribution of transparency with a "who, me?" Self-confident sophisticates will refuse to consider themselves so easily read. Almost all executives underestimate their power and do not recognize deference in others. The import of this, of course, is that a CEO should be conscious of how the position amplifies his or her most casual judgments, jokes, and silences. But an even more important implication—given that people cannot hide their characters—is that the selection of a chief executive (indeed of any aspirant to management responsibility) should include an explicit estimate of his or her character. If you ask how to do that, Emerson would reply, "Just look."

Once a company's leaders have decided that its ethical intentions and performance will be managed, rather than left untended in the corrosive environment of unprincipled competition, they must determine their corporate policy and make it explicit much as they do in other areas. The need for written policy is especially urgent in companies without a strong tradition to draw on or where a new era must be launched—after a public scandal, say, or an internal investigation of questionable behavior. Codes of ethics are now commonplace. But in and of themselves they are not effective, and this is especially true when they are so broadly stated that they can be dismissed as merely cosmetic.

Internal policies specifically addressed to points of industry, company, and functional vulnerability make compliance easier to audit and training easier to conduct. Where particular practices are of major concern—price fixing, for example, or bribery of government officials or procurement—compliance can be made a condition of employment and certified annually by employees' signatures. Still, the most pervasive problems cannot be foreseen, nor can the proper procedures be so spelled out in advance as to tell the person on the line what to do. Unreasonably repressive rules undermine trust, which remains indispensable.

What executives can do is advance awareness of the kinds of problems that are foreseeable. Since policy cannot be effective unless it is understood, some companies use corporate training sessions to discuss the problems of applying their ethical standards. In difficult situations, judgment in making the leap from general policy statements to situationally specific action can be informed by discussion. Such discussion, if carefully conducted, can reveal the inadequacy or ambiguity of present policy, new areas in which the company must take a unified stand, and new ways to support individuals in making the right decisions.

As in all policy formulation and implementation, the deportment of the CEO, the development of relevant policy—and training in its meaning and application—are not enough. In companies determined to sustain or raise ethical standards, management expands the information system to illuminate pressure points—the rate of manufacturing defects, product returns and warranty claims, special instances of quality shortfalls, results of competitive benchmarking inquiries—whatever makes good sense in the special circumstances of the company.

Because trust is indispensable, ethical aspirations must be supported by information that serves not only to inform but also to control. Control need not be so much coercive as customary, representing not suspicion but a normal interest in the quality of operations. Experienced executives do not substitute trust for the awareness that policy is often distorted in practice. Ample information, like full visibility, is a powerful deterrent.

This is why purposely ethical organizations expand the traditional sphere of external and internal audits (which is wherever fraud may occur) to include compliance with corporate ethical standards. Even more important, such organizations pay attention to every kind of obstacle that limits performance and to problems needing ventilation so that help can be provided.

To obtain information that is deeply guarded to avoid penalty, internal auditors—long since taught not to prowl about as police or detectives—must be people with enough management experience to be sensitive to the manager's need for economically viable decisions. For example, they should have imagination enough to envision ethical outcomes from bread-and-butter profit and pricing decisions, equal opportunity and payoff dilemmas, or downsizing crunches. Establishing an audit and control climate that takes as a given an open exchange of information between the company's operating levels and policy-setting levels is not difficult—once, that is, the need to do so is recognized and persons of adequate experience and respect are assigned to the work.

But no matter how much empathy audit teams exhibit, discipline ultimately requires action. The secretary who steals petty cash, the successful salesman who falsifies his expense account, the accountant and her boss who alter cost records, and, more problematically, the chronically sleazy operator who never does anything actually illegal—all must be dealt with cleanly, with minimum attention to allegedly extenuating circumstances. It is true that hasty punishment may be unjust and absolve superiors improperly of their secondary responsibility for wrongdoing. But long delay or waffling in the effort to be humane obscures the message the organization requires whenever violations occur. Trying to conceal a major lapse or safeguarding the names of people who have been fired is kind to the offender but blunts the salutary impact of disclosure.

For the executive, the administration of discipline incurs one ethical dilemma after another: How do you weigh consideration for the offending individual, for example, and how do you weigh the future of the organization? A company dramatizes its uncompromising adherence to lawful and ethical behavior when it severs employees who commit offenses that were classified in advance as unforgivable. When such a decision is fair, the grapevine makes its equity clear even when more formal publicity is inappropriate. Tough decisions should not be postponed simply because they are painful. The steady support of corporate integrity is never without emotional cost.

In a large, decentralized organization, consistently ethical performance requires difficult decisions from not only the current CEO but also a succession of chief executives. Here the board of directors enters the scene. The board has the opportunity to provide a succession of CEOs whose personal values and characters are consistently adequate for sustaining and developing established traditions for ethical conduct. Once in place, chief executives must rely on two resources for getting done what they cannot do personally: the character of their associates and the influence of policy and the measures that are taken to make policy effective.

An adequate corporate strategy must include noneconomic goals. An economic strategy is the optimal match of a company's product and market opportunities with its resources and distinctive competence. (That both are continually changing is of course true.) But economic strategy is humanized and made attainable by deciding what kind of organization the company will be – its character, the values it espouses, its relationships to customers, employees, communities, and shareholders. The personal values and ethical aspirations of the company's leaders, though probably not specifically stated, are implicit in all strategic decisions. They show through the choices management makes and reveal themselves as the company goes about its business. That is why this communication should be deliberate and purposeful rather than random.

Although codes of ethics, ethical policy for specific vulnerabilities, and disciplined enforcement are important, they do not contain in themselves the final emotional power of commitment. Commitment to quality objectives – among them compliance with law and high ethical standards – is an organizational achievement. It is inspired by pride more than by the profit that rightful pride produces. Once the scope of strategic decisions is thus enlarged, their ethical

component is no longer at odds with a decision right for many reasons.

As former editor of HBR, I am acutely aware of how difficult it is to persuade businesspeople to write or speak about corporate ethics. I am not comfortable doing so myself. To generalize the ethical aspects of a business decision, leaving behind the concrete particulars that make it real, is too often to sermonize, to simplify, or to rationalize away the plain fact that many instances of competing ethical claims have no satisfactory solution. But we also hear little public comment from business leaders of integrity when incontestable breaches of conduct are made known – and silence suggests to cynics an absence of concern.

The impediments to explicit discussion of ethics in business are many, beginning with the chief executive's keen awareness that someday he or she may be betrayed by someone in his or her own organization. Moral exhortation and oral piety are offensive, especially when attended by hypocrisy or real vulnerability to criticism. Any successful or energetic individual will sometime encounter questions about his or her methods and motives, for even well-intentioned behavior may be judged unethical from some point of view. The need for cooperation among people with different beliefs diminishes discussion of religion and related ethical issues. That persons with management responsibility must find the principles to resolve conflicting ethical claims in their own minds and hearts is an unwelcome discovery. Most of us keep quiet about it.

In summary, my ideas are quite simple. Perhaps the most important is that management's total loyalty to the maximization of profit is the principal obstacle to achieving higher standards of ethical practice. Defining the purpose of the corporation as exclusively economic is a deadly oversimplification, which allows overemphasis on self-interest at the expense of consideration of others.

Ultimately, executives resolve conflicting claims in their own minds and hearts.

The practice of management requires a prolonged play of judgment. Executives must find in their own will, experience, and intelligence the principles they apply in balancing conflicting claims. Wise men and women will submit their views to others, for open discussion of problems reveals unsuspected ethical dimensions and develops alternative viewpoints that should be taken into account. Ultimately, however, executives must make a decision, relying on their own judgment to settle infinitely debatable issues. Inquiry into character should therefore be part of all executive selection – as well as all executive development within the corporation.

And so it goes. That much and that little. The encouraging outcome is that promulgating and institutionalizing ethical policy are not so difficult as, for example, escaping the compulsion of greed. Once undertaken, the process can be as straightforward as the articulation and implementation of policy in any sphere. Any company has the opportunity to develop a unique corporate strategy summarizing its chief purposes and policies. That strategy can encompass not only the economic role it will play in national and international markets but also the kind of company it will be as a human organization. It will embrace as well, though perhaps not publicly, the nature and scope of the leadership to which the company is to be entrusted.

To be implemented successfully over time, any strategy must command the creativity, energy, and desire of the company's members. Strategic decisions that are economically or ethically unsound will not long sustain such commitment.

STATE YOUR VALUES, HOLD THE HOT AIR

Most corporate values statements are empty rhetoric. A few, though, deliver benefits—like winning customers or keeping you out of jail. Here's how to get a good one.

Alan Farnham

SHH. Quiet, please. We are entering the Corporate Cathedral. To your left, behind the double-dipping font, you will see the Tomb of the Unknown Salesman—poor man actually was pressed flat one day, trying to get closer to his customer. On your right: the Baldrige Chapel. Visit it another time, when it's fixed. And high above us—writ as if in characters of living light upon the windows—you see certain of the Values that sustain us:

"We will strive to achieve average long-term top-quartile performance within our chosen sectors.

"We will promote personal growth through cleanliness.

"We will achieve results in a planful way.

"We will seek and develop long-term relationships with key customers who offer potential for multiple major projects during the Strategic Time Frame.

"We impose on ourselves an obligation to reach beyond the minimal.

"Buy-in from colleagues and supervisors will be sought.

"Our intent is to be the world leader in moving people and material vertically and horizontally, over relatively short distances."

All right—so we invented the Corporate Cathedral. But the values are real, taken directly from corporate values statements, vision statements, mission statements, themes, declarations, mottoes, creeds, pledges, aspirations, oaths, and philosophies that have become as essential to business in the 1990s as a three-martini lunch once was. Robert Levering, co-author of *The 100 Best Companies to Work for in America*, says half of all U.S. corporations have some such statement—double the number he saw ten years ago.

Mark Pastin, a professor at Arizona State University and an expert on business ethics, says, "You have to wonder, Why all this interest in values statements *now*?" Among many reasons, he includes a surprising one: tough new federal sentencing guidelines that kicked in two years ago and increase up to tenfold the fines business must pay for such ethical lapses as paying bribes. Companies can reduce culpability by showing they have a compliance program, including a values statement. Attorney David Zornow of Skadden Arps Slate Meagher & Flom in New York City urges all his clients to write one for protection.

But the biggest reason statements have proliferated is that companies believe them magical. In a way, they are. No matter what they're called (mission, vision, and so on) they are all attempts to capture a company's elusive essence. And consultants who deliver a vision-values combo can get $50,000 to $100,000. Sadly, the results are often duds—empty phrases that become a cause for chuckling by employees. Only a minority pay real dividends.

Lee Edelstein, a management consultant in Westport, Connecticut, says a *good* values statement constitutes the ultimate control system: When everyone agrees on values, you don't need a lot of managers. "What multinational organization has the fewest layers of management?" he asks rhetorically. "The Catholic Church."

John Oertel, president of ME International, a Minneapolis manufacturer of metal grinding balls, agrees. "When you've got people sharing the same values, you've got what amounts to a built-in quality inspector. It used to be our workers picked up ME's values at the company picnic or on the bowling team. Not now. We're growing. Half our people are new. Society itself is becoming scattered. We decided we needed a statement."

Says Don Williams, president of Trammell Crow: "Today life is fired at us point-blank. People don't have time to refer to the Bible or to the company handbook. You've got to have all that internalized."

VALUES assist marketing. Howard Draft, chairman of Chicago-based ad agency Kobs & Draft, wowed the annual meeting of the Direct Marketing Association in October when he delivered a keynote address explaining "the value of values." His audience sat forward in their seats when Draft predicted the most successful marketers of the Nineties would be those who demonstrate an adherence to the values consumers most esteem.

He cited the success of Hanna Andersson, a Portland, Oregon, company that sells children's clothes by mail. Andersson boosted sales and customer loyalty by manifesting one of its corporate values, Social Action *(We will research specific opportunities for Hanna to contribute to the community)*.

It did it through a program called Hannadowns, which gives customers a 20% credit for mailing back clothes their infants have outgrown. The clothes are laundered and given to needy families or to women's shelters.

Besides manifesting Social Action, the program reinforces perceptions of product quality. Says Gun Denhart, Hanna's co-founder and CEO: "We wanted people to know our clothes are well made. One way to do that was to say, 'Our clothes are so good, we'll buy them back from you.'"

New mother Karen Walsh, an Andersson customer who until recently worked as an account supervisor at Los Angeles ad agency Sacks/Fuller, sees Hannadowns as a stroke of genius. "Is it good marketing? Absolutely. It makes you feel like spending your money with them, whether you use the program or not."

So how do you get yourself a good statement? Consultants would have you believe writing one is a daunting task, too tough for you to try unaided. It's not. A little common sense, plus the following tips, will speed you on your way:

From *Fortune*, April 19, 1993, pp. 117-118, 122, 124. © 1993 by Time Inc. Magazine Company. All rights reserved. Reprinted by permission.

1. ETHICS, VALUES, AND SOCIAL RESPONSIBILITY

■ **INVOLVE EVERYONE.** Explains Gary Edwards, executive VP of Conoco: "The process needs to cascade down to the individual departments, to the employees themselves." Everyone who's going to have to live with the statement should get his 2 cents in. Edwards first brought his managing directors together. "We identified the values we felt were important. We basically brainstormed for half a day. Then I asked groups further down to do the same thing. We found threads of consistency. On the core values we got quick agreement. But we struggled with the words. I had to put a time limit on the process—60 days. You can't allow your organization to get too tied up wordsmithing it."

Wordsmithing, however, is essential to your statement's winning wide acceptance. What might strike you as dithering—the choice of a word, or the order in which the words come—is what gets the ditherers engaged enough to commit themselves sincerely to the finished product.

CEO Skip LeFauve of Saturn played wordsmith and felt his time was well spent. He and Saturn's employees considered making "commitment to customer satisfaction" Saturn's No. 1 value. After much discussion, however, they changed it to "customer enthusiasm." Says LeFauve: "We decided 'satisfaction' was just business as usual. 'Enthusiasm' raised the bar."

At ME International, workers are hammering out a statement of their own right now, with help from Rob Lebow, consultant and president of the Lebow Co. in Bellevue, Washington. Subjected to much noodling, here is how one value has evolved:

First draft—*Inspire active participation in the growth of the business to benefit everyone.*

Second draft—*Inspire active participation in the growth of everyone to benefit the business.*

Third draft—*Inspire active participation in the growth of everyone to benefit our business.*

A waste of time? Not to them.

■ **ALLOW CUSTOMIZATION.** There's no better way to draw employees into the process than to allow separate departments to draft their own statements, as long as these don't contradict the company's. Geoff Nightingale, president of SynerGenics, a values-drafting subsidiary of Burson-Marsteller, explains, "Closeness to the customer means something different to billing than it does to sales."

The Ritz-Carlton hotel chain carries this idea to an extreme and has fun doing it. Every department in every hotel writes its own statement. The Ritz parking garage at Amelia Island, Florida, for example, has its mission. Housekeeping and the restaurant have theirs. This spectacle moves values apostle Stephen Covey to exclaim, "Even the front desk has one!"

> **Everyone who's going to have to live with the statement should get a chance to put his 2 cents in.**

A sort of Continental Congress makes sure one statement doesn't war with another. The approach has produced the only whimsical statement FORTUNE was able to find anywhere in corporate America, that of Amelia Island's engineering department: *To boldly go where no hotel has been before—free of all defects.* Says an engineer, who helped draft it: "It made us laugh. But the more we got to talking about it, the more we liked it." Maybe not incidentally, last year the Ritz chain won a Baldrige Award.

■ **EXPECT, AND ACCEPT, RESISTANCE.** An employee of Alltel Mobile Communications whose boss told him to memorize the Alltel Mobile Credo says, "They give you this statement, laminated to a little card. You're supposed to keep it on you at all times, in case somebody from corporate comes by and asks you to recite it.

"It is, in my view, a crock of shit. Not so much because of what's on the card. It's that the company is forcing this on you—they're throwing up all over you with their philosophy. I'm good at my job. I've been promoted three times. All I want is to go out and do it, without some idiot in a leather chair telling me how to think."

Between home, church, and community, workers don't lack for identity. Many are quite freighted with meaningfulness already. It's okay to offer them a little extra spritz at work. The ones who need it most are going to be saying their pledges double-time, voluntarily. The rest? Let 'em be. As University of Michigan professor Noel Tichy observes, "Even the great religions make an accommodation to sin."

■ **KEEP IT SHORT.** Luther needed 95 theses. You don't. Notes Rob Lebow: "The U.S. Constitution is a very short document." Statements should be clear. Here's Domino's Pizza's: "To safely deliver a hot, quality pizza in 30 minutes or less at a fair price and a reasonable profit." Some of history's most effective statements—all shorties—come easily to mind: Carthage must

be destroyed. Death before dishonor. (*Death before dishonor* leaves no room for wondering, "Let's see now . . . do I *die* first, or get dishonored?")

■ **ESCHEW HOKUM.** Statements lend themselves to schlock. Some companies don't stop at laminating them to cards. They go way, way beyond. "Ben & Jerry's has theirs on a cube," says a competitor, admiringly. "We're considering a globe."

The prize, however, must go to PSE&G's electric business unit, which created a values-based shaving kit. The kit contains a pen and a set of disposable razors. Each razor is emblazoned on its back with one of six Core Values. Shave with one, for example, and you are reminded that PSE&G stands for LEAN, COST-EFFECTIVE OPERATIONS; with another, TEAMWORK AND COLLABORATION. The pen has a transparent window, the kind that in naughty pens shows a woman disrobing. Every time its button is depressed, a new value, such as CORPORATE CITIZENSHIP, pops into view.

You don't necessarily need a card, let alone razors or a cube, to win over employees. Says Mary Rabaut, a management consultant with Gemini Consulting in Morristown, New Jersey: "Some of the best value-driven companies don't even have a statement. It's ingrained." Dallas Newman, 86, a Wal-Mart greeter in Marion, Virginia, knows Wal-Mart's values fine without having to carry around a card. "The company explains them to you when you join," he says. "They're not spelled out in black and white, exactly, but they're understood. I'd say them this way: honest, straightforward dealing." He'd say them that way because those happen to be his values too.

So tight is the Newman–Wal-Mart fit that Mr. Newman has often been mistaken for the late Mr. Sam: "It was rumored around here for quite some time that I *was* Sam Walton, in disguise," he says. "Honestly. People would come up to me and ask me to autograph things." Fastidious, he spends three hours every morning getting dressed ("I never wear a dress shirt but once.") and tip-taps his way to work (he's legally blind), not because he needs to (he's well off). He just likes what Wal-Mart stands for.

■ **LEAVE THE SUPREME BEING OUT OF IT.** A surprising number of companies invoke him. Cleaning colossus ServiceMaster, for example, spurring its employees to vacuum more pet hair out of carpets, manages to invoke—in its values statement and annual reports—not just God but Christ and Mother Teresa too. But then, the company's founder, Marion Wade, was very committed to God and to the ideal of selfless service.

The danger to pulling out these stops is that religious references will strike some employees—including the most devout and the atheists—as wildly inappropriate in a business setting. And, as a practical matter, you don't need to do it. If, for example, you wish to instill the Golden Rule, you can do it by talking about "the ethic of fair play" without taking recourse to scripture.

■ **CHALLENGE IT.** If you've already got a statement, put it to a test. That's what James Burke did at Johnson & Johnson to great effect. Burke, back in 1976, noticed his managers were nodding politely at the J&J Credo but didn't take it seriously. "I brought in 32 managers from around the world and told them, 'You're here to challenge this document. If we can't live by it, we should throw it off the wall.' That was a tremendous turn-on. Nobody wanted to get rid of it, and nobody wanted to keep it as it was. Eventually we did that with every one of our managers in the world." Some changes were contended hotly. "There was a terrible battle, for example, over whether we should take out God. In the end we did."

■ **LIVE 'EM.** That's the hardest part. Says Mary Rabaut: "Putting your values into words isn't enough. The company's policies have to be consistent with them." Andrall Pearson, a former president of PepsiCo now teaching at the Harvard business school, calls the void between the real and the ideal a values gap and says it is "the largest single source of cynicism and skepticism in the workplace today." Example: The plaque on the wall says, PEOPLE ARE OUR MOST PRECIOUS ASSET, but the company has just laid off thousands. THE ACME SUITCASE—FINEST IN THE WORLD, says the plaque; on the production line, every tenth handle is being sewn on upside down.

At Levi Strauss, one-third of a manager's raise can depend on how well he toes the value line. At Saturn, employees know that if they blow the whistle on a defect, prompting a recall, they won't be punished for it. Follow-through of that sort is far more important than whether your values are laminated on razors.

And, of course, be sure you observe the values yourself. Don Williams of Trammell Crow says, "These slogan programs—there're a million out there. But making a real values statement is hard. It's as hard as living a good life."

Take comfort in the fact you are setting out on a uniquely American path: the making of a compact. Says Steve Dinkelaker, president of a Washington State insurance agency that hashed out its values last year: "Writing our statement is the closest my employees and I are ever going to get to discussing government. I was up at the Plymouth Plantation last week. I'd never been there before. Their articles, all the stuff they set down, it's there. They were deciding, among themselves, how they wanted to be treated. That's what we did."

Understanding Pressures That Cause Unethical Behavior in Business

O. C. Ferrell, Ph.D. and John Fraedrich, Ph.D.

O.C. Ferrell, Ph.D., is Distinguished Professor of Marketing and Business Ethics in The Fogelman College of Business and Economics at Memphis State University in Memphis, Tennessee. John Fraedrich, Ph.D., is an Assistant Professor of Marketing at Southern Illinois University in Carbondale, Illinois.

Abstract

This paper reviews how personal values, the competitive environment, organizational pressures and opportunity interact to determine ethical decisions in business. An ethically sensitive corporate culture, codes of ethics and enforced ethical policies in companies are seen as the best methods for improving ethical behavior.

Introduction

Ethics in business is a major concern because of the lack of ethical behavior by some individuals and organizations in our society. Dennis Levine at the age of 32 was a managing director of Drexel Burnham Lambert, one of the country's top merger and acquisition specialists. His indictment for insider trading charges ignited the insider trading scandal of the 1980s, forever changing the landscape of American business. Levine was fined $362,000 and agreed to pay the federal government $11.6 million in illegal trading profits. He was sentenced to two years in prison and has since been paroled. Levine received a reduced sentence for helping the federal government in its investigation of insider trading. His testimony helped to implicate Ivan Boesky, who received a $100 million penalty, the biggest ever, for insider trading. Now Mr. Levine is being managed by a public relations agency and receives fees for speaking to MBA students on college campuses. Levine's message to college students is "Don't do it." "It's not worth it," he said of insider trading and other white collar transgressions (*Los Angeles Times,* 1989, part 4).

What causes people like Dennis Levine to behave unethically and even illegally in the business world? There are many scenarios to explain unethical behavior. One explanation is that the individual may be a "bad apple", with poor personal morals, in a good organization. Other explanations for unethical behavior include the nature of the competitive environment, organizational pressures, or even the opportunity to take advantage in the right situation. It is our purpose to explore how both personal and outside pressures on business people can increase the probability of ethical mistakes. In addition, we suggest several ways managers can improve ethical behavior and can avoid the destructive consequences of poor ethical decision making.

Personal Values vs. Corporate Values

The personal dimension of ethics relates to an individual's values and moral philosophies. Individual values are learned from socialization through family, religion, school, and business experiences. These individual values are generally assumed to remain constant in both work and nonwork environments. However, doubt was first cast on this generalization by Carr (1968). He argued that business people have two ethical dimensions that include one ethical value system for home and one for business. Recently, support for Carr's statement has shown that most business persons use one moral philosophy at work and a completely different moral philosophy at home (Fraedrich 1988). This may explain why Dennis Levine says he has strong moral commitments today but could not explain to his five-year-old son a few years ago why he was going to prison. He was a good family man, yet cheated investors out of millions.

The personal value system combines with the corporate culture to affect behavior. In a study conducted by Frederick and Weber (1987) concerning the values of corporate managers and their critics, they concluded that personal values are involved in ethical decisions but are not the central component that guides the decisions, actions, and policies of the organization. They

From *Business Insights,* Spring/Summer 1990, pp. 1-4. *Business Insights,* published by the Center for Business Development and Research, College of Business Administration, The University of Southern Mississippi.

believe that personal values make up only one part of an organization's total value structure. Ethical behavior within the organization relates to the organization's values and traditions rather than solely upon individuals who actually make the decisions.

Consequently, ethical behavior may be a function of two different dimensions of an organization's value structure: the embedded organizational value system or corporate culture, and the personal value preferences of the organization's individual members. An individual member assumes some measure of moral responsibility by agreeing in general to abide by an organization's rules and standard operating procedures. When Dennis Levine stepped over the line into unethical and illegal behavior, it can be assumed that competitive pressures and organizational rewards provided the incentive.

Competitive Pressures

Competition exerts pressure on business decision makers and is a key factor in influencing the ethical environment of the firm. In general, competition helps business and the economy to become more efficient and goal-oriented. However, when competition becomes so intense that business survival is threatened, then employees and managers may view once unacceptable alternatives as acceptable. In other words, pressured employees may engage in unethical practices for corporate survival. The culture of the corporation may encourage and reward unethical behavior because of fear of bankruptcy, possible loss of one's job, or the opportunity for promotion.

Corporate espionage and manipulation to gain insider information are often used in highly competitive industries. One example of such an act involved the acquisition of information on General Electric's turbine parts by a small manufacturing firm. GE employees were offered money in exchange for drawings. By acquiring these documents, the smaller company hoped to save millions of dollars in research and development and to capture a significant share of the more than $495 million turbine parts market (Carley 1988). As this example illustrates, some firms may approve corporate espionage, but society deems such actions as unethical and illegal.

As competition becomes intense and profit margins become smaller, pressures can build to substitute inferior materials or components to reduce costs. Often this is done without informing customers about changes in product quality that involve a form of dishonesty about the nature of the product. Beech-Nut Nutrition Corporation took this concept to an extreme when it changed the contents of its apple juice product. Instead of selling a product made from apples, the company substituted a chemical concoction which has the same taste, smell, and look of apple juice. However, the company continued to label and promote its product as being 100 percent apple juice. In fact, experts found it difficult to distinguish it from pure apple juice. Beech-Nut failed to inform consumers that its apple juice no longer was made from apples (Hall 1989). When companies do not inform consumers that product components are not of the same quality as promoted, ethical issues arise. In this case, Beech-Nut lost millions of dollars, and its executives were sentenced to prison terms.

Other questionable practices, such as increased EPA violations, mechanical devices that periodically increase assembly line speeds, bait-and-switch sales techniques, and bribery to obtain important customers, occur when a firm is in a highly competitive industry. These measures are used because managers are afraid that their company could not compete without using deception and manipulation.

Organizational Pressures

While ethical decision making includes perceptions of how to act in terms of daily issues, success is determined by achievement of company goals. Pressure to perform and increase profits may be particularly intense in middle management. This internal organizational pressure is a major predictor of unethical behavior.

These organizational factors seem to have played a part in several recent scandals. Many insider traders in the Boesky scandal remain uncaught because trading of confidential information in investment banking circles is a routine way of doing business. The E.F. Hutton employees found guilty of 2,000 counts of mail and wire fraud did not understand their company's values. Some may have thought they were doing their company a favor (Dressang 1986). Robert Foman, former chairman of E.F. Hutton, states that, "I thought ethics was something you learned growing up at home, in school, and in church" (Moskowitz 1985, p. 63). Obviously, Foman was wrong in thinking that ethics is only developed at home, school and church. His managers were influenced by pressures to succeed, and by their peers and supervisors in the decision-making process.

The roles of top management and superiors are extremely important in developing the culture of an organization. Most experts agree that the chief executive officer and vice-president level executives set the ethical tone for the entire organization. For example, when Chrysler Corporation President Lee Iacocca learned that several executives of his company were driving new Chryslers with the odometers disconnected and then selling the cars as new, he admitted the company's unethical behavior in a national press conference and developed a program to compensate customers who had bought the pre-driven cars. Iacocca took out two-page advertisements in *USA Today, The Wall Street Journal,* and *The New York Times* to apologize for the ethical mistake and added, "The only thing we are recalling here is our integrity." Messages like this send a signal to all employees in the organization concerning what the firm stands for ethically (Schlesinger 1987). Lower-level superiors obtain their cues from these individuals, yet they too exert some of their personal value system on the company. This interplay between corporate culture and executive leadership helps determine the ethical value system of the firm.

Opportunity Pressures

Opportunity to engage in unethical behavior provides another pressure that may determine whether or not a person will behave ethically. Opportunity is a favorable set of conditions to limit barriers or to provide rewards. Rewards may be internal or external. Internal rewards are those feelings of goodness and worth one feels after an altruistic action. External rewards are what people expect to receive from others in terms of values generated and provided on an exchange basis. External rewards are often received from peers and top management. Opportunity to engage in unethical behavior has been found to be a better predictor of such behavior than personal beliefs (Ferrell and Gresham, 1985). In a survey by Chonko and Hunt (1985), 56 percent of the managers indicated that there were many opportunities for managers in their industry to engage in unethical behaviors.

If an individual uses the opportunity afforded him/her to act unethically and is either rewarded or not penalized, that person becomes more likely to repeat such acts as the opportunity arises. For example, an accountant who receives a raise for preparing financial documents that he or she knows are not completely accurate is being rewarded for this behavior and, therefore, has an increased probability of continuing the behavior.

Several elements within the business environment help to create opportunities, including rewards and the absence of punishment. Professional codes of ethics and ethics-related corporate policy also influence opportunity. Enforcement of these codes and policies should generate the highest level of compliance to ethical standards. The greater the rewards and the less the punishment for unethical behavior, the greater the probability that unethical behavior will be practiced.

It is even suggested that the SEC contributed to the opportunity dimension of insider trading by allowing Ivan Boesky to reduce his partnership's liabilities by $1.3 billion by selling stocks or other securities before the government announced his crimes. This special treatment saved Boesky an additional $100 million in fines. In reality this cut his fines in half. In addition, Congress asked why, if New York Stock Exchange computers flagged 47 suspicious trades by Boesky—many before merger announcements—Boesky was not caught before Levine disclosed his actions. Even after being caught and punished, much opportunity exists for violators to profit from their success.

sentence, Dennis Levine is being paid for public speaking and has started a new financial consulting practice in mergers and acquisitions. A *Barron's* article reports, "We're convinced the venture will be a great success. Mr. Levine's curriculum vita is sure to prove irresistible to any number of companies we can consider." (Abelson, 1989). Apparently, much opportunity continues for those convicted of unethical and illegal activity in the securities industry.

Improving Ethical Decisions

Conflicts between personal values and corporate values, intense competition, organizational pressures and opportunity interact to create situations that can cause unethical behavior. Figure 1 illustrates the pressures that can influence ethical decision making. As discussed previously, both the individual and the organization can influence unethical behavior.

Figure 1

Pressures That Impact Ethical Decisions In Business

Personal Values	Competition
Ethical Decisions	
Organization	Opportunity

One way to sensitize personnel is to create codes of ethics. Trevino and Youngblood (1990) developed a "bad apple", "bad barrel" argument concerning this issue. The "bad apple" argument is that some people are basically bad and will do things in their own self interest regardless of organizational goals. Eliminating unethical behavior requires the elimination of the "bad apples" (individuals) within the corporation. This can be done through screening techniques and through the enforcement of ethics codes. The "bad barrel" argument is that corporate culture becomes unethical not because individuals are bad, but because the pressures to survive competition create conditions that reward unethical behavior. The solution to the "bad barrel" approach is to redesign the corporate image and culture such that it conforms to industry and societal norms of ethical behavior. Robin and Reidenbach (1987) suggest that ethics must be built into the corporate culture and corporate strategy. By sensitizing personnel in an organization to ethical issues and potential areas of conflict, one can eliminate or defuse some of the ethical pressures that occur in day-to-day business activities.

Codes of ethics can be established to help managers deal with ethical situations or dilemmas that develop in day-to-day operations. Top management should provide leadership to operationalize codes. Codes of ethics do not have to be so detailed they take into account every situation; rather codes should have general guidelines that operationalize the main goals and objectives.

If a company is to maintain ethical behavior, its policies, rules, and standards must be worked into its control system. When employees make unethical decisions, the company needs to determine why and to take corrective action through enforcement. Enforcement of standards is what makes codes of ethics effective. If codes are window dressing and do not relate to what is expected or what is rewarded in the corporate culture, then the codes serve no purpose other than to give the illusion that there is concern for ethical behavior.

Conclusion

Ethical behavior in business must be based on a strong moral foundation, including personal moral development and an organizational structure that encourages and rewards desired ethical action. The pressures of competition must be understood and coped with to improve ethical behavior. The idea that ethics is learned at home, in school, and in church does not recognize the impact of the organization on ethical decision makers. Today there is an increasing need for professional associations and corporations to promote and to enforce codes of ethics and eliminate unethical conduct.

Codes of ethics and/or corporate policies on ethics must be established to control the opportunity factor in ethical decision making. Enforcement of corporate policies on ethics brings about more ethical behavior. The establishment of codes of ethics and corporate policies on ethics will enable company employees to better understand what is, and is not, expected of them. Understanding how a person chooses his or her own standards of ethics, and what prompts a person to engage in unethical behavior, may decrease the current trend toward unethical activity in the business world.

For a company to maintain ethical behavior, its ethical policies, rules, and standards must be worked into its control system, including activities related to target setting, measuring and monitoring performance. Increasing ethical behavior in a corporation is similar to increasing earnings. Ethical behavior will happen only after a strategic plan is developed and successfully implemented to achieve the desired results.

References

Abelson, Alan (1989), "Up and Down Wall Street," *The Wall Street Journal,* July 24, p. 43.

Carley, William M. (1988), "Secrets War: GE Presses Campaign to Halt Rivals' Misuse of Turbine Parts Data," *The Wall Street Journal,* August 16, pp. 1, 10.

Carr, Albert Z. (1968), "Is Business Bluffing Ethical?" *Harvard Business Review,* (January-February), p. 145.

Chonko, Lawrence and Shelby Hunt (1985), "Ethics and Marketing Management: An Empirical Investigation," *Journal of Business Research,* 13, pp. 339-359.

Dressang, Joel (1986), "Companies Get Serious About Ethics," *USA Today,* (December), pp. 1-2B.

Ferrell, O. C. and Larry Gresham (1985), "A Contingency Framework for Understanding Ethical Decision Making in Marketing," *Journal of Marketing,* (Summer), pp. 87-96.

Fraedrich, John P. (1988), "Philosophy Type Interaction in the Ethical Decision Making Process of Retailers," Ph.D. Dissertation, Texas A&M University, College Station, TX.

Frederick, William C. and James Weber (1987), "The Value of Corporate Managers and Their Critics: An Empirical Description and Normative Implications," *Research in Corporate Social Performance and Social Responsibility* (9), William C. Frederick, ed., Greenwich, CT, pp. 149-150.

Hall, Mini (1989), "O.J. Wasn't 100% Pure, FDA Says," *USA Today,* July 26, p. A1.

Moskowitz, Daniel B. (1985), "Where Business Goes to Stock Up on Ethics," *Business Week,* (October 14), pp. 63-66.

Robin, Donald P. and R. Eric Reidenbach (1987), "Social Responsibility, Ethics and Marketing Strategy: Closing the Gap Between Concept and Application," *Journal of Marketing,* (January), pp. 44-58.

Schlesinger, Jacob (1987), "Chrysler Finds A Way To Settle Odometer Issue," *The Wall Street Journal,* December 10, p. 7.

Sing, Bill (1989), *Los Angeles Times,* May 24, part 4.

Trevino, Linda K. and Stuart Youngblood (1990), "Bad Apples in Bad Barrels: A Casual Analysis of Ethical Decision Making Behavior," *Journal of Applied Psychology,* forthcoming.

To pose a question of ethics

Do you do "the right thing"? Or do you do what "everyone" does, blurring that sometimes fine line between right and wrong? Indeed, what's become of ethical behavior?

Robert McGarvey

Ours is an era of encompassing ethical issues. There are the passionately debated dilemmas: Is abortion moral? Are there proper limits on immigration? Should high costs ever be a valid reason for denying medical care? And there are, as well, the consuming moral scandals that daily parade across the tabloids and, lately, the mainstream news media too: Is the Duchess of York (alias "Fergie") in the right? What about Princess Di or Prince Charles? *Murphy Brown?* Should Ice-T's rap song *Cop Killer* be censored?

The topics range from the crucial to the trivial—but there they are, fodder for the daily debates in which virtually all persons engage. Yet, it is precisely that preoccupation that may be leading society widely astray.

"We have become moral spectators, not participants," says Christina Hoff Sommers, a philosophy professor at Clark University in Worcester, Massachusetts. "We've put so much emphasis on large-scale moral issues and scandals that we're neglecting our own behavior and the personal ethical choices we make in daily life. Ethics is being turned over to experts, with many of us abdicating our own responsibilities. We are in an era of moral passivity on the part of the individual."

Fellow philosopher Michael Levin of City University of New York elaborates: "Big ethical issues may be routinely faced by the President of the United States and other heads of state. Perhaps corporate CEOs face them too. We do not.

"For most of us, the big decisions are the little ones," Levin continues. "Our issues are: Do you return the extra money when a cashier gives you too much change? Do you throw the gum wrapper on the sidewalk or wait until you get to a trash barrel? Those are the moral issues that fill our lives."

In the grand scheme of things, though, aren't these ignorable, perhaps even irrelevant questions? Not according to Levin.

"Those are the tests of your character," he explains. "Character means: Are you honest? Truthful? Generous? Considerate? The nature of a person's character emerges much, much more clearly from the totality of his little decisions than it does from his position on, say, abortion. When you get the five-dollar bill instead of the $1 you're owed, what you do with the extra money is a test of exactly how good a person you are."

Ethicist Michael Josephson, whose clients include the California Bar Association, the California legislature, and numerous corporations, offers yet another compelling reason to pay close heed to "the little things."

"Little ethical decisions seem unimportant, but so many major social problems are attributable to the cumulative impact of many little sins," Josephson says. "Look at automobile insurance. Some experts say upwards of 25 percent of all claims are way out of line with actual damages. Yet, each of us who steals, steals only a little. When the body shop is repairing the fender that was crumpled in an accident, we ask if they'll replace the molding we lost miles before and add it into the claim. Just a few dollars, but the upshot is that everybody's rate now is much higher than it could be.

"The same is true for littering. If I toss my can on the street, so what? Our society would remain remarkably clean. But I throw out my can, then he does, and you do—and we're in a mess. Little things lead to big things, and the very pettiness of these little ethical missteps magnifies them."

On top of the societal consequences of ethical missteps, there are, of course, the more personal ones.

"A neighbor asks if you'll help him paint his house. You don't want to, so you tell him a family member is sick. A week later he asks how the family member is doing. What do you say?" asks Josephson. "How many times do we have to lie to become a liar? Why would we sacrifice our integrity over such small things?

"Ethics is the plumbing of our lives. When everything is working smoothly, we don't notice plumbing—or ethics either. It's only when things get plugged up that we have a mess."

 From *Kiwanis Magazine*, February 1993, pp. 30-32, 47. © 1993 by Kiwanis International. Reprinted by permission.

T he trouble is, though, that many persons fear exactly that: Society is, indeed, in an ethical mess.

"There's a widespread feeling of malaise, of ethical drift," says Lisa Newton, director of the Applied Ethics Center at Fairfield University in Connecticut, and she points to one particular reason for some of this thinking: "We're in an era when complexities are multiplying. There are more and more gray areas in morals—places where we don't know the right thing to do."

Richard DeGeorge, a philosophy professor at the University of Kansas in Lawrence, expands on that point: "Ethical judgments have been complicated by the fact that today's world is moving so fast. So many things are changing, radically, overnight."

Consider bioethics—the application of ethical reasoning to medical and biological issues. It alone generates dozens of controversies, which, a few decades ago, never would have arisen. Some time in 1993, for instance, research subjects will receive the first public tests of AIDS vaccines. All subjects will qualify as "at high risk" of infection, but perhaps one-half unknowingly will receive placebos, instead of a vaccine. Some, wrongly believing they have been vaccinated, may well die. Is that ethical? Do the long-term public benefits outweigh the suffering of some individuals?

Internationalization also breeds knotty ethical questions. In Western Europe and the US, for example, it is illegal as well as immoral to offer a bribe to a police officer. In much of the developing world, it's accepted practice. So, if a Western European or an American is in a developing country and stopped for a traffic violation, would it be wrong for the person to offer a bribe?

"It's immoral to eat a dog in Virginia; is it in Seoul?" asks Hank Karp, a psychologist based in Virginia Beach, Virginia, who conducts values clarification workshops for corporations. "As we enter into the international arena, moral uncertainties are sure to arise."

Thorny and legitimate as these new moral questions may be, philosophers insist that they are not the problem.

Why are people failing the little tests? For starters, there's the public's ravenous appetite for scandals in the savings-and-loan executive suites, Buckingham Palace, Wall Street, and so forth.

"Paying attention to the scandals is a demoralizing distraction for most of us," Levin says. "It's easy to look around and decide, 'Everybody cheats and lies.' Everybody doesn't, but it's easy to lose sight of that—and to lose sight of doing our own 'little things' right."

Big, uncertain issues undermine society in other ways as well.

"We'll rightly say there are legitimate questions about abortion—with good people debating both sides—and, from there, we'll erroneously jump to the conclusion that there are open questions about cheating on taxes," DeGeorge says. "There are gray areas in ethics, but most aren't."

Newton offers a more concise summation: "Ethical relativism is the refuge of the scoundrel. Some issues are very gray—and we're rightly uncertain. But that is less common than you may think. The ethics of selling pesticides—banned in the US—to Third World countries are debatable. That doesn't mean there's debate about the wrongness of filing a false tax return. Ethics—the fundamental virtues—are fairly unchanged since the time of Socrates."

If the answers are so certain, why do individuals sometimes ignore them? Philosophers, theologians, and psychologists long have debated that question. And while there certainly may be other views, W. Michael Hoffman, director of the Center for Business Ethics at Bentley College in Waltham, Massachusetts, suggests a core reason: "Why don't we do the right thing when we know it? Because we're tempted to put our own best interests before others—at least we think that's the best way to serve our interests."

Most taxpayers know it's wrong to overstate their tax deductions. But if doing it puts cash in their pocketbooks, well, they just may set aside morals, resorting to the "everybody else does it" rationalization.

Newton elaborates: "Ninety-five percent of the time we know the right thing to do. But if it's not in our own immediate, best inter-

---

Codes guide tough decisions

Is it enough to memorize an ethical or a legal code and think that it's an end to all sticky moral dilemmas?

While more and more companies and professions have been busy putting their guiding ethical principles into writing, laws and codes are by no means the cutoff point to ethical problems, according to Hank Karp, a values consultant based in Virginia Beach, Virginia.

"Knowing a code is never enough," Karp claims. "You've still got to get down in the mud and wrestle with the very hard decisions which will arise. A code may be a beginning; it's not the end."

Well-intentioned as they may be, codes may even *cause* moral problems, says Sissela Bok, a philosophy professor at Brandeis University in Waltham, Massachusetts, and author of *Lying.*

"Codes of ethics function all too often as shielfs," Bok contends. "Their abstraction allows many to adhere to them while continuing their ordinary practices. Much more is needed."

The codes must be the starting point for a broad inquiry. In a similar vein, laws cannot be counted on to provide a sufficient ethical framework.

"Compliance with the law is never enough," says W. Michael Hoffman, director of the Center for Business Ethics at Bentley College in Waltham. "There are many cases where there hasn't been illegality, but society retrospectively judged a company or individual to have behaved unethically."

As a case in point, Hoffman cites Ford Motor Company's Pinto, a car with a gasoline tank that was found to be inadequate in accidents. "Nobody believes Ford behaved illegally, but our society nonetheless has judged to be unethical the company's decision to manufacture the car, despite knowing about possible problems with the gas tank," Hoffman says.

Beyond that, says Richard DeGeorge, a philosophy professor at the University of Kansas in Lawrence, laws are reactive—they are passed only *after* injury is incurred.

"Saying that law provides an ample ethical framework is tantamount to saying it's OK to do harm until so much harm is done that a law must be passed," DeGeorge says. "That obviously makes no moral sense.

"Furthermore, there are many areas where societies don't want laws. Lying isn't illegal, except in special circumstances such as under oath in a court of law; but lying, nonetheless, isn't ethical. Laws simply cannot provide a sufficient framework for ethical decision-making."

Adds Karp: "There's no easy way out of moral problems. There will be times when we've still got to do the hard thinking and make the hard choices. Ethics is an ongoing process."

---

ests, we may look for rationalizations to justify what we want to do instead. It's a matter of being human."

Temptation may fuel many ethical misdeeds, but there's another common cause: oversight.

"Many, many times we simply stumble into unethical behavior, because we haven't thought about what we're doing," says Thomas Dunfee, an ethicist at the University of Pennsylvania. "This is more thoughtlessness than a willful violation, and it happens frequently."

California ethicist Michael Josephson shares an anecdote he uses in seminars to support that point: "The father comes home and sees that his child is making a drawing, using an elaborate set of markers, in a rainbow of colors. The father asks where the boy got the markers, and the child says he took them from school. 'Are you allowed to do that?' asks Dad. 'Not really,' the son admits. Responds

Shocking truth jolts morals

If there's a single, most frequent excuse for ethical lapses in business and governmental bureaucracies, it's "I was just following orders." Oftentimes, it's meant quite sincerely too.

A manager will pass down an order to subordinates who soon realize there's no honest way to hit the desired targets, so they'll fudge a bit here and there to make the goal. At the ladder's top, executives may well be blissfully ignorant about what's gone wrong below—until, eventually, so much goes wrong, disaster ensues.

Vivid proof of just how far persons may go in executing orders is provided by psychologist Stanley Milgram in a now classic experiment.

Subjects were provided with a phony shock-generator, an electrical apparatus labeled with dosage increments supposedly ranging from "mild" to "fatal." They were instructed by an experimenter to administer a shock whenever a "student"—out of eyesight but within earshot——gave a wrong answer to a question. With every wrong answer, the punishment shock was increased until eventually the lethal zone would be entered.

Throughout the experiment, the student moaned, cried, and gave every evidence of undergoing torture until they lapsed into silence, likely due to unconsciousness. At this juncture, the experimenter sternly advised the subject to treat silence as a wrong answer and to administer shocks accordingly.

Finally, the moment of experimental truth came: How many of the subjects would administer the killing jolt? The answer is two out of every three delivered the fatal blow when instructed to by the experimenter.

Psychologists Robert A. Baron and Donn Byrne, co-authors of *Social Psychology*, draw a chilling conclusion about the experiment: "This experimental task places subjects in a conflict between their moral values about harming others and their tendency to obey an authority's command. The findings are especially frightening in their implications, because this particular authority figure obviously could do nothing to make them obey and would not be in a position to punish them. In fact, they were unlikely even to see (the authority figure) again."

The relevance to ethics? For everyone whose ever wondered in horror how anybody could have gone along with Adolf Hitler's program against the Jews or, on a much lesser, incomparable scale, the shenanigans that still are unraveling the United States' savings-and-loan system, just remember Milgram.

Granted, the experiment doesn't conclude that deep inside each person lurks a savings-and-loan swindler or a concentration camp guard. But it does mean that unless a society firmly knows, and holds, its core moral values, it always will be subject to tampering from unethical behavior from above.

Somewhere around 400 BC, Socrates built his ethics around the teaching that "the unexamined life is not worth living." The same advice holds true today.

ded values that we're unaware of—we *must* keep talking until those values rise to the top of mind."

Awareness, though, is just the beginning. Once values are understood, actions must be implemented to fulfill the overall objectives of ethics.

"Habits are ethics' core," explains David Glidden, a philosophy professor at the University of California at Riverside. "The word 'ethics' comes from the ancient Greek word *ethiko*, which means habit. Morality, in effect, means having the right habits of living. Our society's root problem is that we are failing to form the right habits—in our children and in ourselves."

It means that when offered a bribe or when an opportunity to cheat arises, a person knows to say "no." And not necessarily because the person knows he *shouldn't* do it, but because he *wouldn't* do it.

"When our moral habits are so ingrained that we wouldn't even think of doing these things, then we know we are ethical," Glidden says.

et, as the habits-ethics equation becomes easier to add up and to associate how one greatly affects the other, the obvious question emerges: How does an individual go about forming strong habits?

"In our guts, we know right from wrong most of the time," Karp says. "We learn our primary values by age fourteen—that's a psychological fact. The knowledge is there, inside; sometimes, though, we lose track of it. Other times we lie to ourselves—we rationalize. In either case, a helpful cure is to talk aloud what we're thinking when we're morally uncertain.

"Oftentimes we just don't know what's inside until we verbalize it. Other times we'll discover just how silly our thinking has been when we hear ourselves say it."

It's one thing, for instance, to cheat on taxes unconsciously; it's another thing entirely to hear oneself saying, perhaps to a child or grandchild, "This year, I'm cheating because everybody else does it."

"Just hearing that is enough to stop most of us in our tracks," Karp says.

Another step endorsed by Karp, though somewhat of a confrontational nature, is to begin holding other persons accountable for their actions.

"The more I overlook their actions, the more I may overlook my own," goes Karp's reasoning. "Either way, despite what may be good intentions, I'm doing nobody any favors. If you don't hold me accountable, you are not helping me."

Newton agrees: "We used to hold people much more accountable than we do today. The con artist who swindles millions of dollars in Massachusetts surfaces tomorrow in Texas with his fortune intact, and few if any questions are asked. A mobile, pluralistic globe has eroded accountability across the board."

Still, when pointing out ethical missteps to other persons, doesn't an individual run the risk of sounding sanctimonious? Perhaps. But as Josephson points out: "Whenever anybody benefits wrongly, somebody else pays for it. When we're talking about honesty and integrity, there really are no little transgressions. Ethical violations come in just two sizes: big and bigger."

Take heart, too, in knowing that "morals are like muscles," Schmidt says. "The more we flex them, the stronger they get. Ethics is a practical skill. If we don't use them, we

the father: 'You know, son, that's against everything I ever taught you. Next time, ask me, and I'll take them from the office.'"

The office, in fact—or any working environment, for that matter—is one area that requires an especially acute sensibility.

David Schmidt, a corporate ethics consultant and one-time head of the Trinity Center for Ethics and Corporate Policy on New York City's Wall Street, points to yet another ethics ingredient: "Awareness is key. So many people get in trouble not because they meant to be unethical, but because they lacked sensitivity and awareness."

Adds Newton: "So many of our decisions involve imbed-

lose them; and the more we use them, the better we get at it."

Which would seem to imply that the longer humans inhabit Earth, the more ethical they should become. Of course, this isn't necessarily the case. Just how bad are today's ethics compared with past eras'? Nobody really knows. A prevailing sense among many experts, though, is that while today's morals seem in greater disrepair, that perception may be rooted more in our proximity than in fact.

"In the '80s we had the savings-and-loan debacle, but in the '20s there was Teapot Dome," Newton says. "Every time has its scandals."

Comparison, though, doesn't necessarily justify a specific era's ethical standards. In today's society, each individual must ask what it is that he or she personally has added or subtracted from a community's values. Only then will the ethical climate become strengthened.

"The road to moral renewal is from the bottom up, not the top down," Glidden says. "It starts person by person, block by block, neighborhood by neighborhood, community by community. That is how morality is reconstituted, and we all are capable of playing our parts.

"Yes, there are problems, but virtue is its own reward and that's the ultimate reason for optimism. People who live virtuous lives live better lives. It's that simple, and, increasingly, that message is getting across."

Adds Josephson: "Doing the right thing is personally rewarding. Often, we find it wasn't such a little thing after all and, beyond that, we just feel better—about ourselves and our world."

The Corporate Ethics Test

Compare your ethical choices
with those of top executives.

RONALD E. BERENBEIM

Ronald E. Berenbeim is senior research associate at The Conference Board and adjunct professor at New York University. This article is adapted, with permission, from *Corporate Ethics Practices*, a Conference Board report.

CORPORATE ETHICS CODES, once regarded as a way for business to deflect cynical outbursts of public distrust, now enjoy a broad base of support within individual companies, a new Conference Board study has found.

The profile of companies participating in the survey suggests that corporate efforts to establish ethical accountability and to improve sensitivity to ethical issues are considerably more sophisticated today than when the Conference Board last surveyed these issues in 1987.

A total of 264 companies responded to the survey of 1,900 firms (186 American, forty European, thirty-four Canadian, and four Mexican). Respondents included chief executive officers, general counsels, senior human resources and financial executives, and auditors.

In many organizations, ethics codes and programs have moved beyond the initial phase of CEO sponsorship and are now part of regular departmental responsibilities — particularly in human resources and the company's legal office.

The increased interest and involvement of senior executives in the creation of ethics policies is due in large part to greater emphasis on four areas of corporate concern:

• *Global management issues.* Companies want to determine their company's core values while at the same time showing respect for local customs and practices. Striking a balance between these competing requirements is not always easy.

As one manager put it, "We are becoming increasingly global. As we do a larger share of business outside the United States, there is a need for a code as a focal point."

Companies pointed to three kinds of external pressures within the international community that can complicate a company's efforts to reconcile its core principles with local business practices: industry standards of behavior; demand for support of movements for social or political change (e.g., the Sullivan Principles); and conventions or regulations promulgated by world or regional multinational organizations (e.g., protection of intellectual property such as literary or artistic work).

 From *Business and Society Review*, Spring 1992, pp. 77-80. © 1992 by Ronald E. Berenbeim. Reprinted by permission.

More Companies Enact Ethics Codes

The Conference Board surveyed ethics practices at 264 corporations in the United States, Europe, Mexico, and Canada. Here are some key findings:

• Among firms with ethics codes, 45 percent have enacted the current statement since 1987

• Some 84 percent of U.S. companies that responded had an ethics code. The figure for non-American firms was 58 percent.

• Financial firms were less likely to have ethics codes than companies in other industries (57 percent versus 82 percent).

• Some 16 percent of American companies said new legislation prompted revisions or additions to their ethics codes.

• One-fourth of the responding companies said they had established new ethics training programs, ethics committees, or ombudsperson's offices during the last three years.

• *Total quality management.* A company must define relationships of trust with employees, customers, suppliers, and local communities to have a successful total quality management program. Corporate ethics statements often include principles of accountability regarding these constituencies.

• *Work force diversity.* Along with representatives from the general counsel's office, senior human resources executives are most likely to be involved with formulating and implementing ethics codes and programs.

The increasing tendency of companies to define the employment contract with greater specificity is a response to increased work force diversity — and to the significant downsizing of corporate departments. In the present competitive environment, companies do not afford the same degree of job security offered in past years. Duties such as maintaining contacts with key suppliers or customers used to be delegated to employees with well-established records of commitment. Now, new and less experienced workers and managers are often responsible for decisions. Thus, no real alternative to increasing the ethical literacy of all employees is available.

• *Inadequate education and training.* American business leaders have expressed serious concern with the quality of public secondary education. The primary focus of this alarm has been on deficiencies in science, math, and literacy. But an educational system that gets poor results in these areas cannot be expected to produce graduates with the analytic power and verbal and social skills needed to make and implement sound ethical decisions.

Evidence of this awareness can be seen in the participation of heads of major departments (e.g., human resources, finance) in the formulation of ethics codes and statements. The increasing involvement of general counsels suggests that codes are viewed as legal documents that establish the accountability of the company and its employees to one another and to the public.

DO MORE CODES MEAN BETTER ETHICS?

The 1991 survey findings show that elements of the employment contract — workplace safety and employee honesty, for example — are the specific subjects most often discussed in codes. This helps explain why senior human resources managers are usually involved in drafting codes.

Companies are also recognizing that in addition to stating their ethical principles, they need to sponsor programs that help employees develop a sensitivity to and an awareness of ethical issues. One-fourth of the participating companies started new discussion programs. Training sessions for middle managers were the most popular initiative in this regard.

None of this documentation of company effort and commitment suggests that business has become more or less ethical. But these data do affirm that senior managers now recognize dealing with ethics issues is part of nearly every employee's job.

To illustrate how senior executives of responding companies would analyze specific situations that might involve ethical issues, participants were also asked for their views on three hypothetical cases, and whether each situation involved ethical as well as business considerations.

"None of this means that companies are any more or less ethical."

They were asked for their own views rather than for statements of their company's policy. Though the facts presented correspond to no particular company or occurrence, each case depicts real issues encountered by managers. The three case studies and ethical choices follow. The survey results are reported at the end of the article. See how your choices match up against those of the managers surveyed.

CASE ONE: ALCOHOL AND ADVANCEMENT

Archer Corporation has an Employee Assistance Program (EAP) that offers counseling for alcohol and substance abuse, mental and psychiatric problems.

In 1985, Bob Spicer, a 15-year sales staff veteran and frequent winner of annual performance awards, told his boss, Joe Sampson, "I have been drinking a lot because I am depressed about my personal problems." Sampson referred him to the EAP. Before, and since that time, Spicer's job ratings have been consistently superior. The company does not have access to his medical records and does not know whether he ever obtained or is currently receiving counseling for depression. Joe Sampson, the manager whom Spicer consulted, is now CEO of Archer.

In November 1990, Spicer applied for the high-stress position of vice president, sales, a job for which his performance merits serious consideration. In reviewing his qualifications:

1. Sampson should (pick one):

A. Ask Spicer if he is still "depressed"; his response is relevant to whether he qualifies for the job.
B. Not discuss the issue with Spicer, but his complaint of being "depressed" should be a factor in considering him for the job.
C. Ignore Spicer's 1985 "depression" complaint because his performance has been excellent and his personal problems are irrelevant in making the promotional decision.
D. Exclude the "depression" incident from consideration in the promotional decision because it occurred more than five years ago.

2. In making his decision Sampson (check one):

A. Is confronting ethical as well as business considerations.
B. Can resolve the issue by limiting discussion to standard personnel policies.

3. Archer's policy with respect to known employee health complaints should be to (pick one):

A. Exclude use in making any assignments or promotions.
B. Consider them when performance related.
C. Consider if performance related, but exclude if they occurred more than three years ago.

CASE TWO: LOCAL CUSTOMS

Dagonet, a diversified manufacturer, is undertaking a major effort to introduce its products in Latin American markets. The company has been asked by several potential distributors to overbill and remit the differences to their company's accounts in Switzerland and the Cayman Islands. The practice is customary in these countries because local taxes are confiscatory and the local exchange rates make it very difficult for local distributors to achieve profitable results. Dagonet has received similar requests in the past from U.S. and European firms and has always refused. Under the circumstances:

Carrot or the Stick?

With all the greed, hubris, and corruption now being showcased worldwide, perhaps it's heartening that a growing number of U.S. corporations are embracing in-house ethics programs. In fact, the Center for Business Ethics at Bentley College in Waltham, Mass., recently found that 45 percent of the 1,000 largest U.S. companies now have ethics programs or workshops, up from 35 percent five years ago. Is some kind of reformist fervor taking hold of corporate America?

Well, not exactly. While many of these programs are doubtless sincere attempts to deter wrongdoing, companies now have a hefty incentive to quickly start an ethics program. Aside from the obvious public relations value in maintaining a commitment to ethics, companies have a wary eye on [tough] new U.S. sentencing guidelines that [took] effect November 1, 1991.

— *Business Week*
September 23, 1991

1. Dagonet should (pick one):

A. Deny the request because what is unethical in one country cannot be ethical in another.
B. Accede to the request because it does not violate the local distributors' standard business practices.

2. In making its decision, Dagonet (pick one):

A. Is confronting ethical as well as business considerations.
B. Can resolve the issue by limiting discussion to accepted local business practices.

3. With respect to ethical considerations in distributor relations, Dagonet should (pick one):

A. Have one policy worldwide.
B. Allow local subsidiaries to formulate policy based on regional customs and practices.

CASE THREE: DEBATING DISBURSEMENTS

Lily Bart's mentor, Lawrence Selden, was promoted and Bart assumed his post as vice president of the general services division of Newland, Inc. Bart continues to report to Selden. In familiarizing herself with her new responsibilities, Bart discovers questionable disbursements for travel and entertainment expenses. The general counsel tells Bart that there has been no illegal conduct and that both Selden and his predecessor routinely approved such reimbursements despite their apparent violation of the company's ethics code. Under these circumstances:

Blacks and Business

Some statistics about black Americans and business:

• Since 1979, the average annual earnings for black women with only a high school education rose $279. For black women with a college degree, average earnings declined $744 in the same period (*Harper's*, November 1991).

• The number of black-owned business increased 38 percent between 1982 and 1987, compared to the 14 percent increase in all firms. Sales for black-owned firms increased 105 percent in the five-year period (*The Wall Street Journal*, April 3, 1992).

• A *Wall Street Journal* poll of black entrepreneurs found that 39 percent believed their business had been hurt by being minority owned. Some 22 percent said minority ownership was helpful; 35 percent said it made no difference.

• At banks across the country, blacks were turned down for mortgages at a rate 2.4 times higher than whites (Federal Reserve Board).

• The top five cities for black-owned businesses, ranked by number and sales: New York, Los Angeles, Washington, D.C., Chicago, Houston, and Atlanta (*The Wall Street Journal*).

• About 70 percent of all black Americans at four-year colleges will drop out at some point in their academic careers. For whites, the rate is 45 percent (*Atlantic Monthly*, April 1992).

• Fewer than 2 percent of the partners in law firms in Chicago, Cleveland, Houston, and Baltimore are minorities (*The Wall Street Journal*, January, 22, 1992).

• About one in seven black families had incomes above $50,000 last year. Nearly one-third of white families exceeded that income level (*Newsweek*, March 23, 1992).

• Statistically, a black child born in the 1980s has a 6 percent chance of living with his biological parents until age seventeen. A white child born at the same time has a 30 percent chance (*Commentary*, April 1992).

1. Bart should (pick one):

A. Launch a formal investigation of all practices to determine real or potential abuses.

B. Issue more detailed policies and enforce them with respect to future conduct.

C. Do nothing. The practices are legal and customary.

2. In making this decision, Bart (pick one):

A. Is confronting ethical as well as legal and business considerations.

B. Can resolve the issue by limiting discussion to legal and business considerations.

C. Is encountering a typical management problem in trying to establish her authority over a new department.

3. The general counsel should (pick one):

A. Only object to employee conduct that exposes the company to legal liability.

B. Object to employee conduct that violates the company's policies and ethics code.

Survey Results		
Case One:		
1A. 37%	1D. 29%	3A. 5%
1B. 1%	2A. 72%	3B. 74%
1C. 33%	2B. 28%	3C. 20%
Case Two:		
1A. 90%	2A. 94%	3A. 82%
1B. 10%	2B. 6%	3B. 18%
Case Three:		
1A. 25%	2A. 80%	3A. 9%
1B. 74%	2B. 12%	3B. 91%
1C. 2%	2C. 8%	

Employees and the Workplace: Ethical Issues and Dilemmas

- Employee Rights and Duties (Articles 9–11)
- Employee Crime (Articles 12 and 13)
- Sexual Treatment of Employees (Articles 14–16)
- Discriminatory and Prejudicial Employment Practices (Articles 17–19)
- Downsizing of the Work Force (Articles 20–22)
- Whistle-blowing in the Organization (Articles 23 and 24)
- Handling Ethical Dilemmas at Work (Articles 25–28)

LaRue Tone Hosmer, in *The Ethics of Management,* lucidly states that ethical problems in business are truly managerial dilemmas because they represent a conflict, or at least the possibility of a conflict, between the *economic performance* of an organization and its *social performance.* Whereas the economic performance is measured by revenues, costs, and profits, the social performance is judged by the fulfillment of obligations to persons both within and outside the organization.

Units 2 through 4 discuss some of the critical ethical dilemmas that management faces in making decisions in the workplace, in the marketplace, and within the global society. This unit focuses on the relationships and obligations of employers and employees to each other.

Organizational decision makers are ethical when they act with equity, fairness, and impartiality, treating with respect the rights of their employees. An organization's hiring and firing practices, treatment of women and minorities, allowance of employees' privacy, and wages and working conditions are areas in which it has ethical responsibilities.

The employee also has ethical obligations in his or her relationship to the employer. A conflict of interest can occur when an employee allows a gratuity or favor to sway him or her in selecting a contract or purchasing a piece of equipment, making a choice that may not be in the best interests of the organization. Other possible ethical dilemmas for employees include espionage and the betrayal of secrets (especially to competitors), the theft of equipment, and the abuse of expense accounts.

The articles in this unit are broken down into seven subsections on different types of ethical dilemmas in the workplace. "Balanced Protection Policies" begins the first subsection by discussing the importance of employers reexamining the balance between employee and employer rights. The next article addresses the issue of an employees' right to privacy in the workplace. The last subsection article presents an ethical dilemma where a manager wrestles with finding a way to help an employee without invading his privacy.

In the subsection entitled *Employee Crime,* two articles explore computer sabotage and employee theft. Suggestions are provided on some ways to deal with these crimes.

The first two selections in the subsection *Sexual Treatment of Employees* take a close look at the sexual treatment of employees in the workplace. The articles reveal various myths about sexual harassment and some forms that sexual harassment and sexual abuse take in office and business environments; they also provide ideas on how to deal with and stop sexual harassment. The last article in this subsection reflects the findings of a survey revealing that women's earnings have only seen meager gains—in comparison to men's—during the past three decades.

The first article in the next subsection provides practical suggestions to help management implement the Americans with Disabilities Act. "Denny's: The Stain That Isn't Coming Out" reveals how Denny's restaurants have recently been barraged by complaints of racial discrimination. The last subsection article discloses that when ethical issues become unclear, managers have a difficult time in their decision making.

The first two articles in the subsection on *Downsizing of the Work Force* suggest key issues to consider and provide possible strategies to be used in revamping and resizing organizational structure and design. "You're Fired" describes an actual situation where an employee is fired unfairly and is in the process of deciding what course of action to take.

The two selections included under the heading *Whistle-blowing in the Organization* analyze the ethical dilemma and possible ramifications of whistle-blowing.

The first article in the last subsection of this unit resonates the benefits of establishing a corporate culture that includes business ethics as an integral part of its ongoing organizational strategy. "Ethical Judgment" provides some thoughtful questions that can provide guidelines for sharpening moral reasoning when facing ethical dilemmas. The last two articles present real-world ethical dilemmas for the reader to ponder.

Looking Ahead: Challenge Questions

Ethical dilemmas occur when a manager or an employee is faced with two or more conflicting ethical choices. In your opinion, what ethical dilemmas do *managers* face most frequently? What ethical dilemmas do *employees* face most often?

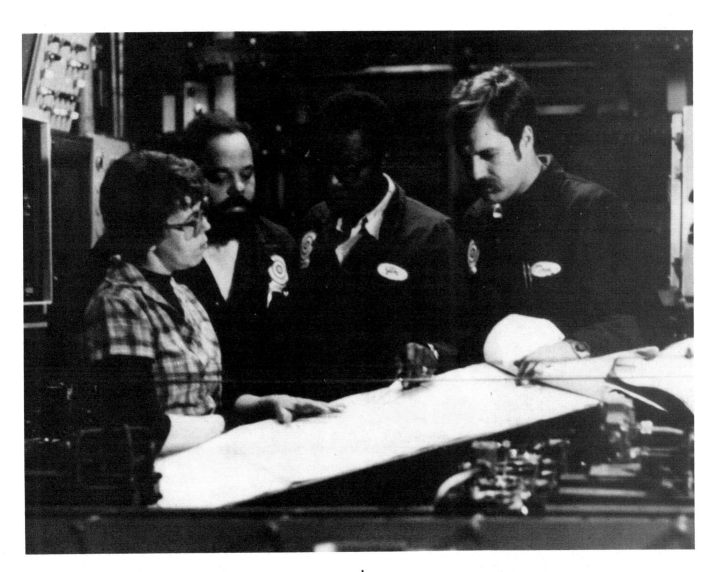

How prevalent do you feel the myths given in "Six Myths of Sexual Harassment" are in today's companies? Explain.

What forms of sexual and minority discrimination are most prevalent in today's workplace? Do you think there are particular job situations or occupations where discrimination is more widespread and conspicuous? Why?

How do you think that Denny's management should have handled the alleged incidents of racial discrimination? Explain.

Whistle-blowing occurs when an employee discloses illegal, immoral, or illegitimate organizational practices or activities. Under what circumstances do you believe whistle-blowing is appropriate? Why?

Balanced Protection Policies

Benson Rosen and
Catherine Schwoerer

Benson Rosen is professor of business administration at the University of North Carolina in Chapel Hill, N.C.
Catherine Schwoerer is assistant professor of business administration at the University of Kansas in Lawrence, Kan.

Corporate human resource specialists currently face the challenge of shaping employment policies for the 21st century. In order to attract and retain the best and brightest workers, organizations must develop new personnel policies that recognize and protect individual rights. A critical element in future HR management policies is the guarantee of employee protection from what might be perceived as any form of arbitrary treatment by management.

Advocates for expanding employee rights warn that management policies that abridge free speech, privacy or due process will surely lead to more government regulation. There is already a movement toward drafting an employee rights law to set national standards for an implicit employment contract between managers and workers.

At the same time that human resource planners face pressures to protect individual rights, pressures are also mounting to maintain a lean, flexible, drug-free work force. Employers argue that to remain competitive, they must protect management's employment-at-will prerogatives, improve the quality of new hires and maintain work force productivity.

Growing international competition and rapid changes in the economy, coupled with increasing numbers of mergers and corporate downsizings,

Striking a balance between the rights of employers and employees is not easy. One study has dealt with this issue and reveals that common protection policies exist.

have made massive layoffs and terminations commonplace. In order to maintain efficiency, quality and productivity, organizations must have little tolerance for dead wood. Accordingly, HR specialists are particularly sensitive about protecting the traditional corporate right to dismiss employees under the employment-at-will doctrine.

Employment-at-will policies permit termination of employees for just cause, no cause or even bad cause at any time. In order to protect their rights under the termination-at-will doctrine, employers have been encouraged to reduce their vulnerability to charges of unjust dismissal resulting from an implied contract. For example, recruiters are warned not to describe employment opportunities as permanent or guaranteed.

Organizations are encouraged to require that job applicants sign a formal statement acknowledging that their employment can be terminated by either party with or without cause or notice at any time. But, the consequences of adopting these protective measures are largely unknown.

A second approach to building a competitive work force centers on improving selection procedures. Growing concerns about the serious consequences of drug abuse and employee theft have compelled many organizations to adopt more stringent selection procedures. Comprehensive background investigations, pre-employment medical screening, drug testing and various psychological tests have been used to improve personnel selection. While acknowledging that some selection strategies risk potential invasion of privacy and violation of other employee rights, employers argue that such measures are necessary in order to screen out high-risk employees.

Finally, in order to improve quality and reduce employee theft, a few organizations have installed various types of electronic surveillance devices. Surveillance may include monitoring of telephone conversations, tapping into computer terminals and installing video cameras in certain work areas. Employers justify electronic surveillance as an important tool for monitoring individual performance and policy compliance.

Reprinted with permission from *HRMagazine* (formerly *Personnel Administrator*), February 1990, pp. 59-61, 63-64.
HRMagazine, published by the Society for Human Resource Management, Alexandria, VA.

Clearly, human resource managers must walk a tightrope, balancing employees' rights of fair treatment and due process against employers' rights to manage the size, quality and productivity of their work forces without cumbersome restrictions. Surprisingly little research is available to help HR professionals evaluate where they stand in terms of employee and employer rights policies.

Survey sample

To determine what policies currently exist, a survey was conducted by a random sampling of 3,800 names drawn from the SHRM national membership. Survey packages containing a cover letter, survey questionnaire and self-addressed, post-paid return envelope were mailed to selected members. By the survey deadline, 785 usable questionnaires had been returned from all regions of the country.

Organizations representing a diverse group of industries responded. Forty-five percent of the organizations employed less than 500 people, 19 percent employed between 500 and 999, and the remaining 36 percent had over 1,000 employees. Less than 30 percent of the organizations were unionized.

Respondents included an almost equal number of men (53 percent) and women (47 percent). The average age of participating human resource professionals was 42.1 and they had an average of 12.7 years of professional experience.

Survey issues

A general question assessed whether organizations currently place greater emphasis on protecting employer or employee rights. Next, a series of specific questions probed what policies organizations currently have in place to protect both employee and employer rights. Participants evaluated the effectiveness of existing policies and reported on the need for additional policies. They also reported on the benefits and costs of existing policies. Finally, survey respondents shared their experiences on the effectiveness of various strategies for revising existing policies or implementing new ones.

The survey included fixed-alternative and open-ended questions. For the fixed-alternative questions, responses were recorded on five-point scales, ranging from 1 (unsuccessful or not needed) to 5 (extremely successful or extremely needed).

Survey results

The present balance. Participants differ on whether their companies' employment policies put more emphasis on employee or employer rights. Slightly more than 44 percent of participating HR professionals characterized their organizations' policies as striking an even balance between employee and employer rights. Of the remaining 56 percent, almost twice as many characterized their organizations as emphasizing employer rights (37 percent) compared to employee rights (19 percent).

In open-ended comments, one participant noted that it may be counterproductive to consider employee and employer rights as mutually exclusive. Another participant pointed out that the challenge for human resource management is to define areas of mutual responsibility with respect to both employee and employer rights. In the next section, we examine specific policies designed to protect the rights of employees.

Employee rights. Experts argue that protecting the rights of employees is both socially responsible and good business. While it is difficult to document conclusively, protecting workers from arbitrary treatment and ensuring basic rights of privacy and free speech are widely believed to build organizational commitment. Moreover, resolving worker conflicts internally should reduce the threat of costly litigation.

Participants were asked to consider eight areas of employee rights. Four policies designed to protect employees from arbitrary treatment were:

- Access to grievance committees.
- Corporate ombudsman to investigate employee complaints.
- Impartial arbitrators for dispute resolution.
- Specific written disciplinary policies.

The remaining policies protected against violation of individual rights:

- Privacy protection with respect to performance, medical and financial information.

- Employee access to personnel records.
- Free-speech protection and safety information.

Respondents indicated whether their organizations currently followed each policy and evaluated the effectiveness of the existing policy. In the absence of a policy, respondents assessed the need for new policies. Findings with respect to employee rights are shown in Exhibit 1.

Survey results suggest a very mixed picture. In the critical area of protecting employees from arbitrary treatment, many organizations have taken a first step, but still appear to have a long way to go.

Written disciplinary policies have been implemented in more than 70 percent of participating companies. These policies guide the administration of discipline, contingent on specific rule infractions. Written disciplinary policies protect both the employee and the employer by ensuring that disciplinary actions are consistent and impartial.

Surprisingly few organizations, however, have taken the next step and supplemented their disciplinary policies with additional measures for resolving disputes between management and employees. Even fewer organizations report using management grievance committees or impartial arbitrators to resolve employment conflicts. Findings indicate that in a majority of organizations, employees have very limited access to internal dispute-resolution mechanisms. Accordingly, when disputes and grievances develop, employees in these organizations may see few alternatives to seeking redress through union grievance procedures or through the courts.

Developing policies to protect employees' rights to free speech is another area where organizations may be lagging. Given current concerns with corporate ethics, it is surprising how few organizations have formal policies protecting "whistle blowers," employees who criticize organizational policies, practices, products or services. Only 26 percent of organizations have implemented policies protecting employees' rights to free speech.

Our survey findings reveal that organizations have been considerably more responsive in protecting employee rights to ensure the accuracy and confidentiality of information contained in employee personnel files. Almost 90 percent of organizations in our sample allow employees to review their own personnel and medical files for accuracy. More than 83 percent have strict rules ensuring the privacy of performance, medical and financial information.

More than three-quarters of participating organizations have explicit policies governing disclosure of health and safety information. In most organizations these policies provide employees with information about potential risks associated with dangerous working conditions. The existence of these policies is no doubt driven in part by "right to know" laws which affect some industries.

Business characteristics and employee rights policies. Two business characteristics associated with the presence or absence of employee rights policies were industry and union status. Industries that were among the leaders in implementing employee rights policies included government, health and education, manufacturing and transportation. Disseminating health and safety information was significantly more likely in transportation, manufacturing and health industries. Government organizations were more likely to use arbitrators and to permit employees access to confidential records. Organizations in banking and finance trailed all other industries with respect to establishing formal grievance committees. Clearly, both the nature of the business and the industry's regulatory environment influence organizational posture on employee rights.

Employer rights

In order to build a competitive, flexible work force, some organizations have implemented new human resource policies to improve personnel selection, monitor performance and preserve management's employment-at-will prerogatives.

We asked survey respondents to indicate which employer rights policies their companies have already implemented, to evaluate the success of existing policies and to indicate areas

where new policies are needed (see Exhibit 1).

Applicant screening policies. Respondents reported a number of policies designed to screen applicants. The most frequently used approach to applicant screening is the background check (used by 80.9 percent). For most organizations, the background check included an investigation to verify education and work history. In other companies, an inquiry into financial background and criminal records was also conducted.

More than 40 percent of organizations in the sample require pre-employment medical examinations. Companies attempt to detect genetic traits that increase employee susceptibility to certain diseases and other pre-existing medical problems. There has been considerable debate over the potential for employment discrimination when genetic testing information is used to influence selection decisions. However, the use of pre-employment medical screening has been justified by some employers as necessary for containing health-care costs.

The survey findings indicate that drug-screening policies have been

---

EXHIBIT 1

Status of Protection Policies
(expressed in percentages)

Employee Protection Policies

	Exist	Successful	Needed
1. Access to records	89.8	93	77
2. Privacy protection	83.2	96	88
3. Health/safety information	79.0	91	78
4. Disciplinary policy	71.7	95	79
5. Company ombudsman	39.8	91	54
6. Free speech protection	26.3	85	45
7. Management grievance committee	24.9	91	46
8. Impartial arbitrators	23.3	87	31

Employer Protection Policies

	Exist	Successful	Needed
1. Background investigation	80.9	89	91
2. Avoid "implied contract"	79.7	95	87
3. Termination at will	51.1	93	71
4. Medical screening	40.6	88	56
5. Drug testing	37.0	93	66
6. Non-competition agreement	28.1	83	43
7. Psych/polygraph testing	10.5	74	24
8. Electronic surveillance	7.4	73	18

implemented by 37 percent of companies in the sample. All of the policies subject applicants to drug screening prior to employment. In addition, some organizations require periodic follow-up drug testing.

Only 10 percent of organizations reported using psychological testing or polygraph screening to identify "high-risk" applicants or employees. In past years, polygraph screening was used as a deterrent to employee theft. However, recent legislation has banned the use of polygraph testing in most employment situations. It appears that use of paper-and-pencil "honesty" tests has not yet been widely adopted in place of polygraph screening.

Electronic surveillance has been justified by some companies as an important tool for feedback, improving productivity and deterring employee theft. However, electronic monitoring and video surveillance have potential for increasing stress and invading employee privacy. Monitoring employee performance by means of computer, telephone or video surveillance is used in 7.4 percent of organizations in the sample. Survey data indicate that only 18 percent of organizations perceive a need for electronic surveillance. At present, the perceived psychological costs to employees scrutinized by electronic monitoring may far outweigh the organizational benefits.

Employment-at-will rights. The majority of organizations are very protective of their employment-at-will rights. Almost 80 percent have implemented new policies to avoid any indication of an "implied employment" contract. In many instances, organizations have deleted from company handbooks mention of permanent employment, promise of annual review or guarantee of a grievance and appeal procedure.

In addition, just over half of the organizations require employees to formally acknowledge that their employment may be terminated with or without cause at any time by either the company or the employee. Protecting against wrongful discharge or implied contract lawsuits and maintaining flexibility to adjust work force size are two frequently cited motivations for preserving management's employment-at-will prerogatives.

The majority of organizations are very protective of their employment-at-will rights.

Non-competition agreements. Non-competition agreements protect employers by prohibiting former employees from working for competitors. They are designed to curtail departing employees from taking valued customers or trade secrets to the competition. Such agreements may be particularly important in certain types of high-technology or sales organizations.

Employees, on the other hand, argue that non-competition agreements unfairly limit their re-employment opportunities. About 28 percent of companies require employees to sign non-competition agreements. Among companies that do not currently have such policies, 43 percent perceive a need to implement non-competition agreements in the future.

Business characteristics and employer rights policies. Industry, organizational size and union status were significantly related to the implementation of employer rights policies. Industries where employer rights policies were most frequently found included transportation, manufacturing and finance.

For example, organizations in the transportation industry were significantly more likely to use drug testing, medical screening and electronic surveillance. Similarly, manufacturing organizations conducted drug testing and medical screening and required non-competition agreements.

Financial institutions emphasized background checks and protected against employment-at-will litigation

by revising company handbooks and requiring employees to sign statements acknowledging the termination-at-will principle. Organizations in the government and education sectors were least likely to develop policies surrounding non-competition or employment at will.

Organizational size also influenced employer rights policies. Relative to smaller organizations, the largest organizations in our sample (more than 1,000 employees) were significantly more likely to implement stringent pre-employment measures. The large organizations were most likely to require pre-employment psychological tests, drug tests and medical exams. Large organizations were more likely to monitor employee behavior through electronic surveillance.

Union status was associated with employer rights policies. Unionized organizations were more likely to conduct both drug testing and medical screening.

The most widely adopted organizational policies focus on ensuring the selection of quality employees and preserving organizations' employment-at-will rights. Comparing existing policies with perceptions of needs, the biggest gaps were found for drug testing and termination at will. In future years, more organizations will likely develop policies aimed at drug screening and reaffirming the employment-at-will doctrine.

Implementing new policies

Organizations have long valued openness, trust, security and employee commitment. Accordingly, these organizations have implemented policies designed to protect employee rights to privacy, free speech and fair treatment. Yet to remain competitive and to ensure a safe work environment, management has also adopted policies and practices that represent potential invasions of employees' rights to privacy, security and due process.

Perhaps the secret for achieving harmony between employer and employee rights rests with the processes by which needs for new policies are identified and with the strategies used to implement these policies.

The majority of survey participants endorsed a strategy that provides education and training to help employees understand the reasons behind new policies. Education and training satisfy the need for communication of new policies in order to break down resistance to change.

Policy implementation based on consultants' advice was evaluated favorably by almost 80 percent of respondents. While this strategy has the potential for capitalizing on the experiences of other organizations, the strategy does not provide for employee input.

About two-thirds recommended policy implementation after negotiation and agreement with employees. Negotiation and agreement allow for modifying proposed policies to account for employee as well as employer needs.

The use of task forces to develop new policy recommendations was evaluated highly by 57 percent of participants. Waiting for a task force to reach consensus on new policy recommendations is clearly the most time-consuming approach. However, the task force ensures maximum involvement of those employees most likely to be affected by the new policies. Accordingly, the task force approach should be very effective in overcoming resistance to change.

In open-ended comments, many participants noted that a combination of approaches represents the most effective way to implement new policy. For example, one participant described an employee task force with management and legal experts serving in advisory capacities. Another participant stressed the importance of communication both before and after policy implementation in order to maintain trust and cooperation.

The challenge is to find a common ground where good business practices do not limit basic employee freedoms.

As organizations strive to balance both employee and employer rights, the process of implementing new policies may be as important as the content of those policies. Our survey findings suggest that human resource professionals appreciate the value of effective communication. Results also suggest, however, that HR professionals may underestimate the importance of employee involvement and participation in overcoming resistance to policy changes.

Implications for the future

The findings reveal that when employer and employee rights clash, many more organizations put the highest priority on preserving and protecting employer rights. The major conflicts between employee and employer rights center on issues of employee privacy and employment at will. The challenge for HR professionals in each of these areas is to find a common ground where good business practices do not limit basic employee freedoms.

In the future, resolving the conflict over employment at will requires that human resource managers accept the concept of an implied contract based on a clearly defined set of responsibilities and rights. Employee responsibilities must include adhering to high standards of honesty, safety, quality and productivity. Employee rights must include security from arbitrary dismissal, channels for dispute resolution and privacy protection. Statements of rights and responsibilities must also specify the mechanisms for settling wrongful discharge claims through binding arbitration before they reach litigation

Many organizations have already revised human resource management policies, often with the input of employees and outside experts. Other organizations have acknowledged the need for new policies, but have not yet taken action. We have offered some guidelines for resolving conflicts over privacy and employment at will. Past experiences in the areas of equal employment opportunity, occupational safety, and pension protection suggest that if companies fail to take the initiative in the area of employee rights, the courts and regulators will surely intervene.

Editor's Note: *This study was funded by a grant from the Society for Human Resource Management. The interpretations, conclusions and recommendations are those of the authors and do not necessarily represent those of the Foundation.*

WHAT THE BOSS KNOWS ABOUT YOU

The right to privacy in the workplace is increasingly under fire. A collision is coming between what companies demand to know and what employees insist on keeping secret.

Lee Smith

Dear Dr. Confidentiality,
  Can the boss look into my head?
              Sincerely,
              Quaking in my cubicle

Dear Q:
  Not yet. But remember that indiscreet message you punched into the computer system and then deleted? Company engineers can retrieve those electronic musings. Also, the spigot overhead that looks like part of the sprinkler system could be a miniature video camera. And your supervisor may have equipped his phone with a voice stress analyzer that detects any suspicious warblings when you defend your expense account.
              Take precautions,
              Dr. C.

PRIVACY IS under stress as never before. As business squeezes out more productivity, companies turn to electronic gadgets to track workers' moves. With health insurance costs soaring, employers offer incentives to workers for round-the-clock clean living. Home and office merge while work and private time blur. At the end of the workday,

REPORTER ASSOCIATE *Edward N. Brown*

Mom and Dad ferry home more work on floppy disks. The next morning they drop off the kids at the company day care center.

Today the companies that employ us seem to know everything from our charities to our cholesterol counts, including how much we save, what our credit rating may be, whether our children are toilet trained (the day care center needs to know), who our heirs are, and what model of car we prefer to rent. That's okay. Maybe. Trouble is, it's becoming increasingly possible for outsiders to tap into that information as well. That's not nearly as okay.

Washington's interest in privacy issues is growing. Proposed legislation that would require credit bureaus to divulge to a consumer free of charge all the information it has collected about him will soon be considered by the House Consumer Credit and Insurance subcommittee. Also, Senator Paul Simon (D-Illinois) is promoting a bill that would restrict employers that eavesdrop on customer service operators.

In this article and the accompanying four boxes, FORTUNE examines current concerns over privacy. The discomforting conclusion: Companies are intruding more deeply into the lives of employees, and even though corporate intentions may be benign, the risk of a backlash is growing. Worker anxiety is likely to rise right along with the surveillance level, possibly hurting performance.

Most companies have failed to take steps to ease that apprehension by explaining to employees how supervisors look and listen in on subordinates, why it's done, and what the limits are. Yes, says the boss, we will canvass all electronic mail if we suspect criminal activity, such as drug trafficking. But no, your supervisor won't be told

---

YOUR EMPLOYER

Can ...
- Peruse your E-mail
- Tap your telephone
- Film you in the restroom
- Fire you for reading this (in most states)

But he can't ...
- Peek into your health records

And he should ...
- Explain what his privacy policy is

From *Fortune*, August 9, 1993, pp. 88–93. © 1993 by Time Inc. Magazine Company. All rights reserved. Reprinted by permission.

you're seeing a psychotherapist twice a week.

Workplace privacy is an issue that reaches beyond employer and employee relations. Business is increasingly vulnerable to corporate espionage (see the box on "Calling All Saboteurs and Swindlers"). The employee who uses a cellular telephone is operating a mobile radio station that may inadvertently be broadcasting confidential information to anyone within radio-wave earshot.

As more electronic routes intersect and as all data go digital, the information highway of computers and telecommunications probably will attract roving brigands, who will waylay the unwary and plunder their secrets—and money. Microsoft Chairman Bill Gates acknowledges that the electronic networks his software helps build are merely "a tool, and like a hammer they can be used to hit a nail or smash someone in the face." Gates and his kind may know how to protect themselves from highwaymen, but the "technically challenged" could get hurt.

Encroachment on employee privacy has strong traditions. Many 19th-century industrialists made sure their laborers went to church. Eighty or so years back, Ford Motor Co. sent social workers to employees' homes to determine whether their habits and finances were worthy of bonuses.

The 1950s added the fashion of psychological profiles to the job interview. Among the 566 questions an applicant had to answer on the Minnesota Multiphasic Personality Inventory were such disturbing and intrusive inquiries as whether the sentence "I deserve severe punishment for my sins" aptly described the candidate's thoughts. Although many companies continue to collect psycho-profiles of their new hires, enlightened employers dumped such tests in the late 1960s. Plumbers with beards and flowered bell-bottoms proved as able to install sinks as the clean-shaven. Says Alan F. Westin, a Columbia University law professor and authority on workplace privacy: "Whether you had an MBA *was* relevant. Your lifestyle was *not.*"

That golden age didn't last beyond the 1970s. In the 1980s victims of assault and other crimes began to target companies as deep pockets. Why didn't Consolidated Crayons know that the security guard it hired was a convicted rapist? So companies

CALLING ALL SABOTEURS AND SWINDLERS

As computer and telecommunications systems become more complex, they grow increasingly vulnerable. All anyone needs to break into most communications networks nowadays is a PC, a modem, and a telephone. Which is why Eddie L. Zeitler, vice president of information services for Fidelity Investments, is so concerned. Although Fidelity has safeguards against interlopers tapping in, once inside the Fidelity system, it would be easy to reroute instructions for trading billions of dollars' worth of securities. Says Zeitler: "The probability of a successful attack is very small, but it would be devastating."

Corporate espionage is easier than ever and paranoia is on the rise. Predators roam Silicon Valley, or so the rumors go, eavesdropping on the cellular phone conversations of passing Mercedes and Range Rovers. The thieves are thought to sell revealing tidbits to competitors and investors. Apple Computer, for one, takes the threat seriously enough to instruct executives never to discuss confidential matters over cellular phones. Other eavesdroppers are likely on the prowl elsewhere, but people with less technical sophistication remain unaware. "They're ostriches," says Donald Norman, an Apple executive who has written on the relationship between man and machine. "If they don't see it happening, they don't believe it."

So why not translate all conversations, voice and data, into code? About 15 years ago, two Stanford professors, Whitfield Duffie and Martin Hellman, created a marvel, the public key code, which makes that possible. Millions of users can have identical scrambling devices installed in their phones and computers, but when Alice addresses a note to Frank only he can unscramble it, not Sandra.

Some international banks now use such codes while shifting piles of money around the world. For example, mathematicians at RSA Data Security Inc. of Redwood City, California, have devised a system for Citicorp. Considering the perils so many companies face by using plain language, it's surprising so few companies have switched to code.

What's impeding this wonder is mostly Washington. If everyone—including drug dealers, terrorists, and inside traders—were to communicate in code, the FBI, the SEC, and other police agencies wouldn't be able to understand their conversations. What good would a wiretap be?

That justifiable worry leads to the great, though esoteric, encryption debate of 1993. The Clinton Administration proposed last April that everyone who wants to communicate in code use a device created by the National Security Agency, a gadget known as the Clipper Chip. A key to breaking the Clipper would be split in two, half given to each of two escrow agents. If the FBI, SEC, or police wanted to eavesdrop on a suspect, they would have to persuade both key holders to give up their halves. But the strategy might not confound criminals at all. The First Amendment would seem to protect the right of citizens to talk to one another in any code they like. The Mafia would likely select a code other than the Clipper.

Legitimate business is not happy with the Clipper Chip. Companies don't welcome the police secretly browsing through their communications. "We're law-abiding citizens," says Zeitler. "If the government has a specific question about something in our system, we'll cooperate. But why let them monitor all my traffic?" In July, Novell, designer of software for business computer networks, announced it had organized an industry group that will produce an alternative to the Clipper.

Still, companies, especially global ones, that want to use the Novell system might find themselves in a difficult bind. The government has the right to prohibit the export of coding devices. So if Dow Chemical, say, wanted to ship a chip based on the Novell system to Paris and Moscow for installation in office computers there, the Commerce Department could prevent it. On the other hand, the French and the Russians might be reluctant to let Dow import the Clipper. The U.S. spy agency that created the chip might have retained the ability to eavesdrop whenever it likes.

DOES THE BOSS KNOW YOU'RE SICK?

And can he fire you if he finds out? The broad answer is no. By federal law, health records must be kept separate from the rest of your personnel file. Your physical condition cannot be grounds for dismissal so long as you can perform your job.

The secrecy of an employee's health record is one area in which workplace privacy seems more secure than ever. That corrects a long tradition. Many employers automatically turned away candidates with disabilities, even one so subtle it could be detected only from medical records. The handicapped have been so discriminated against that their unemployment statistics are staggering. In 1990 some 58% of handicapped men of working age and 80% of women had no jobs, although only a minority were totally incapacitated.

For the employer, of course, confidentiality means a higher risk of hiring and assuming responsibility for a worker with AIDS, degenerative heart disease, or some other calamitous and expensive illness.

What has swung the balance to the employee is the Americans With Disabilities Act. In effect for close to a year, the ADA sets hiring and firing rules for companies with more than 25 employees; those with as few as 15 employees will be included by mid-1994.

Start with the arrival of the job candidate for the interview. The employer may not request the candidate to undergo a comprehensive medical exam. Drug tests are permitted, and any sign that the candidate has been using controlled substances is legitimate reason for tossing his résumé. "However, it's not allowed to ask if someone has had an alcohol problem," notes Mark Rothstein, a University of Houston authority on the reach of the ADA. So there's no probing for the drug that's most prevalent and perhaps most dangerous.

A suspicious employer is not likely to learn much from the applicant's last boss, except dates of employment and positions. It is not illegal to reveal more, but the applicant could sue for defamation and collect if the previous employer cannot prove its case. Insurance companies routinely exchange information about patients. What happens if the prospective employer asks the company health insurer if there's any reason not to hire Social Security number 043-28-8744? The insurer too can be sued for simply answering yes.

After the employer offers a job to the candidate, he can make it conditional upon passing a physical exam. But the employer may rescind the offer only if the physical turns up a defect that prevents the newcomer from doing the job. A curvature of the spine, for example, might be a handicap on the loading dock, but progressive diabetes won't prevent someone from evaluating loan applications—at least not tomorrow. The law doesn't concern itself with whether the apprentice will be effective in a year or so. It also ignores the problems of deteriorating health, missed workdays, and rising medical bills.

Before passage of the ADA, some employers avoided those expenses by abruptly cancelling their health insurance policies and substituting contracts that exclude particular ailments. When H&H Music, a retail chain in Houston, for instance, learned in 1988 that an employee had AIDS, it switched to an insurance plan that put a $5,000 lifetime cap on benefits for an AIDS patient while retaining the $1 million maximum for those who suffered from other diseases. The courts upheld H&H.

Such maneuvers may soon be impossible. In June the Equal Employment Opportunity Commission said it would argue the protection of ADA to win medical benefits for Terrence P. Donaghey Jr., 34, a former New York City construction worker. Donaghey, who needs treatment for sickness brought on by his HIV-positive condition, thought he was covered by his labor union (Mason Tenders Local 23) health plan. But the union quietly changed its policy a year ago to eliminate reimbursements for AIDS. Donaghey and the EEOC claim discrimination and are suing the union.

Denying a worker benefits for AIDS or other catastrophic illness seems cruel. Yet it seems equally unfair to burden a small employer or union with responsibility. Such calamities can cost insurance companies and, ultimately, the insured workers $500,000 or more, and the health insurer might cancel the employer's policy the following year or raise the premiums out of reach. Add the ADA to the long list of reasons why it's high time for health care reform.

---

began to canvass job applicants about criminal records. The forces most responsible for renewed intrusions on privacy were concerns about safety and costs—mostly drugs and health care—as well as the spreading of electronic devices that keep workers wired to the office.

■ **Drug testing.** The goal of a drug-free workplace, set by President Reagan in September 1986, means that an increasing number of workers submit to urinalysis tests that can detect traces of amphetamines, cocaine, heroin, and other controlled substances.

The American Management Association reports that of the 630 members that responded to a survey, 85% will conduct such tests on at least some employees, generally the new ones, in 1993, up from 52% in 1990. Of those tested so far this year, 2.5% showed signs of drug use.

The federal government requires that all contractors who do more than $20,000 worth of business with Washington conduct random tests on a cross section of workers. Some companies go beyond the requirements. Many examine all new hires. Motorola plans to test all employees every three

years no matter how long they have been with the company.

But airlines want Washington to reduce requirements. Carriers must now test at random a number equal to 50% of all their pilots, flight attendants, mechanics, and dispatchers a year, at a cost of close to $100 per test. The debt-burdened airlines argue that a rate of 10% would be adequate.

■ **Health care.** The average cost of providing health insurance has risen to about $4,000 per employee, up from just over

$1,600 a decade ago. Only 10% of employees and their dependents account for about 70% of total medical costs. But the 1992 Americans With Disabilities Act, which protects the handicapped from job discrimination, has made it almost impossible for employers to screen out the riskiest cases (see "Does the Boss Know You're Sick?").

So companies have switched tactics. If you can't jettison them, at least try to keep them healthy. For the most part, such company programs are logical and humane, such as reimbursing workers for Smoke-Enders or Weight Watchers classes. But carried too far, paternalism looks very much like tyranny (see "Can Smoking or Bungee Jumping Get You Canned?").

■ **Electronic tethers**. No phenomenon has more complicated the issue of workplace privacy than the profusion of notebook computers, modems, and similar gadgets in the executive portable office. At times, such devices enhance privacy. A financial analyst can simultaneously crunch numbers and press grapes in the happy isolation of a Napa Valley vineyard.

But the same machines make it close to impossible to remain private. The fax hums into Sunday morning silence as the boss raises a few more questions before Monday's meeting. Beepers and electronic pagers find managers on vacation, in cars, at meetings, at parties, on the golf course—anywhere. The office no longer has walls. Privacy watchers have paid little attention to the electronic monitoring of upscale workers, including production and sales managers (see "Whose Office Is This Anyhow?"). Westin points out that a CEO can tap into a database and find out the progress of a project at any point. But if people know top management is constantly judging their work, it can destroy creativity. Says Westin: "Teams assigned to new undertakings won't take chances because they will worry not about how the project will look in the

---

CAN SMOKING OR BUNGEE JUMPING GET YOU CANNED?

■ Or perhaps just taking in a movie with someone else's wife? Laural Allen, 23, and Sam Johnson, 20, had been working for Wal-Mart in Gloversville, New York, for several months when they began dating last January. Neither was a supervisor, and they were employed in different departments. Says Johnson: "One day in February the store manager called Laural in and fired her. Later she fired me. The reason she gave is that although Laural is legally separated from her husband, she's not divorced. They didn't tell us there's a rule like that." The couple has sued for $4 million, plus back pay and reinstatement on grounds of wrongful discharge. Wal-Mart declines to comment while the case is being litigated.

Assuming Johnson's story is true, Wal-Mart's action seems such an outrageous breach of privacy that it must be illegal. But maybe not. Employers can fire employees or reject job candidates for any reason that a contract or law doesn't specifically forbid. Federal and state laws prohibit discrimination based on race, religion, age, and sex, but Washington does not protect jobs for those who tango, motorcycle, tease pit bulls, play bridge, or otherwise amuse themselves during off hours. And only a handful of states do.

The Wal-Mart case, where morality seems the issue, is unusual. More commonly, employers try to control workers' physical well-being. Why? Cautious, healthy workers cost less. A late 1980s study of 46,000 Du Pont employees showed that each year the average smoker cost the company an additional $960 in medical claims and sick days; the overweight person, $401; the alcohol abuser, $369; a worker with elevated cholesterol, $370; one with high blood pressure, $343. Turner Broadcasting has refused to hire smokers since 1986. North Miami requires applicants to sign an affidavit that they have not used tobacco products for the previous year. Arlene Kurtz, a clerk typist denied a city job because she smokes, has sued. But Florida has no statute protecting smokers.

Twenty-eight other states, including Illinois, New Jersey, and New York, have passed laws shielding smokers from such discrimination, urged on by the strange bedfellowship of the tobacco industry and the American Civil Liberties Union. Eight of those states protect a range of activities. New York, for example, makes it illegal to fire an employee who during off-hours engages in sports, games, hobbies, exercise, reading, or watching TV or movies. Lewis Maltby, an ACLU attorney, argues that all legal activities that are not directly related to work should be protected. Says he: "We all do something dangerous whether it's scuba diving or eating red meat."

He has a point. Firing an employee for having a couple of drinks after his shift is heavy-handed. An Indianapolis manufacturing company, Best Lock Corp., did just that when it discharged Daniel Winn, a machine operator, several years ago. An alternative might be charging workers for bad habits that ultimately take money from colleagues' pockets. General Mills lowers workers' insurance premiums by as much as 20% if they live healthfully. Among the half-dozen measurements: wearing seat belts; not smoking; drinking moderately or not at all; and controlling weight and blood pressure.

Beginning next year, Butterworth Hospital of Grand Rapids, Michigan, will offer its 5,000 employees financial incentives to live healthfully—and will punish those who don't. Staffers who hew to the proper lifestyle will find up to $25 extra in each biweekly paycheck. Employees who do poorly on tests or who refuse to cooperate will be docked up to $25 every two weeks. Some employees consider the policy overbearing. Says one nurse, Julie Ostrander: "I resent *someone else* trying to control my behavior."

Genes determine weight and cholesterol levels as much as diet does. Should workers be penalized for their parentage? And how does the employer find out whether a worker gets tipsy of a Saturday night? Before adopting such programs, companies ought to consider the consequences thoroughly.

WHOSE OFFICE IS THIS ANYHOW?

What rights do you, as an employee, have to make a totally private phone call or to type a completely confidential message into the computer? Virtually none. The Fourth Amendment bars the government from unreasonable search and seizure of your scribblings at home. It does not prohibit the boss from rifling the office he's letting you use.

Consider Bonita Bourke and Rhonda Hall, who traveled the U.S. training car dealers, sales staff, and mechanics on how to use Nissan's electronic mail system. They also logged on for racy conversations with students and some disparaging remarks about a supervisor.

Suspicious, the supervisor overrode the women's passwords to read their E-mail and, among other things, found himself called "numbnuts." He rebuked them. A few weeks later, Bourke and Hall filed a grievance with Nissan headquarters in Los Angeles, arguing they had a reasonable expectation of privacy while using E-mail. Within days Nissan fired them, and the women sued for reinstatement. Nissan says they were dismissed for generally poor performance, but that in any case they had no right to privacy on the E-mail network. So far the California courts have upheld Nissan.

In 1991 two male employees of the Boston Sheraton Hotel were secretly videotaped while changing clothes in the locker room during a hunt for a drug dealer. They were not suspects, simply bystanders. Indignant, they sued. But don't bet on them winning in court.

Legislation that would protect employees in such situations might curtail legitimate surveillance. Companies often have good reason to monitor telephone calls of service operators and of employees who handle customer complaints.

Sometimes, though, monitoring can be excessive or pure harassment. Since 1990, Senator Paul Simon has unsuccessfully tried to pass the Privacy for Consumers and Workers Act. Under that act, an employer could eavesdrop on operators with fewer than 60 days on the job. Over time, employer rights would diminish, so operators with five or more years of service could be monitored only if suspect of a crime. That may sound reasonable, but how do supervisors evaluate veteran operators who might get sloppy?

The key to dealing with employee anxiety about surveillance is to inform workers in writing about policy and the reasons for it. Also, top management ought to keep a close watch on line supervisors who may abuse surveillance privileges.

Electronic snooping is so remote that it doesn't seem harmful at all—examining the patient with a CAT scan rather than cutting him open with a knife. But the practice is nonetheless invasive and sometimes addictive. Al Simon, who designs company security systems in New York, points out that you can acquire a voice stress analyzer or "truth phone" ($2,000 and up) to catch a thief but wind up cross-examining your wife. Supervisors who may hesitate to unlock employee desk drawers are less squeamish about invading electronic mailboxes. *Macworld*, a magazine for computer users, recently surveyed 301 companies from various industries and found that supervisors in 21% have examined employee computer files, E-mail, or telephone voice mail for the stated reasons of investigating larceny or measuring performance.

Reasonable ethics for employer spying seems simple. Says William Moroney, director of the Electronic Mail Association, a trade organization for those who create and use such systems: "Employees have the right to expect that naked pictures of them will not be passed around the office. If, however, you're running an illegal football pool, management has the right to know about it." But the line gets blurry between the poles of voyeurism and police work. Is it all right, for example, to monitor employee whereabouts constantly? Olivetti has recently developed "smart badge," an electronic ID card. Sensors around the building track the bearer as he moves and direct his phone calls to the nearest receiver. Very convenient. Unless you don't want the boss to know you're in a different division inquiring about a transfer. Before installing such devices, employers would do well to think through the ramifications.

end, but how it will look at 3 P.M. on Tuesday."

By and large, continues Westin, workers trust management to use information it collects about them fairly. This year he helped Lou Harris Associates survey 1,000 workers at 300 companies, some with as few as 25 employees, others with more than 1,000. As many as 70% think consumer credit bureaus are far too nosy. "But by overwhelming majorities of 90% or more," reports Westin, "they think employers collect only information that is relevant and necessary."

Employers who let themselves be lulled by such scores are surely shortsighted.

What companies demand to know and what employees insist on keeping private are clearly on a collision course. Attitudes about workplace privacy may seem touchy-feely, but then so are the moods that add up to consumer confidence. And when that heads south, there goes the bottom line.

WHAT WOULD YOU DO?

A Reluctant Invasion

Sam had every right to hide the fact he was HIV positive.
But when Jackie learned of his condition after laying him off, her hands were tied.
How could she help him without invading his privacy?

ILLUSTRATION BY CARL WESLEY.

DOUG WALLACE

Doug Wallace does frequent consulting work on corporate ethics, and was formerly the vice president for social policy at Norwest Bank in Minneapolis.

All cases used in What Would You Do? *depict actual events, although individual and company names are changed to protect privacy. Please contact Craig Cox at the Business Ethics office if you have a case to suggest or if you would like to become a guest commentator.*

THE CASE

He first heard about it during a phone call from Jackie Davies, director of human resources. He remembered because the halting cadence of Jackie's speech seemed strangely out of character. Finally, he stopped her in the middle of one of those painfully hesi-

tant sentences and suggested that they talk face to face over lunch. She seemed relieved.

As they sat down at the restaurant later, Jackie began. "Sorry to bother you with this one, Riley, but I didn't know where else to turn. In a moment, you'll see why."

"Well, that's why I'm here," he replied.

As general counsel of Excel, Inc., Riley Trevor was often sought out by managers of the firm to help them think through tough problems. Over the last few years he had helped this major high-tech contracting firm deal with many sticky and unusual legal arrangements with its clients and, as a result, his judgments were highly respected. He also had increasingly been consulted on personnel issues as the organization navigated through the rocky swells of a whitewater economy.

Jackie described the situation. Because of a continued slow decline in con-

tracts, the company had decided to trim a few people from its 620-employee payroll. One of the positions slated to go was occupied by Sam Spevac, who had been with the firm for a little over a year. Sam had a good record, but efforts to locate him in another position just didn't succeed. He was given the customary two-week termination notice and a severance package that included the extension of health care benefits for six months.

It all seemed fairly routine, Jackie said. But within a couple of hours of notifying Sam, a colleague of his named George contacted Jackie to talk about Sam's situation. He told her, "We really need Sam. His work is important and we can't understand why you are selecting this position to eliminate. Some of us think there may be some politics mixed up in this."

At the time, Jackie wondered why this issue had come up at the last minute. To reassure herself, she checked into it thor-

Reprinted by permission of *Business Ethics*, Vol. 7, No. 1, January/February 1993, pp. 39-40. *Business Ethics*, The Magazine of Socially Responsible Business.

Laying off Sam was a routine matter, until Jackie learned he was HIV positive.

oughly and learned that the decision was squeaky clean. She got back to George, at which time he raised the real issue.

"Sam is HIV infected," he said. "We don't think it's right that he's going without a safety net. There are two of us that know and Sam didn't want it disclosed. He doesn't know I am talking with you. In fact, he doesn't even know that I know."

Jackie looked up from her lunch plate. "That's what I wanted to talk with you about, Riley. Sam is already off the payroll. I am concerned about what happens when his health benefits terminate, but at the same time I'm not supposed to know this information about him—he never told anyone except a close friend at work. You have a professional obligation to keep client information private, and, besides, you have been helpful in the past to me in problem-solving. That's why I came to you." '

After some discussion, Riley came up with a suggestion. "Why don't you ask Sam to come in to review his benefits package and give him an opportunity to reveal the situation himself," he said. "If he does, you have a new ballgame."

A couple of days later, Jackie did just that. But she was disappointed with the results. "He never said boo," she told Riley. "We're back to square one. And now he's already out the door."

They both recognized the conflicting ethical values that were at stake, respecting Sam's autonomy and their own concern for the potential precariousness of his situation, particularly after his health benefits ran out.

"Let's put our heads together and see what we should do," Riley said. "There must be another way."

PAUL JOHNSON
Retired General Counsel for Green Giant and H.B. Fuller Companies, Minneapolis, Minnesota.

The first and obvious thing is Sam's right to keep confidential his condition. It's already been breached and should not be breached further. He has made it clear that he does not want his condition disclosed. And one can't assume greater wisdom than other people and say, "Hey, I'm going to do something for you in spite of yourself."

Second, relative to whether he has been discriminated against because of his HIV condition, Jackie was satisfied that it was fair. Still, I would document all this very clearly for fear that it might turn around on me and I might be involved in a lawsuit.

Next, the obligation to Sam as an employee is not all that great. He's been there for one year. If they took him back, they are exposing the company, the stockholders, and probably other employees to big costs, and the question is whether that is fair to those people.

However, I frankly think they have a greater obligation to him as a person than as an employee. Therefore, what I would do (as Jackie) would be to go back to George and explain to him the fairness of the decision, and tell him that we need to respect Sam's wishes. He has made it clear what he wants to do. Then I would suggest that George go back to the mutual friend of Sam's and say that if he can convince Sam to come forward, that I (Jackie) would like to see what I could do in terms of putting together some help for Sam.

If Sam then does come forward to reveal his condition and ask for help, Jackie should try to tap all the resources that are available to her in terms of helping him as a person.

ED MICKENS
Editor of Working It Out, *a newsletter that focuses on gays and lesbians in the workplace, New York, New York.*

I would have to come down squarely on the side of Sam's privacy. He has the American Bar Association on his side, from a legal perspective. But the fact that Sam didn't tell his employer about his status—even though he has the ABA on his side—demonstrates his mistrust regarding the law. People with positive HIV status know that discrimination is rampant, despite the law.

My heart breaks for Sam. He's afraid and not without good reason. He may not be able to get insurance again. I don't know when he learned his status, but it's common that when people do learn of an HIV-positive status that they go into a state of shock and depression and denial that can last for years. Sam has to learn how to stand up for himself. He must make the choices. What we need to do is protect his right to those choices, starting with his right to privacy.

Now, what's the company to do? Since the information came extra legally—George violated Sam's privacy—the same channels need to be used if the company really wants to do something. George has to go to the originator of the information. There is another party involved here. What we have just seen is that information goes from one to two to four in a very short time. You can be sure that more people know about this. The company is going to have to deal with this secret perception, because other employees are saying, "Oh, how unfair for the company to do this to Sam." This is a classic case where the company was not prepared to deal with an HIV situation.

For the future, what I would do is to set a clear policy that the company does not discriminate on the basis of sexual orientation and to back up this policy with a program of education about AIDS and HIV, to get everything out into the open. It's good practice for all employees in terms of their own health interests and reducing discrimination, and also would reduce fear among those who are HIV positive. This is not the last time the company will come across this issue.

DOUG WALLACE'S COMMENTS
This is as close as you can come to a classic dilemma that ethicists love to debate. On the one hand, a persuasive case can be made on behalf of Sam's right to privacy, which rises from ethical theory that there are some principles (such as individual autonomy) that are essential to the human enterprise, that must be honored, and for that reason they are principles that we have an obligation to keep. A classic deontogical orientation. On the other hand, one can also make the argument (as Paul Johnson does) that we have a responsibility to be beneficent. This reflects another ethical theory (teleological) which asserts that bringing about a good end is the right thing to do, even though in doing so it might violate some principle (such as individual autonomy).

In this real context, both of our commentators went for action that reflected a combination of these points of view. The question about honoring Sam's autonomy, his right to privacy, is answered firmly by both. In the end, both advance very similar approaches—That they would go back through the original chain of communication to provide an opportunity for greater reflection and possible reconsideration on the part of Sam.

Beyond that, Ed makes a strong case for the company to position itself to be better prepared to prevent this sort of dilemma in the future with the development of clear policy and training, what I call anticipatory ethics. Anticipatory ethics requires creative planning skills rather than those needed to manage a crisis, which this has become. He would put a program into place to help establish the integrity of the company in its handling of persons who are

We may have an obligation for caring that transcends institutional and legal boundaries.

HIV positive, and in its fair and even-handed treatment of persons regardless of sexual orientation.

On the other hand, Paul accentuates the need for action based upon one human being's obligation to aid another. He poses an interesting distinction which has been discussed more than once in this column. He reminds us that, beyond our responsibility to the organization, we may have an obligation for caring that transcends institutional and legal boundaries.

Ed also reminds us that, in the midst of trauma, we may not always be acting in our own best interests. In those situations, actions that look like they are autonomous may actually be self-deceptive. Sharing our painful human situation with others may be risky, but sometimes it can also transform the character of the human condition by bringing out the very best in one another.

WHAT ACTUALLY HAPPENED?

RILEY TREVOR, the general counsel, made a decision to extend the health care benefits another year. He did this as a matter of fact, without any fanfare or attention. He and the director of human resources maintained confidentiality about Sam's condition. They also did get back to George and reassured him that the process of selecting Sam as one of the persons whose position was to be eliminated was clean. When Riley told me of how the case ended, he seemed quite pleased with the result and felt that he and the organization had done the best it could under the circumstances.

IN-HOUSE HACKERS

Rigging Computers For Fraud or Malice Is Often an Inside Job

Employees Are More Adept Than Outsiders at Using And Abusing the Systems

Discovering a 'Logic Bomb'

William M. Carley

Staff Reporter of THE WALL STREET JOURNAL

At its London office, American Telephone & Telegraph Co. says, three technicians used a computer to funnel company funds into their own pockets. At General Dynamics Corp.'s space division in San Diego, an employee plotted to sabotage the company by wiping out a computer program used to build missiles. And at Charles Schwab & Co. headquarters in San Francisco, some employees used the stock brokerage firm's computer system to buy and sell cocaine.

As these examples suggest, employees are finding increasingly ingenious ways to misuse their companies' computer systems. Although publicity about computer wrongdoing has often focused on outside hackers gaining entry to systems to wreak havoc, insiders are proving far more adept at creating computer mayhem.

Workers may use company computer systems to line their own pockets, to seek revenge because they didn't get a promotion or because of other perceived slights. Whatever the motive, high-tech misdeeds are creating significant problems for companies large and small.

Means and Motive

Although figures for damages from computer abuse are scarce, some companies report internal frauds involving losses of more than $1 million. Even more costly are losses from disrupted operations, or from repairing the damage.

"Employees are the ones with the skill, the knowledge and the access to do bad things," says Donn Parker, an expert on computer security at SRI International, Menlo Park, Calif. "They're the ones, for example, who can most easily plant a 'logic bomb' [a program triggered by a specific time or event] which can crash your entire computer system." Most companies quietly fire the culprits without publicity, Mr. Parker adds. Dishonest or disgruntled employees pose "a far greater problem than most people realize."

Henry DeMaio agrees. Mr. DeMaio, former director of data security at International Business Machines Corp., now is a partner in Deloitte & Touche, an auditing firm that provides data-protection services to corporations. Mr. DeMaio says that company computers used to be big mainframes in "glass houses" where access was restricted to a few employees. But the systems now include millions of personal computers and laptop units available to most employees. These small units, he adds, are growing rapidly in speed, memory and connections to other company computers, making protection of corporate information systems all the more difficult.

AT&T Dials 900

The booming use of laptops is causing special concern, because they can be used off the premises, for extended time periods, and away from the eyes of fellow workers or superiors. The mobile units "just make it easier for an employee intent on, say, stealing his company's trade secrets," says one security consultant. Eastman Kodak Co., to protect laptop communications from being intercepted either by outsiders or by rogue employees, now uses modems that automatically encrypt certain messages.

Other companies are beginning to adopt a variety of tougher security

Reprinted by permission of *The Wall Street Journal,* August 27, 1992, pp. A1, A5. © 1992 by Dow Jones & Company, Inc. All rights reserved worldwide.

measures. One system allowing only designated employees access to certain computer functions uses a series of encrypted messages developed at Massachusetts Institute of Technology.

Attacks on company computer systems, particularly those designed by programmers or computer technicians, can be sophisticated. At AT&T's British headquarters in London, the three technicians set up their own outside company with a 900 telephone number (which charges anyone who calls that number). Then the technicians allegedly programmed AT&T computers to call that 900 number repeatedly, running up huge bills that AT&T paid.

Trojan Horse

Last year, after the scheme was discovered, the three technicians were charged by Scotland Yard with unauthorized modification of computers and conspiracy to defraud. But the case was dropped due to legal technicalities. The three technicians are no longer with AT&T.

To avoid getting caught, fired—and possibly prosecuted—employees are camouflaging their attacks on computer systems. Even a program designed to act as a devastating logic bomb can be masked. A logic bomb, for example, may be designed to crash a computer system, to plant a virus that will replicate until it jams the computer's memory, or to erase data critical to a company's operations. However it works, the logic bomb program might be hidden within a "Trojan Horse"— that is, the disruptive computer program may be concealed within an ostensibly useful program.

In the incident at General Dynamics Corp.'s space system division in San Diego, the camouflage was so effective that the disruptive program was discovered only by chance.

Michael Lauffenburger, a 31-year-old programmer at General Dynamics, had created a computer program to track the availability and prices of parts that the space division uses to build Atlas missiles, which deliver satellites and other payloads into space.

But Mr. Lauffenburger apparently felt underpaid. So, according to an indictment in San Diego federal court, he schemed to destroy the parts program, quit General Dynamics and then get rehired as a consultant with "substantial" fees to rebuild the computer program.

The plot, the indictment alleges, went like this: In March last year, Mr. Lauffenburger created a second computer program, this one a logic bomb called "Cleanup." It would totally erase the original parts program starting at 6 p.m. May 24, the beginning of the Memorial Day weekend, when few would be around to notice. When the bomb went off, Mr. Lauffenburger wouldn't be around either; he quit March 29.

Cleanup was cleverly designed to lurk undetected in General Dynamics's IBM computers for weeks until it was scheduled to go off. The program had a low priority to run, so it wouldn't attract attention. But once it began running, its priority would escalate rapidly to a very high level so that no other program could supersede it. In addition, the usual notice or "flag" to show that the program had begun to run would be sent not to any programmers on duty but to a nonexistent file. Finally, once Cleanup had erased the Atlas parts computer program, it would erase itself. "It was designed to leave not a trace," says Mitchell Dembin, assistant U.S. attorney in San Diego.

Although there were to have been no clues left pointing to Mr. Lauffenburger, he was caught anyway. Soon after he quit General Dynamics, another technician encountered trouble with the IBM computers. In troubleshooting, he happened to call up all the programs waiting to run—including Cleanup—and saw what it would do. Company security officials were called in, then federal agents. Cleanup was removed before it was schedule to begin destroying files.

Earlier this year, Mr. Lauffenburger pleaded guilty to computer tampering, was fined $5,000 and sentenced to perform community service. It isn't clear how seriously General Dynamics

would have been hurt if the Cleanup bomb detonated. The company had made a backup copy of the Atlas missile parts program, but federal investigators say the backup system apparently wasn't working properly.

General Dynamics declined to comment. An attorney for Mr. Lauffenburger said that his client didn't intend to destroy anything, and that he pleaded guilty to a misdemeanor charge only to avoid the high cost of going to trial.

Sometimes, even security experts are getting caught off guard by computer abuse, including fraud. Pinkerton Security & Investigation Services was hit by an employee's computer scam, according to an indictment filed last year. More than $1 million was siphoned out of the detective agency's bank accounts.

Pinkerton had hired a 48-year-old woman who used the name Tammy Gonzalez in 1988, when she began work in the accounting department at the company's Van Nuys, Calif., headquarters. Ms. Gonzalez was given a computer code which she could use to access Pinkerton accounts at Security Pacific National Bank. Ordinarily, she also would need a superior to type in his approval code before she could use the computer to wire-transfer Pinkerton funds from the bank. But Ms. Gonzalez had been delegated the job of canceling a former superior's approval code. Instead of canceling it, she began using it.

With both the access and approval codes, she began shifting money from Pinkerton accounts at Security to the accounts of "Skyways International" and "Lift Trading" at another Los Angeles bank. According to assistant U.S. attorney Lee Michaelson, both Skyways and Lift were bogus companies.

Normally, a reconciliation of accounts would have caught the discrepancies. But Ms. Gonzalez was also supposed to do the reconciling, and somehow she didn't get around to it. At one point, it was nearly two years behind.

An audit in December 1990 finally uncovered the scheme. Federal investigators also found that "Tammy

Gonzalez" was really Marita Juse, who under that name was also wanted on earlier charges of income-tax fraud. Last August, in federal district court in Los Angeles, she pleaded guilty to computer fraud and embezzling $1,082,307 from Pinkerton. Ms. Juse was sentenced to 27 months in prison. Her lawyer says the sentence was fair.

To protect their operations from both sabotage and fraud, most companies have taken at least basic security measures. Many routinely make backup copies of their files every night to protect against logic bombs that might erase data. (This also protects against a loss of power or other events that can wipe out files.) Companies assign employees passwords, often changing them every 30 days, which enables the employees to gain access only to specified company data banks. And when an employee logs onto the computer system, his user name and password leave an audit trail that investigators can trace back to the individual if he does something wrong.

But passwords can be intercepted and used by others as they travel across computer networks. In one instance in 1989, an outside contractor working on BankAmerica's teller-machine network in California wrote a program that surreptitiously copied thousands of customers' bank account numbers and their passwords into his own file.

After unscrambling the encrypted passwords, the contractor planned to use them to loot the customers' bank accounts. He was thwarted only when an associate tipped off the bank, an industry official says. BankAmerica declines to comment.

Sometimes it is the very advantages of computers, including speed and convenience of communication, that make them tempting tools of abuse. Late last year, officials at Charles Schwab, got a tip that a cocaine ring was flourishing among its headquarters employees in San Francisco. Hal Lipset, a private investigator hired by Schwab, soon discovered that sales were being arranged over Schwab's computer communications system.

Schwab officials secretly began monitoring the messages and copying them for evidence. Two employees who allegedly were selling drugs masked their messages by seeming to talk of tickets to sports events or about a game of pool called eightball. But according to one investigator, a "ticket" represented a half gram of cocaine for $40, and "eightball" represented 3 $1/2$ grams for about $280.

One message to arrange a sale stated: "My buddy says he'd be interested in playing pool at the poker game. He'd like to play eightball. . . . Let me know."

"Whenever you're ready," came the reply from the Schwab employee allegedly supplying the drugs.

An undercover man working for Mr. Lipset, in cooperation with San Francisco police, began buying cocaine to gather more evidence. In April, the police arrested two back-office workers at Schwab for drug dealing. Both pleaded guilty. Schwab has fired them as well as two others allegedly in the drug ring.

Ethics and Employee Theft

William J. Kehoe

It is obvious by now that employee theft is a pervasive problem. *Time* speaks of a "light-fingered work ethic."[1] James Walls, in *Vital Speeches of the Day,* calls the workplace "America's hot bed of crime."[2] Robert Cameron, in *Venture* magazine, says, "You come to the point where you just cross your fingers and hope they won't rob you blind."[3] The "they" to whom he refers are employees, and the "hot bed of crime" is your business.

THE CONCEPT OF EMPLOYEE THEFT

Employee theft may be tangible, as in the case of an employee taking inventory, supplies, or cash moneys from a firm; less tangible, as in the case of an employee falsifying records or expense reports for personal benefit when such benefit has not been earned; or intangible, as in the case of time theft or demotivating colleagues, thereby reducing their effectiveness to the firm.

Whether tangible or intangible, employee theft occurs when an employee takes from the firm something to which he or she is not entitled and that, if known to the firm, would not be granted to the employee. At one extreme is an employee taking a 50-cent box of paper clips for personal use to another extreme of an employee who takes machinery valued at $50,000. Although the profit consequences of the former are not as severe as the latter, both acts of theft have moral consequences to the firm and to the employee, and each will change both the firm and the employee.

ETHICS AND THEFT

To understand the moral consequences of employee theft, an examination of the concept of ethics is a starting point. Ethics have been defined as "a systematic attempt, through the use of reason, to make sense of our individual and social moral experience, in such a way as to determine the rules that ought to govern human conduct and the values worth pursuing in life."[4]

Ethics are concerned with evaluating actions and decisions from the perspective of moral principles and values. In its simplest meaning, being ethical is doing the right thing rather than the wrong thing. It is being moral, honest, correct, and fair in everything a person undertakes. It is living with a set of values and principles that guide the decisions and actions of a person. Such values and principles include the following:

- Obey the law
- Do not harm others
- Respect the rights and property of others
- Never lie, cheat, or steal
- Keep promises and contracts
- Be fair to all people
- Help those in need
- Encourage and reinforce these values and principles in others

These values and principles, at the simplest level of ethics, have been called "moral common sense."[5] When applied to the situation of employee theft, the concept of ethics at the level of moral common sense would suggest that employees should not steal. Such is a principle that is valued. A person, both in personal life and in employment life, should not steal, and when faced with the potential of theft, an ethical person, using moral common sense, does the right thing rather than the wrong thing and does not steal.

But employees do steal, and employee theft is a real problem, noted earlier in this book to be valued at more than $40 billion a year and to be increasing at a 15 percent annual rate. The notion of moral common sense does not stand in the face of the magnitude of employee theft. Moral common sense is a simple, straightforward notion. Its simplicity, however, which would have sufficed at an earlier age, does not hold today. Employee theft is a major problem, a problem not prevented or resolved by applying moral common sense, a problem exacerbated by rationalization, and perhaps better understood by lifting the analysis from the fundamental level of moral common sense to the more complex levels of ethical relativism, rules (deontology), and consequences (teleology).

THE CONCEPT OF ETHICAL RELATIVISM

Rationalization

A justification used by some employees to rationalize their act of theft is that others are doing it too. This is

"Ethics and Employee Theft" by William J. Kehoe, from *Reducing Employee Theft: A Guide to Financial and Organizational Controls,* Chapter 5, 1991, pp. 59-67. © 1991 by Quorum Books, an imprint of Greenwood Publishing Group, Inc., Westport, CT. Reprinted by permission.

the "when in Rome, do as the Romans do" rationalization. Because the employee perceives that other employees are partaking in theft, he or she rationalizes that the act is appropriate. That is, he or she develops the belief that it is morally acceptable to steal from the employer because everyone else is perceived to be stealing as well.

Added to the "everyone is doing it" rationalization are other reasons to justify the act. Examples of some of the reasons employees give for stealing are as follows:

- They are not fairly compensated
- Items taken are of small value (e.g., small parts, office supplies, food stuffs, and the like) and will not be missed by the employer
- The employer expects (i.e., approves) that employees will steal or participate in shrinking the inventory and has arranged insurance coverage to offset the loss
- They will not be caught in the theft and, if detected, will be lightly punished, if at all, by the firm
- The company has engaged in unfair labor practices or is planning a reduction in force; hence they should take (i.e., steal) whatever is available as a form of compensation
- The company is bad or in some other way evil and needs to be justifiably punished by the employee through theft
- The company is big and impersonal, and the employee is hardly known; therefore, stealing is justified to strike back at the big, impersonal entity

These reasons become part of a person's system of belief—a system of belief that is assumed by the person to be widely held, logical, and axiomatic—a system of belief used to justify the act of theft.

Ethical Relativism

In justifying the act of theft on the basis that "everyone is doing it," the employee is applying ethical relativism as the logic in use. The concept of ethical relativism is anchored in the notion that "people in different cultures, as well as people within a given culture, hold divergent moral views on particular issues."[6] For example, in the United States it is morally unacceptable to engage in bribery, but in another country it may be morally acceptable and a common business practice. An example within the United States is the divergent views on the issue of capital punishment. People on each side of the issue have reasons to justify or condemn the practice and are able to articulate reasons in ways they perceive to be logical.

The concept of ethical relativism gives explanation as to why, within a single firm, there may be employed people who hold divergent views on theft. For instance, some employees' system of belief or logic leads them to

morally accept stealing from the firm. On the other hand, some employees have moral standards such that, no matter how they view the firm or how it has treated them, to steal from the firm is wrong and is never considered.

Although the concept of ethical relativism gives explanation as to why, within a single firm, some employees may steal while others do not, the concept does not justify employee theft. Rather, as in most cultures, it may be argued that stealing in our culture is morally unacceptable. Said another way, people in a variety of cultures, including ours, hold the view that theft is morally unacceptable or wrong. Given that theft as a concept is wrong, employee theft also is morally unacceptable and wrong.

RULES AND CONSEQUENCES

The basic argument that employee theft is morally unacceptable and wrong has been framed at the level of moral common sense. The ethical analysis, however, must rise to a higher level to fully explore the concept of employee theft from the viewpoint of ethics and to present ethical theories useful in both understanding and preventing employee theft. Specifically, the higher level of analysis considers rules (deontological theory) and consequences (teleological theory).

Rules

Deontological theory is concerned with the rules used in making a decision or taking an action—in other words, the rules that might be used by a person when deciding whether or not to participate in employee theft. Mere, two rules are considered: the categorical imperative and the golden rule.

- The categorical imperative requires that people never take actions that they would not recommend to others.[7] That is, people should not take an action (e.g., participate in employee theft) unless they believe that it could be recommended to others. In short, would the person be able to stand at the next company meeting, admit employee theft, and recommend it to others? If the answer is no, the action fails the categorical imperative and probably is not ethical. Not being able to tell others is "a clarion call that what is planned or has been done may not be ethical. The categorical imperative, is one of the best and simplest tests of ethics and should, perhaps, be the first test of ethics to be employed when in doubt about a particular action or decision."[8]
- The golden rule—do unto others as you would have them do unto you—advises people to act in the way they would want others to act toward them. Employees considering theft should ask, under the test of the golden rule, whether they would want the firm to

steal from them. If the answer is no, then, under the golden rule, employee theft is not justified.

In each of the deontological theories, the categorical imperative and the golden rule, the person is faced with a *yes* or *no* alternative. If the answer to the ethical question posed by these theories is no, then the action is not ethical and is one in which the employee should not participate. The practice of employee theft fails both the categorical imperative and the golden rule. But what of the consequences of employee theft? Might there be consequences that justify the practice?

Consequences

Teleological theory is concerned with the consequences of an action or decision. Here two concepts are considered—the utilitarian principle and egoism.

- The utilitarian principle asks that an individual act in a way to produce the greatest good for the greatest number.[9] Employee theft produces ill-gotten gain for the individual, but does not produce good for the greatest number. An employee seeking to do an act for the greatest number would do something to benefit the company, its customers, and its community. Employee theft does not benefit the company (i.e., the greater entity) and only benefits the individual in the form of profit from the ill-gotten gain. Here again, an employee, when contemplating a theft, is faced with a yes or no situation under the utilitarian principle. Will the act produce the greatest good for the greatest number? If the answer is no, the act fails the utilitarian principle and, most likely, is not ethical.

- The concept of egoism is about self-interest. It is divided into psychological egoism—that individuals do act to benefit themselves—and ethical egoism—that individuals ought to act to benefit themselves.[10] Some would argue that we are a very egoist society, a society in which individuals put themselves first in all that they do. In the situation of employee theft, individuals are egoists, in that they perceive the act of theft to be in their best interest, no matter how ill-gotten the gain or the hurt to another person. An egoist "does not care about the welfare of others except insofar as it affects her or his own welfare."[11] This explanation fits a thief, a person who, by the very act of theft, demonstrates a lack of care and respect for others.

THE ETHICAL PERSPECTIVE

The consequences of doing good to others (utilitarianism) and self-interest (egoism) give insight to employee theft. A person who has concern for and wants to do good for others (utilitarianism) may be less likely to steal from an employer than a person who is egotistical in orientation. Likewise, people who care about what others would think of them if the theft be known (categorical imperative) and who act in a way they would want to be treated by others (golden rule) are, again, less likely to steal than a person who does not have these concerns. These thoughts, taken together with the earlier discussion of moral common sense, give understanding of employee theft from an ethical perspective.

An application of the ethical perspective in employee theft is found in the written honesty tests reported to be in use in more than 5,000 companies nationwide.[12] These tests, which were administered to 3.5 million job applicants in 1988, cost $5 to $15 each and may be used on a preemployment or after employment basis.[13] Designed from the ethical theories presented above, the tests attempt to measure a person's ethics and morality. Although no single answer in the tests indicates a thief, those who administer and score the tests look for patterns in the answers. Series of questions measure whether the person has concern for others, his or her disposition to honesty in both small- and large-value situations, and his or her logic-in-use, or how he or she reasons through an ethical situation. Scores are determined for each person and placed within a range to indicate whether he or she is more likely to be honest or to be dishonest.

Honesty tests are an application of ethics in dealing with the problem of employee theft. The tests are based on ethical theory and, by posing a series of ethical situations, attempt to measure a person's tendency toward honesty. Ryan A. Kuhn, president of Reid Psychological Systems in Chicago, has done a great deal of research on the psychology of theft, and his company is probably the industry leader in the honesty-test field. His research findings are useful in helping us understand more about the typical thief. For example, he has learned that people who steal believe that others do it frequently, fantasize about committing the act frequently, and do not believe that thieves should be disciplined for their acts. He also says that dishonest people typically bring other problems with them into the workplace. They are far more likely to demonstrate pathological psychological profiles, to abuse drugs, to quit or be fired, to experience hostile encounters, and to file bogus insurance and worker's compensation claims. The *Reid Report,* the original pencil-and-paper honesty test that typically reduces theft incidences and turnover by about 50 percent, costs between $7 and $15 to use—a small price to pay for extremely valuable information.

THE EMPLOYER IN EMPLOYEE THEFT

Thus far, the focus has been on the employee. Of equal importance in an ethical analysis of employee theft is the employer and the ethical obligations of the employer. These include honesty, prevention, fairness, and instilling ethics in the organization.

Management Honesty

We have previously established that management honesty is of paramount importance. In a study that examined management honesty as a factor in preventing employee theft, the conclusion was that "if employees think top management is behaving honestly, they will probably think they are expected to behave honestly. But if employees perceive that top management is dishonest, they will be more inclined to justify and excuse their own dishonesty."[14]

Thus dishonesty in management will, in time, induce employee dishonesty. Through the actions of management, employees will be moved or conditioned toward honesty or dishonesty. It is imperative that management set an example. If managers participate in such things as insider trading, price fixing, check kiting, expense padding, time and material theft, and other acts of white-collar crime, there is a danger that these dishonest actions of management eventually will induce employees toward dishonesty. Management dishonesty, ultimately, will be manifest as employee theft. Therefore, to prevent employees from stealing based on the perception of a dishonest management, leaders in the organization must maintain the highest levels of honesty.

Management Prevention

Management is morally obliged to recognize their responsibility to their employees in preventing the opportunities for employee theft. Managers should "spot the temptations that might induce employees to steal and isolate these temptations so they can be eliminated."[15] As stated before, eliminating temptation can be done by establishing internal controls and security systems within the organization. These controls include inventory systems, security systems, financial controls, employment-screening systems, and the like. Management must be concerned with prevention—this is the second moral obligation of management.

Management Fairness

Management also has an obligation to be concerned about employee theft and to make that concern known in the organization. If management is perceived as not caring about the problem, does not have a clear policy on employee theft, and does not enforce that policy or applies it more leniently to managers, the spirit of fairness necessary to deter employee theft will be eroded. Management must be concerned about employee theft and treat all employees similarly when dealing with the problem.

Management-Instilled Ethics

Management has a moral obligation to instill ethics in the organization. This means that management must nurture ethics in the company and create an open environment for discussion of ethics. A code of ethics should be in place in every company; it should be widely promulgated and discussed with each employee. Meetings and seminars on ethics should be regularly conducted, and ethics and employee theft should be a point of discussion in an employee's annual review with management. Procedures for bringing questions of ethics or of employee theft to management should be established. And violators of the code of ethics should be treated fairly and swiftly. In essence, management must lead by example.

CONCLUSION

Employee theft is a problem of people—a problem of managers and their employees. Both managers and employees have an obligation to deter employee theft. Instilling ethics in an organization is an important process in deterring employee theft. Ethics enhances an individual and an organization. As people and their organizations are enhanced—as the culture becomes one of pride and honesty—employee theft will be deterred.

NOTES

1. "Light-fingered Work Ethics," *Time*, June 23, 1986, p. 64.
2. James D. Walls, Jr., "The Workplace: America's Hot Bed of Crime," *Vital Speeches of the Day*, April 1988, pp. 381–84.
3. "Notice Anything Missing Lately?" *Venture*, November 1988, p. 16.
4. Richard T. DeGeorge, *Business Ethics* (New York: Macmillan, 1986), p. 15.
5. Kenneth E. Goodpaster, "Some Avenues for Ethical Analysis in General Management," *Harvard Business School Note 383–007*, p. 6.
6. DeGeorge, *Business Ethics*, p. 32.
7. Immanuel Kant, *The Metaphysical Element of Justice* (New York: Library of Liberal Arts, 1965).
8. William J. Kehoe, "Ethics for Banking," *VBA Banking News*, December 1985, pp. 10–11.
9. John Stewart Mill, *Utilitarianism* (1863; reprint, Indianapolis: Bobbs-Merrill, 1957).
10. T. L. Beauchamp and N. E. Bowie, *Ethical Theory and Business* (Englewood Cliffs, N.J.: Prentice-Hall, 1988), p. 18.
11. Ibid. p. 19.
12. Harry Bacas, "To Stop a Thief," *Nation's Business*, 75 (June 1987), p. 17.
13. "Honestly, Can We Trust You?" *Time*, January 23, 1989, p. 44.
14. "How to Keep 'em Honest," *Psychology Today*, November 1981, p. 53.
15. Charles R. Carson, *Managing Employee Honesty* (Los Angeles: Security World Publishing Company, 1977), p. 19.

Six Myths of Sexual Harassment

Recognizing that sexual harassment may be alive in your company is the first step to ridding the workplace of this potentially devastating plague.

JAN BOHREN

Jan Bohren is the director of human resources at the Argonne National Laboratory. He has held senior executive positions in the health insurance industry, with the U.S. Office of Personnel Management, the Department of the Navy, and the Federal Labor Relations Authority.

he Anita Hill-Clarence Thomas hearings and the Navy's "Tailhook" scandal were eye-openers for many people in this country—not necessarily for those employers that have worked for years to rid the workplace of outmoded male attitudes, but for all the other employers that had ignored the problem for years.

Enlightened companies recognize that their employees, and especially their management teams, need explanations and education about this relatively new subject, and they have moved quickly to fill the gap in information. Others remain skeptical, chalking up sexual harassment as the latest liberal fad and convincing themselves that "this too shall pass."

But it won't—and the stakes are too high to continue to ignore it. Sexual harassment transgressions will continue to be serious liabilities, and those that are overlooked can bring a corporation to its knees, even cause shareholders to question management's ability to manage. And the liabilities are not just careers, but financial. Managers, especially CEOs, who want to avoid these liabilities, need to understand more about sexual harassment than what they may have seen on television, and they need to recognize and dispel the myths surrounding sexual harassment. Here are six of them:

From *Management Review*, May 1993, pp. 61-63. © 1993 by The American Management Association, New York. All rights reserved. Reprinted by permission of the publisher.

MYTH #1:
IT'S NOT A PROBLEM HERE

Several years ago, a senior executive made a comment in a room of senior executives, including one woman, "Well, this kind of thing isn't happening at the top management level, but we need to make sure that it's not occurring at the worker level." The woman executive remained silent. The top executive of that organization had recently resigned over a sexual harassment scandal.

Flash! Sexual harassment is alive (if not rampant) in every organization that isn't paying attention to the issue. Remember, most sexual harassment complaints are lodged against people who have power over employees' careers. They're called supervisors, managers, vice presidents and, yes, even CEOs! The courts are not blind to managerial hierarchy, by the way. Juries generally hold higher-level managers to higher-level standards. Translation: the higher the level of the harasser, the higher the costs for the company.

MYTH #2:
IT'S HUMAN NATURE.
THEY'LL WORK IT OUT

It's not human nature, but it is prevalent. If you're a woman who has worked for five years or more, it is almost certain that you have been harassed in the workplace. If you're a man, it's just as likely that someone has harassed your spouse, your mother, your sister or your daughter in the workplace.

BRIEFCASE

How often have you heard a senior-level manager claim, "There's no sexual harassment going on in our company"? How often have you seen the subject of sexual harassment dismissed by a business executive with the casual disclaimer, "We're all adults; if there's a problem, we'll work it out"? The fact is, if sexual harassment is going on in your company, you'd better find out about it and act quickly. Ignoring this serious issue is a good way to bring a company to its knees.

The employee who complains and is not heard will either quit or fight. If she quits, the harasser will continue to harass other employees—and the company loses a valuable person in whom time and money has been invested. In either event, the employer loses.

Sexual harassment is not human nature. It is unacceptable behavior, it's learned, it's illegal and, contrary to what many companies would like to believe, by merely leaving it alone, the problem will not disappear.

MYTH #3:
WOMEN HARASS MEN AS MUCH AS MEN HARASS WOMEN

Yes, women can and do harass men. Remember the Biblical story about Joseph, who was taken captive, sent to Egypt and assigned to Potiphar, the captain of Pharaoh's guard? Potiphar's wife harassed Joseph, but she claimed it was Joseph who harassed her and presented her husband with a piece of Joseph's clothing as evidence. Based on this circumstantial evidence, Potiphar would not even listen to Joseph's side of the story. There was no trial. Innocent as he was, Joseph went to jail. But even if there had been an investigation, Potiphar's wife and her "evidence" might have prevailed.

Of course, women can be the harassers. However, the vast majority of sexual harassment cases involve men harassing women. But you will often hear men counter charges of sexual harassment with, "She was the one who harassed me." This is a feeble defense. If he has no documentation, it won't hold up in court. If a man truly is harassed, he can't treat it lightly. He needs to document and report the occurrence immediately.

Some men also counter that the woman dressed or acted provocatively or "came on" to them. That, again, is no defense of the men's behavior.

MYTH #4:
IF THERE'S NO INTENT TO HARASS, YOU'RE NOT LIABLE

This is one of the most common misconceptions and mistakes. Most sexual harassment involves no intended sexual misconduct or activity. Most men accused of sexual harassment will admit to the behavior, but claim they did not *intend* to harass the employee alleging the conduct.

The law, however, does not address intent, but focuses on whether the sexually oriented activity occurred. If it did, and it was unwelcome, there was harassment. If it occurred repeatedly or if it was explicitly objected to and occurred again, some very strong action can be expected. If management was aware of the conduct, you and your general counsel will be spending a great deal of time together.

WORKBOOK

Here's what you can do to help keep your workplace harassment-free:

 Have a clear written policy prohibiting sexual harassment.

 Have mandatory supervisory training progams.

 Ensure that the workplace is free of offensive materials.

 Implement a program for steps to take when a complaint of harassment is received.

 Keep informed of all complaints and steps taken.

 Make sure the commitment is at every level.

MYTH #5:
IT'S HARD TO DETERMINE GUILT; IT'S ONE PERSON'S WORD AGAINST ANOTHER'S

If the Hill-Thomas hearings supported or created support for one myth, it's the one that presupposes that most sexual harassment is one-on-one, secret or hard to determine. The truth is, even where there are no witnesses, most men accused of harassment *admit* the conduct, claim no intent, and/or claim ignorance of the law. The bottom line is, when properly investigated, sexual harassment cases rarely end up as "judgment calls." And, while there are cases in which sexual harassment charges have been totally fabricated, these are rare.

MYTH #6:
THERE'S NOT MUCH
THEY CAN DO TO US

Oh yeah? Ask the automaker that was ordered to pay $185,000 in back pay to a woman whose supervisor told her she was in a male-dominated field and had better get used to her coworkers discussing sex.

Ask the food company that had a manager who commented daily about an employee's breasts, buttocks and physical appearance, who suggested to women that they show him a "good time," and who imposed a dress code designed to show off women's legs. What would they have paid to avoid the court award of $625,000?

Ask the publishing company that was told by the court to pay $800,000 in punitive damages and $85,000 in compensatory damages to an employee who proved that she was subjected to lascivious remarks made by a supervisor about women and passed over twice for promotion in favor of younger men, despite demonstrating exemplary qualifications for the particular promotion.

Ask the grocery chain that settled out of court in a $14 million suit by an employee who charged that her supervisor made constant sexual advances and had sexual encounters with her. One piece of evidence presented to the jury before the out-of-court settlement was the trousers of her supervisor, which she had taken when he was harassing her.

Preventative Steps

If you have responsibility for employees, you need to talk to them, especially the women, and find out how prevalent sexual harassment is in your workplace. If you have employees with "locker-room mentalities," you are at risk.

How do you make sure the myths surrounding sexual harassment don't prevail in your office or workplace?

• First of all, continue the educational process launched by the Hill-Thomas hearings and "Tailhook"—make sure that your company has a clear written policy prohibiting sexual harassment and that it is included in mandatory supervisory training programs.

• Talk to your managers and your employees, including women—personally. Don't leave this to your human resources people or your EEO manager. Employees need to know that concern about this issue is coming from the top. If you have subordinate managers, it is essential that they know where you stand on this important subject—tell them.

• Walk around. You may be surprised with what you see—like nude calendars, sexually oriented cartoons and offensive or pornographic magazines and literature.

• Make sure that your human resources staff is equally committed to your policies, that it understands its role in overseeing the program, and that it knows what steps to take when sexual harassment complaints are received.

• Insist on being kept informed of all sexual harassment complaints in the company, and the outcomes of investigations, including any corrective action or disciplinary action taken (or not taken).

You can't eliminate sexual harassment from your workplace until you first recognize that you are not immune from it. Once you dispel these myths, you are that much closer to eliminating the inappropriate behavior from your workplace. Your employees will appreciate the sensitivity and demonstrated awareness of management, and stockholders will appreciate the money saved by a strongly enforced policy. Besides, it's the right thing to do.

SEXUAL HARASSMENT
WHAT TO DO

Complaints are mounting, confusion is rampant, and almost everybody's a little nervous. But many companies are trying hard to stamp out this form of abuse.

Anne B. Fisher

Tailhook. New rules on college campuses against romances between professors and students. A controversial book that purports to tell the real story of Anita Hill and Clarence Thomas. And of course that staple of late-night-TV jokes, Senator Bob Packwood. In the shift and glimmer of the media kaleidoscope, sexual harassment is a constant glinting shard.

Yet no headline-making subject in recent memory has stirred so much confusion. No doubt you've read your company's policy statement and, from just under its surface, you feel the legal eagles' gimlet stare. But what does sexual harassment really mean? Managers of both sexes are sifting through the past and fretting about next week. Was it all right to say I liked her dress? Is it okay to ask him out to lunch to talk about that project? Should I just stop touching anybody, even if it's only a congratulatory pat on the back? For that big client meeting in Houston, wouldn't it be less risky to fly out with Frank than with Francine? Or, for female managers, vice versa?

If you think you've got reason to worry, you probably don't; the ones who do are usually unaware they have a problem. But right in your own organization, maybe even in your own department, your hallway, your pod, somebody may be so befuddled and self-destructive as to miss the point entirely. Sexual harassment is not really about sex. It's about power—more to the point, the abuse of power.

Imagine it this way. Suppose one of your most senior and valued people has a little problem. Great producer, terrific salesperson, meets every goal, exceeds every guideline, but, well, there's this one glitch: He steals things. Every time he leaves an office he takes something with him—a pen, a coffee mug, a book, some change that was lying around. He's been at it a long time, can't seem to help it and, anyway, he's a good guy, a *great* guy. You're his boss. What are you going to do when he walks off with somebody's $3,000 notebook computer? That's grand larceny, and the victim is hopping mad.

For more and more managers these days, the analogy fits. Let's suppose the fellow isn't stealing material things but rather chipping away at the human dignity and professional self-respect of other people. Can't seem to resist patting fannies and whispering innuendoes. Told a subordinate he'd like to negotiate her raise at the local No-Tell Motel. Cornered a female colleague and loudly compared her physical attributes with those of the current Playmate of the Month. All the time he's producing great stuff. But the whispering behind his back is getting louder; the troops are murmuring about calling the lawyers and human resources people. What do you do with this guy? (Alas, despite a much publicized $1 million jury award in May to a male plaintiff harassed by his female boss in Los Angeles, harassers are, in nine cases out of ten, guys.)

Talk to him, of course. If that doesn't work, and odds are it won't, turn him in to the human resources person in charge of these matters. And do it pronto. Otherwise you could be liable along with your employer. Unsolicited, unwelcome, and downright extortionate sexual demands are as illegal as stealing computers. So are purposeful and repeated efforts to intimidate colleagues by transforming the office into a remake of *Animal House*—what the law calls "hostile environment" harassment. He who steals my briefcase, to paraphrase Shakespeare, steals trash. But the loss of someone's dignity, productivity, and eagerness to come to work in the morning is a theft not only from the person robbed of it, but from the company too.

Sexual harassment is not a compliment on anyone's wardrobe or a friendly pat on the shoulder. It is not the occasional tasteless remark or careless quip. It is not even asking someone for a date the second time, when she's already said no once. To stand up in court, a harassment charge must rest on either a persistent and calculated pattern of antisocial behavior or a single quid pro quo—"You'll never get anywhere in this company unless you sleep with me"—that is so egregious as to leave no room for misinterpretation.

The courts have recognized sexual harassment as an offense under Title VII since 1977. But the number of complaints filed with the Equal Employment Opportunity Commission has nearly doubled in the past five years, to 10,532 in 1992. It's debatable whether that rise occurred because instances of harassment increased or whether events like the Hill-Thomas hearings encouraged people who had long remained silent to speak up. The EEOC doesn't keep a record of how many cases end up in litigation; many are settled on the courthouse steps. One thing is certain. The consequences for corporations are costly.

Research by Freada Klein Associates, a workplace-diversity consulting firm in Cambridge, Massachusetts, shows that 90% of FORTUNE 500 companies have dealt with sexual harass-

From *Fortune*, August 23, 1993, pp. 84-86, 88. © 1993 by Time Inc. Magazine Company. All rights reserved. Reprinted by permission.

ment complaints. More than a third have been sued at least once, and about a quarter have been sued over and over again. Klein estimates that the problem costs the average large corporation $6.7 million a year.

Bettina Plevan, an attorney at Proskauer Rose Goetz & Mendelsohn in New York City, specializes in defending companies against sexual harassment lawsuits. She says employers spend an average of $200,000 on each complaint that is investigated in-house and found to be valid, whether or not it ever gets to court. Richard Hafets, a labor lawyer at Piper & Marbury in Baltimore, believes sexual harassment could be tomorrow's asbestos, costing American business $1 billion in fees and damages in the next five years.

But the costs of sexual harassment go well beyond anything that can be measured on a profit-and-loss statement. Women, often still treated like interlopers in the office, say they feel vulnerable to the myriad subtle—and not so subtle—sexual power trips some men use to keep them in their place. At an Aetna Life & Casualty golfing party last September, four executives vented their resentment of female managers' presence at what had traditionally been an all-male event. Their mildest offense—and the only one we're halfway willing to describe in a magazine your kids might see—was calling women executives "sluts." In response Aetna demoted two of the men and asked the two others to resign.

Jeannine Sandstrom, a senior vice president of the executive recruiting firm Lee Hecht Harrison in Dallas, knows of instances where harassers were caught because they sent X-rated messages to their victims via voice mail or E-mail. Marvels Sandstrom: "How self-destructive do you have to be to do something like this, knowing how easy it is to trace?"

The habitual harasser, fortunately a rare type, is usually a bully in other ways too. Your company can't afford him.

In most cases harassment is more subtle—and far more difficult to prove. As agonizing as it may be, women have an obligation to speak up and tell someone who is hounding them to stop it. Although federal law defines sexual harassment as "unwelcome" behavior, the courts say it doesn't count as such unless the offender knows it's unwelcome. Yet a 1991 study by two professors at the University of St. Thomas in St. Paul, Minnesota, revealed that, among women in a nationwide survey who said they had been victims of sexual harassment, only 34% told the harasser to knock it off; just 2% filed a formal complaint.

With the economy in its current shaky state, many women may be too fearful of losing their jobs to speak up. Or they may be reluctant to be seen as whiners, either by their peers or by the people above them. But if a woman wants to file a grievance, it's important to be able to prove that she told the perpetrator to back off. Some experts suggest tape-recording the conversation or sending a registered letter (return receipt requested) detailing the offending behavior and declaring it not OK. This helps in any follow-up by human resources or legal staff, even in cases where witnesses or other direct proof of the harassment are available.

As for men, the majority of whom wouldn't dream of harassing anybody, they are terrified of being falsely accused—with some reason. "What I'm seeing lately is that companies are overreacting, and accusers are believed on the basis of very little evidence or none at all," says Ellen Wagner, an attorney and author who specializes in labor law. "And the ultimate punishment, termination, is a first resort rather than a last one."

Consider the case of Louis Kestenbaum. From 1977 to 1984, Kestenbaum was vice president in charge of guest operations at a secluded ranch and spa that Pennzoil operated in northern New Mexico. In January 1984, someone wrote an anonymous letter to Pennzoil's top management accusing Kestenbaum of sexual harassment and other misdeeds. Kestenbaum denied the allegations but was fired anyway. He sued Pennzoil and won $500,000 in damages for wrongful discharge. The reason? Pennzoil's in-house investigator admitted in court that she had relied on rumor and innuendo in compiling the sexual-harassment report that got Kestenbaum the ax. "No attempt was made to evaluate the credibility of the persons interviewed," wrote the judge.

Both sexes sometimes feel they're stumbling around in a minefield, lost in enemy territory without a helicopter. What makes the terrain so treacherous is that people have an inconvenient way of seeing the same behavior quite differently. Margaret Regan is a Towers Perrin partner who has conducted a senior-management training program called Respect at Work for dozens of corporations. She points out that some of what might look like sexual harassment is in reality an innocent error arising from past experience. "My favorite example is when we ask a group of men and women, 'How many times is it all right to ask someone out after they've said no once?' " says Regan. "In one class I led, one of the men said, 'Ten.' The women were appalled. They said, '*Ten times? No way! Twice is enough!*' "

As hard, even agonizing, as it may be, victims have a legal obligation to tell someone who's hounding them to stop it.

It turned out, when he got a chance to explain his answer, that the offending fellow had to ask ten or 12 times before the girl of his dreams agreed to go to the senior prom with him in 1959. It worked out fine: They've been married for 32 years. "Naturally ten times seemed reasonable to him," says Regan. "So much of what people think about these things comes from stuff they grew up with—and just never had any reason to question."

Consultants who design sexual harassment workshops, and managers who have attended them, agree on one thing: The best training gives participants a chance to talk to each other, instead of just listening to a lecture or watching a film. In classes where men and women are asked to compare their impressions of the same hypothetical situation, real revelations can occur.

Perhaps not surprisingly, Aetna has stepped up its training program since the infamous golfing incident last fall. Anthony Guerriero, 34, a pension consultant at the company, took the course in January. He says, "The guys in the class were absolutely not resistant to it, not at all. In fact, it's a relief to have someone spell out exactly what sexual harassment is. The men in my session were all saying, 'Its about time.' "

Male managers aren't the only ones who benefit from the classes. Women are sometimes startled to find how widely their perceptions differ from those of other women. Janet Kalas, 45, director of Medicare administration at Aetna, has 300 people reporting to her. "What startled me about the training was how tolerant I am," she says. In one group-discussion exercise, the instructor described an imaginary scenario in which a male and a female colleague, both married to others, are out of town on business. Late in the evening they're still working on a client presentation for the next morning, and they decide to finish it in the female manager's hotel room. Recalls Kalas, "My reaction was. Well, that's practical. What's the big deal? But other people, men and women both, were saying, 'My gosh, don't do that, it's like an *invitation* to this guy.' I was surprised."

Towers Perrin recently queried executives at 600 major U.S. companies and found that about half planned to increase the amount of sexual harassment training they give managers and employees. A dozen or so big corporations have already built shining reputations among consultants and researchers for the quality, creativity, and overall earnestness of their training programs. Among them: Du Pont, Federal Express, General Mills, Levi-Strauss, Merck, and Syntex. But will they talk about what they're doing? Not a chance. "Nobody likes to acknowledge that this problem even exists," says Robert Steed, who runs a consulting firm in Westchester County, New York, that specializes in sexual-harassment training. "It makes people queasy. So their view is, the less said the better." Adds a public relations manager at a FORTUNE 500 company: "The general feeling is, what if we get written up somewhere as having this terrific training program—and then we get sued a week later? In other words, no comment."

For a company's policy to do any good, much less be taken seriously in a courtroom, employees have to understand it. Barbara Spyridon Pope, the

Navy assistant secretary who almost single-handedly exposed the Tailhook scandal, recently established a consulting firm in Washington, D.C., to advise corporate clients on how to communicate their sexual-harassment guidelines to the troops. Her surveys show that 60% to 90% of U.S. workers know there is a policy but haven't the foggiest what it says. "Having a policy is fine, but by itself it isn't enough," says Pope. "The Navy had a policy too."

Sitting people down to discuss their differences on this issue is more than a therapeutic parlor game. Case law over the past decade has established that a company with a well-defined anti-sexual-harassment stance can escape liability for hostile-environment harassment. No wonder, then, that you keep getting all those policy memos and invitations to sign up for workshops. But to prevail in court, companies must also have clear procedures for handling complaints when they arise. Typically, employers choose an impartial ombudsperson, usually in the human resources department, to hear and investigate charges

---

Two managers finish a presentation for an out-of-town client in the woman's hotel room. "What's the big deal?"

---

before the lawyers get into the act. If the complaint seems legitimate, the company must then take what the judge in a pivotal 1986 case, *Hunter v. Allis-Chalmers,* called "immediate and appropriate action." Depending on the circumstances, this might range from transferring the harassed or the harasser to a different department, to docking the harasser a couple of weeks' pay, to firing the guilty party outright.

This fall the Supreme Court will hear *Harris v. Forklift Systems,* its first sexual harassment case since 1986. The suit was filed by Teresa Harris, who left her job at a Nashville truck-leasing company after months of crude remarks and propositions from the firm's president. The mat-

ter was dismissed by a federal judge in Tennessee and ended up in federal appeals court in Cincinnati, where the dismissal was upheld. Reason: Ms. Harris had not proven that she was psychologically damaged by her boss's behavior.

If psychological damage becomes the new standard in harassment cases, which is what the high court has agreed to decide, plaintiffs will have a far harder time winning. Says Anne Clark, an attorney for the National Organization for Women: "You shouldn't have to suffer a nervous breakdown before you can make a claim." Lawyers who represent companies reply that a decision in favor of the psychological-damage standard would cut down on frivolous suits. To which working women are apt to say: "Frivolous? Nobody in her right mind would have her name dragged through the dirt over a frivolous charge!"

No matter how the court rules, managers and employees would do well to keep their own responsibilities in mind. For actual or potential harassers that means: Watch it, buster. For women, it means: Speak up. For their bosses, the best advice is: Get help. Says Susan Crawford, a partner at Holtzmann Wise & Shepard in Palo Alto, California: "I've found that managers too often are reluctant to refer a complaint to human resources. Instead they try to handle it themselves. But bosses need to see that this is a complicated issue with a lot of pitfalls, and it is not a sign of failure on their part to say, 'Hey, I need help with this. I'm not the expert here.' " The people in your company who really know where all the pitfalls are—and who will try to be fair to everybody—are not in your department. They are probably upstairs somewhere. Call them.

For all the seriousness of the issue, it would be a great pity if men and women got to the point of giving up on workplace friendships altogether—a point some men say privately they've already reached. Remember Rob, Buddy, and Sally on the old *Dick Van Dyke Show?* Okay, it was way back in the supposedly benighted early Sixties, but those three were a great professional team, and they were pals. For men and women in corporate America, there could be far worse role models. It will be a sad day, if it ever comes, when people are too nervous to ask a pal out for a drink.

Three Decades After the Equal Pay Act, Women's Wages Remain Far From Parity

Joan E. Rigdon

Staff Reporter of THE WALL STREET JOURNAL

Women have little to celebrate tomorrow on the 30th anniversary of the Equal Pay Act.

Women still earn only 70 cents for every dollar earned by men, according to 1991 median annual wage data from the Census Bureau. (Estimates for 1992 aren't yet available.) That is up a dime from 1963—which means women's earnings have gained on men's by a ratio of one-third of one percent a year over the past three decades.

Minority women fare worse. In 1991, black and Hispanic women earned 62 cents and 54 cents, respectively, for every dollar earned by white men, according to median annual wage data from the Census Bureau.

Those figures are just averages, amalgams of jobs ranging from door-to-door sales to deal making. Numbers for individual professions show that it is often the hourly workers who come closest to parity, while the white-collar crowd earns as little as half.

Female cashiers, for instance, made 95 cents on the male dollar last year, while female securities brokers earned only 52 cents, according to weekly wage figures from the Bureau of Labor Statistics. Female financial managers—including those who close multimillion-dollar deals—earned only 62 cents on the male dollar.

BARELY AN IMPACT

The Equal Pay Act was supposed to close that gap; but, in fact, statistics show it has barely made an impact. Nine times

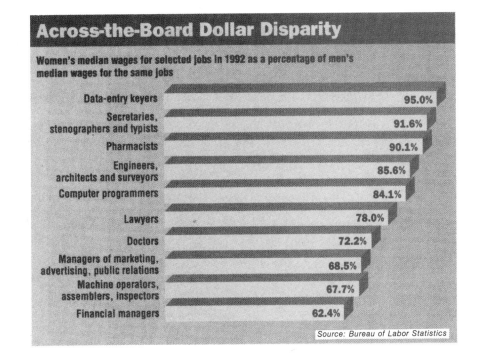

Across-the-Board Dollar Disparity

Women's median wages for selected jobs in 1992 as a percentage of men's median wages for the same jobs

Job	Percentage
Data-entry keyers	95.0%
Secretaries, stenographers and typists	91.6%
Pharmacists	90.1%
Engineers, architects and surveyors	85.6%
Computer programmers	84.1%
Lawyers	78.0%
Doctors	72.2%
Managers of marketing, advertising, public relations	68.5%
Machine operators, assemblers, inspectors	67.7%
Financial managers	62.4%

Source: Bureau of Labor Statistics

since it became law, the pay gap has actually *widened* from one year to the next, according to statistics-bureau figures.

And while the pay gap has narrowed overall, that is mostly because men's wages fell. Measured in dollars, women's median hourly wages were $8.42 last year, up only 31 cents from 1979 (both figures are in 1992 dollars), according to the Economic Policy Institute, a think tank based in Washington, D.C. During the same period, men's median hourly wages fell $1.84 an hour to $11.03 last year.

Is the Equal Employment Opportunity Commission doing much to help? Critics think not. In the government's last fiscal year, which ended Oct. 1, 1992, the EEOC filed only two lawsuits under the act, down from six the year before and from a high of 79 in fiscal 1980. "That sends a message to employers," says Helen Norton, deputy director for work and family programs at the nonprofit Women's Legal Defense Fund in Washington.

Don Livingston, general counsel for the EEOC, says the commission files most sex-discrimination cases under the Civil Rights Act of 1964 because that act has no statute of limitations, while the Equal Pay Act has a two-year limit. In fiscal 1991, the EEOC filed 24 sex-discrimination pay-gap cases under both acts, he says.

A QUESTION OF CREDENTIALS

Companies have long argued that women get paid less because their cre-

Reprinted by permission of *The Wall Street Journal*, June 9, 1993, pp. B1, B10. © 1993 by Dow Jones & Company, Inc. All rights reserved worldwide.

dentials don't stack up to men's. But research from Peter Hammerschmidt pokes holes in that theory. An economics professor at Eckerd College in St. Petersburg, Fla., he analyzed the pay and credentials of 194 corporate managers randomly chosen from 800 who took a leadership course at Eckerd in recent years. His findings: If women were men with the same credentials, they would earn about 18% more.

Most women can't address the pay gap because they don't know what their colleagues earn. And finding out is difficult—pay is a topic more taboo than sex. When they do find out, it is often because they have a friend in payroll, or they have pieced together years of clues about colleagues' spending habits.

That's how Marcia Rafter says she found out. During her eight years at Citibank, Ms. Rafter watched as many of her male colleagues, who brought in fewer profits, purchased boats and expensive homes—things she says she couldn't afford. When she asked for raises, she says she was told that as a single woman she didn't need as much money as a man.

"I was No. 1 or No. 2 in terms of profits, but my compensation never reflected that," Ms. Rafter alleges. She says she was fired in 1988 as a vice president of positioning and arbitrage. Citibank, a unit of **Citicorp,** declines to comment, noting that Ms. Rafter has filed a suit against it.

CLUES FROM GOSSIP

One geologist, who declines to be named, says she got a hint that she was being paid less than less-experienced male co-workers by chatting with drillers on her field site. Then a friend told her that one of her male co-workers, who had only one year on the job, was getting paid about the same as she was, even though she had five years' experience.

To see if the gossip was true, she called a former boss who filled her in on average salaries for workers with her credentials and experience: about $40,000, compared with the $26,000 she was earning at the time. "It really steamed me," she says. She quit this year, and is now looking for a new job.

In running, and not fighting, the geologist wasn't alone. Experts say women are less savvy at negotiating pay than men, and several women who have bargained for raises agree. Among them is Deborah Tannen, the Georgetown University linguistics professor who has coached members of Congress on the different communication patterns of men and women.

Ms. Tannen, author of "You Just Don't Understand," says that girls are taught from an early age not to stand out and that, as women, they make self-deprecat-ing remarks, waiting for friends to build them up. For instance, a woman might remark that she is fat, expecting a reply that she isn't. "Asking for a raise requires a kind of self-promotion" that negates this training, Ms. Tannen says.

That distaste for confrontation applies even to Wall Street women who may thrive on confrontation on the job. Consider Liz Sobol, who resigned as Kidder, Peabody & Co.'s director of corporate finance in 1991. Shortly thereafter, she sued the company in U.S. District Court in New York. She alleges that in 1988, Kidder paid her $655,000 for bringing in about $9 million in fees but that the year before the firm had paid more to a male co-worker who brought in no revenue.

Kidder, a unit of **General Electric Co.,** says that Ms. Sobol was paid in the top one-third of her peer group and that several people helped bring in the fees she says she generated. A spokeswoman says compensation at Kidder is based only partly on fees but declines to elaborate.

Ms. Sobol's first reaction to the pay flap: "I just wanted to hide under the covers and hope the world would go away." It was her husband who encouraged her to sue. And the cost may be great. "Since I've filed my lawsuit," she says, "one headhunter has told me probably no major firm on Wall Street would touch me."

The Americans With Disabilities Act:
The Cutting Edge of Managing Diversity

Robert Ledman, *Department of Social Sciences, Virginia Commonwealth University*

Darrel Brown, *School of Business, Virginia Commonwealth University*

A doctoral candidate at V.C.U., Mr. Ledman had nine years of management experience prior to his teaching career; Dr. Brown, Chairman of V.C.U.'s Management Department, has extensive experience in industrial personnel management and is an active consultant in areas of management, organizational behavior, and human resources management.

In July 1992, the Americans With Disabilities Act of 1990 (ADA) took effect for employers of 25 or more people. The ADA has precipitated much debate, speculation, and analysis centered on its presumed effects on American business. Two diametrically opposed views have been strongly defended.

The view that the ADA will be a burden to employers and is just one more case of government regulation or interference is exemplified by Lindsay.[10] He cites litigation decided under the Rehabilitation Act of 1973 to argue that the ADA will present a greater burden to employers than previously anticipated. Ironically, his conclusions were reached before the bill was even passed. The perspective that this law is another effort to regulate morality and will lead to increased litigation, expensive accommodations, and increased paperwork for documentation seems spurious when compared with the arguments presented by the opposing view of the ADA. In fact, the arguments against the ADA are reminiscent of the arguments presented against workplace safety regulations of the Occupational Safety and Health Administration (OSHA) and other legislative efforts to ensure equal employment opportunities. Today most of those legislative efforts are taken for granted as a way of doing business. It seems time has proven that workplace safety and equal employment opportunity can be beneficial.

The other view of the ADA is that it will not present an undue burden to business and will

more likely be beneficial. This view is the basis for this paper, which is presented in three parts. Part one outlines the historical background of the ADA; part two briefly reviews the major provisions of the law; and part three presents the case for the legislation not being a burden for American business. It also presents suggestions for viewing the ADA as an opportunity to expand the focus of managing diversity programs beyond the traditional one of cultural and ethnic differences.

Throughout this paper, the term "people (or persons) with disabilities" will be used to refer to those to whom the ADA applies. This terminology is used for two reasons. First, it is the commonly accepted usage of professionals in the field of disabilities. Second, and more important, it demonstrates that people with disabilities are people first. Further, the term "disabilities" is commonly preferred over "handicap" by those with disabilities as well as by professionals in that area of human services.

Historical Background

Four reports laid the foundation for the ADA. The first was from The National Council on Disability in 1986. It summarized the prevailing discrimination against people with disabilities. Another report from the Council followed and contained draft legislation.[13]

The third report was drawn from Harris polls concluding that people with disabilities were underprivileged and disadvantaged, with two-thirds of those aged 16-64 not working at all. The last report came from the Presidential Commission on the Human Immuno-Deficiency Virus Epidemic. This one drew attention to the need for legislation to prevent discrimination against those with HIV infection.[13]

Though these reports formed the foundation for the ADA, other societal factors contributed to its evolution. Workers with disabilities have been falling behind the general population both in percentage who are full-time employees and in earnings.[3] Additionally, the advocacy movement for people with disabilities is new and attempting to raise the consciousness of society.[19] The need for consciousness raising is apparent from the work of Loden and Rosener.[11] They asked participants in a management training workshop to identify stereotypes they were aware of. Among the responses relating to people with physical disabilities were:

1. Physical impairment equals intellectual impairment.
2. Charity cases. Fortunate to have jobs.
3. Can't carry own load.
4. Success is qualified with expressions like: Not bad for a handicapped person.[11]

One can only imagine the stereotypes they might have identified for people with other types of disabilities.

Another factor that probably contributed to the passage of the ADA is the inadequate enforcement of the Rehabilitation Act of 1973. Tucker presents a thorough review of the cases during the first ten years' experience under section 504 of that Act and reaches the strong conclusion that government enforcement is lethargic at best and ineffectual at worst. The accumulation of reports on the discrimination against people with disabilities and their lack of progress in employment and earnings coupled with the seemingly limited enforcement of the Rehabilitation Act of 1973 set the stage for the passage of the ADA.

Major Provisions of the Law

The ADA prohibits discrimination (it does not require affirmative action) against people with disabilities who, with or without reasonable accommodation, can perform the essential functions of the position. This prohibition applies to application procedures, hiring, advancement, discharge, pay, training, and terms and conditions of employment.

Persons with disabilities are determined by a three part test to be those who:

1) have a physical or mental impairment that substantially limits one or more major life activity;
2) have a record of such impairment; or
3) are regarded as having such an impairment.[18] Congress did mean for this definition to include muscular dystrophy, HIV infection, mental retardation, mental illness, and alcoholism.[18] The Act further requires employers to meet certain requirements related to exploring the extent of accommodation necessary before rejecting applicants and ensuring that selection criteria are unbiased, job related, and consistent with business necessity.[14] Employers will not have to eliminate essential job functions, create new positions, or even reassign jobs.[1]

The amount of burden imposed by the reasonable accommodations requirement of the Act is perhaps the most frequently debated part of the law. The ADA requires employers to make reasonable accommodations up to and including job restructuring, modified work schedules, acquisition or modification of equipment or devices, appropriate adjustment or modifications of examinations and training materials, and modifications or adoption of procedures or protocols.[18]

Employers are afforded protections in the Act as well. The most significant protection is that an accommodation's effect on the business is considered as an integral part of the reasonable criteria. If making accommodations presents a hardship, the employer can use the "undue hardship" defense. This undue hardship criteria is mitigated by the availability of funding from agencies such as vocational rehabilitation departments.[9] With these protections built into the law, one may question why employers are so concerned that the ADA will create a heavy burden. The following section will suggest that fear is unfounded.

Burden or Blessing?

Any reader by this point could be wondering where the benefits for employers are in the ADA. As Morin notes,[14] selection criteria and mandatory accommodation requirements affect employment decisions and typically include some costs for the employer. However, the benefits of the ADA outweigh the costs by reducing government expenditures on existing programs such as Supplemental Security Income, medical programs, and food stamps. People with disabilities represent an untapped labor pool, and most accommodations are relatively inexpensive. Additionally, most of the accommodations required involve no expenses to the employer. The value to employers and to society of the increased pool of workers is echoed regularly and often, with recommendations for proactive rather than reactive programs.[16,20] The cost effectiveness of employing people with disabilities is also well documented in the supported employment literature.[4,5,6,15] These studies consistently find that employing people with disabilities has clear and overwhelming benefit-to-cost advantages.

It is wasteful not to use available human resources to their fullest. A small investment, relative to return, can turn seemingly unusable human resources into clearly productive ones. Creative partnerships between industry, rehabilitation professionals, and people with disabilities have placed many capable disabled workers in jobs requiring wide ranging skills.[2,12,17] Such successful job placement clearly benefits industry, the worker, and the government budget. Excluding from the work force 10 million people with disabilities who are capable of working costs $300 billion annually. One effort alone has successfully put over 1,200 people to work in real jobs and resulted in a nearly 6-to-1 return on a $2.3 million grant. During those efforts specific cost and benefit data were kept that show a clear benefit.[17]

The National Council on Disabilities has estimated the proportions of workers in different classifications of disabilities. They estimate that 38% are physically disabled, 32% have miscellaneous impairments (heart disease, respiratory/pulmonary disease, cancer, diabetes, and kidney disease), 13% have sensory impairments (hearing, speech or vision), and 12% are mentally disabled (retardation, learning disabilities, brain dysfunction, and senility). The remaining 4% have unknown disabilities.[8]

Of the modifications required to enable workers with disabilities to perform their jobs, 60% cost less than $100 and 90% cost less than $1,000. In fact, most people with disabilities do not require any accommodations, but if they do, the average cost is less than $50.[17] These costs are substantially lower than the costs of employee turnover. Further, large federal budget deficits are reduced two ways when people with disabilities are gainfully employed. The newly employed no longer receive government payments and they pay taxes.

Others have echoed some of these conclusions and identified additional considerations (beyond the cost of accommodations) related to hiring people with disabilities. Tucker lists three:[19]

1. Direct benefits to society by decreased government payments and added productivity.
2. Indirect benefit to employers from increased reliability and productivity of workers with disabilities.
3. Direct benefits to employers from tax credits and other tax incentives. (Many accommodations required by people with disabilities are actually reimbursable from state and federal rehabilitation programs that have, in some cases, existed for many years.)

Recommendations and Conclusion

The evidence presented in this paper suggests there are clearly significant benefits to be realized from the ADA. At the very least there is room for considering the possibility before concluding the ADA is just more government regulation, espe-

cially since the law only prohibits discrimination and does not require affirmative action.

A 1991 Harris survey found 80% of those surveyed said people with disabilities who worked along side them were at least as productive as their nondisabled colleagues. The U.S. Office of Rehabilitation reports that at least 95% of workers with disabilities have the same, or lower, absenteeism, turnover, and job-related accident rates as others.[8] With nearly nine million working age Americans with disabilities and an otherwise declining growth in the number of available workers, it seems imperative that American business recognize that abilities, not disabilities, determine a worker's potential.

In this era of concern for managing diversity in the work force, why not view people with disabilities as one more element in that diversity? Proactive employers can minimize implementation costs by planning. Some excellent suggestions are presented by Postol and Kadue.[18]

1. Notify employees and applicants of the employer's duties under the ADA.
2. Eliminate pre-offer medical examinations except for drug screening.
3. Ensure that lists of forbidden pre-employment questions include inquiries regarding disabilities, diseases, prescription drugs, or worker's compensation claims.
4. Prepare job descriptions that list physical requirements and ensure that they directly relate to essential job functions.
5. Avoid paternalism in employment decisions.
6. Appoint an ADA reviewer to ensure compliance.

Other suggestions might be added to that list, such as:

1. Recognize potential and abilities in applicants and employees by acknowledging they are people (first) who have a disability.
2. Incorporate disability awareness programs into diversity consciousness and management development activities. Educate those who are responsible for training in managing diversity to understand the value of hiring people with disabilities and educate them about the types of disabilities. Public and private agencies are staffed with experts in the area and in many instances are eager to educate the public about the abilities of people with disabilities. Supported employment programs have flourished in the past decade, and the agencies that assist people with disabilities are generally eager to provide employers any assistance necessary.
3. Explore all available government and private mechanisms to help defray costs of ac-

commodations. The Disabled Access [tax] Credit is one mechanism small businesses could investigate. There are numerous state and federal government agencies and programs available to individuals and employers.[19] The Targeted Job Tax Credit is another tax credit available to employers who hire people with disabilities.[4]

4. Adopt a corporate philosophy that recognizes people with disabilities as an element of diversity in the population and the business environment. A computer search of literature on the ADA and literature related to managing diversity disclosed no published works relating the two topics. The search included CD ROM searches of Psych-Lit, ERIC, and ABI-Inform.

Businesses that try to be proactive should have the least difficulty adjusting to ADA requirements. Countless private nonprofit and government agencies have trained professionals ready to provide assistance to employers to facilitate their efforts. The economic concerns expressed in some quarters over accommodations should not become realities because of built-in limits in the ADA.[9]

The most definitive statement to date summarizing the view that the ADA is not another example of useless, burdensome legislation was made by Meyerson, who wrote:

> Twenty-six years after the Civil Rights Act of 1964, our nation has conferred upon people with disabilities the same protections afforded other minorities and women. The ADA marks the right of passage from second-class citizenship to full and equal citizenship for people with disabilities[13] (p. 8).

This paper has suggested that, just as few today would question the benefit of the Civil Rights Act of 1964 to our society, the ADA also can bring positive value. All that is required is a recognition that the benefits of employing people with disabilities outweigh the costs that people with disabilities represent another element of diversity in the workforce.

References

1. Gardner, R. H. and Campanella, C. J. 1991 "The undue hardship defense to the reasonable accommodation requirement of the Americans with disabilities act of 1990." *The Labor Lawyer*. 7 (1): 37–51.
2. Geber, B. 1990. "The disabled: Ready, willing and able." *Training*. (12): 29–36.
3. Hey, R. 1989. "Study finds workers with disabilities losing ground." *Christian Science Monitor*. August 7.
4. Hill, M. 1989. "Supported competitive employment: An interagency perspective." In P. Wehman and M. S. Moon (Eds.), *Vocational rehabilitation and supported employment*: 31–49. Richmond: Virginia Commonwealth University, Rehabilitation Research and Training Center.
5. Hill, M., Banks, P., Handrich, R., Wehman, P., Hill, J. and Shafer, M. 1987. "Benefit cost analysis of supported competitive employment for persons with mental retardation." *Research in Developmental Disabilities*. 8 (1): 71–89.
6. Hill, M. L. and Wehman, P. H. 1983. "Cost benefit analysis of placing moderately and severely handicapped inividuals into competitive employment." Journal of the *Association of the Severely Handicapped*. (8): 30–38.
7. Hofmann, R. L. "The deed makes the difference." *Association Management*. 43 (4): 55–58.
8. Hopkins, K. R. and Nestleroth, S. L. 1991. "Willing and able." *Business Week*. October 28.
9. Lavelle, L. A. 1991. "The duty to accommodate: Will Title I of the Americans With Disabilities Act emancipate individuals with disabilities only to disable small businesses?" *Notre Dame Law Review*. 66: 1135–1194.
10. Lindsay, R. 1989. " Discrimination against the disabled: The impact of the new federal legislation." *Employee Relations Law Journal*. 15: 333–345.
11. Loden, M. and Rosener, J. B. 1991. *Workforce America! Managing employee diversity as a vital resource*. Homewood, IL: Business One Irwin.
12. Martinez, M. N. 1990. "Creative ways to employ people with disabilities." *HRMagazine*. 35 (11): 40–44.
13. Meyerson, A. 1991. "The Americans With Disabilities Act — an historic overview." *The Labor Lawyer*. 7 (1): 1–10.
14. Morin, E. C. 1990. "Americans With Disabilities Act of 1990: Social integration through employment." *Catholic University Law Review*. 40: 189–213.
15. Noble J. 1985. The *benefits and costs of supported employment and impediments to its expansion*. Paper presented at the Policy Seminar on Supported Employment, Virginia Institute for Development Disabilities, Richmond, VA.
16. Noel, R. T. 1990. "Employing the disabled: A how and why approach." *Training and Development Journal*. 44 (Aug.): 26–33.
17. Pati, G. and Stubblefield, G. 1990. "The disabled are able to work." *Personnel Journal*. 69 (Dec): 30–34.
18. Postol, L. P. and Kadue, D. D. 1991. "An employer's guide to the Americans With Disabilities Act." *Labor Law Journal*. 42: 323–342.
19. Tucker, B. P. 1989. "Section 504 of the rehabilitation act after ten years of enforcement: The past and future." *University of Illinois Law Review*. 1989: 845–921.
20. Weirich, C. G. 1991. "Reasonable accommodation under the Americans With Disabilities Act." *The Labor Lawyer*. 7 (1): 27–36.

DENNY'S: THE STAIN THAT ISN'T COMING OUT

Can a pact with the NAACP help it overcome charges of bias?

It's a matter of common sense, says Jerome J. Richardson, chief executive of TW Services Inc. Saddled with $2.2 billion in long-term debt after a 1989 leveraged buyout, his Spartanburg (S.C.) company needs all the money it can earn from its Denny's restaurants. It would be crazy to refuse any customer because of skin color, he says. "Our company does not tolerate discrimination of any kind," says Richardson.

Maybe so. But lately Denny's has been barraged by lawsuits and accusations alleging a pattern of racial discrimination. On Mar. 24, a group of minority customers in San Jose, Calif., filed a lawsuit against Denny's. Among the charges: Denny's required cover charges and prepayment of meals from minorities. On Apr. 1, Denny's agreed to strengthen its policies on equitable treatment to settle a Justice Dept. suit that accused the restaurant chain of discrimination against black customers.

Perhaps most damaging was the highly publicized lawsuit filed on May 24 by six African-American Secret Service agents, who claim they were denied service at an Annapolis (Md.) Denny's because of deliberately slow service. By contrast, the suit alleges, white colleagues were served in a timely fashion.

OBJECT LESSON. In each case, TW claims that if any discrimination did occur, it was in direct violation of corporate policies. But Richardson admits he can't afford to ignore the firestorm of negative publicity. TW's CEO is already in talks with Benjamin F. Chavis Jr., the new executive director of the National Association for the Advancement of Colored People (NAACP) to hammer out a policy that could serve as a model for corporations. Among the possibilities: nation-

---

DENNY'S MENU FULL OF PROBLEMS

MAR. 24 Lawsuit filed by minority customers in California alleges Denny's employees refuse to serve African Americans, impose cover charges, and require prepayment from minorities. Expanded class-action filing expected. Denny's denies allegations.

APR. 1 Federal judge approves consent decree between Denny's and U.S. Justice Dept. Denying any pattern of racial discrimination, Denny's agrees to reinforce policies of equitable treatment and to communicate guidelines to all employees at restaurant chain.

MAY 24 Six African-American Secret Service agents file lawsuit alleging they received such slow service at a Denny's in Annapolis, Md., that they were, in effect, denied service. Denny's denies the slow service was racially motivated.

DATA: COMPANY REPORTS, BUSINESS WEEK

---

wide testing by the NAACP of Denny's restaurants to identify racial discrimination.

In many ways, TW's travails are an object lesson for Corporate America. Often, management consultants contend, senior executives depend too heavily on policy statements instead of active monitoring and training to avoid discrimination complaints.

The issue of racism has already hurt other corporations. In November, the Shoney's Inc. restaurant chain agreed to pay $132.5 million to settle a lawsuit filed by minority workers and job seekers who said they had been discriminated against.

Strains are already beginning to show at TW. In addition to its Denny's chain, the company is also the nation's largest Hardee's franchisee, the parent of the Canteen food-service company, and owner of the Quincy's Family Steakhouse and El Pollo Loco restaurant chains. TW, 47%-owned by Kohlberg Kravis Roberts & Co., was hoping for improved cash flow from its restaurants to pay down more of its debt. But fran-

chisees are afraid that the bad publicity is driving away customers. Don Bohana, Denny's only black franchisee, complains that business at his restaurant in a predominantly black neighborhood in Los Angeles was down about 18%, or $800, on the Sunday following the news of the Secret Service agents' complaint. Bohana says he has similar reports from other Southern California franchisees.

Charges of discrimination at Denny's first surfaced after an incident in late December, 1991, when 18 young African Americans entered a San Jose (Calif.) Denny's and were told they each had to pay a $2 cover charge. What's more, they were told that they had to prepay for their meals. The group later said white teenagers at a nearby table told them they neither paid a cover charge nor were asked to prepay. The African-American youths left without ordering, and they told their story to the *San Jose Mercury News.*

EAT AND RUN? Stung by the negative publicity, several top TW executives went to San Jose in early 1992 and met with NAACP leaders. Richardson said he wasn't aware that local managers had the option of imposing the prepay policy during late-night hours to avoid eat-and-run theft. But he points out that only 35 out of more than 1,000 company-owned Denny's did so because of past trouble. Still, the company quickly agreed to drop the policy and to expand sensitivity training for staffers nationwide. In the past, that apparently hadn't been viewed as a high priority. Much more time was spent preventing discriminatory hiring practices. Indeed, Val E. Christensen, chairman of Denny's Franchisee Advisory Council, says the issue of discrimination was barely addressed when he went through a month-long training program before opening his Victorville (Calif.) franchise four years ago. "We talked about it for some time, 10 minutes or 20 minutes, then we moved on," he says.

That laissez-faire attitude seemed doomed when the hometown Spartanburg newspaper picked up the San Jose story and quoted a local NAACP official, Charles Davis, as saying TW's race relations still had a long way to go. When he read that, Richardson called Davis and invited him to his office. During their talk, Richardson asked Davis if the NAACP would help devise a program to combat discrimination at Denny's. By the summer of 1992, TW and the NAACP were trying to fashion a broad policy.

But if TW's CEO thought the matter would come to a quick conclusion, he made a big misjudgment. To start with, the law firm representing the San Jose

youths filed a lawsuit on Mar. 24 and included new plaintiffs and new allegations. One came from a mother who said her daughter was denied a free birthday meal because of her race. In the meantime, the Justice Dept. had begun its own probe and concluded that the discriminatory practices in San Jose were widespread throughout California. Without admitting guilt, Denny's agreed to sign a consent decree to reinforce its anti-discrimination policies with training programs for Denny's staffers. Then came the lawsuit by the African-American Secret Service agents.

TW apologized to the agents and fired the manager of the Annapolis restaurant. But the company denies that the service snafus were racially motivated. Indeed, TW says the manager wasn't dismissed for discrimination, but for failing to tell a superior of the agents' complaint. Richardson, who plans to fight the suit, says the restaurant was short-staffed on the morning when the nearly two dozen agents showed up.

Looking ahead, Richardson, a 56-year-old former professional football player, hopes to redeem Denny's reputation with the so-called Fair Share pact being hammered out between TW and the NAACP. In addition to random testing, the accord would require TW to hire more minority executives, restaurant managers, and employees and boost its purchases from minority-owned suppliers. The accord also calls for TW to add at least one minority member to its all-white board. A final agreement between TW and the civil rights group could be

announced at the NAACP's July convention in Indianapolis. "This would go far beyond anything we've ever done before with a corporation," says the NAACP's Chavis.

Separately, Chavis says TW's CEO has also agreed to ensure minority participation in the ownership and management of a National Football League franchise that Richardson is seeking for Charlotte, N.C.

RESPECT. So far, Richardson's cooperation has won him respect from civil rights leaders. "I'm impressed with Jerry's level of sincerity," says Chavis. Still, the NAACP says Denny's has more work to do in improving relations with the African-American community. For example, it points to Denny's sole black franchisee, vs. some 400 at McDonald's.

TW's chief hasn't won over all his critics, however. "It's a foxhole conversion, if you ask me," says John P. Relman of the Washington Lawyers Committee for Civil Rights & Urban Affairs, who is representing the Secret Service agents. Relman wants a nationwide settlement similar to Shoney's agreement.

For now, most analysts believe TW, which renamed itself Flagstar Corp. on June 16, can avoid Shoney's fate. The company's conciliatory tone has eased the controversy somewhat. Still, Richardson has a more urgent challenge: convincing the public and his employees that he truly believes in his common-sense notion that discrimination is bad business.

By Chuck Hawkins in Spartanburg, S.C., with bureau reports

TORN BETWEEN
HALO & HORNS

Industry managers grapple with ethics and discrimination issues in a new
INDUSTRYWEEK survey.

David R. Altany

Stealing. Discrimination. Lies. We learned plenty about these as kids at the receiving end of stinging strappings, groundings, and Castro-length lectures from Mother. But now, as industry's "keepers of the code" of moral conduct and appropriate behavior, where do managers stand on these ethical issues? Have today's industry managers, most of whom were in some way influenced by the attitudes and standards of the '60s, created a more liberal and racially progressive organizational environment for themselves and their direct reports? Or have they chosen to adopt the more conservative views and "old-boy" behaviors of previous managerial generations?

To find the answer to these questions, INDUSTRYWEEK surveyed 1,300 middle managers in medium-sized and large companies with at least 500 employees. In a nutshell, middle managers' responses to straightforward ethical questions reflect a pure and steadfast virtue usually reserved for Boy Scouts and clerics. When pushed into gray areas where loyalties, goals, and the desire to be honest don't coincide, however, rationalizations for shady behavior begin working their way into decisions.

At the far end of the spectrum are discrimination and biases, where middle managers make it clear that your advancement odds are best if you're a white male who dates white women who work outside your company. Overall, the vast majority of respondents have extremely slim odds of ever winding up in the slammer for pinching the corporate coffer or pulling an Ivan Boesky on their clients. But in a more telling ethical measure, Mother would still probably cast a disapproving eye on a few of the respondents' answers. One interesting example: As the finale to our survey, we asked if the respondent had lied in answering any of the questions. Despite the fact that the survey was both voluntary and anonymous, 5% of the managers admitted they lied on one or more of their answers.

ILL-GOTTEN GAINS

In response to clearly right/wrong ethical questions, middle managers earn high honors for their stated integrity and un-wavering convictions. Given the scenario that a close business associate asked for preferential treatment on an upcoming contract and has offered you a generous sum of money "for your time and trouble," 99% of survey respondents say they would turn down the tip.

Similarly, given the opportunity to steal $100,000 from their company with absolute certainty that they would not be detected or caught, a similar 98% of the managers maintain that they would not take the money.

The majority of middle managers also say they would not hesitate to turn in an offender who also happens to be the company CEO.

So, even though 5% admitted that they lied on the questionnaire, only 2% would commit a fail-safe theft. One possible explanation is that managers' ethical standards are higher when the gains of deception are enormous (and one's conscience comes into play). Little white lies, however, seem to be more ethically tolerable. "Borrowing" company materials or fudging on one's expense account also appears to elicit a smaller degree of ethical circumspection among industry middle managers than for a full-fledged heist. When asked if they had ever taken anything worth more than $25 from their company, 4% say they have done so—once—and an additional 4% say they have done so repeatedly.

When it comes to others stealing large sums of money from their companies, industry managers have little regard for how close their friendship is with the offender. One-half of all managers say that even if the offender were a close friend or mentor, they would go directly to an executive in their company to report the incident before talking about it with the offender. One-fourth of the managers say they would confront the individual before taking action, and about one-fifth of respondents say

Reprinted by permission of *Industry Week*, March 15, 1993, pp. 15, 18-20. © 1993 by Penton Publishing, Inc., Cleveland, OH.

they would first make contact with the individual with the aim of persuading that person to return the money.

The majority of middle managers also say they would not hesitate to turn in an offender who also happens to be the company CEO. The biggest difference was that fewer of the respondents would confront the CEO directly about the transgression—most likely out of fear. Several respondents comment with only a trace of humor that if they caught their CEO stealing company funds, they would update their resumes *first* and *then* notify the corporate ethics officer or board of directors of the misdeed.

One out of five middle managers has had intimate relations with a co-worker.

In instances where industry managers are confronted with clearcut ethical issues, they agree with near unanimity to abide by and enforce the corporate code. When the ethical waters grow murky, however, consensus on acceptable behavior breaks down. Managers were presented with the scenario that they are in the process of bidding on a contract for the U.S. Navy in which their price is the same as their competitor's; however, company engineers have informed them that it would take several months longer to develop and manufacture than their competitor. We then asked how they would respond if the Navy questioned them about their development schedule. About one-fourth (26%) of the managers say they would describe the advantages of their product and attempt to sidestep the issue. Another 13% say they would tell the Navy they can match the competitor's schedule and worry about finding a solution later. Only a slight majority, 58%, would provide the straight and unaltered facts.

BIAS

In the area of biases, 10% of industry managers say they would prefer to hire a white male over a female. Although that means the great majority of managers (90%) report no preference to either gender, it also means that females in one of 10 hiring situations start off at a disadvantage. Even 2.4% of *women* managers say they would prefer to hire a white male over a female. Although gender bias clearly occurs in only a small percentage of hiring situations, when multiplied by the hundreds of thousands of job openings that are filled each year in the U.S., it is also clear that the incidence of gender bias remains at significant levels.

About the same amount of hiring bias exists against racial minorities as against women, with an overall 10% of industry managers reporting a hiring preference toward white males. Women managers are less biased, but 6% would still prefer to hire a non-minority.

By far the most heavily discriminated against minority group is the gay population. The survey reveals that the level of bias increases with the level of responsibility and public contact that the position in question entails. Yet even for a production-line job with virtually no visibility, 34% of industry middle managers say they would not hire an admitted homosexual. For a management or sales position, 52% say they would not hire a homosexual. The survey thus strongly indicates that it is more acceptable to discriminate against admitted gays than against women or minorities.

Some responses suggest that more subtle forms of bias come into play in the workplace than the responses on outright discrimination indicate. Although 90% of managers say they would not discriminate against women in a hiring situation, 92% nevertheless indicate that they would also prefer to work for a man than a woman. Although a different power relationship exists in the two questions, the obvious influence of preferences on decision-making suggests that subtle forms of bias and discrimination are common.

INTIMACY AMONG CO-WORKERS

You're a single woman in the marketing department. You take a liking to the cute customer-service rep on the third floor, and the two of you start dating. What will the boss think if he or she finds out? Among the 1,300 industry bosses who responded, 27% say they disapprove. But would they actually *do* anything? A little less than half (46%) of those who disapprove say they wouldn't take any action. Among the rest, one-third say they would take whatever actions they could to thwart the budding romance, while about one-fifth (21%) of the managers say it depends on who the lovebirds are and whether the relationship would influence their on-the-job performance.

The situation is perceived as more problematic, though, when the co-workers are married. Almost two-thirds (64%) of industry managers object to intimate relationships between married co-workers. When asked about their own behaviors, on the other hand, one in five managers say they have had intimate relations with a co-worker, and among those individuals, one-half were involved in relationships in which at least one of the partners was married. Does a double standard exist? Among those managers who have had intimate relations with a co-worker in which at least one of the partners was married, 39% say they object to others in their organization engaging in the same behavior.

AGAINST ALL ODDS
HERE'S WHAT INDUSTRY MANAGERS SAY IT
TAKES TO GET AHEAD.

Only a narrow slice of employees makes it into the management ranks of any given company, and the odds of most managers ever holding down a post within the top-executive ranks is wafer thin. To what, then, do middle managers attribute their success to date? And what has most hampered their advancement?

By a large margin, most managers attribute their advancement to their knowledge and on-the-job accomplishments. More than 80% of industry middle managers rank these as being the biggest factors in their promotion to management. Only a small percentage of managers rank other factors as most important, including building relationships with the "right" people (4%), respect of co-workers (3%), respect of supervisor (5%), and appearance and presentation skills (1%).

However, when asked what has most *hindered* their advancement to even higher levels of management, the majority of managers say it was because they hadn't built relationships with the "right" people (56%), followed by insufficient education, intelligence, or knowledge of business area (23%), and insufficient respect of supervisor (11%). Interestingly, respect of direct reports and co-workers isn't reported as a significant help or hindrance to most managers' advancement. Engaging in what many would consider slightly unethical or deceptive behavior also appears to be correlated to advancement.

In the case of the manager bidding for a Navy contract in which his competitor had the shorter production schedule, the survey indicates that the percentage of managers choosing either of the two more questionable ethical options increases steadily with managers' incomes. The percentage of managers responding that they would indicate they could match the competitor's schedule and worry about finding the solution later rises from 5% for those making under $40,000 to 12% among those making between $40,00 and $80,000, to 18% for those making $80,000 to $120,000, and to 22% for those making above $120,000.

The percentage of managers who would report the bare facts as they are falls from 78% for those earning under $40,000 to 59% for those making between $40,000 and $80,000, to 51%

for those making between $80,000 and $120,000 and to 41% for those making in excess of $120,000.

Is deception, then, however slight, a part of "getting ahead?" Is absolute honesty a drawback?

Another potential barrier to "making it," at least in a monetary sense, may be gender. A little more than half of male managers believe that there is not equity in the compensation of women and men doing the same job, while 88% of women managers believe women are underpaid relative to men. The reported salary figures of the managers responding to the survey appear to support this view, although a more in-depth study comparing only managers with the same job titles would be necessary to accurately make that claim. Among the overall legion of women managers responding to the survey, only 17% make more than $60,000 a year, compared with 54% of male managers.

Despite the fact that many managers feel that women employees are underpaid relative to their male counterparts, male and female managers have roughly the same degree of satisfaction with the amount of money that they themselves are paid. Between 40% and 50% of both male and female managers feel they are fairly compensated, and between 40% and 50% of each group feel they deserve a 20% boost in pay. About 9% of managers in each group feel they deserve a pay increase greater than 20%.

What about the people who work for them? When asked about the compensation of manufacturing line workers in their company, only 9% of managers feel these individuals are underpaid. About twice that many (20%) feel production employees are overpaid, and the majority, 71%, feel they are fairly compensated.

After the Layoff: Closing the Barn Door Before All the Horses Are Gone

Robert C. Ford and Pamela L. Perrewé

Robert C. Ford *is a professor of management and chairperson of the Department of Hospitality Management, College of Business Administration, University of Central Florida, Orlando.* **Pamela L. Perrewé** *is an associate professor and chairperson of the department of management, College of Business, Florida State University, Tallahassee.*

> *Financial aspects are not the only criteria management needs to pay attention to during layoffs, restructurings, and mergers.*

For Mega Corporation it had been a momentous year. The economic downturn followed by the loss of an important government contract had led to a merger between Mega Corporation and a former competitor. Now it was time to face the reality of what all these events meant to the future of the organization and its employees—having to downsize the corporation through layoffs.

Although downsizing does not necessarily lead to layoffs, that is most often the case. Mega Corporation faced several problems in its downsizing efforts: it would have to close some of its plants, lay off selected workers at other plants where the work load had diminished, and merge the work forces of two different and previously separate product lines. It would be the task of top management and human resource management personnel to make it all work.

The problem Mega Corporation faces may seem terribly complex. But the story of downsizing and the associated personnel issues such downsizing creates is becoming increasingly common as American industry struggles to remain competitive in the rapidly changing world marketplace. The good news is that there is a fairly large body of literature on layoff strategies that contains sound advice on how to choose which employees stay and which go; how to protect the organization from possible discrimination-related legal challenges; and how to set up effective benefit packages, early retirement systems, transfer policies, outplacement programs, and other procedural issues related to downsizing the corporate payroll.

The future of the newly structured organization, of course, is in the hands of the group of surviving employees who remain after all layoffs have been completed. The bad news is that here, surprisingly, there is not nearly as much research or advice available to either top managers or human resource professionals on how to revitalize an organization after the downsizing. Yet the need to develop programs, policies, and procedures that address the concerns of the survivors and help them cope with the negative effects layoffs have on attitudes and productivity is imperative if the fruits of the downsizing are to ripen. Too often in reorganization processes, managers focus on financial issues; the limited research that exists in this area gives strong indication that the benefits of these types of reorganizations can be realized only if personnel issues are carefully and thoughtfully resolved.

Although there is not much help available in the literature for managers seeking to address non-financial issues effectively, there is a small and growing body of knowledge that identifies issues that are important for surviving employees, what problems are created by downsizing, layoffs, mergers, and acquisitions, and what "best practices" are available to human resource professionals. There is an increasing recognition that it is important to pay as much attention to the "horses" the organization wishes to keep in the "barn" as it does to those it loses. It is too easy to lose the benefits of restructuring if the employees

From *Business Horizons*, July/August 1993, p. 34-40. © 1993 by The Foundation for the School of Business at Indiana University. Reprinted by permission.

who remain behind are demoralized, disorganized, or busy looking for other jobs before they too are laid off. If management forgets the survivors, organizational survival will be even more difficult; employees who can change jobs will do so.

WHAT WE HAVE LEARNED

Although research is limited, some insights have been gained on this important topic. We identify four areas that managers of effective downsizings have foreseen. These areas—the "Four Cs"—include: (1) comprehensive planning for the change, (2) communication, (3) credibility, and (4) consideration (see **Figure 1**). Each plays a critical role in ensuring the successful implementation of a downsizing effort. Our purpose here is to detail the interrelationships of each of these "Cs" and to provide some insights for practicing managers on how they can avoid the problems common to the downsizing efforts of many organizations. This article will also help managers develop strategies to ensure that surviving employees remain with the organization and stay productive.

COMPREHENSIVE PLANNING FOR CHANGE

The most important "C" is comprehensive planning for change. It is the keystone on which the other Cs depend. Management must carefully consider the impact that a downsizing, a layoff, a merger, or an acquisition will have on those laid off, those surviving, and the community in which the downsizing occurs. A number of issues must be resolved.

First, management must communicate its comprehensive plan for change. It must plan on when, where, how, and through what medium it can best communicate its plans to both those inside and outside the organization. How and what it communicates offers great evidence about how thoroughly it has planned for the remaining two Cs.

Second, management ought to show its credibility by planning thoroughly for the variety of details associated with such reorganizations. This can range from the relatively simple—such as new personnel policies on salary determinations, days off, and sick leave—to the more complicated issues of how to lay off people fairly without losing the services of the valued personnel in the newly created organization. This can even extend to more complicated plans that might be necessary to build or recreate the organization's culture and strategic vision effectively. As Siehl and Smith (1991) note, the strategy selected in an acquisition has profound implications on retaining top managers in the newly acquired firm. If

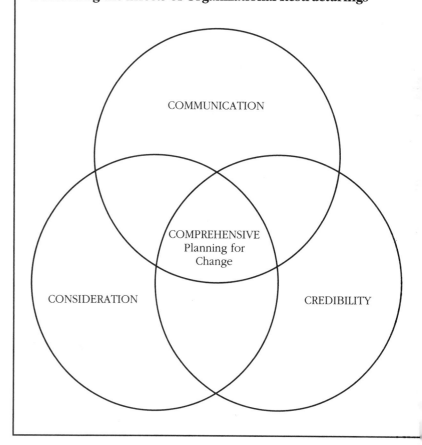

**Figure 1
Foreseeing the Effects of Organizational Restructurings**

COMMUNICATION

COMPREHENSIVE
Planning for
Change

CONSIDERATION

CREDIBILITY

those strategic issues have not been thought through and planned out in advance, the newly created firm runs the real risk of losing its credibility with the "horses" that might have been a primary reason for acquiring the firm in the first place.

Third, management should plan how it will show consideration and caring for the people who stay as well as for those it must let go. The natural focus of managers in such situations is on financial aspects. If there are no expected financial benefits, what would be the point of undertaking the problems of a merger, layoff, or downsizing operation in the first place? Yet financial benefits will likely be elusive if consideration of the human resource problems are not thoroughly planned.

The most frequently mentioned item in a survey of managers whose mergers or acquisitions had failed was "people problems" ("Trends and Findings" 1987). The comprehensive planning for change starts by articulating a future-oriented vision to drive the planning process. A focus on where the organization hopes to go will help the logic of the downsizing decisions and the details of the plans for the future to be more coherent, comprehensive, and reassuring to those who stay than if management merely acts as if it is responding to a problem.

The organization should behave proactively rather than reactively. This enhances credibility, because it shows that management operates on the basis of a vision-focused plan rather than a problem-focused panic, and tends to inspire confidence in the survivors that the future is being competently and completely addressed. Further, as the goals and plans necessary to reach that vision are communicated to employees, the employees regain the sense that their future is more stable and predictable. People are smart enough to know when management is reeling from one crisis to another and when it has damage under control.

> "Full, open, and honest communication is critical for an organization to manage the problems of downsizing successfully."

Comprehensive planning based on a future vision and a clear recognition of the threats and weaknesses faced by the firm breeds confidence by survivors that things will become better. Mirvis and Marks (1986) suggest using an employee survey several months after the downsizing has taken place. This allows managers to obtain the input of surviving employees on how management has been handling the "people problems" such events create. It also shows employees that management is interested in the problems and is seeking effective ways to resolve them.

COMMUNICATION

Once a comprehensive plan for change is developed, management must communicate it effectively. Management must inform its people about what it is doing and how everyone will be affected. Panos (1989) describes a successful downsizing plan based on comprehensive and open communications. Management exhibited trust in the departing employees by sharing with them the legitimate economic rationale for the downsizing. Everyone inside and outside the company was informed about what was going to happen and when; a description of an outplacement and severance package program was made available. Managers responded to every question asked, and demonstrated respect for the departing people by asking for their help in staying on long enough to make the transition from the old organization to the new downsized one. As a result, those who remained appreciated the fairness and consideration management showed to those laid off. Within two weeks after the process was completed, there was evidence of survivors' commitment to move forward.

Rumors thrive when people do not have access to information. The more uncertainty there is, the greater the flow of the informal network. Worse yet, people who do not know what is happening spend time and energy seeking out the information they need. Time spent by the water cooler is time not spent on the job. Employees worry about such things as loss of job, transfer, changes in status, power, responsibility, coworkers, and career path opportunities. Managers must take the time to tell their employees exactly what is happening and how those events will affect them in their jobs. Managers in publicly held organizations face the additional challenge of communicating information to the public. The Securities and Exchange Commission limits what information managers can give their employees without first communicating it to the public. Because timing is part of the meaning of the message, it is critical for employees to hear news that affects them straight from the company rather than on the six o'clock news.

As an added benefit of effective communication, accurate knowledge of what will happen seems to be a positive contributor to the acceptance of the new organizational realities. Marks and Mirvis (1985) relate the significant problems experienced by a bank that first undertook a merger without making an effort to provide relevant information to affected employees. For its second attempt, the bank brought in consultants to design a merger-communication plan that included formal meetings with all members of the work force, informal management-employee discussions, and widespread usage of the company newspaper and the local media. Even though some layoffs were announced, there was no significant increase in absenteeism or customer complaints following the acquisition; financial performance met management expectations.

In spite of the evidence that effective communication with post-trauma employees is important to the continuing success of the organization, a survey by Schweiger and Weber (1989) of human resource practices after acquisitions reveals that between 40 and 80 percent of the responding firms either did not use communication strategies or considered the use of these strategies to be of minor importance.

Most managers prefer not to provide advanced notification of layoffs because they fear a negative impact on productivity—work slowdowns, disgruntled employee sabotage, or notified employees finding new employment before the need for their services has ended. A series of studies reveals, however, that advanced notification is beneficial to both the company and the employee (Feldman and Leana 1989; Leana and Feldman 1989). These studies illustrate that employees spend less time unemployed because they can seek out new jobs before attaining the stigma of being unemployed. They have the opportunity to overcome the shock of being laid off before they enter the job market. Moreover, they spend less energy worrying about the uncertainties created by being laid off, such as termination of health care plans for their families and the threat of an immediate end to their paychecks. The company benefits because, in many cases, productivity increases as employees seek to prove they either are productive enough to be retained or merit strong job references while they seek new employment.

Communication is also needed to reassure those who are told they will not be laid off. They, too, will face the uncertainties of career disruptions, new job responsibilities, and increased work loads with no immediate prospects of additional help. If everyone in an organization is busy doing something important before layoffs occur, survivors must ask themselves the following question, which managers must help them answer: Who is going to do all that work when all those people are gone? Those who remain may even look longingly at those who have gone, see the new challenges they have in their new jobs or careers, and wonder what is so great about staying behind. This can be particularly disconcerting if the survivors feel their own career opportunities are in jeopardy by the new, smaller, often flatter organization.

Communication is also important to ensure that security is rebuilt and further uncertainty eliminated. Those who survive the first round of layoffs are left wondering if there will be more to follow. Communication is critical here to reassure them that the situation will be stable for at least some period of time and further threats to their job security are indefinitely suspended.

This issue is related to the next "C"—credibility. If management reassures the survivors that the situation is stable for the time being and then keeps it stable, some of the trust that a layoff or downsizing inevitably loses will be won back. Full, open, and honest communication is critical for an organization to manage the problems of downsizing successfully.

CREDIBILITY

In a downsizing situation the credibility of the firm with its employees, customers, suppliers, and other stakeholders is at risk. If management has been sending messages and memoranda telling its employees that nothing is going to happen to them and then something does, there is obviously a serious credibility problem. If, in addition, management says it has everything under control and then shows by its subsequent actions that it does not or that it has

been planning to do something different from what it had been saying publicly, credibility is again destroyed. If management tells its survivors that the "deadwood" is gone and the "winners" are left, then the credibility issue is raised once again; the remaining employees wonder why the so-called deadwood had not been pruned out long ago or why they were hired in the first place.

The credibility issue reflects what managers do to aid or destroy whatever existing trust they have with their employees. If there is an announcement that a layoff or restructuring will take place and it will have a certain effect, then it must take place that way and have that effect if management wants to retain the confidence of its remaining employees. If, for example, management tells the survivors that the losers are now eliminated, it calls into question not only the credibility factor but also its judgment as the survivors look across the list of those who lost their jobs. They know these people were not all losers; they know that the reason for the downsizing was not to prune out the low performers but to adjust to a changing structure or marketplace. So the question left in their minds is, "Does management really know what it is doing?" The process for laying off people must be clearly delineated, widely disseminated, and accomplished fairly.

> "Managers should be particularly considerate in dealing with both those laid off and those who remain."

Another sign of a credible management is when layoffs are spread fairly across all levels of the organization. Remaining employees may wonder why many lower-paid operative level employees are laid off if higher-paid managers keep their jobs. The question this creates for employees is, "From where are the savings coming when the expensive managers are retained while the lower paid workers are the ones being laid off?"

The last issue in credibility relates to the degree to which survivors believe managers have considered all alternatives to the layoff or downsizing. There are a number of possible strategies management might consider to avoid the necessity of a layoff. Attrition, early retirements, job-sharing, pay cuts, leaves of absence, and retraining could lead to job transfers. The extent to which managers demonstrate that they do their best to avoid personal difficulties that layoffs and other downsizing strategies hold for the firm's employees affects the credibility they retain after the event.

CONSIDERATION

No one area of research has led to more clear results than the importance of consideration, caring, and compassion in the treatment of employees in organizational restructuring or downsizing. Anecdotes abound of people who have been loyal employees for up to 20 years, then find themselves being escorted to their desks by a security guard immediately after the dreaded and unexpected meeting with human resources, to ensure that only personal effects are removed on the last day at work. The message is clear to both those laid off and those surviving. Suddenly a loyal and respected employee is no longer trustworthy. This person is likely, unless monitored closely, to steal from the company in a parting rage against the injustice of the layoff.

In a series of studies designed to test the effects of different layoff strategies on survivors, Joel Brockner and others have discovered some revealing insights on what effect different layoff strategies have on remaining employees. In one instance in which the layoff was seemingly random, survivors reported feeling guilty; however, they also worked harder. These outcomes were moderated by the survivors' self-esteem. Those who were low in self-esteem exhibited a much greater boost in post-layoff work performance than those with high self-esteem. This may represent a strategy by those with low self-esteem to regain a feeling of control over their work.

In a subsequent study in which the experimental subjects were laid off on either a random basis or a merit basis, there were no increases or decreases in the performance of survivors as a result of the merit layoff condition (Brockner et al. 1986). It is interesting that both conditions produced guilt and remorse in the survivors. Survivors who identify strongly with those laid off may feel a certain sense of illegitimacy about the layoff and a resentment toward management. "Survivor's guilt" seems to be aggravated when management fails to show consideration and compassion for laid-off workers through the provisions it makes to help those terminated.

This body of research suggests that managers should be particularly considerate in dealing with both those laid off and those who remain. Some survivors may feel guilty, others angry, and still others anxious. Managers may want to set up counseling sessions or group discussions to help those affected employees work out their feelings and emotions.

If a layoff or downsizing is the result of an acquisition or merger, then management has other considerations it must address. It is easy for the acquiring firm to treat the acquired as if there were a conquest—a triumph of the good over the bad. One might assume that if the acquired employees were any good, they never would have been in the position of being acquired in the first place. Therefore, for newly acquired employees there may be fear, uncertainty, and a feeling of helplessness as they contemplate who will be retained in the newly emerging organization and who will be let go. They may wonder whom they can trust and to whom they owe allegiance. They may be concerned about their career paths and the value their prior successes, performances, and political debts have in the new organization. They also might wonder "who they are" now that their old corporate identities, statuses, reputations, and positions are gone.

Some writers compare the situation faced by the newly acquired to the classic stages of dealing with tragedy suggested by Elizabeth Kübler-Ross. She argues that people go through stages when confronted with a serious loss in their lives: denial, anger, bargaining, depression, and acceptance. Considerate managers will realize that these stages exist and handle them when layoffs or the loss of old organizational ties are involved (Schweiger, Ivancevich, and Power 1987).

The management of the acquiring organization or the dominant player in the merger must be aware of these repercussions. It ought to ensure that the newly joined employees are treated with the same respect and consideration as the existing employees. At the same time, it must be careful not to send the signal to its old employees that the new people are receiving better treatment than dedicated, long-time employees. It is a delicate balancing act for managers to consider the new with the old.

The need to display consideration is directed two ways. In one direction management must be attentive to the needs of the survivors, as well as to their guilt, relief, anxiety, and feeling of personal loss. In the other direction, management should show consideration to those departing. The way in which management deals with these people sends a strong message to those who remain behind about how management really feels about its people. If management treats these people with disrespect, distrust, and haste, it tells those remaining that deep down the company does not trust its people. Further, it shows that it is insensitive to the personal pain that severing long-time relationships creates between those who leave and those who stay. There is no time allotted to grieve over lost friendships or mark the parting with the customary ceremonies and farewell parties. Those who remain wonder about the years of being told that they were important, vital parts of the organization.

By granting employees control over restructuring, managers may be able to alleviate stress. The stress that survivors experience may ensue partly from the absence of personal control they have over the layoffs. Some believe the job insecurity and the injustice survivors perceive after a corporate restructuring involving layoffs may be part of the more general issue of feeling this loss of control (Brockner et al. 1987). Many employees experience a loss of control not only over their work but also over their lives.

Maintaining a sense of personal control can be positive for both the employee and the firm. Conversely, losing this control can be damaging. The perception of being in control is related to decreased levels of anxiety in demanding situations. Spector (1986) found that high levels of personal control are related to high levels of job satisfaction, commitment, involvement, performance, and motivation. In addition, he found that high levels of personal control are related to low levels of physical symptoms (headaches, insomnia), emotional distress, role stress, absenteeism, and turnover. Given this evidence, it appears that managers who find ways to increase survivors' feelings of personal control will obtain beneficial outcomes for both the employees and the firm.

One appropriate strategy is for managers to implement participatory decision making. By involving employees in making decisions related to the layoffs, management can increase employees' feelings of control and decrease stress. Management sends a powerful message of respect toward those who are affected by the restructuring. Using participation enables management to show that it believes employees have a stake in the outcome of this organizational trauma, have useful ideas to contribute, and are entitled to be involved fully in the process that has a direct bearing on their work lives.

Supporting the important role of participation, Cameron, Freeman, and Mishra (1991) found that employees—not top management—recommended and designed the best downsizing strategies. Using participation to show consideration for employees has the added benefit of expanding the breadth and depth of possible solutions to the problems created by restructuring. Its value in the restructurings is so great that it is listed as one of the "best practices" associated with effective restructurings.

Management that behaves as though it has thoughtfully considered and foreseen the impact the "Four Cs" have on the effectiveness of its restructuring can demonstrate to its surviving employees a great deal about itself and its competence (see **Figure 2**). People are quite able to understand that the world is not likely to stand still. They know that what works today may not work tomorrow.

Management of the work force means that those responsible have the obligation to plan comprehensively for the problems and opportunities caused by changes. They also have the responsibility to communicate the full meaning and impact of corporate restructuring, explain the rationale behind it, and act in ways that will demonstrate credibility. Management has an obliga-

---

Figure 2
The Four "Cs": Managerial Guidelines

Comprehensive Planning for Change
1. Articulate a future-oriented vision to drive the planning process.
2. Communicate the comprehensive change plan to employees.
3. Plan thoroughly for problems ranging from salary determinations to strategic issues.
4. Focus on the human resource problems prior to tackling the financial concerns of the firm.

Communication
1. Use both formal means of communication (e.g., memoranda, company newsletters) as well as informal means (e.g., management-employee discussions).
2. Give advance notice of layoffs and other expected major changes.
3. Communicate fully, openly, and honestly.
4. Communicate frequently.

Credibility
1. Give those laid off and the survivors accurate information about the reasons for the restructuring, downsizing, and layoffs.
2. Try to anticipate the effects of the layoff on surviving employees (e.g., heavier workloads, stress).
3. Share the pain by spreading layoffs across hierarchical levels of the organization.
4. Consider other alternatives to layoffs (e.g., job-sharing, leaves of absence).

Consideration
1. Show consideration and compassion to those departing as well as to the survivors of the layoff.
2. Recognize that employees might view the organizational restructuring as a serious loss.
3. Empower surviving employees by giving them control over their work.
4. Encourage employee participation in decision making.

---

tion to be considerate toward those who are affected by organizational changes created by layoffs, mergers, and employee moves.

Research-based knowledge in this area is still evolving. However, it is clear that firms that do not adequately address the non-financial aspects of restructuring strategies will not likely achieve desired results. This would lead to the ultimate irony of undergoing a radical change to enhance organizational effectiveness that leads instead to ineffectiveness. Focusing on the "Four Cs" will allow firms to capture the benefits expected.

References

J. Brockner, "The Effects of Work Layoffs on Survivors: Research, Theory, and Practice," in B.M. Staw and L.L. Cummings, eds., *Research in Organizational Behavior* (Greenwich, Conn.: JAI Press, 1988), pp. 213-255.

J. Brockner, J. Davy, and C. Carter, "Layoffs, Self-Esteem, and Survivor Guilt: Motivational, Affective, and Attitudinal Consequences," *Organizational Behavior and Human Decision Processes, 36* (1985): 229-244.

2. EMPLOYEES AND THE WORKPLACE: Downsizing

J. Brockner, J. Greenberg, A. Brockner, J. Bortz, J. David, and C. Carter, "Layoffs, Equity Theory, and Work Performance: Further Evidence of the Impact of Survivor Guilt," *Academy of Management Journal*, 29, 2 (1986): 373-384.

J. Brockner, S. Grover, and M. Blonder, "Predictors of Survivors' Job Involvement Following Layoffs: A Field Study," *Journal of Applied Psychology*, 73, 3 (1988): 436-442.

J. Brockner, S. Grover, T. Reed, R. DeWitt, and M. O'Malley, "Survivors' Reactions to Layoffs: We Get by with a Little Help for Our Friends," *Administrative Science Quarterly*, 32 (1987): 526-541.

K. Cameron, S. Freeman, and A. Mishra, "Best Practices in White Collar Downsizing: Managing Contradictions," *Academy of Management Executive*, 5, 3 (1991): 57-73.

D. Feldman and C. Leana, "Managing Layoffs: Experiences at the Challenger Disaster Site and the Pittsburgh Steel Mills," *Organizational Dynamics*, 18, 2 (1989): 52-64.

S. Jackson, "Participation in Decision Making as Strategy for Reducing Job-Related Strain," *Journal of Applied Psychology*, 68 (1983): 3-19.

C. Leana and D. Feldman, "When Mergers Force Layoffs: Some Lessons about Managing the Human Resource Problems," *Human Resource Planning*, 12, 2 (1989): 123-140.

M. Marks and P. Mirvis, "Merger Syndrome: Stress and Uncertainty," *Mergers and Acquisitions*, March-April 1985, pp. 50-55.

P. Mirvis and M. Marks, "Merger Syndrome: Management by Crisis," *Mergers and Acquisitions*, January-February 1986, pp. 70-76.

J. Panos, "Managing the Humane Approach to Post-acquisition Layoffs," *Mergers and Acquisitions*, March-April 1989, pp. 44-47.

P. Perrewé and D. Ganster, "The Impact of Job Demands and Behavioral Control on Experienced Job Stress," *Journal of Organizational Behavior*, 10 (1989): 213-229.

L. Perry, "Least-Cost Alternatives to Layoffs in Declining Industries," *Organizational Dynamics*, 14, 1 (1986): 48-59.

D. Schweiger, J. Ivancevich, and F. Power, "Executive Actions for Managing Human Resource Before and After Acquisition," *Academy of Management Executive*, 1, 2 (1987): 127-138.

D. Schweiger and Y. Weber, "Strategies for Managing Human Resources During Mergers and Acquisitions: An Empirical Investigation," *Human Resources Planning*, 12, 2 (1989): 69-86.

C. Siehl and D. Smith, "Avoiding the Loss of a Gain: Retaining Top Managers in an Acquisition," *Human Resource Management*, 29, 2 (1991): 167-185.

P. Spector, "Perceived Control by Employees: A Meta-Analysis of Studies Concerning Autonomy and Participation at Work," *Human Relations*, 39 (1986): 1005-1116.

"Trends and Findings," *Mergers and Acquisitions*, March-April 1987, pp. 19-20.

J. Walsh and J. Ellwood, "Mergers, Acquisitions, and the Pruning of Managerial Deadwood," *Strategic Management Journal*, 12 (1991): 201-217.

R. Walton, "A Vision-Led Approach to Management Restructuring," *Organizational Dynamics*, 14, 1 (1986): 5-16.

Companies Discover That Some Firings Backfire Into Costly Defamation Suits

Gabriella Stern

Staff Reporter of THE WALL STREET JOURNAL

A company can't be too careful in how it fires an employee.

A $15.6 million Texas jury verdict against **Procter & Gamble** Co. underscores that point. The money was awarded April 23 to Don Hagler, a 41-year veteran of the company, who said P&G fired him after publicly accusing him of stealing a $35 company telephone. Mr. Hagler said that the phone was his property and that P&G libeled him by posting notices accusing him of theft on company bulletin boards. The state-court jury awarded Mr. Hagler $1.6 million in actual damages and $14 million in punitive damages.

P&G says it is reviewing the verdict for a possible appeal. "We're disappointed in the verdict," says a spokeswoman for the Cincinnati-based company.

"I'm not surprised the jury found liability, but the amount of the award is incredible," says Greg Rasin, an employment attorney with Jackson, Lewis, Schnitzler & Krupman in New York.

DEFAMATION LAWSUITS

Lawyers say more ex-employees are using defamation lawsuits to fight firings. "Workers are broadening their allegations to include things like defamation, rather than just claiming unlawful termination," says Jay W. Waks, an employment attorney with Kaye, Scholer, Fierman, Hays & Handler in New York City. "It reflects a lack of care by management in expressing the reasons why the person's been terminated."

This week, the New Jersey Supreme Court held that a former Bell Laboratories manager fired in 1984 for allegedly misusing $250,000 in company funds can sue the company for defamation. The former employee, Barbara A. Williams, won a $670,000 jury award against Bell Labs, the research arm of **American Telephone & Telegraph** Co., in Superior Court in Newark in 1989, but the verdict was overturned on appeal. The Supreme Court reversed part of the appeals-court ruling and said Ms. Williams must prove her case at another trial.

Ms. Williams had worked for Bell for 12 years, becoming manager of the company's Aid to Black Colleges program. In 1984, Bell received an anonymous letter claiming she had embezzled or misused company funds. After an internal investigation, Bell fired Ms. Williams and disclosed the results of the probe to the Essex County, N.J., prosecutor's office. However, the prosecutor's office later dropped its investigation of Ms. Williams.

Ms. Williams sued Bell in 1986, alleging, among other things, that Bell defamed her to the prosecutor's office. After an 11-day trial during which Bell argued it

---

Some Do's and Don'ts of Firing

■ **BE CERTAIN OF THE FACTS** when firing someone. Conduct a thorough investigation and bring in experts in employment law and labor relations either from corporate headquarters or from the outside.

■ **BE FACTUAL AND AVOID INNUENDO** when discussing a firing with other people or when recording what happened. Such caution should extend to personnel files as well.

■ **TELL ONLY THOSE WHO NEED TO KNOW** the details of a worker's firing. Limiting the number of people who know gives the fired employee less ammunition for suing for defamation of character. It shows professionalism and good faith on the part of the company.

■ **AVOID MAKING EXAMPLES** of fired employees. Let the fired employee's behavior and the facts speak for themselves. The details of a firing often seep out in the workplace and indirectly serve as a deterrent.

■ **IF AN EXAMPLE MUST BE MADE** of someone to prevent similar actions, be extremely careful in the wording of any announcement. Accuse someone of something as serious as theft or sexual harassment only if you're sure of the facts.

Reprinted by permission of *The Wall Street Journal,* May 5, 1993, pp. B1, B7. © 1993 by Dow Jones & Company, Inc. All rights reserved worldwide.

had a right to present the results of its investigation to the prosecutor's office, a jury returned a verdict in Ms. Williams's favor on the defamation charge. The verdict was reversed by the appeals court, which cited issues relating to jury instructions and statute-of-limitations. This past Monday, however, the state Supreme Court reversed the statute-of-limitations portion of the appeals court's ruling and remanded the case for trial.

TRIALS, RE-TRIALS AND APPEALS

Another defamation case was filed in federal court in Baltimore by a former Contel Corp. executive, Thomas Hassey, who claimed Contel executives defamed him by blaming him for morale and turnover problems in meetings and speeches before employees, both before and after he was fired in 1987. Contel has since been acquired by **GTE** Corp.

In 1990, Mr. Hassey was awarded $3.5 million by a jury. In a second trial ordered by the judge, who raised the issue of inadequate jury instructions, Mr. Hassey was awarded $7.1 million by a jury, according to his attorney. That judge, however, ordered a third trial, and both sides have appealed aspects of the order to the U.S. Court of Appeals for the Fourth Circuit.

Also moving through the courts is the case of Willard A. Thompson, a former employee of **Public Service Co. of Colorado.** Mr. Thompson sued the utility in state court in Colorado, claiming he was defamed by disciplinary notices sent to his union and several bosses after he was suspended in 1983 for allegedly bothering a customer's female employees with personal questions. About a year and a half ago, the U.S. Supreme Court refused to consider a Public Service Co. appeal of a Colorado Supreme

Court decision setting the case for trial, and it was returned to state court for trial. But a series of snafus involving Mr. Thompson's attorneys have delayed the trial's scheduling.

The firing that led to the P&G case took place on March 4, 1991, six days after security guards at the front gate of the company's detergent plant in Dallas stopped Mr. Hagler at the end of a shift, searched a bag he was toting and found a telephone. Mr. Hagler told superiors he had purchased the phone after a flood damaged a phone on his desk in the plant. He said he hadn't been reimbursed by P&G because he had lost the receipt and his boss had told him he could keep the phone.

P&G fired him after a six-day internal investigation and posted notices on 11 bulletin boards and the plant's electronic mail system saying, in part: "It has been determined that the telephone in question is Procter & Gamble's property and that Don had therefore violated Work Rule #12 . . . concerning theft of company property."

Mr. Hagler filed suit two months later in 101st District Court, Dallas County, Texas, charging that P&G had libeled him. Two years later, witnesses at the trial included a co-worker who had accompanied Mr. Hagler to a mall where he bought the phone with his own cash. Mr. Hagler testified P&G used him as an example to stop a rash of thefts at the plant. He said that since his firing, he has applied for more than 100 new jobs, only to be turned down when prospective employers learned why he had been fired by P&G. After a five-day trial, the jury took five hours to deliberate.

Employment attorneys who represent corporate clients say companies can take

precautions to avoid being sued when firing workers. Bruce Sanford, a libel lawyer with Baker & Hostetler, says, among other considerations, "You have to be careful about what you write in personnel files" when an employee is fired. He adds: "Write it very factually, and don't include gratuitous opinions."

Says Mr. Rasin, the employment attorney: "You'd better be right if you're planning to make an example of someone. The absolute defense to any defamation act is the truth. In a theft situation, unless an employee admits to it, I'd be reluctant to publish it beyond those who need to know. This is a society where people sue when they think they've been wronged."

Mr. Rasin presents another pointer: "Juries will sympathize with workers. They're the little person against the big company."

In the Hagler case, the jury foreman told the Dallas Morning News that jurors never questioned whether P&G was guilty and immediately began discussing how much to award Mr. Hagler. The award for actual damages broke down into $1.3 million for damage to Mr. Hagler's character or reputation, $200,000 for mental anguish, and $100,000 for physical injury. (Mr. Hagler's attorney, Neal Manne of the Dallas firm of **Susman Godfrey,** said his client became depressed after the firing and was diagnosed with dangerously high blood pressure.)

Mr. Hagler says he has strong feelings about his former employer. "I'm not proud of the fact that I had to sue the company I was dedicated to for 41 years," he says. "I sued because they called me a thief and put it on 11 bulletin boards in the plant. I think P&G's a good company. But I think they've changed. They're not as nice to people as they used to be."

"You're Fired."

It was over. Steve had been forced out of the company with little warning, and no one had helped him. What was worse, he suspected the firing might have been because of an ethical stance he had once taken.

DOUG WALLACE

Doug Wallace does frequent consulting work on corporate ethics, and was formerly the vice president for social policy at Norwest Bank in Minneapolis.

THE CASE

Staring numbly at his glistening kitchen table, Steve swirled his spoon in his coffee. He thought about his afternoon—his last hours at the company he had served faithfully for over ten years.

"I'm reorganizing the department, and you aren't a candidate for any position in it," Jeanette Rigley, his thirty-two-year-old boss, had told him. "I've prepared two memos: one describing your severance agreement, and one describing our reorganization and decision to let you go . . . because of a performance problem."

He had quickly scanned the memos. "Can't we discuss this?" he asked.

"There's nothing to discuss," she snapped. "The decision is final."

Steve's mind drifted back to just five days ago when Allied Tech CEO Bruce Ship had introduced him to some 600 managers at the "heads up" session. He had felt confident standing before his colleagues, describing the dynamic plans his public affairs group had devised. It had gone well, Steve thought. But apparently, not well enough, for days later Jeanette had given him the boot.

He stood slouching near the stove, remembering last year's merger and Jeanette's arrival on the scene. Steve remembered the scuttlebutt in the office before Jeanette was hired—women in the office were putting tremendous pressure on Bruce, the CEO, to hire a woman for one of the few remaining executive positions. Steve had thought at the time that Bruce was responding hastily by hiring her, especially since her experience was with a financial services company, not with a technical firm like Allied. Now, look-

In the middle of a recession, Steve found himself unemployed at fifty-two, with only ten weeks severance pay.

ing back, he had probably been right. Steve remembered feeling uneasy when he had first met Jeanette. He had been puzzled by her style, but had made up his mind not to let his feelings hinder their working relationship.

Within six months, though, trouble began. It had started last spring, when Jeanette abruptly handed Steve a performance review as he was on his way out the door to the state capitol. It had been the first negative review of his long career. She ended up changing that evaluation, but only after he sent a documented, follow-up memo. Then, three months later, she had surprised him with another performance memo. Again, Steve documented the inaccuracies in her review. But this time, he also requested the human resources department's assistance with Jeanette. Despite its promise to mediate, no one had ever followed through.

"I should have seen this coming," Steve thought. "There must have been a turning point." And then he remembered. His mind shot back to a meeting last fall. He had questioned the company's proposed international sales policy, at the time thinking others would also recognize the serious ethical implications of the proposal. "I was only doing my job," Steve thought. Members familiar with his work had invited his "thoughtful perspective," because of the potentially volatile public exposure to the company.

As he recalled the reaction he got—blank stares and silence—Steve's stomach sank. He recalled the queasy feeling he had leaving the conference room that day. And he knew why he was fired. "Bruce must have authorized Jeanette's action," Steve thought. "Maybe she was just being a good soldier."

For whatever reason, he hadn't been treated fairly. And almost every ethical principle he held dear had been violated. His dismissal was demeaning. And it left him at risk of joining the unemployed, at fifty-two, in the middle of a recession, with only ten weeks severance pay.

"Should I seek legal help?" he wondered. "Should I protest the decision? What can I do?"

SARA PICARD
Assistant Vice President, U.S. Health Care, Blue Bell, Pennsylvania.

I DO BELIEVE THAT, ethically, Steve wasn't treated fairly, and I would probably be as angry or as shocked as he was. His record shows that he was a fine employee. If I was in his place, I would have confronted Jeanette after the first performance review. I would have taken copies of my previous reviews and sat down with her and had a heart-to-heart. The ten-week severance seemed particularly harsh. If the company was trying to terminate an employee with Steve's background and tenure, I don't understand why some type of retirement package wasn't offered.

Would I leave quietly? Yes. I would not make a large stink about it. Would I seek legal help? If I were in his shoes, I would definitely pursue legal counseling. At Steve's age, I think he has a good case. Would I protest the decision and ask for reconsideration? Yes, I would present some sort of retirement package request to them, in view of the time I had been with the company and my past record

Reprinted with permission from *Business Ethics*, January/February 1992, pp. 41-42. *Business Ethics*, The Magazine of Socially Responsible Business.

of performance. What responsibility do I have? If Steve pursued legal counseling, he might be advised to bring in other employees who were similarly affected, but I wouldn't pursue that on my own. I would try to come up with alternatives to litigation. However, if I didn't get anywhere, I would pursue the legal point and take it as far as I had to.

BERNIE VITTI
Associate Director of Sales Training and Development, Sandoz Pharmaceuticals, East Hanover, New Jersey.

I RECOMMEND SIX STEPS. First, I would ask the human resources and legal departments to help me with Jeanette. In most cases today, HR will get involved with cases like this. Second, Jeanette as a manager must have a sit-down performance appraisal with Steve. That is a must. The role of the enlightened manager today is to get subordinates to work better, to show them how to do the job rather than saying, "What you've done is not acceptable." It's Jeanette's job to show Steve what is not acceptable and to teach him how to do it better. Third, I would develop objectives and projects so that Steve can best do that job. Fourth, Jeanette must agree to set appropriate deadlines, and define what is expected of Steve, so that both parties agree on what the finished projects will look like. Fifth, checkpoints along the way should be determined. Steve's success or failure could be documented at these checkpoints, which would also provide Jeanette every opportunity to help Steve, instead of just approaching him on the end

---

Workers shouldn't acquiesce to an unfair firing. Autocratic managers count on that happening.

---

dates with, "You didn't do your job, so your evaluation is unsatisfactory." Steve has to be given every benefit of the doubt.

Sixth, Jeanette should discuss all options with Steve. A summary of his job should be presented, and if he hasn't met the requirements of the job, Jeanette should recommend another position. But not until Steve has been given every opportunity to become more proficient.

DOUG WALLACE'S COMMENTS

A RECURRING THEME in this column is avoiding Lone Ranger ethics in organizations. Most ethical conflicts are communal in nature. They often involve a variety of persons and groups within the company. Sometimes they erupt because mixed messages about priorities have been sent. But in almost all cases, an ethical conflict is not the result of one person's independent action, and it cannot be understood or successfully resolved without the engagement of those who contributed to the conflict and those who will be affected by its resolution. The art of doing ethics in organizations entails learning how to effectively put an issue on the table, bring together the people who contributed to it (even if they did so unknowingly), and work the conflict through to a good end.

What happens, however, when the one who recognizes the problem no longer has standing in the organization? Steve, a good, productive employee, has been fired. I suspect that the reason Steve was pushed out has more to do with his ethical questions than his performance or his difficulties with Jeanette. But Steve is on the outside looking in. How can he affect anything now?

There are a lot of Steves, or Stephanies, if you will, in this tightening economy, people whose bosses tolerate no debate, and who often find themselves the first to go when an organization restructures. And they aren't necessarily troublemakers. What should, and can, they do?

For starters, people should not simply acquiesce and accept what's occurring. Autocratic managers count on that happening. Both of our guest commentators presume that Steve should take responsibility not only to protect himself, but also to attempt to get the organization to take another look at what it is doing. To do that will invariably involve the assistance of others who still belong to the company or who have access to powerful players within it. This should not be confused with hammering the organization or

individuals in it. Rather, seeking inside assistance aims at encouraging a company to re-examine and improve the way employees are treated—blending caring and fairness into the way people manage.

And if those initiatives fail, there is always the option of litigating the matter.

WHAT ACTUALLY HAPPENED?

S TEVE CONCLUDED that the ethical principles of fairness and respect for dignity had been breached. The next day he wrote a memo to the human resources department requesting copies of all policies on layoffs, termination, and supervisor dispute resolution. He knew such policies existed. Since it was a newly merged company, he wanted confirmation that the company was at least temporarily operating under policies from one of the former organizations.

He then wrote a detailed response to Jeanette's performance evaluation, proposing an alternative severance agreement or a way for him to continue employment with a different reporting relationship. Rather than citing a general statement of unfair treatment, he detailed the history of his relationship with Jeanette and his performance. He sent this memo to the vice president of human resources, with copies to the CEO, chief operating officer, general counsel, and the attorney for human resources.

To get proof of his strong performance, Steve contacted Walt Haverford, a retired executive from the original organization. After explaining his situation, and asking for advice and a letter of reference, Steve leveraged Walt's personal relationship with the COO of Allied to request a meeting. Since Allied's COO was the person at the highest level who hadn't been directly involved in the situation, Steve thought he would be an influential, impartial witness. The COO did write a letter of reference for him, citing Steve's contributions, which in turn helped get human resources to develop a fair and balanced view of the situation.

Finally, Steve solicited legal help to assess whether or not he had a case that could be litigated.

The case is still going forward. As we go to press, the company has not taken action to resolve the issue any differently than where Jeanette originally left it.

Changing Unethical Organizational Behavior

Richard P. Nielsen
Boston College

Richard P. Nielsen is an associate professor in the Department of Organizational Studies, School of Management, Boston College. He has been a faculty member at Boston College since 1980. He has served as a speaker and taught seminars and management development courses in France, Germany, Holland, Indonesia, Mexico, Pakistan, and Switzerland. He has also served as a consultant and presented management development progams to such organizations as Citicorp, GSX/Genstar, IBM, Arthur D. Little, the Society of Friends and the American Friends Service Committee, the United Nations, the U.S. Agency for International Development, the U.S. Office of Education, and the WGBH Educational Foundation.

His research, teaching, and consulting interests are in the areas of ethics practice and cooperative change management. He serves as an editorial board member and referee for the Journal of Business Ethics. Some of his related recent publications include "Limitations of Reasoning as an Ethics Action Strategy" (Journal of Business Ethics, 1988), "Arendt's Action Philosophy and the Manager as Eichmann, Richard III, Faust or Institution Citizen (California Management Review, 1984), and "Cooperative Strategy" (Strategic Management Journal, 1988).

> *"To be, or not to be: that is the question:*
> *Whether 'tis nobler in the mind to suffer*
> *The slings and arrows of outrageous fortune,*
> *Or to take arms against a sea of troubles,*
> *And by opposing end them?"*
>
> William Shakespeare, *Hamlet*

What are the implications of Hamlet's question in the context of organizational ethics? What does it mean to be ethical in an organizational context? Should one suffer the slings and arrows of unethical organizational behavior? Should one try to take arms against unethical behaviors and by opposing, end them?

The consequences of addressing organizational ethics issues can be unpleasant. One can be punished or fired; one's career can suffer, or one can be disliked, considered an outsider. It may take courage to oppose unethical and lead ethical organizational behavior.

How can one address organizational ethics issues? Paul Tillich, in his book *The Courage to Be*, recognized, as Hamlet did, that dire consequences can result from standing up to and opposing unethical behavior. Tillich identified two approaches: *being* as an individual and *being* as a part of a group.[1]

In an organizational context, these two approaches can be interpreted as follows: (1) Being as an individual can mean intervening to end unethical organizational behaviors by working against others and the organizations performing the unethical behaviors; and (2) being as a part can mean leading an ethical organizational change by working with others and the organization. These approaches are not mutually exclusive; rather, depending on the individual, the organization, the relationships, and the situation, one or both of these approaches may be appropriate for addressing ethical issues.

Being as an Individual

According to Tillich, the courage to be as an individual is the courage to follow one's conscience and defy unethical and/or unreasonable authority. It can even mean staging a revolutionary attack on that authority. Such an act can entail great risk and require great courage. As Tillich explains, "The anxiety conquered in the courage to be . . . in the productive process is considerable, because the threat of being excluded from such a participation by unemployment or the loss of an economic basis is what, above all, fate means today. . . ."[2]

According to David Ewing, retired executive editor of the *Harvard Business Review*, this type of anxiety is not without foundation.

> *"There is very little protection in industry for employees who object to carrying out immoral, unethical or illegal orders from their superiors. If the employee doesn't like what he or she is asked to do, the remedy is to pack up and leave. This remedy seems to presuppose an ideal economy, where there is another company down the street with openings for jobs just like the one the employee left."[3]*

How can one *be* as an individual, intervening against unethical organizational behavior? Intervention strategies an individual can use to change unethical behavior include: (1) secretly blowing the whistle within the organization; (2) quietly blowing the whistle, informing a responsible higher-level manager; (3) secretly threatening the offender with blowing the whistle; (4) secretly threatening a responsible manager with blowing the whistle outside the organiza-

From *The Executive*, May 1989, pp. 123-130. © 1989 by The Academy of Management. Reprinted by permission.

tion; (5) publicly threatening a responsible manager with blowing the whistle; (6) sabotaging the implementation of the unethical behavior; (7) quietly refraining from implementing an unethical order or policy; (8) publicly blowing the whistle within the organization; (9) conscientiously objecting to an unethical policy or refusing to implement the policy; (10) indicating uncertainty about or refusing to support a cover-up in the event that the individual and/or organization gets caught; (11) secretly blowing the whistle outside the organization; or (12) publicly blowing the whistle outside the organization. Cases of each strategy are considered below.

Cases

1. Secretly blowing the whistle within the organization. A purchasing manager for General Electric secretly wrote a letter to an upper-level manager about his boss, who was soliciting and accepting bribes from subcontractors. The boss was investigated and eventually fired. He was also sentenced to six months' imprisonment for taking $100,000 in bribes, in exchange for which he granted favorable treatment on defense contracts.[4]

2. Quietly blowing the whistle to a responsible higher-level manager. When Evelyn Grant was first hired by the company with which she is now a personnel manager, her job included administering a battery of tests that, in part, determined which employees were promoted to supervisory positions. Grant explained:

> "There have been cases where people will do something wrong because they think they have no choice. Their boss tells them to do it, and so they do it, knowing it's wrong. They don't realize there are ways around the boss . . . . When I went over his [the chief psychologist's] data and analysis, I found errors in assumptions as well as actual errors of computation . . . . I had two choices: I could do nothing or I could report my findings to my supervisor. If I did nothing, the only persons probably hurt were the ones who 'failed' the test. To report my findings, on the other hand, could hurt several people, possibly myself."

She quietly spoke to her boss, who quietly arranged for a meeting to discuss the discrepancies with the chief psychologist. The chief psychologist did not show up for the meeting; however, the test battery was dropped.[5]

3. Secretly threatening the offender with blowing the whistle. A salesman for a Boston-area insurance company attended a weekly sales meeting during which the sales manager instructed the salespeople, both verbally and in writing, to use a sales technique that the salesman considered unethical. The salesman anonymously wrote the sales manager a letter threatening to send a copy of the unethical sales instructions to the Massachusetts insurance commissioner and the *Boston Globe* newspaper unless the sales manager retracted his instructions at the next sales meeting. The sales manager did retract the instructions. The salesman still works for the insurance company.[6]

4. Secretly threatening a responsible manager with blowing the whistle outside the organization. A recently hired manager with a San Francisco Real Estate Development Company found that the construction company his firm had contracted with was systematically not giving minorities opportunities to learn construction management. This new manager wrote an anonymous letter to a higher-level real estate manager threatening to blow the whistle to the press and local government about the contractor unless the company corrected the situation. The real estate manager intervened, and the contractor began to hire minorities for foremen-training positions.[7]

5. Publicly threatening a responsible manager with blowing the whistle. A woman in the business office of a large Boston-area university observed that one middle-level male manager was sexually harassing several women in the office. She tried to reason with the office manager to do something about the offensive behavior, but the manager would not do anything. She then told the manager and several other people in the office that if the manager did not do something about the behavior, she would blow the whistle to the personnel office. The manager then told the offender that if he did not stop the harassment, the personnel office would be brought in. He did stop the behavior, but he and several other employees refused to talk to the woman who initiated the actions. She eventually left the university.[8]

6. Sabotaging the implementation of the unethical behavior. A program manager for a Boston-area local social welfare organization was told by her superior to replace a significant percentage of her clients who received disability benefits with refugee Soviet Jews. She wanted to help both the refugees and her current clients; however, she thought it was unethical to drop current clients, in part because she believed such an action could result in unnecessary deaths. Previously, a person who had lost benefits because of what the program manager considered unethical "bumping" had committed suicide: He had not wanted to force his family to sell their home in order to pay for the medical care he needed and qualify for poverty programs. After her attempts to reason with her boss failed, she instituted a paperwork chain with a partially funded federal agency that prevented her own agency from dropping clients for nine months, after which time they would be eligible for a different funding program. Her old clients received benefits and the new refugees also received benefits. In discussions with her boss, she blamed the federal agency for making it impossible to drop people quickly. Her boss, a political appointee who did not understand the system, also blamed the federal agency office.[9]

7. Publicly blowing the whistle within the organization. John W. Young, the chief of NASA's astronaut office, wrote a 12-page internal memorandum to 97 people after the Challenger explosion that killed seven crew members. The memo listed a large number of safety-related problems that Young said had endangered crews since October 1984. According to Young, "If the management system is not big enough to stop the space shuttle program whenever necessary to make flight safety corrections, it will not survive and neither will our three space shuttles or their flight crews." The memo was instrumental in the decision to broaden safety investigations throughout the total NASA system.[10]

8. Quietly refraining from implementing an unethical order/policy. Frank Ladwig was a top salesman and branch manager with a large computer company for more than 40 years. At times, he had trouble balancing his responsibilities. For instance, he was trained to sell solutions to customer problems, yet he had order and revenue quotas that sometimes made it difficult for him to concentrate on solving problems. He was responsible for signing and keeping important customers with annual revenues of between $250,000 and $500,000 and for aggressively and conscientiously representing new products that had required large R&D investments. He was required to sell the full line of products and services, and sometimes he had sales quotas for products that he believed were not a good match for the customer or appeared to perform marginally. Ladwig would quietly not sell those products, concentrating on selling the products he believed in. He would quietly explain the characteristics of the questionable products to his knowledgeable customers and get their reactions, rather than making an all-out sales effort. When he was asked by his sales manager why a certain product was not moving, he explained what the customers objected to and why. However, Ladwig thought that a salesman or manager with an average or poor performance record would have a difficult time getting away with this type of solution to an ethical dilemma.[11]

9. *Conscientiously objecting to an unethical policy or refusing to implement it.* Francis O'Brien was a research director for the pharmaceutical company Searle & Co. O'Brien conscientiously objected to what he believed were exaggerated claims for the Searle Copper 7 intrauterine contraceptive. When reasoning with upper-level management failed, O'Brien wrote them the following:

> *"Their continued use, in my opinion, is both misleading and a thinly disguised attempt to make claims which are not FDA approved. . . . Because of personal reasons I do not consent to have my name used in any press release or in connection with any press release. In addition, I will not participate in any press conferences."*

O'Brien left the company ten years later. Currently, several lawsuits are pending against Searle, charging that its IUD caused infection and sterility.[12]

10. *Indicating uncertainty about or refusing to support a cover-up in the event that the individual and/or organization gets caught.* In the Boston office of Bear Stearns, four brokers informally work together as a group. One of the brokers had been successfully trading on insider information, and he invited the other three to do the same. One of the three told the others that such trading was not worth the risk of getting caught, and if an investigation ever occurred, he was not sure he would be able to participate in a cover-up. The other two brokers decided not to trade on the insider information, and the first broker stopped at least that type of insider trading.

11. *Secretly blowing the whistle outside the corporation.* William Schwartzkopf of the Commonwealth Electric Company secretly and anonymously wrote a letter to the Justice Department alleging large-scale, long-time bid rigging among many of the largest U.S. electrical contractors. The secret letter accused the contractors of raising bids and conspiring to divide billions of dollars of contracts. Companies in the industry have already paid more than $20 million in fines to the government in part as a result of this letter, and they face millions of dollars more in losses when the victims sue.[14]

12. *Publicly blowing the whistle outside the organization.* A. Earnest Fitzgerald, a former high-level manager in the U.S. Air Force and Lockheed CEO, revealed to Congress and the press that the Air Force and Lockheed systematically practiced a strategy of underbidding in order to gain Air Force contracts for Lockheed, which then billed the Air Force and received payments for cost overruns on the contracts. Fitzgerald was fired for his trouble, but eventually received his job back. The underbidding/cost overruns, on at least the C-5/A cargo plane, were stopped.[15]

Limitations of Intervention

The intervention strategies described above can be very effective, but they also have some important limitations.

1. *The individual can be wrong about the organization's actions.* Lower-level employees commonly do not have as much or as good information about ethical situations and issues as higher-level managers. Similarly, they may not be as experienced as higher-level managers in dealing with specific ethical issues. The quality of experience and information an individual has can influence the quality of his or her ethical judgments. To the extent that this is true in any given situation, the use of intervention may or may not be warranted. In Case 9, for example, if Frank Ladwig had had limited computer experience, he could have been wrong about some of the products he thought would not produce the promised results.

2. *Relationships can be damaged.* Suppose that instead of identifying with the individuals who want an organization to change its ethical behavior, we look at these situations from another perspective. How do we feel when we are forced to change our behavior? Further, how would we feel if we were forced by a subordinate to change, even though we thought that we had the position, quality of information, and/or quality of experience to make the correct decisions? Relationships would probably be, at the least, strained, particularly if we made an ethical decision and were nevertheless forced to change. If we are wrong, it may be that we do not recognize it at the time. If we know we are wrong, we still may not like being forced to change. However, it is possible that the individual forcing us to change may justify his or her behavior to us, and our relationship may actually be strengthened.

3. *The organization can be hurt unnecessarily.* If an individual is wrong in believing that the organization is unethical, the organization can be hurt unnecessarily by his or her actions. Even if the individual is right, the organization can still be unnecessarily hurt by intervention strategies.

4. *Intervention strategies can encourage "might makes right" climates.* If we want "wrong" people, who might be more powerful now or in the future than we are, to exercise self-restraint, then we may need to exercise self-restraint even when we are "right." A problem with using force is that the other side may use more powerful or effective force now or later. Many people have been punished for trying to act ethically both when they were right and when they were wrong. By using force, one may also contribute to the belief that the only way to get things done in a particular organization is through force. People who are wrong can and do use force, and win. Do we want to build an organization culture in which force plays an important role? Gandhi's

response to "an eye for an eye" was that if we all followed that principle, eventually everyone would be blind.

Being as a Part

While the intervention strategies discussed above can be very effective, they can also be destructive. Therefore, it may be appropriate to consider the advantages of leading an ethical change effort (being as a part) as well as intervening against unethical behaviors (being as an individual).

Tillich maintains that the courage to be as a part is the courage to affirm one's own being through participation with others. He writes,

> "The self affirms itself as participant in the power of a group, of a movement . . . . Self-affirmation within a group includes the courage to accept guilt and its consequences as public guilt, whether one is oneself responsible or whether somebody else is. It is a problem of the group which has to be expiated for the sake of the group, and the methods of punishment and satisfaction . . . are accepted by the individual . . . . In every human community, there are outstanding members, the bearers of the traditions and leaders of the future. They must have sufficient distance in order to judge and to change. They must take responsibility and ask questions. This unavoidably produces individual doubt and personal guilt. Nevertheless, the predominant pattern is the courage to be a part in all members of the . . . group . . . . The difference between the genuine Stoic and the neocollectivist is that the latter is bound in the first place to the collective and in the second place to the universe, while the Stoic was first of all related to the universal Logos and secondly to possible human groups. . . . The democratic-conformist type of the courage to be as a part was in an outspoken way tied up with the idea of progress. The courage to be as a part in the progress of the group to which one belongs . . . ."[16]

Leading Ethical Change

A good cross-cultural conceptualization of leadership is offered by Yoshino and Lifson: "The essence of leadership is the influential increment over and above mechanical compliance with routine directives of the organization."[17] This definition permits comparisons between and facilitates an understanding of different leadership styles through its use of a single variable: created incremental performance. Of course, different types of leadership may be more or less effective in different types of situations; yet, it is helpful to understand the "essence" of leadership in its many different cultural forms as the creation of incremental change beyond the routine.

For example, Yoshino and Lifson compare generalizations (actually overgeneralizations) about Japanese and American leadership styles:

> "In the United States, a leader is often thought of as one who blazes new trails, a virtuoso whose example inspires awe, respect, and emulation. If any individual characterizes this pattern, it is surely John Wayne, whose image reached epic proportions in his own lifetime as an embodiment of something uniquely American. A Japanese leader, rather than being an authority, is more of a communications channel, a mediator, a facilitator, and most of all, a symbol and embodiment of group unity. Consensus building is necessary in decision making, and this requires patience and an ability to use carefully cultivated relationships to get all to agree for the good of the unit. A John Wayne in this situation might succeed temporarily by virtue of charisma, but eventually the inability to build strong emotion-laden relationships and use these as a tool of motivation and consensus building would prove fatal."[18]

A charismatic, "John Wayne type" leader can inspire and/or frighten people into diverting from the routine. A consensus-building, Japanese-style leader can get people to agree to divert from the routine. In both cases, the leader creates incremental behavior change beyond the routine. How does leadership (being as a part) in its various cultural forms differ from the various intervention (being as an individual) strategies and cases discussed above? Some case data may be revealing.

Cases

1. *Roger Boisjoly and the Challenger launch.*[19] In January 1985, after the postflight hardware inspection of Flight 52C, Roger Boisjoly strongly suspected that unusually low temperatures had compromised the performance effectiveness of the O-ring seals on two field joints. Such a performance compromise could cause an explosion. In March 1985, laboratory tests confirmed that low temperatures did negatively affect the ability of the O-rings to perform this sealing function. In June 1985, the postflight inspection of Flight 51B revealed serious erosion of both primary and backup seals that, had it continued, could have caused an explosion.

These events convinced Boisjoly that a serious and very dangerous problem existed with the O-rings. Instead of acting as an individual against his supervisors and the organization, for example, by blowing the whistle to the press, he tried to lead a change to stop the launching of flights with unsafe O-rings. He worked with his immediate supervisor, the director of engineering, and the organization in leading this change. He wrote a draft of a memo to Bob Lund, vice-president of engineering, which he first showed and discussed with his immediate supervisor to "maintain good relationships." Boisjoly and others developed potential win-win solutions, such as investigating remedies to fix the O-rings and refraining from launching flights at too-low temperatures. He effectively established a team to study the matter, and participated in a teleconference with 130 technical experts.

On the day before the Challenger launch, Boisjoly and other team members were successful in leading company executives to reverse their tentative recommendation to launch because the overnight temperatures were predicted to be too low. The company recommendation was to launch only when temperatures were above 53 degrees. To this point, Boisjoly was very effective in leading a change toward what he and other engineering and management people believed was a safe and ethical decision.

However, according to testimony from Boisjoly and others to Congress, the top managers of Morton Thiokol, under pressure from NASA, reversed their earlier recommendation not to launch. The next day, Challenger was launched and exploded, causing the deaths of all the crew members. While Boisjoly was very effective in leading a change within his own organization, he was not able to counteract subsequent pressure from the customer, NASA.

2. *Dan Phillips and Genco, Inc.*[20] Dan Phillips was a paper products group division manager for Genco, whose upper-level management adopted a strategy whereby several mills, including the Elkhorn Mill, would either have to reduce costs or close down. Phillips was concerned that cost cutting at Elkhorn would prevent the mill from meeting government pollution-control requirements, and that closing the mill could seriously hurt the local community. If he reduced costs, he would not meet pollution-control requirements; if he did not reduce costs, the mill would close and the community would suffer.

Phillips did not secretly or publicly blow the whistle, nor did he sabotage, conscientiously object, quietly refrain from implementing the plan, or quit; however, he did lead a change in the organization's ethical behavior. He asked research and development people in his division to investigate how the plant could both become more cost efficient and create less pollution. He then asked operations people in his division to estimate how long it would take to put such a new plant design on line, and how much it would cost. He asked cost accounting and financial people within his division to estimate when such a new operation would achieve a breakeven payback. Once he found a plan that would work, he negotiated a win-win solution with upper-level management: in exchange for not closing the plant and increasing its investment in his division, the organization would over time benefit from lower costs and higher profitability. Phillips thus worked with others and the organization to lead an inquiry and adopt an alternative ethical and cost-effective plan.

3. *Lotus and Brazilian Software Importing.*[21] Lotus, a software manufacturer, found that in spite of restrictions on the importing of much of its software to Brazil, many people there were buying and using Lotus software. On further investigation, the company discovered that Brazilian businessmen, in alliance with a Brazilian general, were violating the law by buying Lotus software in Cambridge, Massachusetts and bringing it into Brazil.

Instead of blowing the whistle on the illegal behavior, sabotaging it, or leaving Brazil, Lotus negotiated a solution: In exchange for the Brazilians' agreement to stop illegal importing, Lotus helped set them up as legitimate licensed manufacturers and distributors of Lotus products in Brazil. Instead of working against them and the Lotus salespeople supplying them, the Lotus managers worked with these people to develop an ethical, legal, and economically sound solution to the importing problem.

And in at least a limited sense, the importers may have been transformed into ethical managers and business peo-

ple. This case may remind you of the legendary "Old West," where government officials sometimes negotiated win-win solutions with "outlaw gunfighters," who agreed to become somewhat more ethical as appointed sheriffs. The gunfighters needed to make a living, and many were not interested in or qualified for such other professions as farming or shopkeeping. In some cases, ethical behavior may take place before ethical beliefs are assumed.

4. *Insurance company office/sales manager and discrimination.*[22] The sales-office manager of a very large Boston-area insurance company tried to hire female salespeople several times, but his boss refused to permit the hires. The manager could have acted against his boss and the organization by secretly threatening to blow the whistle or actually blowing the whistle, publicly or secretly. Instead, he decided to try to lead a change in the implicit hiring policy of the organization.

The manager asked his boss why he was not permitted to hire a woman. He learned that his boss did not believe women made good salespeople and had never worked with a female salesperson. He found that reasoning with his boss about the capabilities of women and the ethics and legality of refusing to hire women was ineffective.

He inquired within the company about whether being a woman could be an advantage in any insurance sales areas. He negotiated with his boss a six-month experiment whereby he hired on a trial basis one woman to sell life insurance to married women who contributed large portions of their salaries to their home mortgages. The woman he hired was not only very successful in selling this type of life insurance, but became one of the office's top salespeople. After this experience, the boss reversed his policy of not hiring female salespeople.

Limitations to Leading Ethical Organizational Change

In the four cases described above, the individuals did not attack the organization or people within the organization, nor did they intervene against individuals and/or the organization to stop an unethical practice. Instead, they worked with people in the organization to build a more ethical organization. As a result of their leadership, the organizations used more ethical behaviors. The strategy of leading an organization toward more ethical behavior, however, does have some limitations. These are described below.

1. In some organizational situations, ethical win-win solutions or compromises may not be possible. For example, in 1975 a pharmaceutical company in Raritan, New Jersey decided to enter a new market with a new product.[23] Grace Pierce, who was then in charge of medical testing of new products, refused to test a new diarrhea drug product on infants and elderly consumers because it contained high levels of saccharin, which was feared by many at the time to be a carcinogen. When Pierce was transferred, she resigned. The drug was tested on infant and elderly consumers. In this case, Pierce may have been faced with an either-or situation that left her little room to lead a change in organizational behavior.

Similarly, Errol Marshall, with Hydraulic Parts and Components, Inc.,[24] helped negotiate the sale of a subcontract to sell heavy equipment to the U.S. Navy while giving $70,000 in kickbacks to two materials managers of Brown &

Root, Inc., the project's prime contractor. According to Marshall, the prime contractor "demanded the kickbacks. . . . It was cut and dried. We would not get the business otherwise." While Marshall was not charged with any crime, one of the upper-level Brown & Root managers, William Callan, was convicted in 1985 of extorting kickbacks, and another manager, Frank DiDomenico, pleaded guilty to extorting kickbacks from Hydraulic Parts & Components, Inc. Marshall has left the company. In this case, it seems that Marshall had no win-win alternative to paying the bribe. In some situations it may not be possible to lead a win-win ethical change.

2. Some people do not understand how leadership can be applied to situations that involve organizational-ethics issues. Also, some people — particularly those in analytical or technical professions, which may not offer much opportunity for gaining leadership experience — may not know how to lead very well in any situation. Some people may be good leaders in the course of their normal work lives, but do not try to lead or do not lead very well when ethical issues are involved. Some people avoid discussing ethical, religious, and political issues at work.

For example, John Geary was a salesman for U.S. Steel when the company decided to enter a new market with what he and others considered an unsafe new product.[25] As a leading salesman for U.S. Steel, Geary normally was very good at leading the way toward changes that satisfied customer and organizational needs. A good salesman frequently needs to coordinate and spearhead modifications in operations, engineering, logistics, product design, financing, and billing/payment that are necessary for a company to maintain good customer relationships and sales. Apparently, however, he did not try to lead the organization in developing a win-win solution, such as soliciting current orders for a later delivery of a corrected product. He tried only reasoning against selling the unsafe product and protested its sale to several groups of upper-level engineers and managers. He noted that he believed the product had a failure rate of 3.6% and was therefore both unsafe and potentially damaging to U.S. Steel's longer-term strategy of entering higher technology/profit margin businesses. According to Geary, even though many upper-level managers, engineers, and salesmen understood and believed him, "the only desire of everyone associated with the project was to satisfy the instructions of Henry Wallace [the sales vice-president]. No one was about to buck this man for fear of his job."[26] The sales vice-president fired Geary, apparently because he continued to protest against sale of the product.

Similarly, William Schwartzkopf of Commonwealth Electric Co.[27] did not think he could either ethically reason against or lead an end to the large-scale, long-time bid rigging between his own company and many of the largest U.S. electrical contractors. Even though he was an attorney and had extensive experience in leading organizational changes, he did not try to lead his company toward an ethical solution. He waited until he retired from the company, then wrote a secret letter to the Justice Department accusing the contractors of raising bids and conspiring to divide billions of dollars of contracts among themselves.

Many people — both experienced and inexperienced in leadership — do not try to lead their companies toward developing solutions to ethical problems. Often, they do not understand that it is possible to lead such a change; therefore, they do not try to do so — even though, as the cases here show, many succeed when they do try.

3. Some organizational environments — in both consensus-building and authoritarian types of cultures — discourage leadership that is nonconforming. For example, as Robert E. Wood, former CEO of the giant international retailer Sears, Roebuck, has observed, "We stress the advantages of the free enterprise system, we complain about the totalitarian state, but in our individual organizations we have created more or less a totalitarian system in industry, particularly in large industry."[28] Similarly, Charles W. Summers, in a *Harvard Business Review* article, observes, "Corporate executives may argue that . . . they recognize and protect . . . against arbitrary termination through their own internal procedures. The simple fact is that most companies have not recognized and protected that right."[29]

David Ewing concludes that "It [the pressure to obey unethical and illegal orders] is probably most dangerous, however, as a low-level infection. When it slowly bleeds the individual conscience dry and metastasizes insidiously, it is most difficult to defend against. There are no spectacular firings or purges in the ranks. There are no epic blunders. Under constant and insistent pressure, employees simply give in and conform. They become good 'organization people.' "[30]

Similar pressures can exist in participative, consensus-building types of cultures. For example, as mentioned above, Yoshino and Lifson write, "A Japanese leader, rather than being an authority, is more of a communications channel, a mediator, a facilitator, and most of all, a symbol and embodiment of group unity. Consensus building is necessary to decision making, and this requires patience and an ability to use carefully cultivated relationships to get all to agree for the good of the unit."[31]

The importance of the group and the position of the group leaders as a symbol of the group are revealed in the very popular true story, "Tale of the Forty-Seven Ronin." The tale is about 47 warriors whose lord is unjustly killed. The Ronin spend years sacrificing everything, including their families, in order to kill the person responsible for their leader's death. Then all those who survive the assault killed themselves.

Just as authoritarian top-down organizational cultures can produce unethical behaviors, so can participative, consensus-building cultures. The Japanese novelist Shusaku Endo, in his *The Sea and Poison*, describes the true story of such a problem.[32] It concerns an experiment cooperatively performed by the Japanese Army, a medical hospital, and a consensus-building team of doctors on American prisoners of war. The purpose of the experiment was to determine scientifically how much blood people can lose before they die.

Endo describes the reasoning and feelings of one of the doctors as he looked back at this behavior:

> "At the time nothing could be done. . . . If I were caught in the same way, I might, I might just do the same thing again. . . . We feel that getting on good terms ourselves with the Western Command medical people, with whom Second [section] is so cosy, wouldn't be a bad idea at all. Therefore we feel there's no need to ill-temperedly refuse their friendly proposal and

hurt their feelings. . . . Five doctors from Kando's section most likely will be glad to get the chance. . . . For me the pangs of conscience . . . were from childhood equivalent to the fear of disapproval in the eyes of others — fear of the punishment which society would bring to bear. . . . To put it quite bluntly, I am able to remain quite undisturbed in the face of someone else's terrible suffering and death. . . . I am not writing about these experiences as one driven to do so by his conscience . . . all these memories are distasteful to me. But looking upon them as distasteful and suffering because of them are two different matters. Then why do I bother writing? Because I'm strangely ill at ease. I, who fear only the eyes of others and the punishment of society, and whose fears disappear when I am secure from these, am now disturbed. . . . I have no conscience, I suppose. Not just me, though. None of them feel anything at all about what they did here.' The only emotion in his heart was a sense of having fallen as low as one can fall." [33]

What to Do and How to Be

In light of the discussion of the two approaches to addressing organizational ethics issues and their limitations, what should we do as individuals and members of organizations? To some extent that depends on the circumstances and our own abilities. If we know how to lead, if there's time for it, if the key people in authority are reasonable, and if a win-win solution is possible, one should probably try leading an organizational change.

If, on the other hand, one does not know how to lead, time is limited, the authority figures are unreasonable, a culture of strong conformity exists, and the situation is not likely to produce a win-win outcome, then the chances of success with a leadership approach are much lower. This may leave one with only the choice of using one of the intervention strategies discussed above. If an individual wishes to remain an effective member of the organization, then one of the more secretive strategies may be safer.

But what about the more common, middle range of problems? Here there is no easy prescription. The more win-win potential the situation has, the more time there is, the more leadership skills one has, and the more reasonable the authority figures and organizational cultures are, the more likely a leadership approach is to succeed. If the opposite conditions exist, then forcing change in the organization is the likely alternative.

To a large extent, the choice depends on an individual's courage. In my opinion, in all but the most extreme and unusual circumstances, one should first try to lead a change toward ethical behavior. If that does not succeed, then mustering the courage to act against others and the organization may be necessary. For example, the course of action that might have saved the Challenger crew was for Boisjoly or someone else to act against Morton Thiokol, its top managers, and NASA by blowing the whistle to the press.

If there is an implicitly characteristic American ontology, perhaps it is some version of William James' 1907 *Pragmatism*, which, for better or worse, sees through a lens of interactions the ontologies of being as an individual and being as a part. James explains our situation as follows:

"What we were discussing was the idea of a world growing not integrally but piecemeal by the contributions of its several parts. Take the hypothesis seriously and as a live one. Suppose that the world's author put the case to you before creation, saying: 'If I am going to make a world not certain to be saved, a world the perfection of which shall be conditional merely, the condition being that each several agent does its own 'level best.' I offer you the chance of taking part in such a world. Its safety, you see, is unwarranted. It is a real adventure, with real danger, yet it may win through. It is a social scheme of co-operative work genuinely to be done. Will you join the procession? Will you trust yourself and trust the other agents enough to face the risk? . . . Then it is perfectly possible to accept sincerely a drastic kind of a universe from which the element of 'seriousness' is not to be expelled. Who so does so is, it seems to me, a genuine pragmatist. He is willing to live on a scheme of uncertified possibilities which he trusts; willing to pay with his own person, if need be, for the realization of the ideals which he frames. What now actually are the other forces which he trusts to co-operate with him, in a universe of such a type? They are at least his fellow men, in the stage of being which our actual universe has reached." [34]

In conclusion, there are realistic ethics leadership and intervention action strategies. We can act effectively concerning organizational ethics issues. Depending upon the circumstances including our own courage, we can choose to act and be ethical both as individuals and as leaders. Being as a part and leading ethical change is the more constructive approach generally. However, being as an individual intervening against others and organizations can sometimes be the only short or medium term effective approach.

Acknowledgements

I would like to acknowledge and thank the following people for their help with ideas presented in this article: the members of the Works in Progress Seminar of Boston College particularly Dalmar Fisher, James Gips, John Neuhauser, William Torbert, and the late James Waters; Kenneth Boulding of the University of Colorado; Robert Greenleaf; and, Douglas Steere of Haverford College.

Endnotes

1. Paul Tillich, *The Courage to Be.* New Haven, CT: Yale University Press, 1950.
2. See Endnote 1, page 159.
3. David Ewing, *Freedom Inside the Organization.* New York: McGraw-Hill, 1977.
4. The person blowing the whistle in this case wishes to remain anonymous. See also Elizabeth Neuffer, "GE Managers Sentenced for Bribery," *The Boston Globe,* July 26, 1988, p. 67.
5. Barbara Ley Toffler, *Tough Choices: Managers Talk Ethics.* New York: John Wiley, 1986, pp. 153-169.

6. Richard P. Nielsen, "What Can Managers Do About Unethical Management?" *Journal of Business Ethics*, 6, 1987, 153-161. See also Nielsen's "Limitations of Ethical Reasoning as an Action Strategy," *Journal of Business Ethics*, 7, 1988, pp. 725-733, and "Arendt's Action Philosophy and the Manager as Eichmann, Richard III, Faust or Institution Citizen," *California Management Review*, 26, 3, Spring 1984, pp. 191-201.

7. The person involved wishes to remain anonymous.

8. The person involved wishes to remain anonymous.

9. See Endnote 6.

10. R. Reinhold, "Astronauts Chief Says NASA Risked Life for Schedule," *The New York Times*, 36, 1986, p. 1.

11. Personal conversation and letter with Frank Ladwig, 1986. See also Frank Ladwig and Associates' *Advanced Consultative Selling for Professionals*. Stonington, CT.

12. W. G. Glaberson, "Did Searle Lose Its Eyes to a Health Hazard?" *Business Week*, October 14, 1985, pp. 120-122.

13. The person involved wishes to remain anonymous.

14. Andy Pasztor, "Electrical Contractors Reel Under Charges that They Rigged Bids," *The Wall Street Journal*, November 29, 1985, pp. 1, 14.

15. A. Ernest Fitzgerald, *The High Priests of Waste*. New York: McGraw-Hill, 1977.

16. See Endnote 1, pp. 89, 93.

17. M. Y. Yoshino and T. B. Lifson, *The Invisible Link: Japan's Saga Shosha and the Organization of Trade*. Cambridge, MA: MIT Press, 1986.

18. See Endnote 17, p. 178.

19. Roger Boisjoly, address given at Massachusetts Institute of Technology on January 7, 1987. Reprinted in *Books and Religion*, March/April 1987, 3-4, 12-13. See also Caroline Whitbeck, "Moral Responsibility and the Working Engineer," *Books and Religion*, March/April 1987, 3, 22-23.

20. Personal conversation with Ray Bauer, Harvard Business School, 1975. See also R. Ackerman and Ray Bauer, *Corporate Social Responsiveness*. Reston, VA: Reston Publishing, 1976.

21. The person involved wishes to remain anonymous.

22. The person involved wishes to remain anonymous.

23. David Ewing, *Do It My Way or You're Fired*. New York: John Wiley, 1983.

24. E. T. Pound, "Investigators Detect Pattern of Kickbacks for Defense Business," *The Wall Street Journal*, November 14, 1985, pp. 1, 25.

25. See Endnote 23. See also Geary vs. U.S. Steel Corporation, 319 A. 2nd 174, Supreme Court of Pa.

26. See Endnote 23, p. 86.

27. See Endnote 14.

28. See Endnote 3, p. 21.

29. C. W. Summers, "Protecting All Employees Against Unjust Dismissal," *Harvard Business Review*, 58, 1980, pp. 132-139.

30. See Endnote 3, pp. 216-217.

31. See Endnote 17, p. 187.

32. Shusaku Endo, *The Sea and Poison*. New York: Taplinger Publishing Company, 1972. See also Y. Yasuda, *Old Tales of Japan*. Tokyo: Charles Tuttle Company, 1947.

33. See Endnote 32.

34. William James, *Pragmatism: A New Name for Some Old Ways of Thinking*. New York: Longmans, Green and Co., 1907, p. 290, 297-298.

Why *Your* Company Should Have A Whistleblowing Policy

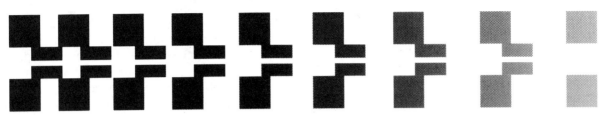

Tim Barnett, *Assistant Professor of Management, Louisiana Tech University*

Dr. Barnett has published in The Journal of Business Research, Journal of Business Communication, *and others, and is a member of the Academy of Management and Southern Management Assn.*

Whistleblowers, those individuals who call attention to possible wrongdoing within their organizations, are the subjects of much controversy. Some say that whistleblowers are noble characters, willing to sacrifice personally and professionally to expose organizational practices that are wasteful, fraudulent, or harmful to the public safety. Others suggest that whistleblowers are, by and large, disgruntled employees who maliciously and recklessly accuse individuals they feel have wronged them in order to attain their own selfish goals.

The truth, as is often the case, probably lies somewhere between these two extremes. Whistleblowers do call attention to genuine abuses of power by decision-makers in business and government. They do often suffer retaliation for their ethical resistance. However, whistleblowers may often be wrong in their accusations and their motives are not always pure. Their actions can disrupt a workplace, and may cause serious harm to individuals wrongly accused.

Whatever your personal view of whistleblowers and whistleblowing, as an organizational policy-maker you must consider the issue objectively. It is not an issue that can be ignored, due to the possible negative consequences for both your employees and your organization. For example, a recent review of whistleblowing incidents shows that among the whistleblowers surveyed, 62% lost their jobs, 18% felt that they were harassed or transferred, and 11% had their job responsibilities or salaries reduced. Fifty-one percent of the incidents resulted in external investigations of the companies involved, 37% in man-

agement shake-ups, 22% in criminal investigations, and 11% in indictments.[1] Although these outcomes may not be typical, they do point out the potential seriousness of whistleblowing.

Recent whistleblowing cases further demonstrate the potential problems facing companies that do not adequately address the issue. For example, after an employee of the entertainment company MCA notified his supervisor of a possible kickback scheme, he was fired. The employee filed a wrongful discharge suit, alleging that he was fired because of his attempt to stop the scheme. He recently received a favorable ruling in a California appellate court. In another California case, a jury awarded a former employee of a large drug company $17.5 million when he was fired after expressing concerns about product safety. Both companies have appealed the rulings.[2]

In each of these cases, the employee expressed concern about possible organizational wrongdoing to members of management, thus providing the company an opportunity to investigate and take corrective action if necessary. Yet, management was apparently unresponsive, even hostile, to the employees' concerns, with unfortunate results. What can you do to ensure that your company handles whistleblowing more effectively?

Whistleblowing research suggests several conditions that are necessary if whistleblowing is to be effectively managed. First, your employees must be informed of the appropriate steps to take in communicating their ethical concerns internally. Studies of federal government employees indicate that there is a significant association between employees' knowledge of appropriate internal channels and the likelihood that they will report perceived wrongdoing.[3] Second, your employees must believe that their concerns will be taken seriously and will be investigated. Studies suggest that many employees who first report their concerns internally later go outside the company with their information if they perceive their organizations to be unresponsive.[4] Third, your employees must feel confident that they will not suffer personal reprisals for using internal channels to report percieved wrongdoing. Whistle-blowing studies suggest that employees who believe that management will retaliate for expressing concerns may be more likely to blow the whistle outside the organization.[5]

In this paper, I will argue that organizations should develop formal whistleblowing policies as a way to create the conditions necessary for the effective management of whistleblowing. These policies should provide standard guidelines within which organizations respond to the ethical or moral concerns of their employees. Whistle-blowing policies should have the following components as a minimum:

(1) A clear statement that employees who are aware of possible wrongdoing within the organization have a responsibility to disclose that information to appropriate parties *inside* the organization;

(2) The designation of specific individuals or groups *outside* the chain of command as complaint recipients;

(3) A guarantee that employees who in good faith disclose perceived wrongdoing to the designated parties inside the organization will be protected from adverse employment consequences; and

(4) The establishment of a fair and impartial investigative process.

To succeed, policies must have the commitment of top management and must be adequately communicated to employees.

I believe that the whistleblowing research mentioned earlier points to legal, practical, and ethical imperatives that compel organizations to develop whistleblowing policies. The following discussion explains why I believe this, and presents the legal, practical, and ethical imperatives that make whistleblowing policies advisable.

The Legal Imperative

The legal trends developing in the United States make whistleblowing policies an important part of organizations' overall ethics code. Increasing statutory protection at the federal and state levels, and court decisions that protect whistle-blowers under the public policy exception to employment-at-will, lead to the statement of a legal imperative regarding whistleblowing.

1. *Increasing Federal protection for whistle-blowers.* Employees of most organizations are expressly guaranteed protection against reprisals from their employers when they disclose actions that violate specific federal statutes. Title VII of the Civil Rights Act, the Age Discrimination in Employment Act and the Occupational Safety and Health Act all contain anti-retaliation provisions.[6]

In addition, in 1989 President Bush signed a federal "Whistleblower's Protection Act" which extends protection available to federal employees who disclose government waste, fraud, and abuse. This law does not directly affect private sector employers. However, numerous legal scholars have recommended comprehensive federal legislation protecting both public and private sector whistleblowers. Congress is expected to consider legislation in 1992 that will extend federal whistleblower protection to private sector employees.[2]

2. *The increasing number of state whistle-blower protection laws.* In the meantime, states are moving quickly to fill the void left by the lack of comprehensive federal legislation. Michigan passed the first "Whistleblower's Protection Law" in 1981, and the majority of states now have such statutes. Many of these apply equally to public and private sector employees. Most of these laws specify that employees have a right to report the illegal or illegitimate actions of their employers to regulatory agencies, government officials, law enforcement officials, and the like. They generally provide remedies, including reinstatement and back pay, for employees who can show that they have suffered adverse employment consequences as a result of their whistleblowing activities. Some states also allow successful plaintiffs to collect punitive damages. Organizations should be aware of the law regarding employee whistleblowers in states in which they operate.[7]

3. *The increasing erosion of the employment-at-will doctrine.* In addition to the legal trends toward whistleblower protection at the federal and state levels, the courts are increasingly recognizing exceptions to the traditional at-will doctrine which has governed most private sector employer-employee relationships for well over 100 years. For example, courts have found "implied contracts" in employee handbooks or in statements made by company officials when hiring individuals which limit the right to terminate except for "just cause." Some courts have found that some employers have shown "malice and bad faith" when discharging employees and have provided relief to the employees. Other courts have held that certain personnel decisions by employers violate "public policy" and that such actions are exceptions to the traditional doctrine of employment-at-will.[8] All of these exceptions have, in some jurisdictions, been cited to protect whistle-

blowers from discharge. The public policy exception probably offers the broadest potential protection for whistleblowers. Therefore, I will examine it in slightly more detail.

Essentially, the public policy exception means that employees performing acts that are consistent with public policy or refusing to perform acts that public policy discourages are protected against reprisals. The term "public policy" is vague, and has been interpreted differently by different courts. Some courts have ruled that the whistleblower who in good faith discloses perceived organizational wrongdoing is acting in a manner consistent with public policy, and therefore is protected from discharge. Other courts, however, have denied relief to whistleblowers, even while acknowledging that employers' disciplinary actions were unfair.[9]

So, while there is no certainty that at-will employees can find protection under one of the exceptions to the doctrine, courts in many jurisdictions have provided relief to whistleblowers. Organizations must be aware that even if there is no federal or state statute expressly protecting whistleblowers, there is a possibility that adverse personnel actions against whistleblowers may backfire because of the increasing limits the courts are placing on employment-at-will.

So what exactly is the legal innovative? Nothing in federal or state law, and no court decision, suggests that your organization is required to develop an internal whistleblowing policy. Does it follow that because whistleblowers may be protected from reprisals that your organization should have such a policy?

I believe it does. Research indicates that many organizations retaliate against whistleblowers.[10] In the absence of a clear organizational directive against such retaliation, it may happen in your company. Such personnel actions may put your organization in violation of federal or state law protecting whistleblowers, or may make you vulnerable to employee lawsuits based on exceptions to the doctrine of employment-at-will.

Whatever your personal views toward whistleblowers, the prudent course is to formalize a stance toward whistleblowing that outlines your company's opposition to reprisals against whistleblowers. *The legal imperative is to prevent adverse personnel decisions that may be linked to whistleblowing.* Such retaliation, even when not specifically prohibited by law, has the potential for creating damaging lawsuits. A policy that expressly forbids such conduct is probably advisable for this reason alone.

The Practical Imperative

Although the legal factors discussed make a good case for the need to treat whistleblowing as a policy issue, I believe there is a practical imperative also. In the following discussion, I explain why I believe this, and then state the practical imperative.

1. The inevitability of wrongdoing. One executive, responding to my questions concerning whistleblowing policies, said words to this effect; "We don't have a policy. We don't have any need for one in our company, because no one is engaged in wrongdoing." This seems a particularly naive view considering what we know about the state of ethical behavior in business and government.

In a perfect world, wrongdoing would be nonexistent, employees would never disagree with the actions of organizational leaders on ethical or moral grounds. This is not a perfect world, however. Wrongdoing, or at least the perception of wrongdoing, is almost sure to occur. When it does, there are often employees who will desire to stop it. Whistleblowing policies that provide internal disclosure mechanisms for employees offer a viable alternative to employees who wish to express concerns of an ethical nature.

2. The likelihood of increased whistleblowing. Although empirical evidence is difficult to come by, there is a general perception that whistleblowing is on the rise, for several possible reasons.

First, there is a continuing problem of unethical conduct in business and government. One cannot read the newspaper or turn on the television without hearing of a new scandal, and there is little need to list the numerous well-publicized cases of recent years. We can probably assume that for every case of unethical behavior we hear about, many others do not make the headlines. It seems obvious that despite all the lip service we give to business ethics, we still have a long way to go to achieve ethical behavior in the workplace.

The second reason whistleblowing may be increasing is that our society seems to sanction blowing the whistle as a way to promote more ethical behavior in business. Big business and government are generally regarded as too powerful, and as exercising too much control over our lives. Whistleblowers are regarded as the underdogs, taking on powerful organizations for society's well-being. They are held up as heroic figures by the media. Academics praise their actions and call for comprehensive protection for them. And, as they discussed earlier, such legal protection is indeed increasingly available.

Finally, the world is becoming increasingly complex. Business organizations must deal with diverse and demanding stakeholder groups. More and more conflict between business and these groups can be expected concerning controversial issues such as the environment, civil rights, product safety, animal rights, and many other issues. Employees who sympathize with activists in various interest groups may be torn between their feelings toward these groups and loyalty to their organizations. When confronted with ethical conflicts which force them to choose between competing loyalties, they may choose actions which are consistent with their perceived obligations to individuals and groups outside the organization.

3. The ineffectiveness of retaliation. Although it seems that organizations sometimes punish whistleblowers to silence them or to persuade other employees to keep silent, there is little if any empirical evidence that such tactics work. In fact, employees who blow the whistle to parties outside the organization generally do so because their efforts at internal resolution have been frustrated by unconcerned or hostile supervisors, top managers, etc. They are aware that their actions may bring adverse personal consequences, but are willing to run the risk to call attention to what they believe is morally or ethically unacceptable.

Whether whistleblowers' actions are justified or not, and whether their concerns are legitimate or not, retaliation accomplishes little and may cost much. It is simply not a viable long-term strategy for dealing with employee dissenters.

4. The potential for internal resolution. As the cases cited earlier clearly show, when organizational "dirty laundry" is exposed publicly, it can do great harm. The reputation of the firm suffers. The financial performance of the company may be affected. The organization may find itself sued by those who feel they have been harmed by the actions of the company.

Whistleblowing policies offer the opportunity for internal resolution of sensitive issues. Employees who use the internal channels established by such policies actually do organizations a great favor by giving them the chance to investigate employees' concerns before those concerns become public. If investigation reveals legitimate problems, at least organizations have the chance to correct them without the glare of publicity.

Many times, illegalities or morally dubious activities are taking place in organizations without the knowledge or consent of top executives. The internal communication channels established by whistleblowing policies may prevent top management from being blindsided by public disclosures of alleged wrongdoing.

Now we can define the practical imperative. You cannot expect that wrongdoing, or the perception of wrongdoing, can be entirely eliminated in your company, even if you develop ethics codes, preach ethical behavior to employees, and practice what you preach. If unethical behavior is occurring, the possibility of whistleblowing is very real. Neither taking an inactive stance toward whistleblowing, nor actively retaliating against employees who blow the whistle, are successful long-term strategies. Your organization should take proactive steps to resolve ethical and moral conflicts.

The practical imperative is to prevent public disclosure of alleged wrongdoing. Establishing a whistleblowing policy that creates internal communication channels through which employees can express their concerns about questionable activities is one of the more useful steps you can take to protect your organization from unexpected public disclosures. If employees can be persuaded that you are serious about responding to their ethical concerns, it seems unlikely they will feel compelled to blow the whistle on your company. Ethical problems may be solved internally, instead of showing up on the front pages and television news shows.

The Ethical Imperative

So far, I have offered both a legal and practical imperative for organizations to establish whistleblowing policies. I also believe there is an ethical imperative, which I will explain next.

1. The potential for improving the ethical climate. I have already noted the continuing problem of unethical behavior in business and government. Many business leaders express concern about improving the ethical climate within their organizations but do not know how to do it. As academics, we have told executives to develop ethics codes which spell out standards of conduct. Many have done this, only to find that they seem to make little genuine difference in the behavior of employees. What else can be done?

I believe that whistleblowing policies can "put teeth" in ethics codes by institutionalizing both the process employees can use to share their ethical concerns and the process by which organizations respond. Effective whistleblowing policies may improve the ethical climate by increasing employees' confidence that their ethical concerns will be taken seriously and that they will not be punished for good-faith attempts to report perceived violations of the ethics code.

2. The need for fairness. Most companies develop a wide variety of policies concerning issues such as selection, performance appraisal, promotion, and compensation. One of the key reasons for developing such policies is the need to provide equitable treatment to employees. In other words, the objective of many personnel policies is to ensure that employees are treated fairly.

Whistleblowing policies also should be motivated by the desire to treat employees fairly. First, individuals concerned about possible wrongdoing within the organization, who honestly express their concerns, should be treated fairly. Those who find themselves the target of whistleblowers' accusations should be treated fairly. Whistleblowing policies can help ensure that all employees concerned receive equitable treatment by standardizing the way such situations are handled.

Whistleblowing policies can also ensure that employees' right to free speech isn't violated. This right is not absolute. Employees do not have the right to make malicious or irresponsible charges of wrongdoing that are not supported by facts. They do not have the right to disrupt the workplace just because they think organizational actions are unwise or because they disagree with company policy. But they should not be expected to go along silently when they are aware of probable wrongdoing, or when they are asked to do something they feel violates the law or generally accepted moral standards.

Recognizing employees' right to speech does not imply that organizational leaders must abandon traditional authority structures or abdicate their responsibilities as managers. What it does mean is that organizations recognize employees' legitimate right to express concerns with organizational practices that they believe violate the law or generally accepted moral standards.

Now we can summarize the ethical imperative. It is a rare organization indeed that does not pay lip service to ethical conduct among its employees. And yet we are constantly besieged by reports of scandals in business and government. Obviously, more is required of your organization than writing an ethics code and distributing it once a year to your employees. You must take proactive steps to improve your company's ethical climate.

The ethical imperative is to create a just workplace. In this context, I consider a just workplace to be one where:
- your organization is committed to high standards of ethical conduct;
- employees' right to express concern about perceived moral or ethical problems to appropriate parties inside the organization is protected; and
- all employees are treated fairly when questions of unethical or immoral behavior are raised.

I believe that whistleblowing policies can contribute to a just workplace by helping to improve the ethical climate and by helping to ensure that employee rights are respected.

Wrongdoing cannot be corrected unless organizational leaders are aware of it. Whistleblowing policies should promote more open communication about sensitive ethical and moral issues. One research study suggests that formal whistleblowing policies do indeed encourage such communication.[11] The policies should make your organization's code of conduct more relevant by making it more likely that violators will be held accountable.

A primary goal of personnel policies is the fair treatment of employees. Whistleblowing policies should increase the chances that both whistleblowers and those who are targeted by their accusations will be treated equitably.

A Final Word

I have discussed briefly the essential components of whistleblowing policies and have presented what I believe to be three imperatives that compel your organization to consider adopting such a policy. In summary, I believe that organizations should establish whistleblowing policies in order to:
- prevent retaliation against employees for expressing concerns about perceived wrongdoing (the legal imperative);
- prevent public disclosures of alleged organizational wrongdoing, (the practical imperative); and
- create a more just workplace (the ethical imperative).

In closing, let me point out that I certainly do not believe that whistleblowing policies are a panacea for all ethical problems. Indeed, establishing such policies is just the first step. Communicating to employees the policy is equally crucial, and this means more than just an annual letter from the CEO. Ethical training sessions should be undertaken to acquaint employees with ethical dilemmas unique to your organization. Concrete examples of the types of activities that should be disclosed through internal whistleblowing channels should be discussed with employees. Employees should understand that they must be responsible in making accusations of wrongdoing, and that malicious or reckless charges are not sanctioned. Employees should understand how the organization will respond to their concerns in terms of an investigative process.[12]

The policy must be more than words on paper. Writing a policy, adopting it, and then going on with business as usual will do nothing to protect your company or to improve ethical conduct. The policy must reflect the real commitment of your organization to prevent retaliation against employee whistleblowers; encourage employees with ethical concerns to discuss them internally rather than externally; and create an overall environment within which employees have the opportunity and desire to behave ethically and responsibly.

References

1. Jos, P. E., Tompkins, M. E., and Hays, S. W. (1989), "In Praise of Difficult People: A Portrait of the Committed Whistleblower," *Public Administration Review*, November–December, 552–561.

2. Hamilton, J. (1991), "Blowing the Whistle Without Paying the Piper," *Business Week*, June 3, 138–139.

3. Miceli, M. P., and Near, J. P. (1985), "Characteristics of Organizational Climate and Perceived Wrongdoing Associated with Whistleblowing Decisions," *Personnel Psychology*, 41, 525–544.
   Miceli, M. P., Roach, B. L., and Near, J. P. (1988), "The Motivations of 'Deep Throat': The Case of Anonymous Whistleblowers," *Public Personnel Psychology*, 17, 281–296.

4. Miceli, M. P., and Near, J. P. (1988), "Individual and Situational Correlates of Whistleblowing," *Personnel Psychology*, 41, 267–281.

5. Near, J. P. and Jensen, T. C. (1983), "The Whistleblowing Process: Retaliation and Perceived Effectiveness," *Work and Occupations*, 10, 3–28.
   Keenan, J. P. (1988), "Communication Climate, Whistleblowing, and the First-Level Manager: A Preliminary Study," Paper presented at the *Southern Academy of Management*, Atlanta.

6. Boyle, R. (1990), "A Review of Whistle Blower Protections and Suggestions for Change," *Labor Law Journal*, 41, 821–831.

7. Parliman, G. C. (1987), "Protecting the Whistleblower," *Personnel Administrator*, 32, (July), 26–32.

8. Hames, D. S. (1988), "The Current Status of the Doctrine of Employment-At-Will," *Labor Law Journal*, 39, 19–32.

9. Malin, M. H. (1983), "Protecting the Whistleblower from Retaliatory Discharge," *University of Michigan Journal of Law Reform*, 16, 277–318.
   Massengill, D. and Petersen, D. J. (1989), "Whistleblowing: Protected Activity or Not?" *Employee Relations Law Journal*, 15, 49–56.

10. Near, J. P. and Miceli, M. P. (1986), "Retaliation Against Whistleblowers: Predictors and Effects," *Journal of Applied Psychology*, 71, 137–145.

11. Barnett, T. R., Cochran, D. S., and Taylor, G. S. (1990), "The Relationship Between Internal Dissent Policies and Employee Whistle-Blowing; An Exploratory Study," Paper presented at the *National Academy of Management Meeting*, San Francisco.

12. Barnett, T. R. and Cochran, D. S. (1991), "Making Room for the Whistleblower," *HRMagazine*, January, 58–61.

Implementing Business Ethics

Patrick E. Murphy

Patrick E. Murphy is an Associate Professor of Marketing in the College of Business Administration at the University of Notre Dame. He is coeditor of Marketing Ethics: Guidelines for Managers, *Lexington Books, 1985 (with G. R. Laczniak). His articles on ethics have appeared in* Journal of Marketing, Review of Marketing *and* Advances in Marketing and Public Policy. *Professor Murphy currently serves as editor of the* Journal of Public Policy and Marketing.

ABSTRACT. This article outlines an approach for *implementing* business ethics. A company should both organize for ethical business policies and execute them. The organizational dimension refers to structural components including codes of ethics, conferences and training programs and an ethical audit. The corporate culture must support these structural elements with top management playing a central role in implementing ethics.

The execution of ethical business policies includes implementation responsibilities and tasks. These responsibilities are leadership in ethics, delegation, communication and motivation of the company's ethical position to employees. Execution tasks are delineated for the marketing function. Although many company examples are provided, a program in place at McDonnell Douglas is highlighted as a model of ethics implementation.

Introduction

Most organizations have learned that it is not enough to have a well designed corporate strategy in place. Equally important is to be able to *implement* this strategy. In fact, one projection is that only about ten percent of all strategies are effectively implemented. If implementation is to succeed, the entire organization must be committed to the strategy and even the smallest detail should not be overlooked. The same is true with ethics. Implementing ethics is not just a concern of managers setting the firm's overall strategic direction, but should pervade all levels of the business.

Recent events concerning unethical business practices not only on Wall Street, but also in many other places, appear to highlight the lack of attention to implementation of ethical policies. The existence of a carefully defined ethical code does not guarantee ethical behavior. A good example is General Electric (GE). The company has long had a formal, written code of conduct that is communicated to employees and perceives itself as a leader in subscribing to ethical business practices. Yet, GE ran into trouble in 1985 for having time cards forged at a Pennsylvania defense plant. This situation caused a suspension of new defense contracts for a time and much embarrassment for the firm. More recently, their Kidder Peabody subsidiary was implicated in the insider trading scandal even though GE was assured before their June, 1986 acquisition of Kidder that the firm faced no major problems with the SEC or Justice Department. These events lead to a management shake-up at Kidder. GE found that it is quite difficult to implement ethics in their far flung range of businesses.

What can be done to make sure that ethical policies are implemented and that the firm will steer clear of wrongdoings that result in legal problems and/or bad press? The answer is not an easy one. This article outlines steps that companies might use in carrying out ethical business practices. Implementing business ethics involves organizing for and executing ethical policies.[1] The organizational aspects of implementation are covered initially and then we will turn our attention to executing ethical strategies.

This paper takes a pragmatic, rather than a philosophical, approach to examining ethics. The manager is pulled from several directions — personal, organizational and market — in reconciling ethical dilemmas.[2] Making good moral judgments requires frank discussions and ethical sensitivity. This point was well articulated by B. H. McCoy (1983): "In contrast to philosophy, business involves action and implementation — getting things done. Managers must come up with answers to problems based on what they see and what they allow to influence their decision making process."

Organizing for ethical business policies

Figure 1 lists the organizational dimensions of business ethics and procedures that will bring about the implementation of ethical company practices. *Structure* refers to formal organizational mechanisms that foster ethical decisions. *Culture* pertains to the informal organizational climate.

Structure

Corporate codes have long been viewed as the major organizational structure in which to implement ethical policy. Research indicates that approximately 90 percent of *Fortune 500* firms and almost half of all companies have codes in place (Center for Business Ethics, 1986; Murphy, 1986). Several writers, the first being the late Ted Purcell, S. J. (1978), have viewed ethical codes as the cornerstone to "institutionalizing" ethics. However, codes of conduct continue to be criticized as being too general, containing too many platitudes, serving purely as public relations ploys or being designed strictly to avoid legal problems (Berenbeim, 1987; Wartzman, 1987). Cressey and

---

Organizing for Ethical Business Policies

Structure: the formal organization | Culture: the informal organization

Corporate codes | Open and candid
  Specific
  Public documents
  Blunt and realistic | Management role
  Revised periodically

Committees, conferences
and training

Ethical audit
questions

- -

Executing Ethical Business Policies

Implementation responsibilities | Implementation tasks

Leadership | Product alteration
Delegation | Price negotiation
Communication | Place determination
Motivation | Promotion presentation

Fig. 1. Implementing business ethics.

Moore (1983) found that codes give more attention to unethical conduct likely to decrease firm's profits than to conduct that might increase profits. After closely examining over 50 corporate codes of ethics, several observations can be offered.

If codes, are to serve as a foundation for implementation, they should possess the characteristics listed in the Figure 1. Corporate codes should be *specific*. Employees need guidance in interpreting their actions. Motorola gives specific examples (i.e., A Motorolan traveling on Motorola business may accept the courtesy of free lodging in a customer facility so long as properly noted on the Motorolan's expense records) after each of the sections of its code. IBM lists three types of activities — mandatory, acceptable and unacceptable — in its Business Conduct Guidelines.

An area needing specificity is gifts and entertainment. Several companies state that employees can give or receive gifts of "nominal," "token" or "modest" value. However, it is very difficult to determine what is nominal or token and when a gift becomes a bribe. A number of companies have made their codes more specific in this area. Ford and GM stipulate that employees cannot give or receive gifts exceeding $25. Waste Management defines nominal value as "not exceeding $100 in aggregate annual value." Donnelly Mirrors gives the following guidelines: "If you can't eat it, drink it or use it up in one day, don't give it or anything else of greater value."

Second, codes should be *public documents*. Some corporate codes are exclusively for internal corporate use. If a code is worth developing, it should demonstrate to customers, suppliers, stockholders and others interested in the company the organization's commitment to fair and ethical practice.

Corporate codes should also be *blunt and realistic about violations*. For example, Baxter's code states that violators will be terminated. Gellerman (1986) indicated that the most effective deterrent is not to increase the severity of the punishment, but to "heighten the perceived probability of being caught." Therefore, active enforcement of existing codes should enhance compliance. Firms also need to consider how employees should react when confronted with violations of the code. Several codes instruct them to talk to their supervisor. Difficulties arise when the supervisor is the violator. Marriott tells employees to "see your manager or department head" if the issue cannot be resolved with the immediate supervisor.

Finally, codes should be *revised periodically*. That is, they should be living documents and updated to reflect current ethical problems. Caterpillar has revised its code three times since 1974. Investment banking firms likely would want to revise their codes in light of recent events. Specifically, Goldman Sachs now lists fourteen business principles and the last one states: "Integrity and honesty are at the heart of our business. We expect our people to maintain high ethical standards in everything they do, both at work for the firm and in their personal lives." This point probably should be placed much higher on the list and given greater emphasis in future revisions.

Ethics committees, training and conferences are a second structural method for implementing ethical business policies (see Figure 1). Only 15 percent of firms have ethics modules in their training programs and about 30 percent discuss ethics in management or policy sessions (Murphy, 1986). Motorola has a Business Ethics Compliance Committee that is charged with interpreting, clarifying, communicating and ajudicating the company's code. Some firms have used ethical consultants or speakers at dealer meetings on ethics. Cummins Engine for a time had an in-house ethicist. Polaroid held day long in-house conferences on ethics in '83 and '84 as part of a major ethics program.[3]

The Drackett Company, a subsidiary of Bristol Myers, recently implemented an ethics module in their 1987 Market Research Conference. Attendees at the meeting submitted in advance their responses to sixteen ethical scenarios. During the meeting small groups met to discuss three of the eleven scenarios where there was the greatest disagreement. According to the manager who led this activity, it was enthusiastically received. Many of the participants were surprised by their colleagues' judgments, but enjoyed the interchange in analyzing these issues.

Another structural suggestion for implementing business ethics listed in Figure 1 is an ethical audit. Just as financial and marketing audits seek to gain information about these functions, an ethical audit would pose questions about manufacturing practices, personnel policies, dealings with suppliers, financial reporting and sales techniques to find out if ethical abuses may be occurring. It might be argued that the answers to such questions are less important than raising and grappling with the issues.

Dow Corning instituted a face-to-face audit in their firm over ten years ago at company locations throughout the world. The agenda has shifted over the years from a standard one of 8–10 items for each site to a tailored discussion of specific questions about functional areas. At sales offices, issues such as kickbacks, unusual requests from customers and special pricing terms are examined. John Swanson, who heads this effort as Manager of the Corporate Internal and Management Communications Division, explained that the benefit of their innovative audit approach is "to make it virtually impossible for employees to consciously make an unethical decision."[4] Swanson (1987) indicated that twenty-one meetings were led by one of the four Business Conduct Committee members in '86–'87 and a report was prepared for the Audit Committee of the Board. He emphasized that there are no shortcuts to implementing this program and it requires time and extensive interaction of the people involved.

Culture

The informal organization or corporate culture is the second component of the organizational dimension of ethics implementation (see Figure 1). Some commentators have indicated that the informal organization is much more important in the development of the firm's ethical posture than the formal organization. The informal organization creates the culture and formal policies are then a reflection of that culture. It works well at Hewlett-Packard, where the firm follows policies of liberal health benefits and no layoffs, because Bill Hewlett and David Packard want to remain true to the ideals on which the firm was founded. On the negative side, the recent revelations of nepotism and bribe taking by executives at Anheuser Busch was at least partially explained by observers who criticized the Busch family for perpetuating a corporate culture that condoned these activities. Therefore, the informal organization must reward ethical activities and give signals to managers that the company is committed to integrity in all business dealings.

A candid and ethical culture is one where communication freely flows within the organization (Serpa, 1985). This type of culture can help to reduce "moral stress" (Waters and Bird, 1987) and achieve "moral excellence" (Hoffman, 1986). A number of individuals including a CEO of a Big Eight accounting firm have advocated this approach to dealing with ethical problems. A climate where ethical issues can be openly discussed can lead to this type of culture. Spending time in management meetings is one avenue that has been used effectively. This sort of ethical training should ideally occur before problems arise and not after the fact such as the instance of E. F. Hutton and General Dynamics

contracting with the Ethics Resource Center for ethics training after running into serious problems.

The role of top management is crucial in creating the culture of an organization. The tone starts at the top. The CEO and other Vice-President level executives are extremely important in setting the ethical tenor of the firm.

Executing ethical business policies

Figure 1 also shows the two components of the executing phase of business ethics implementation. It is not enough to have the structure and culture that support ethical decision making. These organizational dimensions must be combined with implementation responsibilities and tasks so that a firm is ethical in its execution of strategies.

Implementation responsibilities

Although there are four execution responsibilities listed in the Figure, the over-arching one is leadership. As Bennis and Nanus (1986) have stated: American corporations are over-managed and under-led. Leadership is important in all aspects of the business, but it is critical in the ethics area.[5] Horton (1986) examined characteristics of CEOs and listed integrity as an "indispensible ingredient." A good example is James Burke of Johnson & Johnson who had managers evaluate the J & J Credo (which is often given as the reason for the swift and ethical reaction to the Tylenol poisonings). Basically, they reaffirmed the company's longstanding commitment to ethical business practice. A recent illustration is Lee Iacocca's stance regarding Chrysler's questionable practice of disconnecting odometers during testing by executives. He admitted that the company made mistakes in judgment and set forth a program to rectify them and promised that they would not happen again in a two page national ad. Mr. Iacocca did not view this as a product recall, but added "the only thing we're recalling here is our integrity."

Delegation follows from leadership, but is an essential responsibility for effective implementation to occur. Middle and lower level managers are sometimes placed in difficult ethical situations because high level executives are unclear in their delegation of ethical responsibilities. Statements such as "I don't care how you do it, just meet or beat your quota" or "Ship more to that customer this month than you did last" or "Find a way to fire that person" often give subordinates the impression that any tactic can be used to reach organizational objectives. Several years ago managers in a truck plant installed a secret control box to override the speed of the assembly line because they felt it was the only way to achieve production objectives set by upper management. If the delegation responsibility is to be dispatched properly, executives must be more explicit about what are acceptable and ethical practices.

Communication is an essential responsibility if ethical policies are to be executed in any organization. Formally, this communication can happen in many ways through the ethical code and seminars/ training programs that deal with ethical issues. New employees of most companies are asked to read and sign the ethical code upon their employment. In many instances, however, little communication follows the initial exposure. To overcome this potential problem, Caterpillar requires its managers to report annually about its implementation of the code within the division/department. Similarly, Michigan National Bank requires that employees sign off on the ethical code every year.

Informal communication is also a potentially effective implementation responsibility. The grapevine can disseminate information that formal vehicles cannot. For instance, the fact that a salesperson lost his/her commission for padding the expense account may not lend itself to discussion in the company newsletter. However, the word can get through informal channels and consequently influence future behavior.

The last, but certainly the not the least important, implementation responsibility is motivation. If companies are to be successful in executing ethical marketing policies, individuals must be motivated to do the right thing. This means that higher level executives must look closely at how performance is measured. Managers who engage in exorbitant entertaining of clients or informally practice discrimination should not be rewarded for these activities. One of the problems with the Wall Street scandal was that top managers did not look closely at the large profits their firms were earning. How did these large returns happen? Unfortunately, we know the answer in many cases. Employees are motivated by higher level executives and their expectations regarding ethical business practices.

Implementation tasks

Implementation tasks relate to specific functional areas within the firm. One area that has received

much attention in the academic and popular press is marketing implementation (Bonoma, 1984; Enis and Murphy, 1987; Peters and Waterman, 1982). Since marketing is charged with external relations with customers where many ethical issues arise, it will serve as the focal point for this discussion. Other functional areas could be treated similarly. For example, if human resources were the focus, tasks relating to hiring, training and promoting employees would be relevant.

Figure 1 lists the relevant implementation tasks for the marketing mix variables of product, price, channel and promotion. Product alteration is intended to get the consumer to make the intended exchange. Ethical issues result when minor adjustments are promoted as being significant changes to the product. Furthermore, the development of me-too products could be questioned from an ethical standpoint. One other product alteration issue relates to the product manager. Does this person, who is usually on the fast-track, make needed modifications to a brand to insure its long-term marketplace staying power or only perform cosmetic changes to improve next quarter's market share or profit picture?

Price negotiation is often at the heart of marketing implementation. Those sales executives and marketing managers who can effectively negotiate on price win many contracts. An ethical problem occurs in this process when one of the participants has much more power than the other. An example is a large Midwestern department store chain which dealt with a small candy producer and told the company that they would pay 70 percent of the negotiated price and the small firm could keep the account or pay 100 percent and they would lose the account. These types of practices are unethical, but not illegal. They possibly might be curbed by the small firm taking its case to the top echelon of the larger company.

Place determination refers to getting the product to the place it is demanded in an expeditious manner. Here marketers often promise more than they can deliver. It becomes an ethical issue when there is economic or psychological harm to the client/consumer. In health care or other life threatening situations, execution of place determination is critical. Greater emphasis on marketing by these organizations may heighten the ethical problems they face. Furthermore, large retailers may coerce other members of the channel to achieve their objectives in getting products to the market.

Promotion presentation is often viewed as a

crucial function of marketing. Both selling and advertising have persuasive, informative and reminding components. The persuasive area is most often associated with ethical abuses. In selling, ethical problems often arise when persuasion is too intense or competitors are unscrupulous in their appeals. What the ethical salesperson should do is to insure that the buyers are making decisions on what he/she believes are the most important evaluative criteria. If the unethical marketer cannot deliver on their promises, the ethical firm has a good chance to gain the business. Even if the business is lost once, there is sometimes an opportunity to gain it later. For example, a communications firm sought a contract with a defense contractor, but found the defense company only wanted entree to newspaper editors. The consultant indicated that he could not meet these unrealistic goals and ". . . walked out. Several months later he got a $50,000 contract" (Davidson, 1986).

Some companies even identify the types of sales tactics that are acceptable in their firm's code of ethics. For instance, ADP, a computer software company, states: "Aggressive selling should not include defamation of competition, malicious rumors or unsupportable promises." IBM's code makes a similar point: "It has long been the company's policy to provide customers the best possible products and services. Sell them on their merits, not by disparaging competitors."

The advertising area is one where persuasion is often criticized for being unethical. If the message includes puffery, but not deception (which is illegal), then it falls into an ethical gray area. One type of advertising that is receiving growing criticism is advertising to children, especially for war toys and highly sugared products. Furthermore, the current debate about advertising beer and wine on television centers on free speech vs. potential negative effects of product usage on consumers, especially teenagers who find the lifestyles portrayed in these commercials to be rather desirable.

In examining a number of codes of conduct, it was surprising to find that very few list a specific posture with respect to advertising. An exception is Ford which provides explicit policies for the use of comparative advertising. This might be an area where consumer products marketers consider developing explicit guidelines. Some have ad hoc policies regarding sponsorship of shows dealing with sensitive subjects or containing large amounts of sex/violence. It appears that thought should be given to appropriate advertising messages and possibly even

media in implementing the ethical policies of the firm.

An illustration of business ethics implementation

In 1987 one firm, McDonnell Douglas, has engaged in an extensive business ethics implementation program.[6] Their effort even has a theme — "Always take the high road." The corporate code has been revised for the third time in the 1980s. A series of three ethics books were distributed to all employees at their home address in June. The "Code of Ethics" book features ethical decision making guidelines, a short version of their code and the ethical decision making checklist. The latter two are also available in pocket size cards and are shown in Figure 2.

The "Standards of Business Conduct" book lists five overriding standards and several areas pertaining to each of them. Discussion of these standards is treated in three sections — *In General* (states the overall principle), *Specifically* (contains specific rules, laws and requirements applicable to each standard) and *Where to Go* (where to turn to for help). This book concludes with a section on procedures for reporting possible violations including employees' obligation to report, confidentiality and absence of reprisals.

The third book, "Questions and Answers," shows how selected standards apply in potentially difficult work situations through a question and detailed answer format. This publication is written in layman's terms and cross referenced to the longer standards book. The company also has a corporation-wide ethics training program that all management and blue collar employees attend. A seven person ethics committee is formally charged with implementing all facets of the program.

The informal organization is involved in several ways. An extensive ombudsman program is operational as well as a number of instructions to employees to openly discuss and air ethical abuses they see occurring. At the end of the "Questions and Answers" book, employees are asked for their comments or questions on ethical issues. These informal responses are to be returned directly to the Corporate Ethics Committee. Another alternative for responding about ethical problems and violations is a hotline number used exclusively for reports to this committee.

The role of top management is instrumental in making the program work. S. N. "Sandy" McDonnell,

McDONNELL DOUGLAS CODE OF ETHICS

Integrity and ethics exist in the individual or they do not exist at all. They must be upheld by individuals or they are not upheld at all. In order for integrity and ethics to be characteristics of McDonnell Douglas, we who make up the Corporation must strive to be:

- *Honest and trustworthy in all our relationships;*
- *Reliable in carrying out assignments and responsibilities;*
- *Truthful and accurate in what we say and write;*
- *Cooperative and constructive in all work undertaken;*
- *Fair and considerate in our treatment of fellow employees, customers, and all other persons;*
- *Law abiding in all our activities;*
- *Committed to accomplishing all tasks in a superior way;*
- *Economical in utilizing company resources; and*
- *Dedicated in service to our company and to improvement of the quality of life in the world in which we live.*

Integrity and high standards of ethics require hard work, courage, and difficult choices. Consultation among employees, top management, and the Board of Directors will sometimes be necessary to determine a proper course of action. Integrity and ethics may sometimes require us to forgo business opportunities. In the long run, however, we will be better served by doing what is right rather than what is expedient. (From MDC Policy 2, *MDC Policy Manual*).

ETHICAL DECISION MAKING CHECKLIST

Analysis

- *What are the facts?*
- *Who is responsible to act?*
- *What are the consequences of action? (Benefit-Harm Analysis)*
- *What and whose rights are involved? (Rights/Principles Analysis)*
- *What is fair treatment in this case? (Social Justice Analysis)*

Solution development

- *What solutions are available to me?*
- *Have I considered all of the creative solutions which might permit me to reduce harm, maximize benefits, respect more rights, or be fair to more parties?*

Select the optimum solution

- *What are the potential consequences of my solutions?*
- *Which of the options I have considered does the most to maximize benefits, reduce harm, respect rights and increase fairness?*
- *Are all parties treated fairly in my proposed decision?*

Implementation

- *Who should be consulted and informed?*
- *What actions will assure that my decision achieves its intended outcome?*
- *Implement.*

Follow up

- *Was the decision implemented correctly?*
- *Did the decision maximize benefits, reduce harm, respect rights and treat all parties fairly?*

Fig. 2. McDonnell Douglas ethical code and check list.

the former CEO, has been on the forefront in advocating ethical practices in the aerospace industry. He has taken a leadership role as evidenced by the following comment made in 1984:

A company has to go beyond just tacking an ethics code up on the wall. You have to make sure that everyone knows and understands it — from the chairman on down through supervision (Miller 1984);

and this statement which appeared in a 1987 company publication describing his commitment to the current ethics program:

What I hope all this will lead to is a business environment in which the issue of ethics remains in the forefront of everything we do. If we always make the ethical choice, if we always take the high road, we will be doing not only what is right, but also what is best for McDonnell Douglas and ourselves as individuals.

A procedure is delegated and communicated throughout the organization in the form of the company's "ethical decision making" check list in Figure 2. The steps outlined are analysis, solution development, selection of the optimum solution, implementation and follow-up parallel closely those advocated by Nash (1981) several years ago. These mechanisms have motivated employees to become more active in providing comments and suggestions on how ethics can be improved in the firm. This complete ethics implementation program can serve as a model for other companies.[7]

Conclusion

The major premise articulated here is that firms can ethically implement their business strategies. Several conclusions can be drawn.

1. Codes of ethics must be more than legal or public relations documents. They must provide specific and useful guidance to employees. Firms are urged to rethink their codes to make them more viable by including specific practices, examples or answers to often asked ethical questions.

2. Visible signs must exist that ethics matters to the firm. This can be accomplished by spending time in formal meetings discussing ethical issues and working through the corporate culture. Both the carrot and stick methods should be used. Employees should be rewarded for making ethical choices and at the same time the code must be enforced. These actions must be communicated throughout the firm, so that the commitment is understood.

3. Top management must pay attention to detail on how results are accomplished. The same scrutiny should be employed when examining profits as costs. Similarly, management should not give vague or unrealistic goals to subordinates without some explanation of how they are to be attained.

4. Ethics implementation needs a champion. Someone must make it happen. It is essential that the CEO be in support of it, but in companies like McDonnell Douglas and Polaroid the ethics cause had a champion. This is likely most effective if the job title in not solely related to this task.

In implementing business ethics, attention must be paid to both the organizing and executing components (see Figure 1). Only if managers and top executives are consciously committed to carrying out ethical policies will implementation actually occur. Tough questions must be asked and appropriate answers should be given at all levels of the organization. We can improve the ethical posture of business, but everyone must be committed to it.

Notes

The author would like to thank Gerald Cavanagh, S. J., Stephen Greyser, Gene Laczniak, Lee Tavis, Clarence Walton and Oliver Williams, C. S. C. for their helpful comments on an earlier version of this article.

[1] This definition and format of the article are partially adapted from "Marketing Implementation," in Murphy and Enis (1985).
[2] The following discussion of implementing business ethics relies primarily on structural or organization procedures. An alternative approach which focuses on individual responsibilities is outlined by Nielsen (1986).
[3] For a discussion of Polaroid's program, see Godfrey (1987) and Godfrey and Williams (1985).
[4] For more detail on this program, see Swanson (1984) and ("Dow Corning" . . . 1986).
[5] A recent in-depth examination of the ethical leadership issue appeared in Enderle (1987).
[6] McDonnell Douglas is a participant in the eighteen point voluntary industry agreement, "The Defense Industry Initiatives on Business Ethics and Conduct." The company's commitment to ethics is the driving force for this program, not industry or governmental pressure.
[7] Although McDonnell Douglas was implicated in recent U.S. Defense Department contract problems, the company feels that its policies are sound and set up a high level task force to determine whether additional guidelines are needed. The CEO stated: "We want to leave no doubt that McDonnell Douglas believes in and acts in accordance with the highest ethical standards" (Schachter 1988).

References

Bennis, Warren and Bert Nanus: 1985, *Leaders*, New York: Harper & Row.

Berenbeim, Ronald E.: 1987, *Corporate Ethics*, New York: The Conference Board.

Bonoma, Thomas V.: 1984, 'Making Your Marketing Strategy Work', *Harvard Business Review* (March—April), 69—76.

Center for Business Ethics: 1986, 'Are Corporations Institutionalizing Ethics?', *Journal of Business Ethics* 5, 85—91.

Cressey, Donald R. and Charles A. Moore: (1983), 'Managerial Values and Corporate Codes of Ethics', *California Management Review* (Summer), 53—77.

Davidson, Jeffrey P.: 1986, 'The Elusive Nature of Integrity', *Marketing News* (November 7), 24.

'Dow Corning Corporation: Ethics, "Face-to-Face" ': 1986, *Ethics Resource Center Report* (Winter), 4—7.

Enderle, Georges: 1987, 'Some Perspectives of Managerial Ethical Leadership', *Journal of Business Ethics* **6**, 657—663.

Enis, Ben M. and Patrick E. Murphy: 1987, 'Marketing Strategy Implementation', in G. L. Frazier and J. N. Sheth (eds.), *Contemporary Views on Marketing Practice*, Lexington, MA: Lexington Books, pp. 159—173.

Gellerman, Saul W.: 1986, 'Why "Good" Managers Make Bad Ethical Choices', *Harvard Business Review* (July—August), 85—90.

Godfrey, Joline: 1987, 'Ethics as an Entrepreneurial Venture', *Training News* (June).

Godfrey, Joline and R. Williams: 1985, 'Leadership and Values at Polaroid Corporation', unpublished paper.

Hoffman, W. Michael: 1986, 'What Is Necessary for Corporate Moral Excellence?', *Journal of Business Ethics* **5**, 233—242.

Horton, Thomas R.: 1986, *What Works for Me: 16 CEOs Talk About Their Careers and Commitments*, New York: Random House.

McCoy, Bowen H.: 1983, 'The Parable of the Sadhu', *Harvard Business Review* (September—October), 103—108.

Miller, William H.: 1984, 'Business' New Link: Ethics and the Bottom Line', *Industry Week* (October 29), 49—53.

Murphy, Patrick E.: 1986, 'Marketing VPs Views Toward Marketing Ethics', Working Paper, University of Notre Dame.

Murphy, Patrick E. and Ben M. Enis: 1985, *Marketing*, Glenview, IL: Scott-Foresman.

Nash, Laura: 1981, 'Ethics Without the Sermon', *Harvard Business Review*, (November—December), 79—90.

Nielsen, Richard P.: 1987, 'What Can Managers Do about Unethical Management?', *Journal of Business Ethics* **6**, 309—320.

Peters, Thomas J. and Robert H. Waterman, Jr.: 1982, *In Search of Excellence*, New York: Harper & Row.

Purcell, Theodore V., Jr.: 1978, 'Institutionalizing Ethics on Corporate Boards', *Review of Social Economy*, December, 41—53.

Schachter, Jim: 1988, 'McDonnell Douglas to Probe Use of Defense Officials as Consultants', *Los Angeles Times* (August 5, 1988), Part IV, 3.

Serpa, Roy: 1985, 'Creating a Candid Corporate Culture', *Journal of Business Ethics* **4**, 425—430.

Swanson, John E.: 1984, 'Developing a Workable Corporate Ethic', in W. M. Hoffman, J. M. Moore, and D. A. Fedo (eds.), *Corporate Governance and Institutionalizing Ethics*, Lexington, MA: Lexington Books, pp. 209—215.

Swanson, John E.: 1987, Personal communication with the author, June 21.

Wartzman, Rick: 1987, 'Nature or Nurture? Study Blames Ethical Lapses on Corporate Goals', *The Wall Street Journal* (October 9), 21.

Waters, James A. and Frederick Bird: 1987, 'The Moral Dimension of Organizational Culture', *Journal of Business Ethics* **6**, 15—22.

Ethical Judgment

We can stimulate and sharpen moral reasoning and ethical judgment by considering decisions in light of certain questions.

SHERRY BAKER

Sherry Baker, a Ph.D. candidate at the University of Utah, Department of Communication, is Assistant Academic Dean at LDS Business College in Salt Lake City, UT (801) 363-2765.

ETHICS IN THE WORKPLACE (applied ethics) has become a hot topic in recent years. Business book titles and academic textbooks and journals are now replete with volumes on ethics.

Why all the concern? We live in a world where new technologies and communication systems have given rise to new ethical questions; where concern for profits often come into conflict with concern for principles; where professions and specializations recognize a need to identify and encourage professional values; and where society is demanding an ethic of social responsibility for corporate action.

Also, there is disturbing evidence of patently unethical behavior all around us—from employee theft of time and materials, to corporate social and environmental irresponsibility, to the unethical and illegal activities of our political and religious leaders. Professionals and scholars have responded with professional codes of ethics, articles about ethics, and courses in ethics, all resulting in more discourse about ethical issues and a greater availability of ethics-related material.

Moral Dilemmas

Despite all this new discourse, executives who face troubling decisions are often confused about how to arrive at the right—the moral—the ethical course of action. This is not surprising since by definition a "moral dilemma" is one where there is no clear right and wrong, only positives and negatives.

Tip-of-the-tongue guidelines such as "Love thy neighbor" rarely suffice when one is faced with an ethical dilemma where no course of action seems to satisfy all ethical responsibilities.

Writers disagree about how to reach an ethical decision or about what criteria must be met for a course of action to be ethical. Some ethicists, for example, stress the need to be concerned with ethical outcomes or consequences, while others are interested in basing action on ethical principles regardless of the outcome; some stress the importance of developing a sterling character while others focus on issues of justice.

While it may be problematic to come up with a set of principles that apply in all cases, we can be guided in our moral reasoning by the insight that comes from asking ourselves the tough questions about personal principles and codes of conduct; respecting the moral rights of others; justice; consequences and outcomes; explaining and defending the decisions we make; and intuition and insight. I include intuition because our judgments often must be rough and intuitive and made, as Manuel G. Velasquez says, at "the edges of the light that ethics can shed on moral reasoning."

Questions to Ask

Assuming a difficult management decision, consider how the following questions might be helpful in identifying points of ethical concern.

Principles and Codes of Conduct
• Does this decision or action meet up to my standards about how people should interact with each other?

• Does this decision or action agree with my religious teachings and beliefs (or with my personal principles and sense of responsibility)?

• How will I feel about myself if I do this?

• Do we (or I) have a rule or policy for cases like this?

• Would I want everyone to make the same decision and take the same action if faced with these same circumstances?

• What are my true motives for considering this action?

Moral Rights
• Would this action infringe or impinge on the moral rights or dignity of others?

• Would this action allow others freedom of choice in this matter?

• Would this action involve deceiving others in any way?

Justice
• Would I feel that this action was just (ethical or fair) if I were on the other side of the decision?

• How would I feel if this action were done to me or to someone close to me?

• Would this action or decision distribute benefits justly?

• Would it distribute hardships or burdens justly?

Consequences and Outcomes
• What will be the short- and long-term consequences of this action?

• Who will benefit from this course of action?

• Who will be hurt?

• How will this action create good and prevent harm?

Public Justification
• How would I feel (or how will I feel) if (or when) this action becomes public knowledge?

• Will I be able to explain adequately to others why I have taken this action?

Reprinted with permission from *Executive Excellence*, March 1992, pp. 7-8. *Executive Excellence*, The Magazine of Personal Development, Managerial Effectiveness, and Organizational Productivity.

• Would others feel that my action or decision is ethical or moral?

Intuition and Insight

• Have I searched for all alternatives? Are there other ways I could look at this situation? Have I considered all points of view?

• Even if there is sound rationality for this decision or action, and even if I could defend it publicly, does my inner sense tell me this is right?

• What does my intuition tell me is the ethical thing to do in this situation? Have I listened to my inner voice?

Moral Reasoning

These questions are a good reference tool that could be helpful for decision-making and for fruitful group discussions when considered in light of specific cases or hypothetical scenarios. Examples of actual difficult cases to discuss can be found in a company's own experience, in newspapers or periodicals, or in books about business ethics.

Just as we stretch and expand our minds through mental exercise, we can stretch and expand our moral reasoning and ethical judgment, and sharpen our ethical sensitivity and moral awareness by thinking through particular dilemmas in light of the questions above.

While all of the questions suggest important ethical considerations, the difficulty is that often what appears to be an ethical decision in light of one consideration might appear to be less ethical in light of another. Eventually we must weigh all alternatives and decide which criteria deserve the highest priority in the particular circumstance facing us.

Submitting an ethical dilemma to a set of questions such as this allows us to identify and to verbalize to ourselves and to others why a particular situation is, in fact, an ethical dilemma, and what basic issues are involved. Identifying the points of difficulty with clarity also allows us to decide what values or considerations must have the most weight in our deliberations and decisions. When we achieve clarity as to the issues of the dilemma, we are better prepared to make a decision that is both right and defensible. (We must remember that our goal is to achieve an ethical course of action, not to find a way to construct a rational argument in support of an unethical decision.)

Ethical dilemmas are poignant in ways that other dilemmas are not because they are concerned with the positive or negative impact of people's actions on other people; with issues of right and wrong, good and bad. We have a basic moral obligation not to cause harm, and we must always weigh our obligation to prevent and alleviate harm. The answers are never easy or absolute, and well-meaning people can disagree on a proper course of action. Still, when faced with an ethical dilemma we can be confident that if we consider all the questions discussed above with real intent and pure motives, our moral reasoning and insight will lead us to basically sound and ethical decisions.

Pepsi Faces Problem in Trying to Contain Syringe Scare

Michael J. McCarthy

Staff Reporter of THE WALL STREET JOURNAL

Pepsi-Cola Co., up and running after what some critics call foot dragging, is mounting a massive public-relations offensive against widespread reports of tampering with its soft drinks.

With more than three dozen reports in at least 20 states of Pepsi cans containing syringes, hypodermic needles—even a bullet—the company has assembled a 12-member crisis-management team at headquarters in Somers, N.Y. The building's sixth floor, where the team has assembled, is being called "the bunker."

The unusual nature of the product-tampering claims has created a dilemma for Pepsi. For one thing, no one as yet has been injured—a situation that might require such action as a limited recall or closing a plant. Moreover, there still hasn't been a single confirmed case of a syringe found in an unopened Pepsi can.

Indeed, the Food and Drug Administration has said it can't find any connection among the growing number of syringe reports.

But to calm mounting fears, Pepsi-Cola President Craig Weatherup has taken to the airwaves in a TV-news blitz that included "Nightline" on Tuesday night and all three network morning shows yesterday to reassure the public that the company's beverages are safe, and to calm mounting fears. He was scheduled to appear last night on "Larry King Live" and the McNeil-Lehrer show, as well.

"We've gone through every can line, every plant, numerous records," Mr. Weatherup said in an interview. "All the evidence points to syringes going into the cans after they were opened." Calling it too early to tell whether there has been any effect on sales, he said the company hasn't moved to recall any products because "there is no health issue."

By contrast, when Perrier Group of America Inc. pulled its bottled water from store shelves in 1990, it was after regulators found bottles with traces of benzene, a poisonous liquid shown to cause cancer in laboratory animals.

Pepsi, a unit of **PepsiCo** Inc., is faxing daily morning updates to its 600 offices, distribution centers and bottlers nationwide, asking them to reassure retailers that Pepsi products are safe and should be kept stocked on store shelves.

"Pepsi is really on the horns of a dilemma," said Steven Fink, president of Lexicon Communications Corp., a Los Angeles crisis-management consulting and public-relations firm. "It's not clear how many of these cases are hoaxes and how many, if any, are real."

Some crisis-management experts, however, think Pepsi should have moved more swiftly when the first two reports of syringes arose in Washington state last week. "They were a little late in getting out in front of it," said Bill Southard, president of Earle Palmer Brown Public Relations in New York, who has helped several companies manage through crises. "Initially they tried to low-key it." And it wasn't until fully a day after reports of tampering popped up in several areas of the country that anyone more senior than a Pepsi spokesman appeared in the media to respond to the problem.

Mr. Southard and others think Pepsi's tack of deflecting blame doesn't combat consumer-confidence problems. In interviews and TV appearances, Mr. Weatherup and other Pepsi officials have emphasized that the speed of the company's production lines and the cleaning methods used in its plants make it virtually impossible to insert objects into cans in a bottling operation.

"Fear is a consumer-sensitivity issue," said Mr. Southard. "It's very important, regardless of the circumstances, to position yourself as a company that is concerned, and to outline specific steps you'll take to get to the bottom of the issue."

Some crisis-management specialists think the sheer amount of negative publicity leaves Pepsi with little choice but to order up a recall, at least in states where reports have been made. "In the Tylenol scare in 1982, you find that Johnson & Johnson was very effective in convincing the American people that it cared as much about customers as money," through its product recall, says Jack Levin, a professor of sociology and criminology at Northeastern University in Boston. "That message hasn't gotten through in Pepsi's recent actions."

Indeed, Mr. Fink, the crisis specialist, said big consumer-product companies periodically experience tampering claims, and he typically advises them to temporarily suspend sales in the immediate area of the incident. "You nip it in the bud in a low-key way—investigate it, fix it, then reintroduce the product without fanfare," he says. "Pepsi had an opportunity to do that early on, and they missed it."

What started as two cases of reported syringes in Diet Pepsi cans in the Seattle-Tacoma area last week quickly mushroomed into more than 35 claims in about 20 states in 48 hours. To date, a single

Reprinted by permission of *The Wall Street Journal*, June 17, 1993, pp. B1, B6. © 1993 by Dow Jones & Company, Inc. All rights reserved worldwide.

person, in Pennsylvania, has been arrested on federal charges of making a false report of finding a syringe in a Pepsi can. Other syringe sightings could well be hoaxes, too. Yesterday, a spokesman for **Coca-Cola** Co. in Atlanta said the company had received two reports of tamperings with its drinks, both of which it believed were false. Still, the FDA is advising people to pour their Pepsi into a glass before drinking it, just to be sure.

David A. Kessler, FDA commissioner, said his agency is investigating each claim seriously. In an interview, he noted that, of the cans the FDA has examined so far, "none has been tampered with, or the packaging altered." He added: "If you go back to the Girl Scout Cookie tampering case in 1984, there were 487 complaints after the first [report]—none of which were substantiated or verified."

Nonetheless, Pepsi may have to contend with public emotion rather than reason. "There's an arm wrestling for the belief of the public," says Tom Pirko, president of BevMark Inc., a beverage consulting company. "And if the public senses that there are so many incidents that that many people couldn't be faking it, then Pepsi could have a disaster."

Most stores seem to be taking a wait-and-see attitude. Vons Cos., the big Los Angeles-based grocery chain, said it hasn't had any noticeable impact on sales. But some customers clearly are wary. At a soft-drink vending machine in an Atlanta Kroger store, Carla Smith, a 28-year-old Kroger employee, said she normally drinks Diet Pepsi. "I was going to buy one today," she said. But, the syringe reports left her uneasy. "Now I'm drinking diet Coke," she says.

Mr. Pirko thinks Pepsi's best defense is to hang tough, and to continue to rely on the FDA as its best ally. Even if Americans have doubts about what a big corporation is telling them, he said, the blessing of the FDA should be convincing.

Mr. Weatherup, who has talked with Dr. Kessler, said it has been frustrating trying to manage through a problem that he believes is wholly out of Pepsi's control. Mr. Weatherup said he expects further arrests in the tampering claims. "We have a fair amount of information in hand that shows that at least in several incidents it was a hoax," he said. He added that it is too early to gauge the effect on Pepsi sales.

In composite trading on the New York Stock Exchange yesterday, PepsiCo stock closed at $35.625, unchanged.

Pepsi's trick will be to convince the public that it is taking the situation seriously and that it cares more about the safety of consumers than sales. If they can accomplish that, said Frederick Koenig, a professor of sociology at Tulane University who has studied business rumors, "they might even get a sympathy backlash because they'll be viewed as a victim."

WHAT WOULD YOU DO?

Promises to Keep

The new employee incentive plan Janice helped design had worked:
Productivity and profits were soaring. How then could she allow the promised bonuses
to be diverted to company executives?

DOUG WALLACE

Doug Wallace does frequent consulting work on corporate ethics, and was formerly the vice president for social policy at Norwest Bank in Minneapolis.

All cases used in What Would You Do? *depict actual events, although individual and company names are changed to protect privacy. Please contact Craig Cox at the Business Ethics office if you have a case to suggest or if you would like to become a guest commentator.*

THE CASE

It was one of those conversations that feels more like nine rounds with a heavyweight boxer than ship talk between two corporate managers. "Well, maybe on second thought," Janice mused, "There are moments when the boxing metaphor is closer to the reality of this place."

Janice Matson wasn't sure how this bout would turn out. She did know, however, that the issue was too important to let someone else decide without trying to do something more. It was the now sorting through.

She recalled how it all began. Her company, Sheridon Computer Services, had gone through a significant reorganization and recognized it needed to change the way employees benefited when the organization reached its growth and profitability goals. As a compensation manager in the human resources department, Janice had been part of a team that eleven months ago recommended a competitive excellence program. The plan would make employees eligible for year-end lump-sum bonuses if Sheridon met predetermined operating profit objectives.

The executive committee had responded enthusiastically to the proposal and promptly approved it. When the news was announced in the employee newsletter there were smiles all around.

But Janice's smile had vanished a few minutes ago, with a sudden turn taken in her hallway banter with Dick Stevens, Sheridon's vice president of finance. Dick had stopped by to discuss another matter, and then abruptly changed the subject. "I just came from a meeting with the executive staff where I provided a peek at preliminary year-end

---

"Are you telling me that executive bonuses come first and that won't leave anything for the employees?"

---

numbers, which basically are good," he said. "I did some calculations and discovered that your competitive excellence bonus program for employees has got a problem. I wanted to give you a warning, and recommend that you dampen the expectations of the folks below."

"What's the problem," Janice asked.

"The executive bonus plans are based on company operating profit, and if the employee bonuses are to be paid before the executive bonuses, the operating profit objective would not be met," Dick explained. "As a result, the executives would not receive their bonuses, which are a major source of their income. We can't disappoint them. They're counting on that bonus as part of their compensation."

Janice was stunned. "Wait a minute, Dick. Are you telling me at the eleventh hour that the executive bonuses come first and that won't leave anything for the employees?"

"Well, I wouldn't put it exactly in those terms," Dick replied. "That sounds abrasive."

She sensed his defensiveness, but pushed ahead. "Do you think that's fair?" she asked. "That's really going to go over well when the employees read that in the newsletter. I wonder what they will think."

Their voices rising in the empty hallway, the two managers sparred fiercely until Dick angrily reminded Janice who held the power here. He was, after all, light years above her in the company hierarchy. "Just bite the bullet, and take the tough action," he barked. "After all, that's what you're paid to do."

He stormed off, leaving Janice fuming outside her office. Damn the ultimatum, she thought, slamming her door and retreating to her desk. She *had* to do right by the employees, didn't she? After she'd calmed down, though, it didn't seem so clear. Some knee-jerk, self-righteous action might make her feel better, but would it save the employee bonus program?

Later, she recounted the conversation with human resources VP Jim Steckel. They acknowledged that executive salaries had been frozen during a couple of lean years, and they were probably counting on this year's bonuses. But so were the employees.

"If there ever was an ethical principle at stake, this is it," Janice said. "A promise was made to the employees. They have been producing better than ever as a result. I think the question is, how can we be effective in pressing the issue? What is our responsibility?

Reprinted by permission of *Business Ethics*, July/August 1993, pp. 35-36. *Business Ethics*, The Magazine of Socially Responsible Business.

EDWARD MILLER
Vice President of Human Resources, Lear Jet, Wichita, Kansas.

THE FIRST THING I would do is recognize the fact that the VP of finance is putting a burden on the human resources department that is probably at least a shared burden between human resources and finance. A decision was made eleven months ago to put the plan in and it was communicated to every employee. I made the assumption they have crossed a budget planning year given the time that plan's been in place and communicated. Therefore, shame on the finance VP for not recognizing what that plan entails from a cost standpoint and incorporating that as part of his financial plan for the year.

Setting all of that aside, what do you do as the comp manager with this issue? Janice needs to go back to Jim Steckel and further discuss the problem. It is really the human resources VP's responsibility to act on the matter. All she can do is to provide him with technical advice. If he reports to the VP of finance, we've got a basic problem. But assuming that he does not, then it becomes clearly an issue that's got to be brought back to the executive committee who approved that plan. They also have to share some responsibility for not having a clear understanding of that financial obligation. It was approved by the executive committee, and I am sure at least as a one-year priority, they can make an accommodation.

But the underlying philosophical question is: Who comes first, the employees or the corporate executives? I can tell you that if the HR department chose, they could go out and explain to the employees, "Here's the dilemma. The executive bonus plan does not pay if you get yours." And then the employees will make sure that the executive bonus plan does not pay. So, I don't think that is a legitimate option.

I think the employee bonus plan comes first. If it's an either/or question, the executive group is the one that has to suffer for one more year. They weren't smart enough to recognize in their plan design that they were designing themselves a problem, so shame on them. And if they try to make a different decision now they won't get their bonus either, and the company will come apart at the seams.

RICK JACKSON
Vice President for Operations, Seattle Metropolitan YMCA, Seattle, Washington.

I think Janice's closing questions—about how can she be effective in pressing the issue and what's her responsibility—are exactly the correct questions. After the blow-up she had with the finance person, somehow they need to re-establish the fact that they work for the same organization, and that they've got to come up with a solution that addresses both the needs of the executives and the employees.

It sounds like there were commitments made to that group that were not fully acknowledged to the committee that worked on the employee compensation package. But clearly the company is going to suffer if they renege on the commitment to the employee compensation plan.

It sounds like this work was done well by the committee, was presented to the executive group, and they signed off on it. It's not as simple as just sending their finance person back to say, "Oh, never mind." It is the kind of issue in which they need to get the CEO involved, somebody with vision and a sense of responsibility for the overall enterprise.

Also, I am left wondering where Jim Steckel is. It sounds like Janice is the one who is pressing the issue. Good for her. But Jim's the VP of human resources. He ought to be the guy who goes back into the boss' office with the message that, "We've got a problem here, and here's how I suggest we solve it." Somehow, Jim has got to either take it on himself and/or support Janice in getting to the top and getting this thing resolved. Otherwise, he's the problem.

> **If the executive committee makes a different decision now they won't get their bonus either, and the company will come apart at the seams.**

DOUG WALLACE'S COMMENTS

Thank goodness for the Janice Matsons in our lives and in our organizations. What she has done is to provide an enormous opportunity for taking leadership in strengthening the climate of integrity for this company.

Our guest commentators have pointed out several of these opportunities. The first is for the VP of human resources to knit together an initiative that brings the finance person into jointly producing a good solution. A second is for the CEO to use this as a wonderful chance to skillfully engage the entire executive committee in thinking through the ethical issues and working out a fair solution. After all, as Edward Miller so eloquently observed, they had a hand in fashioning the problem because of their inattention and prior approval of the plan. Now they have an opportunity to address it in a new way. Demonstrating his/her capability to put the matter on the table for a thoughtful review provides the CEO with an opening to elevate certain ethical values in the management of the place while modeling how a problem of this sort can be carefully worked through.

Under certain circumstances, there is a third opportunity for ethical leadership, as well (which Rick Jackson alludes to). Janice has taken some important responsibility by raising the issue and not retreating. And she has brought the matter to her boss. It would be an extremely important chance in her professional development to continue to play a role in taking the problem forward. She could learn more of what it takes to bring it to the CEO (or the executive committee) along with practicing a new way to invite someone who seems adversarial (Dick Stevens) into a joint approach toward a solution. This is a developmental opportunity for the head of human resources, and it would demonstrate to other employees a good way in which someone who does confront an ethical problem will be treated.

In this case there are major ethical questions, about potentially violating the standards of promise-keeping and justice, that beg to be addressed. The potential consequences for the greater good of the organization and its members are at stake, as well. It isn't often that something so ethically dicey can serve up so many leadership opportunities at the same time.

WHAT ACTUALLY HAPPENED?
When Janice presented the problem to Jim Steckel, his initial reaction was, "We can't do that." He knew he had to work it through. He took the issue, with Janice's background on the problem, to the top of the organization. When he brought it to the executive staff, their joint reaction was that the commitment to the employees must come first. Edward Miller's comment: "It was approved by the executive committee, and I am sure at least as a one-year priority, they can make an accommodation," was prescient. That's exactly what they did. Interestingly, the company did so well at the end of the year that there was enough bonus money for both groups.

Business and Society: Contemporary Ethical, Social, and Environmental Issues

- Changing Perspectives in Business and Society (Articles 29–33)
- Major Contemporary Dilemmas (Articles 34–36)
- Global Ethics (Articles 37–39)

Both at home and abroad there are social and environmental issues that have potential ethical consequences for management. Incidents of insider trading, deaths resulting from unsafe products or work environments, AIDS in the workplace, and the adoption of policies for involvement in the global market are a few of the issues that need to be seriously addressed by management.

This section will investigate the nature and ramifications of some of the prominent ethical, social, and environmental issues facing management today. The unit articles are grouped into three subsections. "The New Crisis in Business Ethics" describes how, during tough economic times, managers are being tempted to put more pressure on subordinates and cut ethical corners. "Work and Family" reveals the importance of organizations helping employees balance work and family. The next article suggests that for women to achieve equality in the workplace, a cultural revolution must occur. The last article in this subsection explains how "the green movement" is increasing in many organizations as the working world learns that recycling makes both dollars and sense.

The second subsection addresses some of the major dilemmas that contemporary business has recently been forced to reckon with. The first two articles in this subsection consider the impact of drugs and AIDS in the workplace and suggest ways to establish sensitive policies and ongoing programs to help deal with each problem. The last article relates to how the Stride Rite company is wrestling with some difficult questions: What makes a company socially responsible? How far can social responsibility be expected to go?

The last subsection, on *Global Ethics*, includes three articles that provide helpful insight on ethical issues and dilemmas inherent in multinational operations. They describe adapting ethical decisions to a global marketplace, discuss European businesses trying to put corruption scandals behind them, and offer guidelines for helping management deal with ethical issues in international markets.

Looking Ahead: Challenge Questions

How well do you feel organizations are responding to issues of work and family—e.g., via flexible schedules, day care, job sharing, telecommuting?

Is it fair to bring criminal charges against corporations and executives for unsafe products, dangerous working conditions, or industrial pollution?

How do you feel management should deal with drugs in the workplace? Should management deal with alcohol-related problems in the same way? Why or why not?

What types of ethical dilemmas is management likely to face when conducting business in foreign environments? How can management best deal with these dilemmas?

Unit 3

The Moral Audit

Or, why having a company fulfill its financial obligations is not enough.

S. Andrew Ostapski

S. Andrew Ostapski is Assistant Professor of Business Law in the School of Business Administration at the University of Miami. The author thanks Camille N. Isaacs for her help in preparing the groundwork for this article.

The legal and moral justification for the existence of any corporation is that it benefit society. Corporations exist, not by right, but by privilege. This privilege is conferred by law in the form of corporate licenses.

Society nurtures corporate existence by establishing laws that limit the liability of corporate owners to the amount invested. In most cases, society repays corporations with revenues for the benefits they supply. In return, the corporation, at the very least, has a moral obligation to shield society from the ill effects of its operations. As an inducement for corporate self-regulation, corporate licenses can be revoked or fines and other sanctions imposed under the law, or society can withhold its patronage, compelling the corporation to cease its operations.

Beyond the regulation of corporate creation and existence, the law is used also to encourage and mandate moral behavior. However, law and morality are not always synonymous. Society mandates minimally acceptable moral standards through its laws, which are enforced by sanction. But moral conduct often requires behavior at a level well above the law, because some actions that are legally acceptable may be morally unacceptable. Although moral responsibility may not always be legally enforceable, society generally expects its members, including business entities, to act for the common good.

Corporations often maintain a favorable public image by performing philanthropic acts. While such deeds do enhance a firm's status in the community, they do not address the corporation's basic moral responsibility to prevent any harm that may result from its operations. A corporation cannot fulfill its moral obligations by merely engaging in external acts of philanthropy. Instead, it must identify any harm it could inflict on society and respond to that harm.

Those organizations that do act responsibly to protect the public have been successful in the long run. A good case in point is Johnson & Johnson (J&J) and its handling of the Tylenol crisis.

In 1982 and 1986, when lethally-contaminated packages of the painkiller Tylenol reached the public, J&J voluntarily and unreservedly

> ". . . law and morality are not always synonymous."

withdrew the product from the market. Revenue losses totaled $100 million in 1982 and $140 million in 1986.

The company took swift action. Capsule use was stopped. Tamper-proof packaging was introduced. The company committed itself to widely-publicized cooperative efforts with the Food and Drug Administration and other regulatory agencies. It used press releases and toll-free telephone hot lines to disseminate information on the company's preventive and remedial

From *Business & Economic Review,* Vol. 38, No. 2, January-March 1992, pp. 17-20. *Business & Economic Review,* College of Business Administration, The University of South Carolina, Division of Research.

action.[1] Subsequently, Tylenol reemerged as one of the most popular over-the-counter analgesic medicines.[2]

These responses are strong evidence the company put public safety above profits. J&J recognized its self-imposed obligation to avoid harming the public through its products, even though the company was not the direct cause. The catalyst for such action was J&J's Corporate Credo, which stresses service for the public good.[3]

If properly formulated and implemented, a Code of Ethics is a useful tool for reinforcing corporate moral responsibility. Beyond the general guiding principles of a Code of Ethics, each corporation should also have an internal system of checks and balances that systematically and continuously evaluates the extent to which its specific moral obligations are being met. To achieve this objective, corporations should establish a well-structured and effectively-implemented Moral Audit, which focuses on the ethical and legal im-

duct and profit clash. The committee should report directly to the Board of Directors in its capacity as initiator of corporate policy and protector of the interests of shareholders, customers, and the public.

Ideally, the Moral Audit Committee should consist of a representative of the company's Board of Directors, an "independent" member from management (i.e., someone not answerable to management regarding what decisions are made by the committee), and several representatives from the community. This broad spectrum of participation minimizes any potential abuse of authority within the corporation when only corporate agents are involved.

The Board's representative would chair the committee and be responsible for its overall operation. The Chairperson would see to it that fact-finding was conducted and reports made on a periodic, timely basis to the Board of Directors, who, subsequent to taking appropriate action, would release the

The Moral Audit

The Moral Audit Committee must devise a strategy of preventive measures, responses, and compensations. Every aspect of the corporation's operations must be subject to review. New trends in industry as well as changes in market demand and government regulation must be analyzed. This pervasive scrutiny would challenge corporate agents to consider thoughtfully the consequences of their actions.

As an independent consulting entity within the firm, the committee may also provide guidance to employees faced with ethical dilemmas.

The Moral Audit Committee should refer to the corporation's Code of Ethics for its guiding principles. The Code of Ethics must contain a set of precepts with which employees are expected to comply. The code must be regulatory, prescribing sanctions for legal and ethical misconduct by the corporation's employees, and yet foster a cooperative spirit. Employees, fully aware of the standard set for corporate morality, should ensure that their actions do not harm those directly or indirectly affected by the corporation.

Admittedly, a Code of Ethics and Moral Audit cannot make employees intrinsically moral. However, these mechanisms do enforce the value system of the organization by providing a collective sense of right and wrong against which specific issues can be systematically assessed.

Any description of the nature of a Moral Audit may not be as illustrative as exposure to an actual model. The following case applies the Moral Audit concept to an existing corporation, whose name and other identifying data have been changed to preserve its anonymity. The essential factual basis has not been materially altered to preserve actual business conditions. The scenario depicted is not intended to portray either effective or ineffective management.

"Those organizations that . . . act responsibly to protect the public have been successful in the long run."

plications of actions and the harm they might cause. A Moral Audit Committee can be established to deal with the specific moral issues faced by the corporation.

Moral Audit Committee Profile

The corporation's Moral Audit Committee should be structured so it can assess most effectively the corporation's operations and communicate its recommendations to the appropriate level of corporate authority. The committee must be unbiased toward management to avoid possible conflicts of interest when considerations of moral con-

information for public scrutiny. Management's representative would be responsible for implementation of committee decisions approved by the board.

The other committee members, involved in the actual implementation of the audit, must be well respected in the community, with reputations for high moral and professional conduct. They should be familiar with the technical and regulatory aspects of the company's operations, and at least one of these public members should possess exceptional quantitative and analytical skills to facilitate the committee's investigations.

Moral Audit Review of Dynamic Disposal, Inc.

The Issue

The discharge of corporate moral responsibility has always created public controversy, particularly when corporate operations are profitable at the expense of society. News reports indicate that Dynamic Disposal Inc. (DDI), a leading corporation in the waste disposal industry, has violated safety standards. Additional questions have been raised concerning the company's moral obligations to protect the interests of its shareholders and clients and the general public.

The company's present record may be attributed to the absence of an ongoing Moral Audit which would have provided DDI with the necessary guidance to address moral issues.

The effectiveness of a Moral Audit depends largely on corporate awareness of the specific moral obligations that arise from the nature of its operations. Companies that participate in the waste disposal industry for profit have the self-imposed obligation to ensure that their operations are not a source of harm. Unsafe disposal practices have long-term, and often irreversible, effects on the public and the environment. Profit making, as a goal of any business enterprise, is an acceptable pursuit — within the bounds of moral responsibility. A truly ethical firm in this hazardous field will not disregard its moral obligation of ensuring environmentally-safe disposal practices which may, in fact, diminish its profit margin. In view of technological limitations, total prevention of harm is an unattainable goal. Yet, this ideal should serve as an objective in the relentless effort to achieve the highest level of safety in waste disposal management.

The Charges

In 1982, DDI paid more than $1.5 million in fines for anti-trust violations in the United States. The illegal conduct involved collusion in the allocation of garbage collection territories that resulted in the artificial control of prices. An additional $15 million was paid in fines and remedial cleanup costs at one of its disposal facilities. In the period 1981-'86, 16 grand juries investigated cases involving DDI's waste disposal practices.

DDI failed to inform its shareholders of the nature of its pending lawsuits. The annual reports for those years contained only a few sentences to the effect that lawsuits are a normal result of conducting business. DDI's 1983 and 1988 annual reports stated the company did not believe the legal proceedings taken against it were "material to [its] business or financial condition." George Booty, President and Chief Executive Officer of DDI, reported that, despite increased government scrutiny, there was virtually no impact on profits even after the payment of heavy fines. Profits had grown at an annual rate of 20 percent in the last 20 years.

The Concerns

At least three specific concerns can be found in the official reports on the company's operation. The Moral Audit will focus on these concerns to ascertain whether DDI is honoring its moral obligations to its shareholders and clients and the general public.

1. **The relentless pursuit of profits at the expense of public safety.** George Booty stated that, despite heavy fines and increased government scrutiny, the company's profits were unaffected. The pursuit of profits is a reasonable business goal, of course. Businesses require profits to continue their operations. But financial data should not be used as the sole measure of corporate performance. Measurements of daily business activities that safeguard society from harm may involve financial, social, legal, and ethical scrutiny. Ideally, corporate success delivers "zero harm" to society.

If harm does result, the corporation is legally and morally obligated to compensate those affected and to institute remedial measures to ensure, at the very least, future company compliance with the minimum requirements set by law. In addition, the corporation has a higher ethical obligation to diminish harm in any form, whether legally mandated or not, because the law is merely asocially mandated minimum standard.

The Moral Audit Committee would make three recommendations.

a. That an internal examination be conducted to determine the agents responsible for violations of law and to ensure that the culpable parties are appropriately punished.

b. That a program of ongoing training be instituted for all company employees to reinforce awareness of their legal and moral responsibilities.

c. That company operations be monitored to ensure full contract performance and legal compliance.

2. **Full disclosure to shareholders of pending lawsuits and legal action taken against the company.** Statements made in the DDI annual report indicated that expenditures on lawsuits were not "material to [its] business or financial condition." Consequently, the costs of these transactions were not disclosed. The accounting principle of materiality holds that "the accountant should be concerned primarily with those transactions which are of real significance or concern to the users of financial information."[4] Although the nondisclosure of "immaterial financial information" is generally accepted in financial reports, the omission of information regarding the use of shareholders' investments to finance lawsuits is morally unacceptable. From a moral context, "material information" consists of those facts that would influence the characterization of an action as being harmful or not.

The nondisclosure of morally

material information on lawsuits and fines by corporate financial officers deprives DDI's Board of Directors, management, and shareholders of the opportunity to assess fairly the harm the company has caused. Without adequate information at its disposal, the corporation cannot remedy the harm resulting from its operations. Unmitigated harm becomes silently perpetuated, and the corporation no longer benefits society to which it is legally and morally obligated.

On this basis, the Moral Audit Committee would make three recommendations.
a. That information reflecting the company's goals, policies, and activities be published in trade and business journals.
b. That a communication network, including the use of a toll-free telephone number, be established for the report of harmful corporate activity.
c. That financial officers be required to state explicitly in financial statements the nature of lawsuits and the costs of fines.

3. Top management's attitudes toward moral responsibility. DDI's Chief Executive has been entrusted by shareholders to implement corporate policy and mobilize subordinates to achieve corporate goals. If his comments fail to recognize corporate moral responsibility, his subordinates will not feel constrained to consider the legal and moral dimensions of their actions. In this context, employees will not believe punitive measures will be enforced against them or that moral conduct is preferred over profit making. The Chief Executive's comments are not merely a reflection of his personal opinions: when he speaks, he represents corporate policy and sets an example for others to follow.

The Moral Audit Committee would recommend that statements be reviewed for their legal and moral implications prior to dissemination.

Conclusion

The DDI case indicates that fulfillment of legal obligations does not guarantee discharge of corporate moral responsibility. Although DDI paid its fines, it has fallen short of preventing harm to society.

The courses of action recommended by the Moral Audit Committee require corporate agents to act in deference to the good of society. Most of the recommendations require that communication be maintained with the public concerning the company's moral actions. Increased respect for the company and public patronage will be the corporate dividends.

"Increased respect for the company and public patronage will be the corporate dividends."

[1]John B. Cullen, Bart Victor, and Carroll Stephens, "An Ethical Weather Report: Assessing the Organization's Ethical Climate," *Organizational Dynamics* (Autumn 1989): 50.
[2]Clark H. Johnson, "A Matter of Trust," *Management Accounting* (December 1989): 12.
[3]The views of J&J's founder General Johnson on public and social responsibility were formalized in the 1940s as the company's Corporate Credo. This statement underscored the company's responsibilities to its customers, employees, communities served, and stockholders. J&J's managers consider it to be the unifying philosophy guiding all important decisions.
[4]Benjamin Schugart et al., *Survey of Accounting,* 6th ed. (Homewood, Ill.: Richard D. Irwin, Inc., 1988).

THE NEW CRISIS IN BUSINESS ETHICS

To meet goals in these tough times, more managers are cutting ethical corners. The trend hurts both the culprits and their companies, even if they don't get caught.

Kenneth Labich

As this economic slowdown lingers like some stubborn low-grade infection, managers are putting the heat on subordinates. Many of the old rules no longer seem to apply. Says Gary Edwards, president of the Ethics Resource Center, a consulting firm in Washington: "The message out there is, Reaching objectives is what matters and how you get there isn't that important."

The result has been an eruption of questionable and sometimes plainly criminal behavior throughout corporate America. We are not dealing here so much with the personal greed that propelled Wall Street operators of the Eighties into federal prisons. Today's miscreants are more often motivated by the most basic of instincts—fear of losing their jobs or the necessity to eke out some benefit for their companies. If that means fudging a few sales figures, abusing a competitor, or shortchanging the occasional customer, so be it.

People lower down on the corporate food chain are telling the boss what they think he wants to hear, and outright lying has become a commonplace at many companies. Michael Josephson, a prominent Los Angeles ethicist who consults for some of America's largest public corporations, says his polls reveal that between 20% and 30% of middle managers have written deceptive internal reports.

At least part of this is relatively harmless—managers inflating budget pro-

posals in the hope of ultimately getting what they really need, for example. But a good share of it will almost surely hurt the people and the companies involved, in some cases grievously. The U.S. press, broadcast and print, has become increasingly adept at uncovering corporate misdeeds. Witness the frenzy of reports raising questions about Dow Corning's breast implants. The stock of Corning Inc., one of the two corporate parents of Dow Corning, has declined by about 15% since the scandal erupted, even though the implants represented only around 1% of Dow Corning's revenues and its insurance coverage seems adequate to cover potential litigation.

The Justice Department has become far keener on catching and punishing white-collar criminals since the S&L crisis and the BCCI scandal. Last November tough new sentencing guidelines for corporate crimes went into effect. Warns Josephson: "We are going to see a phenomenal number of business scandals during the 1990s. We are swimming in enough lies to keep the lawyers busy for the next ten years."

The faint sign of good news is that many big U.S. companies have begun to respond to the crisis. According to a survey of FORTUNE 1,000 companies conducted by Bentley College in Boston, over 40% of the respondents are holding ethics workshops and seminars, and about one-third have set up an ethics committee. Some 200 major U.S. corporations have recently appointed ethics officers, usually senior managers of long experience, to serve as ombudsmen and encourage whistleblowing.

Regrettably, such actions won't put an end to ethical dilemmas—or to the current spree of shoddy practices. Dow Corning had a substantial ethics program in place for 18 years before the breast-implant scandal, but no questions about safety or testing of the implant materials were ever raised to the ethics committee.

The problem, says Kirk Hanson, a Stanford management professor and president of an ethics research group called the Business Enterprise Trust, is extreme pressure to perform. "Quite simply," he says, "the individual who isn't perceived as a top achiever is a candidate for a layoff." Under such circumstances, flirtations with impropriety are hardly surprising.

Virtually every day we read about the hapless folks who get caught. Citicorp fires the president and senior executives of a credit-card-processing division for allegedly overstating revenues. American Express cans several executives for failing to write off accounts of customers who had filed for bankruptcy, as required by company policy. Alamo Rent A Car agrees to refund $3 million to customers who were overcharged for repair costs to damaged vehicles.

There is clearly quite a bit more iceberg down there. No one knows how many top managers are intentionally overlooking questionable acts because they are paying off. Josephson tells of a bank whose executives one day discovered that a large number of customers had been overbilled for mortgage payments. "There's no doubt what you ought to do in a case like that," says Josephson. "You come clean and you take your hit." That's what the bank

REPORTER ASSOCIATE *Temma Ehrenfeld*

From *Fortune,* April 20, 1992, pp. 167-168, 172, 176. © 1993 by Time Inc. Magazine Company. All rights reserved. Reprinted by permission.

eventually did—but only after regulators discovered the error.

Some practices born of competitive excess fall into a kind of gray area. Last autumn Toys "R" Us managers sent employees to rival Child World stores around the country to buy up large quantities of heavily discounted items, which were then resold in their own stores. Misrepresentation? Other acts now taking place clearly cross the line. Gary Edwards tells of one struggling company that recently placed fake want ads in the hope of luring competitors' employees to job interviews where they might reveal trade secrets. Stanford's Hanson reports that three of his returning students were asked by summer employers to call up competitors and seek information under the guise of doing academic research.

Many top managers desperate for profits have turned to emerging markets overseas, a trend that presents a fresh set of ethical dilemmas. Far too often, a company will send off its team with no directive other than finding new business. Bribery and sloppy accounting may be a fact of business life over there, the customer base may be riddled with questionable characters, and yet the sales force is supposed to find its way with no ethical compass. Mark Pastin, an Arizona State University management professor who has consulted with many companies seeking to go global, suggests that the confusion overseas could later lead to problems at home. Says Pastin: "Don't forget that you eventually are going to re-import those managers. Once they've come back, do you think they're going to put on their old ethics like a new suit?"

As Pastin notes, ethics begin at home, in the nexus between employer and employee. The recent layoffs at many big companies carry a slew of ethical implications. Many job reductions have clearly been necessary, the result of lousy business. But at least some top managers have axed employees to pump up profits for the short term or impress Wall Street. Says Hanson: "Unfortunately, layoffs have sometimes become a way to buy a multiple." At such companies much of the work load may still be there, while many of the bodies are not. Middle managers end up pressuring the remaining employees to work unconscionable amounts of overtime. What are the ethics of that?

Compensation for top executives has become a hot-button ethical issue during this recession as well, especially at those companies where workers are being fired and the big guy's salaries appear excessive or unrelated to job performance. In such cases the old argument that companies need to bestow grand wealth on chief executives to prevent them from fleeing to a more beneficent competitor seems especially flimsy. The market for the overpaid chiefs of losing or minimally profitable enterprises is not a large one. In effect, the top dogs are isolating themselves—but not their employees—from the brutal realities of the marketplace. The basic injustice involved is obvious.

In tough times it's all the more important to remember that ethics pay off in the end, and the bottom line. Ten years ago James Burke, chief executive of Johnson & Johnson, put together a list of major companies that paid a lot of attention to ethical standards. The market value of the group, which included J&J, Coca-Cola, Gerber, IBM, Deere, Kodak, 3M, Xerox, J.C. Penney, and Pitney Bowes, grew at 11.3% annually from 1950 to 1990. The growth rate for Dow Jones industrials as a whole was 6.2% a year over the same period.

The case is probably easier to make in the negative: Doing the wrong thing can be costly. Under the new federal sentencing guidelines, corporations face mandatory fines that reach into the hundreds of millions for a broad range of crimes—antitrust violations, breaking securities and contract law, fraud, bribery, kickbacks, money laundering, you name it. And that's if just one employee gets caught.

Even if you don't land in court, you might find yourself on the front page or the evening news, which could be worse. In the past few years, most media have given much more coverage to business. Newspapers and magazines all over the U.S. now employ investigative reporters with MBAs and business experience to dig into the affairs of companies. The old advice is still the best: Don't do anything on the job you wouldn't want your mother to read about with her morning coffee.

Even if a company's slippery practices go undetected, there is still a price to pay. Successful enterprises are inevitably based on a network of trust binding management, employees, shareholders, lenders, suppliers, and customers—akin to the network that Japanese call keiretsu. When companies slip into shoddy practices, these crucial relationships start to deteriorate. Says Barbara Ley Toffler, senior partner of a Boston ethics-consulting firm called Resources for Responsible Management: "The effects aren't obvious at first. People may feel bad about what they're doing, but they rationalize it somehow." Eventually a kind of moral rot can set in, turning off employees with higher personal standards and stifling innovation throughout the company. She adds: "People in these situations feel frightened, constrained. They are not in the proper frame of mind to take prudent risks."

Companies that depend heavily on customer service are especially vulnerable. A company that jacks up prices unfairly, skimps on quality, or beats up on employees can hardly expect its salespeople to treat customers properly. Says Arizona State's Pastin: "You can put on a happy face for only so long before reality intrudes. I don't believe employees can deliver superior service if they don't think their company is treating customers with respect." Ultimately, many of the most effective managers and most productive workers will find a way to work somewhere else. When the economy turns up again, companies with a sorry reputation for ethical behavior will have a harder time attracting top-quality people.

Among the scariest aspects of the current situation, ethicists say, is how unaware many top managers are of what is going on. Michael Josephson, who is usually called in after a company has landed in the headlines, begins by circulating questionnaires among top and middle managers to determine what's happening. More often than not, the CEO expresses shock and disbelief at the results of the anonymous survey. Adds Josephson: "There's very often a sort of 'kill the messenger' attitude, which may have led to some of the problems in the first place."

Once the scope of the problem is clear, the next step is to communicate in no uncertain terms what is expected of managers and other employees. Hewlett-Packard, for example, works hard to ensure that all employees are familiar with its extensive standards for business conduct, which cover everything from conflicts of interest and accounting practices to handling confidential informatio̳ and accepting gratuities. The standaᵣ are high; salespeople are instruct̳ avoid commenting on a comᵣ character or business practices, even to refrain from mentioning the fact that a competitor might be facing a lawsuit or government investigation.

A little innovation helps in getting the message across. Citicorp has developed an ethics board game, which teams of employees use to solve hypothetical quandaries. General Electric employees can tap into specially designed interactive software on their personal computers to get answers to ethical questions. At Texas Instruments, employees are treated to a weekly column on ethics over an international electronic news service. One popular feature: a kind of Dear Abby mailbag, answers provided by the company's ethics officer, Carl Skoogland, that deals with the troublesome issues employees face most often. Managers at Northrop are rated on their ethical behavior by peers and subordinates through anonymous questionnaires.

More and more companies are appointing full-time ethics officers, generally on the corporate vice-presidential level, who report directly to the chairman or an ethics committee of top officers. One of the most effective tools these ethics specialists employ is a hot line through which workers on all levels can register complaints or ask about questionable behavior. At Raytheon Corp., Paul Pullen receives some 100 calls a month. Around 80% involve minor issues that he can resolve on the spot or refer to the human resources department. Another 10% of callers are simply looking for a bit of advise. But about ten times a month, a caller reports some serious ethical lapse that Pullen

must address with senior management. Says he: "Most people have high standards, and they want to work in an atmosphere that is ethical. The complaints come from all levels, and they are typical of what you would find in any business: possible conflicts of interest, cheating on timecards, cheating on expense reports."

Some companies have been motivated to set up an ethics office after a spate of unfavorable publicity. Nynex took the step in 1990 following a series of scandals, including revelations of lewd parties in Florida thrown for suppliers by a Nynex executive. Later 56 middle managers were disciplined or discharged for allegedly receiving kickbacks, and the SEC accused a former unit president of insider trading. The company has since been beating the drum about ethics, but Graydon Wood, Nynex's newly appointed ethics officer, says the job requires a realistic view of human behavior. Says he: "You have to recognize that even with all the best programs, some employees do go wrong. Last year some marketing people didn't report properly, resulting in unjustified commissions. We fired them."

In the current crunch much deception and unethical conduct can be avoided if top managers make sure that the performance goals they set are realistic. Ethicists often cite a classic case that occurred at a GM light-truck plant several years ago. The plant manager got caught with a device in his office that periodically speeded up the line beyond the rate designated in union contracts. Confronted with the evidence, he pointed

out that the company's production specifications were based on the line running at maximum allowable speed 100% of the time. He was simply trying to make up for inevitable down time.

Managers must be sure that what they actually do fosters rather than impedes ethical conduct. One sure way to send the word is by rewarding admirable behavior. No code of ethics and no amount of cajolery by the chief executive will have much effect if promotions regularly go to the people who pile up big numbers by cutting corners. Says Kirk Hanson: "Senior management has got to find a way to create heroes, people who serve the company's competitive values—and also its social and ethical values."

These role models could be especially important for younger employees who are trying to survive in what seems to be an increasingly hostile business environment. Michael Josephson reports some dispiriting news about the start that the new generation are off to. He cites surveys of Americans 18 to 30 years old that show between 70% and 80% cheated in high school and between 40% and 50% cheated in college. And—are you ready for this?—between 12% and 24% say they included false information on their résumés.

Commenting on Americans' ethical standards in the 19th century, Alexis de Tocqueville declared that the nation had become great because it was good. He may have overstated a bit, but in pursuit of profits today we may indeed be losing an element vital to our long-term success tomorrow.

WORK & FAMILY

COMPANIES ARE STARTING TO RESPOND TO WORKERS' NEEDS— AND GAIN FROM IT

Josephine C. Pigg, a former clerk with U. S. West Inc. in Grand Junction, Colo., was 14 months from retirement when her daughter, Tammie, 32, was diagnosed with cancer. The prognosis was not good, and Pigg decided to stay with Tammie in Denver rather than travel the 250 miles back and forth. At many other companies, Pigg would have been forced to leave. But her former boss, Penny Larson Hubbard, a director in the small-business services unit, figured out a way to keep Pigg working while she was sitting at her daughter's bedside. With the help of a human-resources manager, Hubbard found Pigg a job with U. S. West in Denver. While it was a good deed, Hubbard wasn't just trying to be nice. "Jo is valuable to our company," she says. "If our employees have done a good job, we try and accommodate their situation."

Bosses such as Hubbard aren't typical. But in many companies, they're fast becoming the model of what a manager ought to be. With record numbers of working women, single parents, two-career couples, and an aging population, more managers are coming face-to-face with the problems and demands of a diverse work force. Now, the question is: How can managers meet those demands and make sure the work gets done? "We know what it's like to sacrifice family for career and the reverse," says management guru Peter M. Senge. "Now, we're creating a middle ground—success at home and at work—and everyone has to work together. It's tough."

Yet not all share the view that corporations must adapt so workers can have it all. Many companies say they can ill afford family-oriented programs in an era of heightened global competition. In fact, many are cutting such core benefits as health insurance and pensions. For small businesses especially, family-friendly policies can breed resentment among the workers who have to pick up the slack. And for every company that embraces a family-friendly working environment, there are others that merely say they do.

Increasingly, though, the evidence shows that managers who get results aren't tough but flexible. From Aetna Life & Casualty Co. to Alden Merrell Dessert Co., a cheesecake maker in Newburyport, Mass., they're helping employees resolve work and family conflicts through such arrangements as job sharing and compressed workweeks. In the process, they're increasing productivity, reducing turnover and absenteeism—and reinventing how work gets done. "It's time for business to get in step with this country's evolving social patterns," says Continental Corp. CEO John "Jake" Mascotte. "Corporate America can't afford to ignore or pay lip service to the work-family agenda anymore."

Changing demographics and the growing emphasis on worker competitiveness are only some of the reasons that companies are becoming more responsive to workers' personal needs. At least 20 states already require employers to provide unpaid parental and medical leaves, and the rest will follow when the federal Family & Medical Leave Act takes effect in August. Even the Clean Air Act is prodding such large companies as Pacific Bell to get commuters out of their cars, in part by promoting telecommuting.

MORALE BOOSTER. Helping employees balance their personal lives with work seems like common sense: A worker who isn't distracted by worries over babysitting or caring for a parent is better able to focus on the job. But the benefits of a family-friendly environment go beyond making life easier for employees or boosting a company's reputation with recruits.

Recent studies of such companies as Johnson & Johnson and American Telephone & Telegraph Co. show that helping employees resolve work and family conflicts boosts morale and increases productivity. The J&J study found that absenteeism among employees who used flexible time and family-leave polices was on average 50% less than for the work force as a whole. It also found that 58% of the employees surveyed said such policies were "very important" in their decision to stay at the company—the number jumped to 71% among employees using the benefits. At AT&T, the company found that the average cost of giving new parents up to one year of unpaid parental leave was 32% of an employee's annual salary, compared with 150% to replace the leave-taker altogether.

Some companies have been reluctant to offer these programs out of fear that workers would abuse them. But those fears have not been realized. At AT&T, 60% of new parents were back on the job within three months, and all but 10% returned to work within six months.

And at Fel-Pro Inc., a Skokie (Ill.)-based auto-parts maker, University of Chicago researchers recently found a strong link between high benefit users and high performers—indicating, in part, that "workers perform best when they use and appreciate workplace supports." The researchers—who approached the 1,800-employee company because of its family-responsive policies—also found that the high benefit users were more active in team problem-solving and were almost twice as likely to submit suggestions for improving products and processes. "The research is pretty clear," says Ellen Galinsky, co-president of the New York-based Families & Work Institute, which did the studies of J&J and AT&T. "There's a cost to not providing work and family assistance."

"BREAKTHROUGH." At some companies, CEOS such as Continental's Mascotte (page 136) and NCR Corp.'s Jerre L. Stead are driving changes. They're convinced that workplace flexibility is not an accommodation to employees but a competitive weapon: It frees workers to use their full potential on the job instead of, say, fretting about taking a child to the doctor. "Everything we do must start out with a recognition of a balance between work and family," says Stead. "The only sustainable competitive advantage a company has is its employees." To show he is serious, Stead ties 25% of his managers' pay to how well they help workers meet personal objectives—as measured by employee-satisfaction surveys—including balancing family and work demands. And, he says, the percentage will go up.

For many other companies, line managers are the critical agents of change. From vice-presidents such as Duke Power Co.'s Sharon Allred Decker (page 137) to work-and-family champions such as Aetna's Michelle M. Carpenter (page 135), they're finding creative ways to solve common problems. The Conference Board's Work & Family Council, made up of about 30 top companies, calls such pioneers "breakthrough managers." It is studying the qualities that set such managers apart, including a willingness to focus on results, not procedures (table).

But whether it's an attorney at Aetna who ovesees job sharers or a plant man-

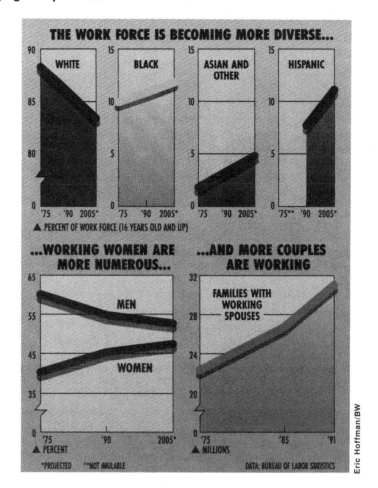

THE WORK FORCE IS BECOMING MORE DIVERSE...

WHITE · BLACK · ASIAN AND OTHER · HISPANIC

▲ PERCENT OF WORK FORCE (16 YEARS OLD AND UP)

...WORKING WOMEN ARE MORE NUMEROUS...

MEN · WOMEN

▲ PERCENT

...AND MORE COUPLES ARE WORKING

FAMILIES WITH WORKING SPOUSES

▲ MILLIONS

*PROJECTED **NOT AVAILABLE

DATA: BUREAU OF LABOR STATISTICS

Eric Hoffman/BW

ager at Menlo Park (N. J.)-based Engelhard Corp. who lets workers vote on their hours, the managers share one crucial trait: They get results by bending to their employees' needs—and demanding a high level of performance in return.

Plenty of managers reject such an approach. To them, flexibility means working nights and weekends, not going home every night at 6. Even some bosses who can afford to be more flexible

don't feel they have to be. "It's still a buyer's market," says Barbara Provus, a Chicago-based executive recruiter. "The good jobs and the good companies can still get whoever they want."

NEW THINKING. That's certainly the case at Microsoft Corp. The nation's No.1 personal-computer software maker has a "hard core" work ethic: flexible but long hours and seven-day workweeks for those finishing big projects. Chairman

---

BALANCING WORK AND FAMILY

TRADITIONAL ATTITUDES VS. FLEXIBLE MANAGER

▶ Fairness means treating all employees the same

▶ Must sacrifice personal needs to get ahead

▶ Flexibility is accommodation to specific employee

▶ Assesses performance largely based on hours at the office

▶ Seeks equitable, not uniform, treatment

▶ People perform better free of personal pressures

▶ Flexibility is competitive issue, and management tool

▶ Measures performance based on value added, not hours worked

QUALITIES OF INNOVATIVE MANAGERS

▶ Meets business objectives by helping employees meet personal needs

▶ Willing to take risks or take a stand

▶ Results oriented, not hung up on rules and procedures

▶ Respects the individual, but acknowledges and responds to differences

▶ Often gains top-level support, plus backing from peers

▶ Produces change within the organization that outlives the manager

DATA: FAMILIES AND WORK INSTITUTE, WORK & FAMILY COUNCIL

ERIC HOFFMANN/BW

MICHELLE CARPENTER
AETNA'S FAMILY-FRIENDLY EXECUTIVE

Michelle M. Carpenter is living proof that employees who ask for reduced schedules can get promotions. Five years ago, Carpenter, 34, began working 30-hour weeks at Hartford-based Aetna Life & Casualty Co. after the birth of her first son. Two years later, she changed her schedule to a compressed week: 40 hours in four days. But that didn't stop Aetna from promoting Carpenter in September, 1991, from a senior consultant in its human-resources department to manager of its Work/Family Strategies unit.

The new job showed just how far Aetna had to go in the work-and-family area. Creating Carpenter's unit in 1988 was recognition of a serious problem. Aetna was losing hundreds of talented female employees—70% of its workers are women—who weren't returning after pregnancies. But for the unit's first three years, Carpenter says, employees only

called "when they wanted information on child care."

GRUMBLINGS. Since Carpenter took over two years ago, she has tried to shed the unit's "babysitter" image to reflect an employee's need to balance work and home. She has talked up the benefits of flexible schedules to business units and helped employees find job-share partners. When a manager nixes an employee's request for flexibility, Carpenter will often intervene on the worker's behalf. But promoting flexibility hasn't been easy: Managers grumble about how such jobs are reported in their budgets, and non-Hartford employees say it's harder for them to get flex-time approval than for those in the home office.

Carpenter's biggest success was convincing Aetna that it's cheaper to keep trained workers—even in limited schedules—than to hire new ones. Now, roughly 2,000 of its 44,000 employees

work part-time, share a job, work at home, or work a compressed workweek. The results: Aetna estimates it saves $1 million per year in not having to train new workers. And from July, 1991, to June, 1992, 88% of its workers who took family leave returned to work. An added benefit is good publicity. Aetna was named one of the top four "family-friendly" companies by the Families & Work Institute.

But Carpenter's work is far from over. "People have been resistant," says Leo Taylor, Carpenter's boss. Carpenter wants to "create a culture change" at Aetna about flex time. She also plans on using her experience in Aetna's offices in Denver, Syracuse, and Philadelphia to show that flexible schedules can work in far-flung business operations. Just don't look for her in the office on Fridays. That's the day she spends with her kids.

By Chris Roush in Hartford

William H. Gates III sets the pace, getting to work at 9 a.m. and often not leaving before midnight. At home, he often spends a few hours zapping computer memos to his staffers. The result: Most programmers follow suit by putting in 60- to 80-hour weeks, and, typically, not griping, especially given Microsoft's big bonuses and stock options. Employees also work such long hours because they're young and single—the average age is 30, only half the employees are married, and only half of the married workers have any kids.

But as Microsoft's work force ages, the company says it will have to look at parental issues more closely. Already, it is trying to get away from such long hours. "In the old days, the longer you worked, the bigger bonus you got," says Mike Murray, vice-president for human resources and administration at Microsoft. Now, the company is "encouraging" managers to look at pure performance.

At least Microsoft is honest about what it expects of workers. Other companies say they have family-friendly programs but tacitly discourage employees from using them. Even at companies that make a real effort, the ideal falls short of reality. For one thing, programs such as on-site child-care centers may be unavailable to most employees because of their location or size. SAS Insti-

tute Inc., a software maker in Cary, N.C., has two child-care centers with capacity for 328 kids—and a two-year waiting list on average for the company's 2,800 employees, most of them of child-bearing age. As for popular benefits such as dependent-care spending accounts, Lincolnshire (Ill.) consultants Hewitt Associates found that 95% of employees don't use them because of Internal Revenue Service rules.

"AT RISK." At cutting-edge companies where benefits are widely available, employees must be encouraged to take advantage of them. Corning Inc. has been committed to benefits such as flexible hours for years. But an employee survey nearly three years ago showed that many corners of the company were only paying lip service to workplace flexibility: About 40% of senior managers were judged by employees as not supportive of work and family issues. "Here we had all these policies, but people were afraid to use them because they thought their careers were at risk," says Sonia S. Werner, work/life balance consultant at Corning. Part of the problem was that senior managers weren't experiencing the same concerns. Says Werner: "Ninety percent of our senior managers were males who had spouses at home taking care of the kids. But 75% of the staff were in dual-career households."

Corning and other companies are finding they have to teach managers why flexibility is good for business. And that requires embracing a new way of thinking. For example, instead of linking job performance to the number of hours at the office, managers must evaluate employees based on their contribution to the company. Employees also must be taught that they have a role to play. And they must understand that flexibility means that not everyone will get the same treatment (table).

However flexibility is attained, viewing workers as individuals puts new demands on managers. No one knows that better than Brian G. Thiele, vice-president and manager of Bank of America's employee-transportation programs, which subsidize workers for using car pools or mass transit. Thiele manages seven employees, including four in four different offices who telecommute on a part-time basis. Thiele says his big problem is trying to reach workers during the day, reminding himself that "it's no worse than in the office when they go to lunch or if they worked in satellite offices."

Such inconveniences are well worth it. Before the telecommuting program started in March, Thiele's unit was typically three to five days late in sending checks to commuters. Now, it hasn't had any late payments, he says, because em-

135

SAM RIVERA
AN EASYGOING BOSS—AND A MASTER MOTIVATOR

Ten years ago, when Sam Rivera became an assistant foreman at 1,800-employee Fel-Pro Inc., a Skokie (Ill.) auto-parts maker, his supervisor said the secret to success was to be just like him. "He was really tough," recalls Rivera. "I said, 'My name is Sam Rivera. I have to be in my heart what it says to me to be.' At that moment, I made up my mind that I was going to be a different kind of manager."

For Rivera, 48, being himself meant giving factory worker Edwin Carrera three days of emergency leave so he and son Erwin could meet with Fel-Pro's on-site psychologist. Carerra needed help to extricate his son from Chicago's Latino gang culture, just as Rivera did with his eldest son, Sam, eight years ago. It meant finding another job for Pedro Hernandez, who wasn't able to operate a forklift truck, the job he was hired for. Rivera knew Hernandez, then 45, would have a tough time getting hired elsewhere. Hernandez is now one of his best punch-press operators, he says.

"PEOPLE WORK HARDER." Instead of acting dictatorially, Rivera tries to place himself in his employees' shoes. He gives his workers plenty of flexibility and discretion. "As long as the job gets done, that's the bottom line," he says. And 95% of the time, according to Rivera and the company, Rivera's unit exceeds its objectives. On June 2, for example, instead of producing 95 hours' worth of parts, Rivera's unit produced 112.

Rivera's management style also motivates workers to go the extra mile, they say. Carrera is so grateful Rivera helped rescue his son that in his spare time he has devised ideas—now being implemented—to increase machine productivity and safety. "People work harder in the department because of the way Sam is," says Carrera, who has worked for him for two years. "He makes you feel comfortable on the job."

Rivera says his philosophy is a result of his poor childhood in Puerto Rico. "I know what people have to do to survive," he says. Another factor is Rivera's own experience at Fel-Pro. Twenty-five years ago, when he had been with the company just three months, his wife, Elva, had their first child. He hadn't worked at Fel-Pro long enough for company insurance to cover their medical expenses, but Bob O'Keefe, the human-relations manager, arranged to have insurance cover part of the hospital bill.

Juggling work and family requests isn't easy for Rivera, especially given his unit's diversity, say his workers and his supervisor, Ricky Justus. His 50 workers include 29 Latinos, 11 Caucasians, 9 African-Americans, and 1 Asian Pacific Islander. There are 4 women and 46 men. Justus says that if Rivera "has a fault, it's that he hates saying no to special requests and disciplining." Rivera agrees. But he adds: "I'd rather be soft than be hard, because hard people are hated and can't accomplish anything."

By Ann Therese Palmer in Chicago

JOHN MASCOTTE
'BUSINESS IS STILL STRUCTURED LIKE FOURTH GRADE'

Do business and family issues mix? John "Jake" Mascotte, CEO of Continental Corp., thinks they do. What's more, he believes companies that fail to balance the two may be jeopardizing their future. "So much of business is still structured like fourth grade," says Mascotte. He thinks results are better when employees have flexibility and freedom. And he's pushing Continental to prove him right.

Three years ago, Continental's management began studying just how flexible the New York insurer—with $5 billion in revenues and more than 12,000 employees—really was. From focus groups, Mascotte learned that employees saw the company as fairly rigid—and that work and family conflicts often distracted employees from their jobs.

OUT OF CONTROL? As a result, Continental in early 1990 rolled out a series of family-friendly programs, including job-sharing and telecommuting. Continental also eliminated "occurrences"—the practice of tracking employee absences no matter what the reasons and using the results in performance reviews.

Mascotte's biggest challenge was getting management to buy on. Many managers worried that flexible rules would give them less control, making it tougher to get the work done. "Frankly, I was skeptical," says David Bates, an assistant vice-president in Cranbury, N.J. "Who needs this? We need employees."

But Doreen A. Horvath, vice-president of Residual Markets Center, a unit of Continental in Glens Falls, N.Y., needed no convincing. Of her 207 employees, 200 are now on an alternative schedule. Horvath says scheduling can be a real pain. But, she says, the extra trouble is worth it. Since starting the new schedules 15 months ago, productivity has jumped 15%.

Mascotte is leaving implementation of his vision to managers such as Horvath. "We tried not to do anything so uniform that we would be substituting new rigidity for old rigidity," he says. That doesn't mean that work and family issues are optional concerns. Mascotte tracks each department to see where flexibility is being achieved, and he evaluates managers partly on employee development. What about the bottom line? Although it's hard to quantify the results in dollars, Continental says it has halved its voluntary employee turnover rate to less than 5% a year.

By Lori Bongiorno in New York

SHARON ALLRED DECKER
'WE HAD TO RECOGNIZE THAT PEOPLE HAVE LIVES'

In 1990, Duke Power Co. in Charlotte, N.C., gave Sharon Allred Decker a critical assignment: consolidate the customer-service functions of its 98 local offices and make the once-sheltered monopoly more responsive to customers. Decker jumped at the chance. She launched a service center that operates 24 hours a day, seven days a week. But Decker quickly realized that for Duke Power to be more responsive to customers, it had to become more responsive to employees, too. "I saw an opportunity to create an environment I wanted to work in," says the vice-president for customer service. "We needed to recognize that people have lives."

"THEY'RE ADULTS." Decker sought to bring about an atmosphere where the 500-person staff could handle family matters more easily. Her first move: getting her bosses to combine with other local employers, such as IBM and Allstate Insurance Co., to build a child-care center. She also campaigned successfully for a fitness center.

Early on, Decker got an earful from employees who hated working swing shifts: days one week, evenings the next, and then nights. So she came up with 22 separate schedules and let workers bid on them yearly, based on seniority. Some are traditional weeks of five 8-hour days, but there also are weekly schedules of four 10-hour days and three 12-hour days. She did away with swing shifts, making it easier to arrange care for children—and parents: The staff is 75% female, 33 years old on average, and earns starting pay of $19,000 a year. Decker dropped the requirement that supervisors—called coaches—had to give approval before staff swapped shifts. "They're adults," she says. "They know they're responsible for someone being here."

Decker, 36, knows how tough juggling work and family can be. At her last peer review, colleagues remarked that she was working too hard—and not practicing what she preached. The mother of two boys, 7 and 4, and a 2-year-old daughter (an adopted son, 24, is no longer at home) says she got the message.

Decker's boss, Executive Vice-President William A. Coley, has nothing but praise for her work. Why not? The employee-to-manager ratio has gone from 12 to 1 to 20 to 1. And even though turnover in telephone-call centers nationwide usually runs at 40% a year, Decker says her center's attrition is running at only 12% annually—and 75% of those transfer within the utility. Her moral is fairly simple: "As I treat my team, that's how they're going to treat the customer."

By Chuck Hawkins in Charlotte, N.C.

ployees can work a whole day uninterrupted at home. Morale also has improved. Just ask Pam Centoni, who sets up car pools. A telecommuter one day a week, she also works a "9-80" schedule (80 hours over 9 days). Every other Monday, she either has the day off or works at home. "I ride my bike, go to the pool, or do errands," she says. "There are not a lot of lines on Monday."

SURVIVAL. When employees are on odd schedules, managers have to work around them. Kate Sullivan, an attorney at Aetna, is responsible for the day-to-day operations of a 280-person legal department. But if she wants to meet with her support staff, it must be on Wednesdays, which is tricky because she travels often. The reason is that her assistants, Lisa Trusch and Leeann Barrieau, both mothers, are in a job share. Barrieau works Monday through Wednesday lunch, and Trusch works Wednesday through Friday. They keep in touch by phone and electronic mail: When one gets a message, it is automatically sent to the other. Without the job share, both women say they would have been forced to quit. While Aetna has to pay for 5½ days a week instead of 5, Sullivan, a mother herself, welcomes the schedule because "two heads are better than one on the job. They can

bounce ideas off each other and can work on two separate projects at once."

For some managers, flexibility is a matter of survival. When Joseph Steinreich became plant manager of Engelhard's two Huntsville (Ala.) plants in 1981, he was given six months to turn the chemical plants around or see them closed. The plants had a 150% turnover rate, 18% product waste, and 22 people were injured so seriously that they couldn't come back to work. A big part of the problem, managers and employees say, was excessive absenteeism, largely among workers who had drinking and other problems. "There were some Friday nights we couldn't even run," says Sharon Hobbs, a plant superintendent. "It was horrible."

Steinreich began by focusing on employees' problems, both at work and at home. He also established an employee-assistance program and hired an on-site psychologist, who is available one day a week and by beeper. Those changes laid the foundation for other innovations. In 1985, Steinreich allowed employees to vote on adjusting and distributing overtime and on setting lunch and break schedules. Recently, a majority of the plants' 290 workers voted to work four days of 10-hour shifts ending at 3 p.m., when their children get out of school.

The earlier schedule means that Steinreich, who likes to sleep late, is up at 5 a.m. But he's satisfied: Absenteeism per worker has dropped from an average of 20 days a year to 3 days, and turnover has dropped to under 1% annually. There's also less than 1% product waste, and on Sept. 13, the plants will have had 10 years without a serious injury.

Other managers respond to workers' personal needs because a determined employee won them over. Karen Tanklow, a social worker in Salem, Mass., wanted a job-sharing arrangement after the birth of her son in August, 1991. But her bosses at Massachusetts General Hospital were skeptical that a crisis-oriented job such as hers could be split. Tanklow drew up a detailed proposal, including how the job would be divided and who would cover what shifts, when. She even found a candidate of equal experience. It also didn't hurt that Tanklow's record was superb.

The arrangement has since convinced Tanklow's boss, Evelyn Bonander, the hospital's director of social services, that job sharing can be done. But she wouldn't grant the option to anyone: "You need people who are willing to be flexible, not just in their schedules but also in their willingness to do something the way someone else would do it."

Tanklow isn't totally happy with the way things worked out. Despite all her efforts, her partner got first crack at the schedule and Tanklow was passed over for a promotion. Bonander says Tanklow has taken on more responsibilities, which could lead to a management position down the road. "We are still learning to be less rigid," Bonander says.

Ultimately, flexibility for many managers means treating employees the way they would want to be treated. Sam Rivera, assistant foreman at Fel-Pro, tries to put himself in his workers' shoes (page 136). For Tenneco Gas Co.'s Claude Cox, an information-service specialist, the goal is to maximize his employees' strengths, however involved he must become in their personal lives to do so. In late 1988, one of Cox's 10 employees was asking for more and more time away from the office during normal working hours. At first, he made up excuses but then revealed this: His partner was dying of AIDS, and he had tested positive for HIV, the virus that causes AIDS.

RAPID CHANGE. Cox rearranged the employee's schedule to give him time off during the day to care for his partner: The employee worked before and after hours instead. When he got sick, Cox cut his workload from 50 or 60 hours a week to 40, then to 30. His performance didn't suffer. After a year, he went on long-term disability—but not until Cox made sure his salary lasted until the benefits kicked in. "You can have all the machinery in the world, but without this thing called an employee, you aren't going to make money," Cox says.

While bosses such as Cox may still be the exception in Corporate America, the business world is rapidly changing. Says Continental's Mascotte: "If we don't spend the time to create and foster a worker-friendly agenda, won't we contribute to the erosion of the very values we say we can't do without?" Many managers already know the answer: They realize that employees are also parents and children. Now the question for companies is no longer "Can we afford to offer these benefits?" but "Can we afford not to?"

By Michele Galen in New York, with Ann Therese Palmer in Chicago, Alice Cuneo in San Francisco, Mark Maremont in Boston, and bureau reports

The (R)Evolution of the American Woman

Catherine M. Daily, Guest Editor

Catherine M. Daily is an assistant professor of management at the College of Business, Ohio State University, Columbus.

To give a woman the vote, according to a U.S. senator in 1866, would be to put her "in an adversary position to man and convert all the now harmonious elements of society into a state of war, and make every home *a hell on earth*" (Rosenberg 1992; emphasis added). Here is an attitude that provides some insight into the difficulty of women's struggle for equality. And nowhere has this struggle been more visible than in the workplace, as generations of women have historically fought to create harmony between their jobs both inside and outside the home. Although the level of participation by women in the work force has fluctuated during the 1900s, their contributions and progress cannot be discounted.

The economic contributions of women have increased substantially over the past century as the influx of women into the workplace has swelled. The recently released Department of Labor report, *Workforce 2000*, noted that by the end of the century women will constitute nearly half of the work force. This is more than twice the rate of participation recorded in the early 1900s, when just over 21 percent of the work force was women (Edwards et al. 1991).

Several factors have contributed to this more than double the number of working women over the past century. Such technological innovations as washing machines and dishwashers have freed them from the time-consuming tasks necessary to managing the home environment. The fertility rate has steadily declined and has recently leveled off. Medical advances have shortened the amount of time spent caring for sick children. The rise in single-parent families and the increasing need for dual-income households to maintain reasonable living standards have made income-generating work less a choice than a necessity for most women.

Although for many of us our most vivid memories of progress begin with the social and sexual revolution of the 1960s, working women are clearly not a novelty of the past 30 years. Little progress was realized, however, until this struggle affected middle- and upper-class women seeking advancement into the professional ranks—a trend that has risen since the 1920s. Until the 1960s, however, the contributions of these work force participants were typically transitory. Women worked while they were young and unmarried. Two world wars provided employment opportunities for them. With marriage and peace, however, women exchanged their jobs in the marketplace for those in the home.

To begin to understand the evolution of the role of American women, we must appreciate the difficulty of cultural change, as found in the barriers to progress. At the same time, we must recognize and capitalize on those factors that have enabled progress.

A cultural revolution must occur for women to achieve equality within the workplace.

A Chronology of Progress

Rosenberg (1992) recently chronicled the history of working women in America during the twentieth century. Until very recently, women were largely considered a reserve work force used to fill positions that were either undesirable, be-

From *Business Horizons*, March/April 1993, p. 1-5. © 1993 by The Foundation for the School of Business at Indiana University. Reprinted by permission.

cause of low pay or status, or needed in times of crisis, such as that experienced during times of war. Dr. Alice Hamilton, a physician in the early 1900s and one of a handful of pioneers in the women's movement, commented on this mentality, noting that "[t]he American man gives over to the woman all the things he is profoundly disinterested in, and keeps business and politics to himself."

Whereas approximately 40 percent of unmarried women over the age of 14 worked for wages in 1900, the overall participation of women as a percentage of the work force was 21.2 percent. The typical woman's experience involved working while she was a young woman living under her parents' roof—but only until she got married, whereupon she assumed responsibility for the care and maintenance of the home.

Women who sought a life independent of men had few options. Typically they were relegated to communities of women. Jane Addams, an activist in the early 1900s, was one of the initiators of this independent lifestyle. At the turn of the century, she created a Chicago settlement community designed to meet the needs of unmarried, educated women. The women who joined these communities provided each other with the emotional support to lead the women's movement and challenge other women to become active in transforming the role expectations that society placed upon them.

Not surprisingly, these choices were radical in their time. As has been the case throughout this century, women did not speak in a unified voice. Various factions gained followers. The women striving for change at this time in our history typically fell into one of two categories: suffragists and anti-suffragists. A common denominator shared by both groups was the reliance upon argumentation, which emphasized the differences between men and women. The suffragists argued that the differences between the sexes made political support essential. Anti-suffragists, however, believed sex differences meant that women were destined to remain in the home while men participated in business and politics.

The women's movement continued to be plagued by these factions, preventing any widespread, unified effort for bringing equality between women and men into the workplace. Even today, women support the platforms of various groups professing to speak for the majority opinion. Conservative factions left over from the early 1970s, spearheaded by Phyllis Schlafly's campaign to prevent the ratification of the Equal Rights Amendment, are still at loggerheads with such feminist groups as the National Organization for Women. The perpetual infighting of women can easily obscure the progress that began with such women as Alice Hamilton and Jane Addams.

Progress, however, has not been consistent. The stock market crash in 1929 all but obliterated any gains realized during the previous several decades. With unemployment levels reaching 25 percent, few were interested in the economic or social gains of women. In fact, the opinion that working women were the cause of the crash by virtue of taking away men's jobs gained considerable momentum.

The growth of the service sector and the onset of World War II brought some measure of relief from the backlash of the stock market crash. During the war, women's participation in the work force rose to 35 percent, with a doubling of the numbers of married women who worked outside the home. With the recognition that women were essential to the functioning of the economy, employers responded to the needs of women in the workplace as well as in the home. To accommodate married women with children, day care centers were established and employers provided hot meal programs. But as the war ended and the men returned home, not only were these services discontinued, but men rapidly began displacing the women from the higher-paying jobs they had filled during the war. Once again, the backlash was felt.

The most recent gains occurred as a result of the social unrest of the country during the 1960s. Women's resolve to fight for equality was revitalized. The progress made during the modern women's movement has led to a work force composed of 41 percent women, with projections of an even split by the year 2000.

A Woman's Place

Every push forward has been answered with resistance. Faludi (1991), in the bestseller *Backlash: The Undeclared War Against American Women*, documents evidence of a societal backlash occurring whenever women appear to be achieving the still elusive goal of workplace equality. With each incremental gain, the push for equality has met cultural resistance strong enough to halt the advance.

As evidence of the difficulty of widespread progress, even when economic necessity forced a married woman to work outside the home, she was castigated by men and women of all social classes. A 1936 Gallup Poll found that 82 percent of respondents, including 75 percent of the

> *"With each incremental gain, the push for equality has met cultural resistance strong enough to halt the advance."*

women, believed a woman should not work if her husband held a job. These numbers barely changed after World War II, when 80 percent of women and 84 percent of men felt similarly. Remnants of these attitudes persist even today.

A common denominator underlying these attitudes is an unsettling ambiguity of what defines appropriate gender roles. Eleanor Roosevelt, widely believed to be an ardent supporter of women's rights, struggled with the definition of appropriate primary and secondary roles for women:

> It seems to me perfectly obvious that if a woman falls in love and marries, of course her first interest and her first duty is to her home, but her duty to her home does not of necessity preclude her from having another occupation.

More recently, Degler (1980) noted that this conflict still exists:

> Women are still the primary child rearers, even when they work, and the purpose of their work in the main is to support and advance the family, not to realize themselves as individuals.

The biological fact of childbearing has provided the basis for an occupational segregation that has persisted into the 1990s. Even today, parenting is still perceived as primarily a female role; conversely, a full-time, uninterrupted career is still perceived as a male role. It is, however, the persistence of this segregation that remains an inexplicable element of today's culture. Childbearing may be a biological function unique to women, but child care is an issue that transcends gender.

Building Glass Walls

The coining of the term "mommy track" recently ignited debate based on the premise that women are responsible for the two full-time roles of mother/wife and wage earner. Career interruptions as a result of family commitments have led to the stereotype of women who leave organizations to bear and care for children.

Once again, perception is greatly divorced from reality. One recent examination (Garland 1991) found that most of the turnover among women in large firms was a result of some factor other than the desire to "rock the cradle." In fact, 73 percent of these women moved to another company, presumably to seek greater career opportunities or a better working environment.

Role segregation is just one of the barriers that prevents women from advancing to the top levels of organizations. Without access to top management positions, women are relegated to a permanent second-class status in organizations. Any disruption in the organizational status quo threatens the economic lock men hold on these senior-level positions. In 1968, women represented 15 percent of managers, yet today a mere 3 percent of senior executives are women, compared to 1 percent in 1981—a net gain of only 2 percent at the senior level in the past decade. If women were advancing at a rate comparable to that of their male peers, we would expect significantly more women (closer to 15 percent) to occupy senior-level positions 25 years later. Complicating this slow pace is men's resistance to change and women's historical reluctance to create change.

> "Change brings with it costs, some of which are deliberately built into organizational systems to discourage women from persisting when faced with artificial barriers."

Change brings with it costs, some of which are deliberately built into organizational systems to discourage women from persisting when faced with artificial barriers. Such barriers are constructed based on stereotypes and biases that do little to enable the performance of women in the workplace and much to detract from the consistently high levels of performance that women are capable of achieving.

A recent and notable example of one of the most pervasive barriers women face was the resignation of Dr. Frances Conley, professor of neurosurgery at Stanford University. In an act providing evidence that success in the professions remains difficult for women, Conley resigned her tenured faculty position following 16 years of "gender insensitivity," manifested in such indignities as being called "honey" by her male colleagues.

This incident exemplifies a barrier that has received scant serious attention—language differences between men and women. Gilligan (1982) suggests that women and men speak different languages, which each group assumes to be the same. Men, for example, use language to structure hierarchies, whereas women use language to build relationships. The resulting confusion when these two language styles collide often results in unintentional barriers.

Stylistic differences contribute to an array of tradition-bound stereotypes that women continue to face in organizations. The totality of these attitudes and prejudices transcend the proverbial "glass ceiling" and include "glass walls" as well (Lopez 1992). These barriers refer to the subtle biases that have prevented women from advancing in organizations. The lack of upward mobility demonstrates "the abiding . . . sexism of the corporation" (Bradsher 1988). Not only is women's upward mobility stifled, but lateral mobility is limited as well.

The costs to organizations supporting these role distinctions are significant. Mary Rowe, adjunct professor at the Massachusetts Institute of Technology's Sloan School of Management, has termed this treatment "microinequities" (Edwards et al. 1991). Microinequities occur when stereotypes, not actual performance, constitute the basis for workplace treatment. The outcome is often exclusion from critical information (via exclusion from the "old boy network") and skewed performance appraisals based exclusively on subjective measures of performance.

As evidence of stereotypes operating more powerfully than fact, a recent Department of Education report, entitled *Women at Thirtysomething,* found that women consistently outperformed their male counterparts at both the secondary and undergraduate educational levels. Nevertheless, these same women faced a tougher labor market than men, experienced higher levels of unemployment, and suffered gross pay inequities (Koretz 1992). Clearly, the skills and abilities of a significant portion of the work force are being grossly underutilized, if not ignored.

The bias continues to exist, in part, because of differences in preparing individuals for advancement in organizations. Those in positions of power typically encourage and advance individuals most like themselves. Exclusion from these formal and informal networks provides some explanation for the abysmal percentage of women in top management positions.

Exploiting the Cracks

Women who have broken into the corporate elite have relied to a large extent on familial ties. Marion O. Sandler, CEO of Golden West Financial, for example, shares her position with her husband. Katherine Graham, chairperson of The Washington Post Co., inherited her position after the death of her husband. While these women have excelled in these positions, the avenue by which they gained access to the corporate elite is a narrow street that very few have the opportunity to travel. Reliance upon familial ties will not benefit the vast majority of qualified women desiring top corporate positions. Being born into privilege is much like being born into royalty—a privilege of nature, not a barometer of one's ability to lead.

Faced with this reality, significant numbers of women elect alternatives to the traditional organization. The growth of women-owned businesses

has ballooned. During the years between 1974 and 1984, the rate of women-owned startups was six times that of men. Some of these businesses are born out of the desire to integrate work and family life successfully, an accommodation that few large firms are willing to make.

The trend toward self-employment, though an attractive alternative at an individual level, does little to address the inequities that continue to plague corporate America. Large-scale organizations must work to manage the diversity that women bring to the workplace. Continued pressure to conform to tradition-bound ideals may only drive more women from large organizations, at a cost to both parties.

Some 15 years ago Kanter (1977) suggested that to manage inequities effectively, organizations must alter systems, structures, and management practices to eliminate any subtle barriers that may prevent employees from reaching their full potential. By focusing on these issues, the burden of blame is removed from any given individual. This orientation enables behavior to be explained more as a function of the position one holds in the organization than as a general attitudinal predisposition. Systemic change, however, is unlikely without cultural revolution.

Removing existing barriers in the workplace is an issue that confronts women and men alike. Challenging opportunities, which provide visibility and the potential for success, are crucial to women's advancement. Incentives must be created so that all organizational members approach issues of equality with a progressive mindset. Rather than perpetuate blame, we must embrace change as a vehicle to equality. As Faludi (1991) suggests, those fearful of progress may, in the short term, have the strength to push back advances. It is unlikely, however, that they possess the endurance to outlast those seeking a cultural (r)evolution.

This special issue of *Business Horizons* is designed as a mechanism for opening the door to such progress. As you read the following articles, be mindful of Gilligan's observation (1982) and make the effort to hear the message:

> As we have listened for centuries to the voices of men and the theories of development that their experience informs, so we have come more recently to notice not only the silence of women but the difficulty in hearing what they say when they speak.

References

K. Bradsher, "Women Gain Numbers, Respect in Board Rooms," *The Los Angeles Times,* March 17, 1988, p. 1.

C. Degler, *At Odds: Women and the Family in America from the Revolution to the Present* (New York: Oxford University Press, 1980).

A. Edwards, S.B. Laporte, and A. Livingston, "Cultural Diversity in Today's Corporation," *Working Woman*, January 1991, pp. 45-61.

S. Faludi, *Backlash: The Undeclared War Against American Women* (New York: Crown Publishers, Inc., 1991).

S.B. Garland, "How to Keep Women Managers on the Corporate Ladder," *Business Week*, September 2, 1991, p. 64.

C. Gilligan, *In a Different Voice* (Cambridge, Mass.: Harvard University Press, 1982).

R.M. Kanter, *Men and Women of the Corporation* (New York: Basic Books, 1977).

G. Koretz, "America's Neglected Weapon: Its Educated Women," *Business Week*, January 27, 1992, p. 22.

J.A. Leavitt, *Women in Administration and Management: An Information Sourcebook* (New York: Oryx Press, 1988).

J.A. Lopez, "Study Says Women Face Glass Walls as Well as Ceilings," *Wall Street Journal*, March 3, 1992, pp. B1, B8.

A.M. Morrison and M.A. Von Glinow, "Women and Minorities in Management," *American Psychologist*, February 1990, pp. 200-208.

E. Roosevelt, *It's Up to Women* (New York: Franklin A. Stokes, 1933).

R. Rosenberg, *Divided Lives: American Women in the Twentieth Century* (New York: Hill and Wang, 1992).

F.N. Schwartz, *Breaking with Tradition* (New York: Warner Books, 1992).

A.T. Segal and W. Zellner, "Corporate Women," *Business Week*, June 8, 1992, pp. 74-78.

D. Tannen, *You Just Don't Understand: Women and Men in Conversation* (New York: William Morrow and Co., Inc., 1990).

Business rethinks, refines, recycles, and recoups

Ted J. Rakstis

"The green movement" branches further into offices, shops, and factories as the working world learns that recycling makes both dollars and sense

Americans are being buried under an avalanche of trash that shouldn't even exist.

According to waste-collection industry estimates, people in the United States each year throw away more than 1 million tons of aluminum cans and foil; 4.5 million tons of office paper; 10 million tons of newsprint; and earth-rupturing quantities of glass bottles and jars, metals, and plastics.

Landfills in many US communities are near capacity, and only 23.4 percent of the garbage consists of food and yard waste. The remainder is divided as follows: paper and paperboard, 42.1 percent; glass, 9.4 percent; metals, 9.2 percent; plastics, 6.5 percent; and other waste, 9.4 percent.

Moreover, most landfill waste is unnecessary, because nearly all such material could be recycled. Marcy R. Wydman, president of WITT Company, a manufacturer of recycling containers in Cincinnati, Ohio, observes: "The recovery and reuse of one ton of paper saves seventeen trees, diverts

From *Kiwanis Magazine*, August 1993, pp. 40-43, 49. © 1993 by Kiwanis International. Reprinted by permission.

ninety-six gallons of water from the pulping process, and reduces the energy required to make the paper from virgin materials by the equivalent of two-and-one-half barrels of oil. With the average office worker throwing away at least a half-pound of paper each day, or more than 125 pounds a year, recycling makes good environmental sense.

"Including high-grade paper and beverage cans, businesses generate valuable office recyclables. Their recovery means less waste, less use of landfill space, and reduced trash-disposal costs."

There aren't enough recycling facilities in the US to handle what's already being hauled away by curbside collection programs (*see related story, page 146*). Still, processing capability is bound to increase as organizations realize the economies that can be attained through recycling.

Public concern at last is mounting. Michael Peters Design, a New York marketing firm, learned that 78 percent of the consumers it surveyed in 1990 would be willing to pay more for "environmentally benign" products. And in the three years since that study was conducted, curbside programs in the US have burgeoned by more than 600 percent.

Another significant study was carried out by Gerstman + Meyers Inc., a New York City-based design-consulting organization. In 1989, Gerstman + Meyers found little consumer interest in environmentally clean packaging.

Only a year later, a second survey turned up a complete reversal in attitudes. Ninety-four percent of those questioned in 1990 said they believed that buying products in such packaging would contribute to the struggle to save Earth.

Companies that have established recycling policies are attracting and retaining top-quality employees.

"If you have a reputation for being a responsible business, people will be proud to work for you," says Jeffrey Hollender, chairman of Seventh Generation, a supplier of recycled paper in Colchester, Vermont.

Recycling doesn't represent an additional cost of doing business. By making your staff aware of why it's important, you'll *save* money, because you'll buy fewer supplies. If your company churns out substantial waste, you might even profit by selling it to a commercial recycler.

"Making a company 'green' can sound intimidating, indeed, to a small-business owner with too many things to do and too few people to do them," Mary Rowland writes in Your Company magazine. "But there's a lot of help and information available. You'll find handbooks, recycling services, and suppliers of 'benign' products.

"A good way to start, if you have the resources, is to have a consultant do an environmental audit, which may cost several thousand dollars. If you can't afford an audit, there are simpler things to do. You

must try to reduce waste, replace inefficient items, reuse whatever you can, recycle what you must dispose of, and buy recycled products. You can save the most money just by generating less trash."

WITT Company's Marcy Wydman lists these as the most essential steps:
• Make a firm personal commitment. Appoint a program coordinator, invest in recycling containers, and educate your employees as soon as the program begins.
• Instruct your coordinator to choose a waste-paper dealer, develop a collection system, select collection containers, meet with maintenance personnel, track the program to ensure that it runs smoothly, and analyze cost savings.
• Install recycling containers at locations where trash is thrown away most frequently. The most obvious areas are around copy machines, computers, common work centers, and individual desks and workstations. The best place for beverage-can-collection receptacles is near your cafeteria or lunchroom and in waiting rooms. To simplify separation and collection, color-code all containers.
• Organize your central storage area so that there's no chance for accidental mixing of trash with recyclable paper. Be certain that the location meets fire-code requirements. Many companies keep their main storage bins in the basement or near loading docks.
• Get everyone in the organization to participate. Begin with a signed kickoff memo that highlights the program's benefits and explains the separation and collection procedures. Explain where the revenue from the program will go. A share for an office party, for example, will build enthusiasm. After the memo is circulated, conduct a brief information session.
• Reinforce the recycling habit. In follow-up memos or on bulletin boards in heavy traffic areas, provide information on the amounts recycled, cost savings, and any problems that may exist.
• Besides a disposal program, put into effect other methods to reduce waste and reuse products. These include re-inking printer cartridges instead of throwing them away, eliminating unnecessary packaging, and circulating memos rather than making a copy for each employee.
• Because colored paper isn't collected in many programs, buy only white paper. Most important, purchase recycled white paper. When organizations express a preference for recycled products, more disposal companies will build recycling facilities to meet the market demand.

"Another approach to recycling that has been adopted by some companies is shredding paper for use as packing material," Patrick J. O'Connor reports in The Office magazine. "Some firms that didn't have shredders are buying them for that purpose.

"Aluminum and glass, as compared to paper, have very few categories. In offices,

the (recyclables) are mainly beverage containers. If they aren't returnable for a deposit or covered by a mandatory recycling program, these containers usually can be recycled locally through a commercial vendor or voluntary organization."

Some offices have too little waste to interest a recycling company. John Ortbal, author of *Buy Recycled! Your Practical Guide to the Environmentally Responsible Office*, recommends that firms with offices in multitenant buildings enter into cooperative recycling ventures.

> **Companies that have recycling policies are attracting top-quality employees**

Ortbal, president of Services Marketing Group in Chicago, also suggests that you use as few photocopy sheets as possible by copying on both sides and using your copy machine's reduction features. In addition, written memos can be all but eliminated through telephone and voice-mail messages. If your company has a direct-mail list, Ortbal further advises that you weed out the names of prospects who haven't responded.

Some big American companies are racking up huge savings through recycling.

Employees of Coca-Cola in Atlanta, Georgia, for instance, recycle nearly everything in sight. In one three-year period, they raised $50,000 for charity by selling otherwise useless junk. At AT&T's headquarters in New Jersey, the company saves $1.3 million a year from the recycling of office paper alone.

Bellcore, the New Jersey-based research arm of the Bell Telephone companies, makes $300,000 a year through the sale of recyclables and lower haul-away expenses. The company, which launched its recycling program in 1988, sells a videotape and other how-to-do-it materials to businesses that want to begin their own programs.

United Telephone of Florida (UTF), a Sprint company headquartered in Altamonte Springs, places its recycling focus on telephone directories. Through programs in thirteen counties, UTF in 1991 recycled more than 1,200 tons of directories. As a company publication points out, that kept 20,400 trees upright and saved 3,960 cubic yards of landfill space.

A UTF-sponsored program in Hardee County recruited the aid of schoolchildren and resulted in the return of 50 percent of all used directories. According to UTF, that's one of the highest return rates ever achieved in a voluntary collection program.

Steelcase Inc., based in Grand Rapids, Michigan, is one of the world's largest manufacturers of office furniture. In 1991, the company stopped sending fabric scrap to landfills. Instead, it was processed and used by the automobile industry as sound-dampening insulation. During the program's first six months, nearly forty tons of fabric were recycled.

The plan was set into motion when a forklift operator complained about the volume of discarded waste. Tom Hyde, a Steelcase project coordinator, organized a team of workers who knew that phase of production. Meeting weekly, they devised a collection system while management searched for and found a marketplace for the fabric scrap.

The Great Lakes Recycling Journal observes: "Fabric recycling at Steelcase is part of a large commitment to waste reduction. Other items now being recycled include office paper, corrugated (paper), sawdust, pallets, office ribbons, lubricants, tin, Styrofoam, telephone books, small batteries, plastics, foam, coatings, chemicals, and paint."

Long before US President Bill Clinton mandated drastic reductions in military expenditures, some armed-forces facilities were slashing costs through recycling projects.

Time magazine tells of one such effort that began in 1989: "J.J. Hoyt, recycling manager at the US Naval Base in Norfolk, Virginia, took over a solid-waste disposal program that had been costing taxpayers $1 million a year.

"A shrewd businessman, Hoyt was sensitive to hauling managers' needs and negotiated lucrative deals. Now, says one US Navy officer, 'not a tin can or newspaper falls to the ground on base.' (In 1992), Hoyt's program (earned) close to $800,000. 'The key is knowing the market,' he says."

 n a more limited scale, entrepreneurs and small-office professionals can achieve the same kind of results.

Recycling programs often begin with a single idea. As one example, Levine/Schneider Public Relations in Los Angeles recycles all the paper, press releases, envelopes, cards, and labels that pass through its office each day.

"My challenge to all businesses is to get involved in doing something to recycle and conserve," says Michael Levine, the firm's president. "If not, we aren't meeting our obligations as good corporate citizens."

The Equity Group Inc., a financial public-relations firm in New York, has found an easy way to get second usage of most of its paper. Says spokeswoman Linda Latman: "We issue and print news releases on behalf of our clients and include them in the background kits we mail. Sooner or later, those releases become dated and obsolete.

"Instead of dumping them, we use the printless side of the press releases in our plain-paper fax machine and for drafts in

Process produces paper recycling

The Great Lakes Recycling Journal suggests a six-step process to make paper recycling successful in your office:

1. Appoint one of your most reliable employees to act as recycling coordinator. Working with him or her, motivate your employees to make recycling a commitment.

2. Talk to a waste-paper dealer or a local recycling center to determine what type of paper can be collected. Then, enter into a contract with a recycling hauler.

3. Set up a system that will enable your employees to separate paper at their desks quickly. For example, ask them to place computer paper in one bin, white office paper in another, and colored office paper in a third.

4. Prepare and distribute a list that describes which papers are "recyclable" and which are "trash." Most important, stress that recycling bins aren't garbage cans. Coffee grounds and the like must be disposed of elsewhere.

5. Publicize the results. Generate enthusiasm by calculating the total weight of the paper recycled by your staff in the past month. Even more compelling, estimate how many trees have been spared and how much landfill space has been conserved.

6. Buy recycled paper. Show your employees the end product of their efforts. And remind them that such paper can be recycled again and again.

Curbside collection ahead of its time?

Between 1989 and 1992, Time magazine reports, the number of curbside trash-collection programs in the United States alone soared from 600 to 4,000. Yet, much of what's being hauled away never is recycled.

According to testimony given before a US Congressional committee, 100 million tons of newspapers are in storage nationwide because there are no places to recycle it.

Time remarks: "The problem is that the economics of recycling are out of whack. Enthusiasm for collecting recyclables has raced ahead of the capacity in many areas to process and market them. In recent years, many states and municipalities have passed laws mandating the collection of newspapers, plastics, glass, and paper. But arranging for processing—and finding a profit in it—has proved tricky."

The situation, however, may be only a short-term one. Some savvy processors have reaped substantial profits through the recycling of steel, aluminum cans, paper cartons, and cardboard.

Facilities to remove the ink from newsprint before it can be pulped to make new paper are tremendously costly. Still, smart deals can be made.

Many customers of Champion International Corporation, a major paper manufacturer, demand recycled paper. Champion Recycling Corporation, a subsidiary in Houston, Texas, built an $85 million de-inking plant. In turn, the city agreed to give Champion all its collections of old newspapers and magazines.

Says Champion International president Andrew Sigler: "This is a market-driven operation that's great for

Houston and gives us the assured supply we need for a profitable operation."

By the end of this century, recycling may be an economic necessity.

"Our members recognize that if you're not into recycling, you'll be out of business in ten years," says Allen Blakey, public relations director for the (US) National Solid Wastes Management Association. Based in Washington, DC, the trade group represents America's trash collectors.

Critics of recycling maintain that it will weaken the US economy, but Germany is thriving with a well-advanced national effort.

In December 1991, German retailers became obliged by law to reclaim such transport-packing materials as pressed foam and cardboard boxes. And, by mid-1995, German manufacturers will be required to collect 80 percent of their packaging waste.

The Duales System Deutschland, a recycling program initiated by private industry, had distributed collection bins to more than half of Germany's 80 million people by late 1992. Its goal is to reach everyone in the nation.

In Japan, recycling results are somewhat mixed. Time notes: "Japan's recycling rate is almost double that of the US—40 percent of municipal waste versus 17 percent. But the Japanese program shares some of the problems familiar to American recyclers. Milk cartons, one of the favorite recycling items, are piling up high in warehouses."

Hiroshi Takatsuki of Kyoto University compares his land's plight with that of the US: "Japan emphasized collection before coming up with an appropriate infrastructure for reuse."

our laser printer. In addition to releases, we use the other side of bad photocopies in the fax machine and the printers."

Manko, Gold, & Katcher, an environmental and land-use law firm in Bala-Cynwyd, Pennsylvania, initiated a basic recycling program that has become a model for many practices. It began when Jonathan Rinde, one of the firm's attorneys, commented to his associates: "Since we're an environmental law firm, maybe we should really try to use both sides of paper to reduce the paper flow.

"Perhaps we shouldn't use colored paper because it's more difficult to recycle. And what about those eight-and-one-half-by-fourteen-inch *yellow* pads that lawyers have been using for hundreds of years?"

The firm discovered that few of its vendors sold recycled legal pads. That prompted Rinde to recommend a radical departure from legal-profession tradition. He wanted to use *eight-and-one-half-by-eleven-inch white* pads. Rinde claimed that the smaller size would be both a paper reduction and recycling aid.

"But lawyers have *always* used eight-and-one-half-by-fourteen-inch yellow pads," one colleague argued. Another protested: "Let's not get carried away with all these new ideas!" Even though recycled paper at that time was more expensive, Rinde eventually won his point. Manko, Gold, & Katcher made the apparently unprecedented switch to small, white legal pads.

"All of us are feeling pretty terrific about what we're doing," says Mary McCullough, one of the firm's employees. "We now recycle newspapers, cans, and bottles. Also, we found legal pads with good-quality recycled paper. We use ceramic mugs or glasses instead of paper cups whenever possible. And our building recently started a recycling program. We like to think we had something to do with that."

NIBCO Inc., based in Elkhart, Indiana, manufactures faucets, industrial valves, and other flow-control devices at nine plants. Its recycling program involves each of its 4,500 employees.

Every work area is supplied with two wastebaskets: one for recyclable office paper and computer paper, the other for office-generated trash. Discarded office and computer papers are picked up each night by a commercial hauler and taken to a recycling firm hired by the company.

Aluminum cans are placed in lined containers throughout each NIBCO factory and emptied into a central aluminum-recycling bin once a week. Employees who live in areas not served by Elkhart's extensive

city recycling program are encouraged to bring all their home recyclables to work.

NIBCO buys only recycled paper products for office use. The office-supply requisition sheet itself is printed in soy-based inks on recycled carbonless paper. Further, the advertising department selects recycled paper for catalogs, price sheets, stationery, and all in-house printing.

Global Turnkey Systems Inc., a sixty-five-employee maker of customized computer software and hardware systems, went all out when it launched a recycling program at its facility in Waldwick, New Jersey. Laura Madaras, Global's corporate communications manager, conceived the plan and brought it to chief financial officer Michael Winer. What began as a recycling effort later turned into a wide-sweeping conservation campaign.

Madaras was named to head the drive. The early steps included the use of personal ceramic mugs bearing the corporate logo to replace paper and foam coffee cups, installation of bins and individual receptacles for various types of paper, pass-along memos in place of individual ones, centralized collection of aluminum cans, and a company policy of buying only recycled paper whenever possible.

Early in 1991, Winer decided to go beyond recycling and into total energy conservation. Heading a ten-employee volunteer cost-cutting team, he saw potential savings everywhere.

"By recycling paper," Winer notes, "you're saving energy, because paper producers don't need to create new paper. But you also can save your own electricity, water, and utilities in-house by initiating conservation procedures."

The team met every two weeks at lunch to discuss such energy-saving topics as high-efficiency light bulbs, energy audits, and water usage. Soon, conservation efforts swept through the company.

Initially, the energy-savings blueprint included the elimination of inefficient personal heaters, air-vent balancing, a strict policy of shutting off all unused lights and computers, and the installation of sun film on windows. That added up to a five-month saving of nearly $3,000.

Next, Global Turnkey cut its water usage by 40 percent when it installed low-flow faucet aerators on sinks and in the lunchroom. The sale of eighteen tons of used paper a year brought in monthly revenue of about $150. And with less trash going out, disposal services were slashed by $442 a month.

It all added up to about $10,000 in annual savings. Global used the money to buy

rolls, doughnuts, and bagels for employees; purchase recycling containers and energy-saving mechanisms; and make donations to local charities.

Companies whose products require packaging and glass are coming forth to do their share. Dry Creek Vineyard in Healdsburg, California, for example, has asked glass suppliers to buy only recyclable cardboard boxes for its bottles.

Peterson and Sons Winery in Pavilion Township, Michigan, is the state's smallest winery. Even so, it has its own home-devised bottle-washing equipment and a recycling program. The company pays a refund of twenty-five cents for each of the 3,000 or so wine bottles that it sells annually.

Printers also are becoming aware of the need to recycle what they sell. In Kalamazoo, Michigan, TS Print Center operates two shops. Several years ago, Suzanne Cook, the company's president, volunteered to print brochures promoting Earth Day events in Kalamazoo. She inserted recycling tips in each envelope.

About 30 percent of her customers, Cook says, request that their printing be done on recycled paper. She suggests that they have all of it done that way, explaining that printers like recycled paper because it folds and dyes more easily.

"It looks beautiful," she adds. "There's even gloss-finished recycled paper. Many people are unaware that recycled paper exists. Once the demand increases, costs will go down and the stock will be easier to obtain."

Recycling has emerged as a popular community-service activity. One of the most spectacular events unfolds on the second Saturday of every month at the American Mall in Allen County, Ohio. Some 500 pickup trucks, vans, and other vehicles head for the mall to donate their garbage to the Tri-Moraine Audubon Society.

"We fill two forty-five-foot tractor trailers with about 35,000 pounds of newspapers, glass, and aluminum cans each month," says an enthusiastic Audubon officer. "It gets pretty lively. Our volunteers unload six cars at a time, but it still gets backed up."

Does that give you an idea for a Kiwanis club project? And, what about your own business or practice? Have you looked at ways to buy and sell recycled products? It's good citizenship, and, in the "green-conscious" 1990s, it's also an extremely smart business strategy.

Combating Drugs In the Workplace

MINDA ZETLIN

Minda Zetlin is a New York-based writer.

George was one of the owners of a small, family-run business in the Midwest. One day, while walking around his manufacturing plant, he found a package of suspicious-looking white powder.

Bewildered, he summoned the local police; their investigation turned up an entire cocaine-dealing ring operating on his premises. In fact, the drug was being transported inside the stuffed animals his company manufactured.

Although names and identifying details have been changed, the above story is true. The point is a simple one: No matter who you are or what your company does, your workplace can be affected by drug abuse. And if your image of the typical drug abuser is a minority, inner-city teenager, think again. "Sixty-eight percent of drug users are currently employed," says Lee Dogoloff, executive director, American Council for Drug Education. "Seventy-six percent are white, which you would never know by watching the evening news." This, he says, explains the current concern with drugs in the workplace: "That's where they are."

Corporate America is beginning to think so too. Five years ago, an American Management Association survey of human resources managers showed that less than half their companies had addressed the issue of drugs at all; this year, the same survey showed 85 percent had established specific drug-abuse policies. Sixty-three percent were conducting some form of drug testing. (The possibilities include random testing of all employees,

testing for "cause," as when an employee presents suspicious behavior or is recovering from a drug problem, testing as a routine part of post-accident investigation, or as a condition of hire.)

"Most major corporations now do pre-employment testing," Dogoloff says. Some managers only began such testing because most other companies in their communities were doing it. "They started thinking, 'Gee, what kind of candidates are coming to us?' "

Though most human resources managers believe testing is an effective weapon against workplace drug abuse, it does have passionate opponents. "Drug testing is an invasion of privacy," says Shelly Ginenthal, director of human resources at Macworld Communications Inc. "Besides, the accuracy is often in question, and a false positive can do a lot of damage to a person's reputation."

Whether or not you are in favor of it, drug testing alone is not enough, experts say. That belief is echoed by respondents of the AMA survey: Less than 9 percent of its survey respondents depend on testing alone to combat drug abuse. Most also provide drug education, supervisory training, employee assistance programs, or some combination of these.

Drug education is particularly effective, many companies have found. According to the survey, those companies that conducted drug education had a 55 percent lower test-positive rate than those that didn't. "A person who understands how a drug like marijuana interferes with coordination will have a different view of the crane operator's pot break—especially if he or she is on the receiving end of a bucket of concrete," Dogoloff explains.

PROCESS OUTWEIGHS POLICY

The foundation of an effective anti-drug program, experts agree, is a clear and coherent drug pol-

icy. "The first thing a company's management needs to do is figure out why drug use is unacceptable in its workplace and what it's going to do about it," Dogoloff explains. "To me, the process by which you figure your policy out is more important than what the policy is at the end. The thing not to do is hire some expert to come sit alone in a room and write up a policy for your company."

Instead, he suggests bringing together those areas of the company that must deal directly with drug problems: human resources, legal, safety, an EAP or a health department, and a representative who can speak for employees—whether or not they're represented by a union.

For one thing, he adds, you're more likely to create a policy that fits your company's philosophy, corporate culture and the industry it's in. Besides, "these are the same people who will have to live with the policy and implement it when it's done."

Whatever drug program or policy you wind up with, experts caution against ignoring the most common workplace drug: alcohol. Most do not make a distinction between alcohol abuse and illegal drug abuse—since drug abusers often use both at once.

"Alcohol is the overwhelming drug of choice," notes Jim Kelley, a partner in the Washington, D.C., law office of Morgan, Lewis & Bockius. Unfortunately, he says, many companies see alcoholism as a "run-of-the-mill" addiction. And because the media focus has been on illegal drugs, many companies have had a tendency to overlook alcohol abuse.

THE CORPORATE QUANDARY

Whatever you do, when faced with a drug abuse problem, "the first rule is: don't do nothing," Dogoloff says. "If you leave it alone, it's going to get worse."

From *Management Review*, August 1991, pp. 17-24. © 1991 by The American Management Association, New York. All rights reserved. Reprinted by permission of the publisher.

MANAGED CARE—DOES IT WORK?

Talk to employee assistance program (EAP) professionals about drug rehabilitation, and you'll often hear the same complaint: a substance abuser comes to them for help and they recommend treatment—only to find the company's insurance won't pay for it.

At issue is the concept of managed care: reducing medical expenses, and thus insurance premiums, by ensuring that employees receive only such treatment that is deemed medically necessary. The idea has spawned an industry: Most major companies now have managed care companies overseeing employees' medical expenses and ruling out those seen as inappropriate; many of these managed care companies are subsidiaries of insurance firms. HMOs, though fundamentally different, operate on managed care principles, as well.

Managed care's detractors claim that this kind of care serves to treat employees only when they're really ill, and refuses treatment earlier, when illness might be prevented. Further, they point to the fact that both managed care companies and HMOs profit most by denying treatment. (HMOs can cut expenses, and thus raise profits, by denying treatment. And, although managed care companies may not gain directly by denying treatment, every time they do, they save money for the company that hired them.)

Managed care providers argue that it is the complete lack of control on medical spending that has driven insurance premiums into the stratosphere. Further, they claim, each individual case is evaluated according to the patient's needs and *not* the bottom line. So how can they produce these savings that companies hire them to create? "If you're making decisions based on the client's needs, you're going to save money, because there's been a lot of inappropriate hospitalizations, people staying in the hospital longer than they need to, and that type of thing," says Jeff St. Romain, national account manager consultant for Human Affairs International, a managed care company and subsidiary of Aetna.

Whether good or bad, managed care has a profound effect on the treatments available to drug abusers. Most often at issue is an EAP's recommendation of inpatient treatment, which is frequently turned down in favor of much less expensive outpatient sessions. Frustrated EAP professionals are left scrambling for free beds at government-sponsored facilities, or finagling free beds from programs they've sent paying clients to in the past. In extreme cases, some have even doubled as social workers, counseling substance abusers themselves after coverage was turned down.

"The whole idea is to deny treatment," says Tom Ruggieri, LCSW, coordinator of the faculty-staff assistance program at the University of Maryland in College Park. "We've had employees who stay at home detoxing, in withdrawal for three or four days because we can't get inpatient treatment approved."

"HMOs, in particular, want the financially easy way out," says Valetta Evans, EAP manager for the American Red Cross. "Some have programs that don't do much at all, with only one meeting a week. Others will say: 'Okay, even if the person needs inpatient treatment, they have to fail at outpatient treatment first.' This is a tragedy. It just doesn't make sense."

Another EAP manager described one employee receiving drugs at home from a live-in boyfriend who was also physically abusing her. An insurance company denied inpatient treatment. Here was one case, he claimed, where inpatient treatment was clearly needed to get her out of a home environment in which going straight would be all but impossible.

But managed care professionals question this assessment. "You don't put someone in an inpatient program for housing reasons," St. Romain says. "What is insurance for? It's for medical conditions, not for housing. Companies can't afford to take on these kinds of situations."

Further, they argue, inpatient programs, especially ones of fixed duration, too often have been used as a rather costly panacea. "The idea is to go in for 28 days to straighten out—as if there were something magic about that length of time," St. Romain says. "I guess the magic is that insurance companies usually cover about 30 days of treatment."

"HMOs invariably want to manage treatment case by case," notes Glenn Young, chief operating officer of Health New England, an HMO in Springfield, Mass. "A program that automatically runs 28 or 21 days is not managing case by case."

And, he adds. "There's another aspect to this that EAP managers don't always talk about. The same company that instituted the EAP also decided to offer healthcare through an HMO or another managed care program. When the company's executives contracted for it, they knew what it meant. Often the two programs clash."

—M.Z.

As an employer, you are in a good position to help a drug abuser face reality, adds Ginenthal. "A lot of companies are quick to fire a drug abuser, but once that person is at large, the chances that he or she will get treatment diminish greatly." Often, the threat of dismissal will get a drug user into treatment when nothing else can, she adds. "So much of your identity and self-worth is tied to your job."

What's more, says Tom Ruggieri, LCSW, coordinator of the faculty-staff assistance program at the University of Maryland in College Park, "There are plenty of studies that show it's cheaper to rehabilitate someone than recruit, hire and train a new person."

Some job-related drug problems have straightforward solutions. Let's say an employee comes to work drug-impaired and relapses several times despite repeated rehabilitation treatment. You'd probably fire him: You'd have little choice. Or let's say someone stopped by your office to tell you she'd seen one of your employees smoking a joint at a private party Saturday night. You'd probably ignore this rumor without further substantiation.

But some drug-abuse incidents are not so clear-cut, presenting problems not only of good management, but also of good ethics. Following are five such dilemmas, each drawn from real life, though names and identifying details have been changed. *Management Review* asked for comments from four experts: a corporate manager (**Norm Bush,** president and chief operating officer at ENSCO Inc., a Virginia-based research and development company), a human resources executive (**Shelly Ginenthal,** director of human resources at Macworld Communications Inc., located in San Francisco), an employee assistance program professional (**Dale Masi,** D.S.W., professor at the University of Maryland School of Social Work and president of Masi Research Consultants Inc.) and an attorney who specializes in this area (**Jim Kelley** of Morgan, Lewis & Bockius). Their answers illustrate the conflicting concerns of safety, fairness, productivity and compassion that confront managers when dealing with this difficult issue.

CASE 1

Charles operates heavy equipment for a power company. One evening, on his own time and away from company premises, he is arrested for driving while intoxicated. A search of his car turns up packets of cocaine, a loaded gun and drug paraphernalia. Under police questioning, he admits he's been dealing drugs. Without Charles' arrest and confession, the company would have no knowledge of his dealing, and there was no evidence that he has been using or selling drugs at work. But the power company has recently instituted a drug-abuse policy forbidding employees to sell drugs. The policy does not specify whether this stricture applies only to the workplace, or to outside locations as well. Charles promises to go straight and offers to subject himself to drug testing. Should he be allowed to keep his job?

NORM BUSH:

Although this is a serious charge, I would hate to condemn him on his first incidence without understanding what history was involved. A lot would depend on *how* we learned about the problem: If he was hiding it and we found out through other means, it would indicate that he wasn't trying to correct the situation.

If he came forward, though, and I felt he was being honest, I would want to give him a chance through drug testing—which would be reasonable in this situation—and counseling. Then, because the case is so severe, I would talk to his counselors and get their opinion as to whether we should retain him or not. I would at least want to look at the possibility that the employee may change.

DALE MASI:

Selling drugs is a separate issue from taking drugs. How you found out about it doesn't matter. If your company has a policy that says drug dealing will not be permitted, then you should follow the policy.

If the policy doesn't specify that drug dealing is only prohibited on company premises, then that policy needn't be limited to company premises. And, unless you're part of the federal government, you have the right to write a policy that applies to employees' off hours.

SHELLY GINENTHAL:

I would assume the policy refers only to the workplace. Employers don't really govern what you do outside, so I don't think the company's policy could be enforced. I would have stayed out of this entirely and really stuck to the performance issues: Has the employee's arrest affected his attendance? If it has, he might be suspended and referred to an EAP, which could suggest a drug program. Although the company can offer assistance, it cannot demand that he receive treatment. Then I would continue to monitor his performance carefully.

JIM KELLEY:

Is Charles protected by a union contract or not? That will become the major point. In the absence of a union contract, most employers would terminate him, especially if they were serious about eradicating drugs in the workplace. There is particular concern about drug dealers: The theory is that employees who sell drugs are likely to sell to their coworkers, since that's an obvious, accessible market. And even though Charles was caught off company premises, the policy is enforceable; most state laws don't protect illegal conduct.

But if Charles has a union contract, the picture changes. Under most common contracts, it's questionable whether the company can enforce his termination, un-

less it can prove some relation to job performance.

THE REAL-LIFE OUTCOME

This is the only case in this article in which names and details have not been changed, because they are a matter of public record. In 1985, the Florida Power Corp. dismissed Charles Waters under the circumstances described. However, Waters *was* protected by a union contract, and his union, the International Brotherhood of Electrical Workers, filed a grievance. A labor arbitrator reviewed the case, found that the anti-drug policy was unclear in its application to off-premises activity and ordered Waters reinstated with back pay.

Florida Power fought the arbitration by filing to have it vacated in district court. The company won its filing, but the union appealed to the U.S. Court of Appeals, Eleventh Circuit, and that court reinstated the arbitrator's decision.

CASE 2

Andrea is a brilliant, young computer designer who recently won an award for her work. However, she has been showing up to work with bloodshot eyes and slurred speech. Her company sends her to its EAP for testing, and her system is found to contain painkillers for which she has a prescription. She had started taking them to help with a back problem, which has long since improved, but she has now become dependent on the painkillers. She lies about her symptoms to get more drugs. EAP professionals send her to a rehabilitation clinic. After staying clean for four months, she again comes to work impaired. Should she be fired?

NORM BUSH:

I would consider the circumstances of Andrea's situation. She didn't get into this for kicks. She got involved because of a real problem, and *then* she got hooked. I would be more sympathetic to her than to someone who started taking drugs recreationally.

I would probably put her on probation and give her more time. I might invite her to work part time while getting treatment. In general, I would hang in there longer before I gave up on this situation. But she'd have to be working toward getting off the dependence. I hired her to do the work at a certain quality level, and she's not meeting that level.

DALE MASI:

It depends on what the policy is. If the policy says that a drug user who has a relapse should be fired, then you should follow the policy. If she were the porter that cleaned up the plant, would you give her another chance? I don't think so. And all employees obviously have to be treated equally.

I don't think firing on the first relapse is a good policy. It's better to give employees a second chance and fire on the third incidence of drug use. But even if you have a bad policy, you can't start making exceptions. You shouldn't give mixed signals. It's not fair to the other employees.

SHELLY GINENTHAL:

I would let her know in what areas her performance wasn't satisfactory and give her a referral back to the EAP. We would go through all the counseling again, and we would have many conversations about how important it is to stay off the drugs. Then I would warn her that this was her last chance.

It doesn't really matter whether the drug is legal or illegal. I'm not looking at the drug problem. I don't see a big difference between a person using drugs, or having a marital problem, or working a second job during the night and coming in too tired to function. What I care about is her performance, and she's not performing. She needs to get that fixed, and I'm willing to supply her with whatever she needs to do it.

JIM KELLEY:

The drugs Andrea is using are not legal: They were fraudulently obtained, even if she does have a valid prescription. Abuse of prescription drugs is a major problem in the workplace, and many drug policies address this circumstance exactly. If you don't have a specific policy, essentially, you have to evaluate the relationship between Andrea's lapse and her job performance. You might want to accommodate her if she's still doing a good job.

You might also have legal problems if you fire her: Under many state disability statutes and the federal Rehabilitation Act (which applies to government contractors), she might qualify as disabled. If she were an alcoholic, most courts would say you have to give her another chance. They are less understanding about drugs, but they might still take that view with a drug user who was in a rehabilitation program.

THE REAL-LIFE OUTCOME

The policy in Andrea's company is that an employee who tests positive for drugs within a year of rehabilitation is terminated, and so it was determined that she had to leave. However, because the drugs she was abusing were legally obtained, she was allowed to resign, rather than be fired.

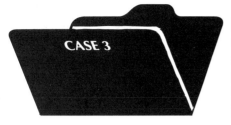

CASE 3

Nancy is a security guard in a manufacturing plant. For several months, she has been coming to work impaired by marijuana and depressants. Laura, Nancy's immediate supervisor, has discussed the problem with her several times, each time suggesting that Nancy seek counseling at the company's EAP. To let Nancy know that she cares, Laura has even gone to Nancy's home. Laura has the power to fire Nancy if she does not go to the EAP, but she lets the situation drag on. Laura is not doing her job effectively. Is it time for Laura's boss to step in?

DALE MASI:

It's very common for supervisors to avoid confronting drug users and holding them responsible for their behavior. Laura has got to remain uninvolved in Nancy's problem, while dealing with Nancy's performance. Going to Nancy's home is inappropriate; Laura is not a social worker.

As Laura's supervisor, I would tell Laura that she is responsible for Nancy's behavior. It's going to affect Laura's performance evaluation unless she handles the situation quickly. And that's the only way you'll get Laura to move.

SHELLY GINENTHAL:

I would try to get Laura some training. But because this is a safety issue, I would probably go over Laura's head and deal with the employee first. If it weren't a safety issue, I would coach and counsel Laura, give her an opportunity to handle the situation, or show her how it's done by meeting with her and Nancy together. I would send Laura to the EAP, and I would certainly want her to learn how to use the EAP in supervising people in crisis.

JIM KELLEY:

I would deal very severely with both supervisor and employee, es-

pecially given the nature of the job. At a minimum, I would give Laura a very serious counseling session. While she may believe she's being compassionate, she isn't helping Nancy—and she's harming the company.

As for the employee, this guard is worse than no security at all; I would get her off the job very quickly. Then I would give her a reasonable period of time to think about it—say, three days or a week—either without pay or as sick leave. During those few days, Nancy must decide whether she wants to go to the EAP. If not, she should be subject to disciplinary action, including discharge. Remember, an individual has to have an element of choice in going to an EAP—even if the option is losing her job.

NORM BUSH:

Because Nancy is in a position where security is paramount, she would be terminated immediately. When we hire someone in security, that person has to understand better than anyone how important it is. Because we deal with the Defense Department, we cannot tolerate any deviations at all that might jeopardize our classified material. If that happens, and the government decides we're not secure, they can cancel our con-

tract and put the entire company out of work.

As for Laura, I would counsel her and tell her I want Nancy removed. I'd explain that by trying to be understanding and sympathetic with Nancy, she'd failed to understand my concerns for the company. If she delayed further, I might have to put someone else in charge of security in the future.

THE REAL-LIFE OUTCOME

After several months of inaction—during which she'd been patiently briefed by her company's EAP head—Laura still had not dealt effectively with Nancy's drug problem. One day, Laura's boss, fed up with the situation, simply appeared at the security department and ordered Nancy to accompany him to the EAP. According to the EAP head, this forced Nancy to deal honestly, both with her counselor and herself, about what she was doing. As a result, he has high hopes for Nancy's recovery.

CASE 4

David is a former drug user who has spent time in jail. For the past three years he has been straight, and he now operates a forklift at a small construction company. Lately, however, he's begun having seizures, or "flashbacks," as a result of his earlier use of the drug PCP. He has been carefully evaluated by EAP professionals, and found to be clean of current drug use; indeed, they say flashbacks of this nature are quite common in ex-addicts. Mishandling of David's machine could be potentially dangerous to him and his coworkers. However, he has already had flashbacks while at the controls, and in each case the seizure caused him to release a handle, which simply stopped the machine. It is the only work he is qualified to do within this company. Should he continue on the job?

SHELLY GINENTHAL:

That's a tough one. I'd go right to David himself and really enlist his help in solving this problem. Then I'd put the situation to his coworkers—I'd maintain confidentiality about his prison record—and try to have them come up with a solution, rather than try to impose one. For instance, a coworker could be assigned to keep an eye on him at all times, ready to react if something happened. I would probably ask them to try this on a trial basis, so the situation could really be monitored.

NORM BUSH:

What I'd be tempted to do is retrain him for a different job and get him out of a potentially dangerous situation—where he could cause harm to himself and his coworkers. Even if it involved a cut in pay, it might mean a more permanent future.

JIM KELLEY:

Terminate him. You have no choice: He is physically unable to do the only work you have for him. Just because he's been lucky a couple of times doesn't mean this is a risk you or your company should take. It's unfortunate because he's clearly made an effort to stay away from drugs.

This is the kind of thing you tell high school kids about when you're warning them about the dangers of drugs.

DALE MASI:

I would not let the EAP make the decision. It's a medical decision, and I would want a brain scan and a full medical examination. I'd want to see what a psychiatrist who specializes in flashbacks had to say. I'd do that before assuming the seizures are flashbacks. It's a mistake people make often, and many patients are misdiagnosed. If the seizures aren't flashbacks, it may be possible to treat them.

If the people who do the examination are willing to sign off on him, and give him a clean bill of health, I'd let him go back to the forklift. Otherwise he might have to be retrained for another job in the company. If not, my hunch is you're eventually going to have to let him go.

THE REAL-LIFE OUTCOME

Company executives took a good look at David's history with seizures, including the fact that all of his seizures had been non-violent, and carefully considered the workings of the forklift he was operating. They took into consideration that he was drug-free. Eventually, executives decided that he posed no threat and allowed David to continue working the forklift. There have been no accidents so far.

CASE 5

Joe has been working at a large manufacturing company for about 20 years. Seven years ago, he had a serious alcohol problem. The company does not have a formal EAP, but Craig, his manager, gave Joe a referral to a rehabilitation program. With Craig's support, Joe stopped drinking. Recently, in the wake of a divorce, Joe has begun appearing at work under the influence again. This time, Craig has decided to fire him. The company's HR department wants to veto Craig's decision: Joe is only nine months away from retirement. Early retirement might be a solution, but Joe refuses that option, claiming the benefits are too low. How would you handle this?

NORM BUSH:

If the guy has been productive all these years, there is no way I would fire him with retirement only nine months away. I would try to get a bit more creative and figure out what to do, even if I had to keep him on the payroll at $1 a week until he retired. I would also make an evaluation as to whether he intended to continue working past retirement. And I would try to get the EAP to help him. If Craig insists that he still wants Joe out of the workplace, I would respect his decision, but tell him that we can't fire Joe.

SHELLY GINENTHAL:

I wouldn't allow Joe to be fired. Instead, I would somehow negotiate a deal that would get him out of the office. I would counsel Joe on what help was available and explore other options. It seems Craig should be satisfied just having Joe out of the picture. After all, the problem isn't that he needs to fire Joe, it's that he needs someone who can do the job.

JIM KELLEY:

I'd bring him in and say, "Look, Joe, you're late, you're often absent, and we can't deal with your unreliability. We would like to put you in a treatment program, or at least have you diagnosed." Whatever you do, Joe won't be left with nothing. Under federal law, you become vested in your retirement benefits after five years, although the benefits are much higher if he makes it to retirement.

But just because he's eight or nine months shy of retirement is no basis to say that we'll carry him so he can vest completely. If he looks you in the eye and says, "I don't have a problem," then you have to apply your disciplinary rules as if he were anyone else. As a manager, there's no common-sense reason to do otherwise.

DALE MASI:

The chances are probably still very good for rehabilitation. Joe's been clean for years, and it was a crisis that caused him to drink again. What you need to do is get him back to the EAP—and he will go back there if he knows that his only other choice is going on early retirement. Even if rehabilitation takes up almost all of Joe's remaining work time, it will pay for itself in lower medical expenses, since medical benefits are usually part of a retirement package.

As for Craig, he's getting involved emotionally when he shouldn't be, and he needs help. He's taking it personally that his employee is drinking again, even though Joe's just been through a personal crisis.

THE REAL-LIFE OUTCOME

Angry both at Joe and the HR department, Craig made it his personal mission to fire Joe before the nine months were up. Eventually, he succeeded.

AIDS in the Workplace: The Pandemic Firms Want to Ignore

Rose Knotts and J. Lynn Johnson

Rose Knotts is an associate professor of management, and **J. Lynn Johnson** is an associate professor of business administration, both at the University of North Texas, Denton.

"Acquired immuno-deficiency syndrome is the final stage of an infection caused by the human immuno-deficiency virus. HIV cripples the body's defenses, allowing cancers and life-threatening infections to develop."
— From "AIDS in the Workplace," Texas Department of Health brochure, June 1991.

A dmitting to an unprofitable quarter is more popular than confessing to employing a person with AIDS—or at least it seems that way. Current corporate mentality appears to consider that employing a person with AIDS (PWA) is a "malady" worse than sexual harassment, computer fraud, employment discrimination, or insider trading. Our cultural, religious, moral, and ethical taboos typically exclude it from being discussed openly. Companies simply wish to ignore the reality that AIDS is an organizational problem that must be addressed.

AIDS issues that were formerly ignored or concealed are finally being dealt with by a few pioneers in progressive organizations. Earvin "Magic" Johnson stunned the world in November 1991 with his announcement that he, a heterosexual basketball celebrity, had tested positive for HIV. *Fortune* sparked controversy with a feature on "Gays in Corporate America" (Stewart 1991) in which the AIDS issue was discussed. An even more conservative *Business Week* (Fitch 1992) described the prejudices encountered by Sean Strub, an HIV-positive entrepreneur. More recently, Arthur Ashe's reluctant announcement and subsequent death shed new light on the importance of AIDS awareness.

Though many "successful" business people and CEOs wish the dilemma would remain in the closet, corporate America has no such option. Despite industry's fantasy, ignoring the problem will not make it disappear. The primary corporate concern currently identifies the massive cost of caring for those infected as the most devastating effect. In reality, the most devastating effect will be the loss of valuable human resources. Any non-believers should ask the Los Angeles Lakers if they miss the talent and charisma of Magic Johnson.

> *Corporations cannot sidestep the problems generated by the AIDS pandemic.*

ORGANIZATIONAL AIDS ISSUES

A IDS is a critical concern for every organization. Even when the workplace is free of AIDS, it is likely to influence human resource management (HRM) organizational decisions and policies. The epidemic raises at least two pivotal questions for managers:

1. How should the firm treat an individual who has tested positive for the AIDS virus?

2. What policies and decisions should it address in coping with the impact of AIDS in the work force—loss of human potential, discrimination of infected workers, education and safety of coworkers, and provision of health benefits?

To address these questions, enterprising organizations are taking innovative approaches as more knowledge about the disease is discovered. An active firm will establish a responsible AIDS policy, implement a comprehensive educational program, and—most difficult of all—change attitudes about the disease.

A Responsible AIDS Policy

A responsible corporate AIDS policy will provide a mechanism for preparing the firm to handle the effects of the AIDS epidemic. A well-conceived policy addresses four basic concerns: equal treat-

From *Business Horizons*, July/August 1993, p. 5-9. © 1993 by The Foundation for the School of Business at Indiana University. Reprinted by permission.

ment, legal responsibility, education, and confidentiality for all employees. These important principles are explained as follows:

Equal Treatment. Employees infected with AIDS should have the same status as others with life-threatening illnesses. The stigma or discrimination associated with the possibility that the disease may have been contracted from socially unacceptable behavior does not justify discrimination practices toward the AIDS employee. AIDS is not a moral issue.

Legal Responsibilities. Organizational policies should comply with federal, state, and local laws and guidelines. Federal legislation affecting AIDS in the workplace are:

• The Vocational Rehabilitation Act of 1973 (VRA): 29 U.S.C. Section 701, et seq.;

• Section 5 (a) of Americans with Disabilities Act of 1990 (ADA): Pub. L. No. 101-336, Section 101, et seq.;

• Occupational Safety and Health Act of 1970 (OSHA): 29 U.S.C. Section 651, et seq.;

• Section 510 of the Employee Retirement Income Security Act of 1974 (ERISA): 29 U.S.C. Section 10001 et seq.;

• The U.S. Consolidated Omnibus Budget Reconciliation Act of 1986 (COBRA): Pub. L. No. 99-272, Section 10001, et seq.

Education for All Employees. Policies must be based on current scientific evidence. The U.S. Centers for Disease Control provides the most current information on the transmission and treatment of AIDS. A manager must be responsible for an effective education program based on this information as well as the latest updates.

Confidentiality of Employees. Establishing and maintaining employee confidentiality is critical in an effective AIDS policy. The failure of a firm to safeguard employee confidentiality may result in legal liability—as well as rendering the whole AIDS policy process ineffective.

These four principles must permeate the organization. For such saturation to occur, AIDS awareness, policies, and procedures should be reinforced frequently using a variety of media. At a minimum, they will be reinforced through assignment of credible corporate managers or officers for AIDS-related issues and a comprehensive health benefit program.

Figure 1 provides a sample AIDS policy statement. However, organizations should develop their own statements within the context of their corporate environments, organizational needs, task demands, and employee norms. In constructing a policy statement, a thorough self-analysis will help identify the distinctive characteristics to be considered in customizing the statement to the organization. Another consideration in constructing the AIDS policy is an assessment of the potential exposure of the organization to AIDS-related problems and the environment. Health care providers, public service blood centers, and related organizations provide excellent examples of programs that can serve as corporate models for AIDS awareness programs.

The sample provided will serve as a guide only. Firms must spend the time and energy to design AIDS policies that provide a solid foundation of support for the composite organization.

Assignment of Corporate AIDS Responsibility

To centralize the awareness campaign, an individual in the organization can be appointed to function as a corporate AIDS liaison or spokesperson. Each employee should have access to this individual. For larger organizations, responsibility can be shared depending on number of locations and dispersion of employees. These managers can be responsible for establishing and administering a conscientious AIDS policy.

Comprehensive Health Care Coverage

A comprehensive benefit package that provides a broad spectrum of coverage for all catastrophic illnesses must be part of an organization's health care coverage. Though some insurance companies are limiting coverage for PWAs, legal decisions contesting these limits have had mixed results. A written statement that AIDS is part of the company's catastrophic benefit package and affiliation with a health insurance company that does not discriminate is recommended.

Managing the Impact of AIDS on Coworkers and Other Employees

In the past, open-minded companies attempting to be sympathetic to PWAs have seen their efforts backfire. In the 1980s, one bank convened its employees and carefully explained that one of their colleagues had AIDS. Officials discreetly outlined their supportive position and asked that his coworkers extend the same support and compassion. Instead of condolence, three employees recoiled hysterically and threatened litigation if they had to work with the colleague. Controversy ensued, and the officials quickly realized that their compassionate efforts had turned sour.

Other firms attempting a politically correct solution have been penalized instead of praised by homosexuals and AIDS groups. One New York executive, whose firm had one of the most liberal AIDS policies in existence, used incorrect vocabulary in a press conference about the AIDS policy and was picketed by a local group. In light of some of the negative publicity experienced by well-intentioned people, it is little wonder that some firms are hesitant to address the issue.

We have come a long way, and we have assumed a more humane attitude about AIDS. Heterosexual groups are aligning with homosexual groups to combat AIDS-phobia; many have little concern about a person's sexuality but are merely interested in eliminating a devastating disease. Many "non-exempt" companies have voluntarily established AIDS policies and many more are in the process of doing so. Most important, companies are beginning to realize that having an effective AIDS program is simply the "right thing to do."

How a company prepares for an AIDS program is not simple because it requires a change of attitude. Because of the nature of public reaction to the disease, unfortunately, AIDS sensitization is not the same as for other debilitating diseases such as cancer. The public still does not perceive AIDS as it does other devastating diseases. The stigma of the disease is a reality, so eliminating the fear and stigma is one of the first battles in which we must engage ourselves.

Education of Employees

Employees should become comfortable in talking about AIDS. Encouraging employees to discuss their candid fears and feelings about the disease is beneficial for organizations. If people are penalized for expressing their genuine feelings, they will avoid revealing their apprehensions and inhibitions. Coworkers of PWAs may have unfounded fears about working with the infected workers; some may wish to make a moral statement. In either case, the ability and opportunity

---

Figure 1
An AIDS Policy Statement: XYZ, Inc.

1. **Purpose:** This policy statement is provided to help prevent the spread of Acquired Immune Deficiency Syndrome (AIDS) to XYZ employees, to provide a healthier working environment, and to help limit the spread of AIDS through the general population.

2. **Policy:** XYZ, Inc. is concerned about the increasing incidence of AIDS, AIDS-related-complex (ARC), and infection with human immuno-deficiency virus (HIV). It is important that the XYZ corporate community understand and be prepared to deal with this serious problem. Every effort needs to be made to ensure the rights and well-being of individuals, but it is equally important to safeguard the corporate community as a whole. This policy statement is intended to provide a fair and equitable method of responding to the occurrence of AIDS in the corporate community.

3. **Definition:** AIDS is the acronym for Acquired Immune Deficiency Syndrome. The disease is caused by the human immuno-deficiency virus. AIDS is characterized by a loss in an individual's natural immunity against disease. Loss of the immunity response allows an individual to be vulnerable to diseases that would normally not be life-threatening. These diseases are called opportunistic diseases and can be fatal to AIDS victims. HIV also causes an illness called AIDS Related Complex (ARC). Individuals with ARC may develop the same chronic symptoms as AIDS victims but they are not inflicted with some very specific opportunistic infections that AIDS patients may have. ARC—as well as AIDS—can be fatal. In this policy, the term AIDS will refer to AIDS, ARC, and HIV infections.

4. **General Issues for this Policy Statement:**

   a. *Education:* Because prevention is currently the only method of limiting the consequences of AIDS, XYZ, Inc. will direct its major efforts toward educating the corporate community regarding the cause, methods of transmission, and prevention of AIDS. [Follow this with statements indicating what educational activities will be provided and by what office.]

   b. *Safety of Coworkers:* Medical evidence indicates that people with AIDS pose no risk of transmitting the virus to others through ordinary, casual, or interpersonal contact. Research identifies transmission of the disease through blood, semen, vaginal secretions, birth, and breast milk. Any employee who may come in contact with blood or other body fluids should contact the immediate supervisor for job-specific AIDS-related work procedures.

   c. *Employee Rights:* XYZ, Inc. recognizes that employees who have or may be perceived as having AIDS may wish to continue in their normal work activities as long as their physical condition allows them to do so. No difference in treatment should be accorded these individuals so long as they are able to meet work standards and so long as medical evidence indicates that their condition is not a threat to themselves or others. In addition to the above rights, XYZ, Inc. recognizes the following:

   • *Confidentiality of Information:* Our corporation will comply with federal and state laws, regulations, and policies that protect the confidentiality of medical records. People who are infected by the AIDS virus should be urged to share that information on a confidential basis with [name of responsible corporate official].

   • *Hiring and Promotion:* Consideration of the existence of AIDS will not be part of the employment decision or any promotions awarded by XYZ, Inc.

   • *Right of Employment:* Employees infected, or who may become infected, with the AIDS virus will not be excluded from employment, services, or benefits of XYZ, Inc. The corporation will make reasonable accommodations to assist employees with AIDS as it would other handicapped employees. If a reasonable accommodation cannot be made, the corporation may take other appropriate action as provided by law after reviewing the skill level of the infected employee.

Other Possible Provisions
• Prohibition Against Inquiries and Mandatory Testing
• AIDS Committee
• Responsible Behavior

Figure 2
Beware of AIDS Buzzwords!

AIDS buzzwords misinform, insult, and promote ignorance. Jody Powell, former White House press secretary, has identified the following terms as "buzzwords" (Powell 1988). These words either should not be used by reporters or should require explanation.

Bodily fluids

". . . should never be used without an explanation of which bodily fluids actually contain the HIV virus in concentrations sufficient to transmit the disease. . . . Sweat, saliva, and tears are all bodily fluids, but do not carry a threat of HIV infection. Reports on AIDS should make it clear that semen, vaginal fluids, and blood are the concerns here."

General population

". . . artificially divides the American people into those who have the disease and those who do not. Everyone who has AIDS—regardless of sexual orientation, race, gender, or manner of exposure to the virus—is part of the 'general population.'"

High-risk groups

". . . implies that some kind of demographic trait, rather than behavioral practice, is responsible for AIDS exposure." Appropriate term: high-risk behavior.

AIDS victims

"People with AIDS are not victims; they are people struggling to live normal lives in the face of a fatal disease. We don't refer to people with other diseases as victims. . . ." Most preferable phrase: people with AIDS.

HIV virus vs. "AIDS"

"Many people still confuse exposure to the HIV virus with the disease itself. More than one million people are believed to have been exposed to the virus; some 50,000 actual cases have been reported. Coverage should always explain the difference."

Condoms

"Reports recommending condom use to reduce the risk of HIV exposure should clearly state that latex condoms with a spermicide are preferable (natural lamb condoms may not provide the necessary protection)."

Intimate sexual behavior

". . . a polite phrase that doesn't tell the reader anything useful (many people regard kissing and fondling as intimate). Certain sexual practices—especially unprotected anal intercourse—are known to pose a much greater chance of HIV transmission than others. News articles should make this clear."

AIDS Services of Dallas believes that the following terms also pose problems:

Innocent victims

A term sometimes applied to children with AIDS or those who contracted AIDS through blood transfusions; a value judgment that implies that some people with AIDS may be guilty of something. "Victim" is also a problem (see above).

AIDS carrier

The term "carrier" is reminiscent of the typhoid hysteria of the 1920s, and can incite similar reactions. Appropriate terms: HIV (anti-body)-positive person or person with AIDS (depending on the condition).

AIDS activism vs. gay rights

AIDS activist groups are sometimes incorrectly called gay rights groups. Although AIDS activists also campaign for gay rights, and some issues may overlap, the two subjects should not be confused.

Having sex

Also vague; see *Intimate sexual behavior* (above).

---

to express such opinions and feelings will allow managers an opportunity to provide the most reliable information available.

This education can start by examining the vocabulary used daily to describe opinions and feelings about AIDS. Words are important because they reveal our feelings and convey hidden meanings. Organizations and managers must provide leadership in using words that avoid "moral" judgments about PWAs. **Figure 2** presents some suggestions for vocabulary to be used when discussing AIDS.

Information Sources for Employees

Employees should be kept informed about AIDS. Although the national and local media are important, it is just as important for an organization to create a source of information for those who

wish to know more about the disease. This should include information about places, sources, and locations for help for those who might have questions or require assistance. **Figure 3** lists national sources of information. FIrms should distribute the hotline numbers of national, state, and local sources of information. Be sure to in-

---

Figure 3
Information Sources

National Resources Telephone Numbers:
- AIDS Hotline: 1-800-342-AIDS
- AIDS Spanish Hotline: 1-800-342-SIDA
- AIDS Hotline for Hearing Impaired: 1-800-AIDS-TTY
- AIDS Helpline: 1-800-548-4659

---

clude the organizational resource committee or officer within the information display or packet.

Have a Crisis Program in Place

Firms should consider the suggestions and implications discussed in this article, and be prepared to acknowledge and manage the reality that PWAs live and work within organizations. Within the framework of being prepared, firms must be ready to deal with the fears and concerns of external groups—customers, suppliers, and the general public.

A crisis program's primary objective is to provide solutions and protection for employees. A secondary objective is to provide accurate and appropriate information in the event a public statement is necessary. In the event that an AIDS-related questions arises, a crisis plan needs to be in place. Because rumors are often more difficult to control than the actual facts of a situation, a crisis program should also include the capacity to react to rumors with accurate and appropriate information.

The Center for Disease Control estimates that there were more than 270,000 AIDS cases in 1992; the American Council on Science and Health believes that 60,000 people will die each year if the spread of AIDS is not

reduced. Once AIDS develops, 80 percent of the PWAs die within two years. Finally, most PWAs are between the ages of 20 and 49 years.

The potential devastation on organizations is obvious. Firms that prepare for the AIDS threat will be able to minimize the devastation. The decision for preparedness rests solely with the decision makers who wish to face the reality that AIDS is a pandemic of today, not tomorrow.

References

"AIDS in the Workplace," Texas Department of Health pamphlet, Stock No. 4-148, revised June 1991.

Peter Fitch, "Running a Business in the Shadow of AIDS," *Business Week*, February 3, 1992, pp. 62-63.

Marilyn Chase, "Corporations Urge Peers to Adopt Humane Policies for AIDS Victims," *Wall Street Journal*, January 20, 1988, p. 29.

Thomas A. Stewart, "Gays in Corporate America," *Fortune*, December 16, 1991, pp. 42-56.

Geralyn McClure Franklin, Alicia Briney Gresham, and Swen F. Fontenot, "AIDS in the Workplace: Current Practices and Critical Issues," *Journal of Small Business*, April 1992, pp. 61-73.

Social Responsibility And Need for Low Cost Clash at Stride Rite

Shoemaker Does Good Deeds But Closes Its Facilities In Depressed Inner Cities

Most Jobs Move Overseas

Joseph Pereira

Staff Reporter of THE WALL STREET JOURNAL

CAMBRIDGE, Mass.—At the gleaming headquarters building of Stride Rite Corp. in bustling Kendall Square here, plaques on the walls honor the shoe company for its good deeds.

In the past three years alone, Stride Rite has received 14 public-service awards, including ones from the National Women's Political Caucus, Northeastern University, the Northeast Human Resources Association and Harvard University, which praised it for "improving the quality of life" in its community and the nation.

While doing good, Stride Rite also has done well. It has posted a profit, usually a record, for the past 32 quarters. This year, its sales are expected to top $625 million, more than double the 1986 level. Its stock has increased sixfold since then, making it a favorite on the New York Stock Exchange and among socially conscious investors.

A VERY DIFFERENT SIGHT

But just a few miles away, in Boston's rough inner-city Roxbury neighborhood, stands another Stride Rite building: a weather-beaten, red-brick structure surrounded by empty lots, crumbling roads and chain-link fences. It once housed corporate headquarters and employed 2,500 people making the company's Keds sneakers and Sperry Top-Sider shoes.

Today, the building is just a distribution center employing only 175 workers. Next year, even they will be gone. Stride Rite plans to close the warehouse—and another one in New Bedford, Mass.—and move the operations to Kentucky.

In Roxbury, so close to corporate headquarters but yet so far, Stride Rite's citations for corporate citizenship ring hollow. With the local unemployment rate estimated at nearly 30%, the soon-to-be-jobless workers see a bleak future.

"Where are you supposed to go?" wonders Miguel Brandao, a 46-year-old Cape Verdean immigrant who has worked at the plant 11 years. "There is no place to go."

BITTERNESS IN NEW BEDFORD

In New Bedford, where unemployment runs about 14% of the labor force, Stride Rite's plan to leave stirs bitterness. Since the company's announcement earlier this year, two suspicious fires have caused plant damage estimated at more than $750,000, and three workers are under investigation.

And last June, Stride Rite closed another plant, in Tipton, Mo., and laid off 280 workers. The unemployment rate is grim there, too. Three other shoe companies also closed nearby factories at about the same time, idling 1,400 workers.

Angie and Stanley Shewmaker, who both worked for Stride Rite in Tipton, are still unemployed. They have been in job training—and in counseling for a marriage strained by money worries. "I'm all nerves," Mrs. Shewmaker says. "I'm on tranquilizers. I can't sleep at night. It's been hard. I'm fighting depression all the time."

In the past decade, Stride Rite has prospered partly by closing 15 factories, mostly in the Northeast and several in depressed areas, and moving most of its production to various low-cost Asian countries. The company still employs 2,500 workers in the U.S., but that is down from a peak of about 6,000.

DIFFICULT QUESTIONS

So yet-another departure from yet-another inner-city neighborhood such as Roxbury is hardly surprising. Neither is the transfer of work to the Far East. But when the company behind the moves is a Stride Rite, one that has received so many accolades, it raises difficult questions: What makes a company socially responsible? And how far can social responsibility be expected to go?

Is it sufficient to do good deeds, as everyone agrees Stride Rite has done? It has contributed 5% of its pretax profit to a foundation, sent 100,000 pairs of sneakers to strife-torn Mozambique, paid Harvard graduate students to work in a

Reprinted by permission of *The Wall Street Journal*, May 28, 1993, pp. A1, A6. © 1993 by Dow Jones & Company, Inc. All rights reserved worldwide.

Cambodian refugee camp, given scholarships to inner-city youths, permitted employees to tutor disadvantaged children on company time and been a pioneer in setting up on-site day-care and elder-care facilities.

Or is something more basic needed, such as providing jobs in depressed areas even at the expense of profits? To many who have watched much of corporate America leave inner cities, the answer is clear. "The most socially responsible thing a company can do is to give a person a job," argues Donald Gillis, executive director of Boston's Economic Development and Industrial Corp., which tried to persuade Stride Rite to stay.

Adds Gilda Haas, an economic and urban-planning lecturer at the University of California at Los Angeles: "It strikes me as strange that we're having this conversation about inner-city jobs only a year after the civil unrest in South Central Los Angeles. What exactly did the corporate sector mean when they spoke of the need for inner-city jobs last year as Los Angeles burned?"

Stride Rite contends that it has been socially responsible but nevertheless has to balance the demands of two masters—shareholders and society. If a company doesn't stay competitive, its executives contend, it can't grow, it would provide even fewer jobs, it would earn too little to afford its community programs, and, at worst, it might jeopardize its survival. "Putting jobs into places where it doesn't make economic sense," Chairman Ervin Shames says, "is a dilution of corporate and community wealth."

So, even while Stride Rite was nurturing social programs, it slowly and reluctantly began closing plants in Maine and New Hampshire in the late 1960s and shifting production overseas. And as the quality and efficiency of foreign workers improved, Stride Rite, and its competitors, started to export jobs more rapidly. Higher-priced American workers simply weren't competitive; even Stride Rite's efforts to run small, cost-efficient factories in rural New England failed.

Nike Inc., too, briefly tried running a factory in Maine in the late 1970s, but gave up after losing more than $5 million a year. "Athletic shoes are best made in parts of the world other than the U.S.," a Nike spokesman says. "If the Air Jordan shoe were to be made in the U.S. today, it could retail for $280 to $310 a pair." The Taiwan-made shoe costs about $100.

By the early 1980s, only half of Stride Rite's shoes were U.S.-made. "You could stay in the U.S. if you were doing high-end shoes," a niche Stride Rite wasn't in, says Myles Slosberg, a director and former executive vice president. "Otherwise, it was going to be pretty darn difficult."

One of the company's biggest layoffs, of 2,500 people, came in 1984. Stride Rite closed three plants, including its children's shoe factory in Roxbury, and moved the jobs overseas. It had to, it says, to survive. That year, its net income plummeted 68% to $5.4 million from $16.8 million in 1983—the first drop in 13 years. In 1986, the company closed two more Massachusetts plants, in Brockton and Lawrence. It still operates two factories in Missouri, but it now makes only 10% of its shoes in the U.S. It doesn't own the overseas factories or directly employ the workers; instead, it contracts with local companies.

The labor savings are huge. Andy Li, a Taiwan contractor who has found subcontractors to work for Stride Rite, says skilled workers in China earn $100 to $150 a month, working 50 to 65 hours a week. Unskilled workers—packers and sorters—get $50 to $70 a month. By comparison, Stride Rite's U.S. workers average $1,200 to $1,400 per month in wages alone, plus modest fringe benefits.

"It has become virtually impossible to manufacture sneakers in the U.S. and still be in the competition," says Carl Steidtmann, chief economist at Price Waterhouse's merchandise-consulting division. The obvious consequence in Missouri: Shoe-making jobs dwindled to 8,250 last year from a peak of 25,000 in 1968.

Even overseas, Stride Rite continues its quest for labor bargains. In recent years, it has switched from factories in South Korea as pay rose there to lower-wage Indonesia and China. "It has become sort of Holy Grail for us," Mr. Slosberg says.

Stride Rite also contends it has little choice but to pull its distribution centers out of Roxbury and New Bedford. "It was a difficult decision," Mr. Shames says. "Our hearts said, 'Stay,' but our heads said, 'Move.'" Stride Rite will save millions of dollars, he adds, by going to the Midwest. When the company profiled its retailers, he says, "the average customer tended to be in the Midwestern or Southern part of the nation."

Moreover, the central location will make shipping generally more efficient. Now, most Stride Rite shoes are shipped from the Far East to Los Angeles and Seattle and then trucked to Boston and New Bedford, where they are sorted and labeled and then dispatched to retailers nationwide. The new distribution center in Louisville will eliminate 800 to 1,200 miles on some truck routes, speeding delivery by 2 1/2 to four days. "After the numbers were added up, it wasn't even a close decision," says Mr. Slosberg, who is now a Massachusetts assistant attorney general.

Within Stride Rite's top management, however, the decision has caused soul-searching. Arnold Hiatt, a former chairman who retired last year but remains a director, says, "I objected to that decision as much as I could. I was overruled." He passionately espoused a "Jeffersonian vision" linking corporate and social responsibility. When Stride Rite joined 54 other companies to form Businesses for Social Responsibility last year, he said, "If you're pro-business, you also have to be concerned about things like jobs in the inner city and the 38 million Americans living below the poverty line."

But Mr. Hiatt concedes that the issue is complicated. For three months, officials reviewed offers in connection with the warehouse from Indiana, Ohio, Massachusetts and Kentucky. Kentucky won mainly because of a $24 million tax break over 10 years, vs. a $3 million offer from Massachusetts. Lower wage rates also played a role.

Mr. Hiatt acknowledges that he himself moved many jobs out of Roxbury in his 24 years as a top officer. "To the extent that you can stay in the city, I think you have to," he says. But "if it's at the expense of your business, I think you can't forget that your primary responsibility is to your stockholders."

It was under Mr. Hiatt, a staunch liberal who served as treasurer for Sen. Eugene McCarthy's 1968 presidential campaign, that Stride Rite became known for progressive policies. In 1971, he opened a day-care center at the Roxbury plant, a move that cost some money but more than paid off in goodwill. In 1988, another day-care center, at the Cambridge headquarters, was expanded to become a widely praised "intergenerational center," caring for the aged as well.

Stride Rite also contributes heavily to charity. In 1991, its board decided to allot 5% of pretax profits—or about $5 million last year—to the Stride Rite Charitable Foundation. Part of that money helps 40 inner-city students attend Harvard; in return for the $5,000-a-year scholarships, the students serve as mentors to other inner-city youths, helping them with school work and spending summers in housing projects. After graduation, the scholarship recipients can continue their public service for a year under a fellowship offering a $15,000 stipend. One student who last year was headed for a Wall Street job chose instead to work in a New York hospital that serves many AIDS patients.

Stride Rite has won admirers among many business critics. The company "is a case study of giving something back to the community," says Peggy Charren, a Cambridge resident who founded Action for Children's Television, which lobbies for better TV programming for kids.

For a long time, the Roxbury site, then the company headquarters, was relatively unscathed despite the sharply deteriorating neighborhood. Then, in 1981, came a stunning blow: Stride Rite moved its offices to Cambridge. "We held out as long as we could," Mr. Hiatt says, "but it became clear that people that had the more skilled jobs at Stride Rite were coming from other parts of the city and were increasingly reluctant to go into Roxbury." One day, a bullet smashed through his window, he says, "and I knew it was time to go."

To soften the impact on Roxbury, Stride Rite moved in distribution centers from Atlanta and Salem, N.H. But the respite was brief. In 1984, it closed the factory.

Now, the departure of the warehouse compounds Roxbury's problems. Ames Department Stores Inc. closed its Roxbury store in March and Digital Equipment Corp. shut its factory in the neighborhood this month.

"It is very devastating," says Roderick Dowdell, a worker at the nearby Common Bostonian restaurant. "It is like back-to-back grand slams by the opposing team." A few doors from Stride Rite in Roxbury, Edward Williams says his Hair Salon is struggling. "We did 150 clients a week; now, I'm lucky to do 25," he says.

In the wake of the closings, community leaders called a huddle, seeking ways to stimulate new businesses and hold onto existing ones. But one ray of hope, a proposed biotechnology center that will create 150 jobs, is little consolation to Stride Rite employees; many speak little or no English and lack the skills that even entry-level jobs at the center will require. Stride Rite employees need "$3,000 worth of education" to have hope of getting in the door, says Sue Swartz, director of the Boston Workers Assistance Center. But her project allows for only half that.

"How can I hope to find a job?" wonders Alberto Andrade, a 60-year-old native of Cape Verde whose eight years at Stride Rite don't qualify him for a pension.

The talk of schooling draws looks of amusement from a few workers. With eight children, Mr. Brandao, a sorter at the warehouse, says he must work an average of 14 hours overtime a week to make ends meet. "Who will feed my children?" he asks in thickly accented English.

The approximately 500 employees at the Roxbury and New Bedford facilities could request transfers to Kentucky but would compete with local applicants for the 275 positions. Many probably won't even try. "Why would we want to go there?" says Carol Pitta, an inventory controller at New Bedford. "There won't

be a union, the pay will be less and what happens if in two months they don't want you? Who'll pay my way home?"

Realizing that about 250 co-workers will soon flood an already-tight job market, Tom Camara, a shop steward in New Bedford, is already pounding the pavement. He was unemployed more than a year before landing a job at Stride Rite two years ago. What will life be like after Stride Rite? "Don't know," he shrugs. "One thing's for sure: It's going to be tough."

Mr. Camara won't get much disagreement from people in Tipton, even though the federal government offered them retraining because the jobs lost in Missouri went abroad. Not all the unemployed could take advantage of the programs.

"It costs $80 a week for a baby sitter, and I'm getting $175 a week in unemployment assistance," explains Anita Bracht, a former Stride Rite employee in Tipton who has four children. Her husband, Donny, worked at Stride Rite, too, and also is unemployed. "He's tried everything," Mrs. Bracht says. "The union tells him there are 500 people on the waiting list" for jobs contracted by the union. With their unemployment benefits nearing an end, she adds, "I'm about ready to panic."

Among the many lessons learned from the closings, one has struck especially close to home for Mr. Brandao in Roxbury. A 70-year-old Irish immigrant, who rented a room from him, died recently, leaving behind a 32-year-old mentally disabled son. "I don't have the heart to ask him to leave," he says with the help of a translator. "If I did, I would be doing to him what my company is doing to me."

Is U.S. Business Obsessed With Ethics?

That's the view of many foreign managers who resent distinctive American ethical practices being forced upon them.

David Vogel

DAVID VOGEL is professor of business and public policy at the University of California at Berkeley. This is adapted from an article that appeared originally in the fall 1992 issue of *California Management Review*.

In a number of important respects, the increased globalization of the economies of the United States, Western Europe, and Japan is making business practices more uniform. The structure and organization of companies, manufacturing technologies, the social organization of production, customer relations, product development, and marketing—all are becoming increasingly similar throughout the advanced industrial economies. One might logically think that a similar trend would be taking place with respect to the principles and practices of business ethics.

But business ethics have not yet globalized; the norms of ethical behavior continue to vary widely in different capitalist nations. During the past decade, highly publicized incidents of misconduct on the part of business managers have occurred in virtually every major industrial economy. Yet, while interest in business ethics has increased substantially in a number of countries in Europe, and to a lesser extent in Japan, no other capitalist nation approaches the United States in the persistence and intensity of public concern with the morality of business conduct.

During the past 15 years, more corporate officers and prominent businessmen have been jailed or fined in the United States than in all other capitalist nations combined. Likewise, the fines imposed on corporations in the United States have been substantially greater than in other capitalist nations. This both reflects the high standards that exist for corporate conduct in the United States and also serves to reinforce the perception that business misconduct is more pervasive in the United States. The American penchant for evaluating and comparing corporate social and ethical performance also informs consumer judgments of business. Various private, nonprofit organizations in the United States regularly "rank" corporations in terms of their behavior on such dimensions as women and minority employment, military contracting, concern about the environment, and animal testing; one annual guide, the Council on Economic Priorities' *Shopping for a Better World*, has sold close to 1 million copies since 1989. Such rankings are virtually unknown outside the United States, as are awards for "excellence in ethics." The Japanese may be obsessed with ranking corporations, but they appear to have overlooked this particular dimension of corporate performance.

Similarly, the number of companies that have been subject to consumer boycotts on the basis of their social policies has increased substantially in the United States in recent years. By contrast, consumer boycotts are much less com-

From *Across the Board*, November/December 1993, pp. 31-33. Adapted from *California Management Review*, Vol. 35, No. 1, Fall 1992. © 1992 by The Regents of the University of California. Reprinted by permission.

mon in Europe and virtually unknown in Japan (the most recent took place in the early 1970s and it involved the prices of televisions). A number of consumer boycotts have taken place in Britain, but far fewer than in the United States—even after taking into account the relative sizes of the two economies.

More generally, the debate over the role of business in Europe has focused on how to organize the economy, while in the United States it has emphasized standards of conduct for companies whose private ownership is assumed. This in turn may be due to another distinctive characteristic of American society: namely, the considerable emphasis that historically has been placed on the social obligations of business. Because corporations played a critical role in the development of cities and the shaping of communities in the United States, they long have been perceived as social institutions with substantial responsibility for the moral and physical character of the communities in which they have invested. Both the doctrine of corporate social responsibility and the practice of corporate philanthropy date back more than a century in the United States. By contrast, in both Europe and Japan, the responsibility of business historically has been defined more narrowly.

Ironically, it may be precisely because the values of "business civilization" are ingrained so deeply in American society that Americans tend to become so upset when the institutions and individuals they have looked up to—and whose values and success they have identified with—betray their trust.

Protestant Work Ethics

An important key to understanding the unique interest of Americans in the subject of business ethics lies in the United States' Protestant heritage: "The United States is the only country in the world in which a majority of the population has belonged to dissenting Protestant sects," according to Samuel P. Huntington's *American Politics: The Promise of Disharmony* (Harvard University Press). This has important implications for the way in which Americans approach the subject of business ethics. By arguing that one can and should do "God's work" by creating wealth, Protestantism raised the public's expectations of the moral behavior of business managers.

Thus, thanks in part to the role played by Reformed Protestantism in defining American values, the United States remains a highly moralistic society. Compared to the citizens of other capitalist nations, Americans are more likely to believe that business and morality are, and should be, related to each other, that good ethics is good business, and that business activity both can and should be consistent with high personal moral values.

While the high expectations of business conduct shared by Americans have a strong populist dimension, this particular understanding of the proper relationship between business and morality is not in any sense anti-business. It also is shared by much of the American business community. Indeed, the latter appear as concerned about the ethical lapses of their colleagues as is the American public. A survey of key business leaders that was conducted by Touche Ross (now Deloitte & Touche) in 1987 reported that more than two-thirds believe "that the issue of ethics in business has not been overblown in the current public debate."

Admittedly, some of these expressions of concern about business ethics amount to little more than public relations. But it is impossible to read through the various reports on business ethics in the United States without being struck by the sincerity of the concerns of the executives whose views they report.

Where else but in the United States would a group of nationally prominent executives establish and fund an organization such as the Business Enterprise Trust in order to offer annual awards for outstanding ethical behavior by corporations and individual managers? While the belief that good ethics and high profits go hand-in-hand certainly is not confined to American businessmen, they seem to articulate it more frequently than do their counterparts in other capitalist nations. One senses that many of the latter are a bit more cynical about the relationship between ethics and profitability. For example, in Germany: "Insider trading doesn't have much of a stigma. Tax evasion is a gentleman's sport," according to a March 23, 1987 *BusinessWeek* article.

Because the moral status of capitalism in Europe traditionally has been problematic, there appears to be much more cynicism about the ethics of business in Europe and in Japan. Europeans, in part due to the legacy of aristocratic and precapitalist values, have tended to view the pursuit of profit and wealth as somewhat morally dubious, making them less likely to be surprised—let alone outraged—when companies and managers are discovered to have been "greedy." For their part, "some Japanese seem almost inured to the kind of under-the-table favors whose disclosure sparked the [1991 Nomura Securities Co. Ltd. and The Nikko Securities Co. International Inc.] scandals," according to an Aug. 26, 1991 *BusinessWeek* article. As one Japanese investor told the magazine, "It's so much a part of Japanese culture and tradition that the people don't think they're doing anything wrong."

A Japanese political consultant mused to the *Washington Post National Weekly Edition* in September 1991: "I wonder sometimes when the Japanese people will rise up and say, 'We've had enough.' But the only answer I can give for sure is, 'Not in this century, at least.'"

Not surprisingly, many Europeans regard the current level of interest of Americans in the ethics and morality of business conduct—to say nothing of other aspects of American society—as somewhat excessive. Corporate codes of conduct, ethics-training programs, lists of "ethical" and "unethical" companies—all are seen as signs of an "unusually moralizing society," one that "people in old and cynical Europe often find difficult to take . . . seriously," according to the *Washington Post* article. The extent of moral scrutiny and self-criticism that pervade contemporary American society prompted *The Economist* to publish an editorial titled, "Hey, America, Lighten Up A Little."

Is the Whistle-Blower Always a Traitor?

The United States is distinctive not only in the intensity of public concern with the ethical behavior of business, but also in the way in which business ethics are defined. For one, Americans tend to emphasize the role of the individual as the most critical source of ethical values, while in other capitalist nations relatively more emphasis is placed on the corporation as the locus of ethical guidance.

Business ethics in the United States have been affected strongly by the "tradition of liberal individualism that . . . is typical of American culture," according to the *Journal of Business Ethics*. Not surprisingly, a frequent characteristic of business-ethics cases developed in the United States is that they require the individual to decide what is right on the basis of his own values. While the company's goals and objectives or the views of the individual's fellow employees are not irrelevant, in the final analysis they are not intended to be decisive. Indeed, they often may be in conflict.

By contrast, "in European circumstances it is not at all evident that managers, when facing a moral dilemma, will navigate first and foremost on their personal moral compass," the *Journal of Business Ethics* said. Rather, managers are more likely to make decisions based on their shared understanding of the nature and scope of the company's responsibilities. The legitimate moral expectations of a company are shaped by the norms of the community, not the personal values or reflections of the individual.

One possible outcome of the tension between the interests and values of the company and those of the individual employee is whistle-blowing. Critics of business in the United States have urged increased legal protection for whistle-blowers—and, in fact, some regulatory statutes in the United States explicitly protect those who publicly expose violations of various company policies.

By contrast, the idea that there could even be such tension between the individual and the organization is thoroughly alien to Japanese business culture, where whistle-blowers would be regarded more as traitors than heroes. Only a handful of European countries have laws protecting whistle-blowers. And few non-American companies have established formal mechanisms, such as the appointment of ombudsmen, to enable employees to voice their moral concerns about particular corporate policies. Workers in many other capitalist nations may well feel a greater sense of loyalty toward the businesses for which they work and greater respect for those in authority.

Check Checklists at the Door

A second critical difference between business ethics in the United States and other capitalist countries has to do with the role of law and formal rules. Notwithstanding—or perhaps because of—its traditions of individualism, Americans tend to define business ethics in terms of rules; the writing on business ethics by Americans is replete with checklists, principles, and guidelines for individual managers to follow in distinguishing right from wrong.

Americans' tendency to think of ethics in terms of rules is reflected in the widespread use of corporate codes among U.S.-based companies. Such codes are much less common in Europe, although their use recently has increased in Britain. One French observer notes: "The popularity of codes of ethics in the United States meets with little response in Europe. America's individualism does not correspond to the social traditions of Europe. These large differences make fruitless all desire to imitate the other's steps."

One French manager, whose company recently had been acquired by an American company, stated at an executive-training session I taught in 1991: "I resent having notions of right and wrong boiled down to a checklist. I come from a nation whose ethical traditions date back hundreds of years. Its values have been transmitted to me by my church and through my family. I don't need to be told by some American lawyers how I should conduct myself in my business activities."

Henri-Claude de Bettignies, who teaches business ethics at the French business school INSEAD, added at the 1991 Tokyo Conference on the Ethics of Business in a Global Economy: "Some European leaders perceive corporate codes of conduct as a device which deresponsibilizes the individual, i.e., he does not have to think for himself, he just needs to apply the codes of conduct which he has learnt and which—through training—have programmed him to respond in a certain 'corporate' way."

By contrast, European businesses appear to place greater emphasis on informal mechanisms of social control within the company. Indeed, European managers frequently profess astonishment at the apparent belief of many American executives and government officials that a company's adoption of a code actually can alter the behavior of its employees.

Is Bribery Always Unethical?

There is a third critical difference between business ethics in the United States and other capitalist nations around the world. Americans not only tend to define business ethics in terms of rules and procedures, but also believe that American rules and procedures should be applied universally.

For example, no other nation requires the foreign subsidiaries of its multinational corporations to follow the laws of their home country as frequently as does the United States. Thus, the United States is the only nation that restricts its companies from making payments to secure contracts or other benefits outside its borders.

A survey of European executives that was reported in *The New York Times* in March 1978 stated that, "Nearly 40 percent would never complain about bribery by a business rival—or answer charges of bribery against themselves." Similarly, in no other nation have corporations been criticized so frequently for exporting products that do not conform to the health and safety standards of their "home" country.

Universalism also has a second dimension having to do with the importance of the distinction between "us" and "them." American business culture—and American society—attaches considerable importance to treating everyone in the same arm's-length manner. By contrast, the Japanese—and, to a lesser extent, the citizens of Southern Europe—define their responsibilities in more particularistic terms: Managers and government officials place less value on treating everyone equally and attach much more importance to fulfilling their obligations to those individuals and institutions with whom they have developed longstanding and long-term relationships. (Significantly, it is very difficult to translate the phrases "equal opportunity" and "level playing field" into Japanese.) On this dimension, the United Kingdom and much of northern Europe are much closer to the United States.

All these dimensions are, in fact, interrelated. To summarize the American approach: Business ethics is about individuals making moral judgments based on general rules that treat everyone the same. By contrast, business ethics in Europe and Japan have more to do with managers arriving at decisions that are based on shared values, often rooted in a particular corporate culture, applied according to specific circumstances, and strongly affected by the nature of one's social ties and obligations.

Regulatory rules and standards, especially within the European Community and between the United States and Western Europe, certainly are becoming more similar. For example, a strengthening of environmental regulation has occurred in virtually all capitalist nations, while legal restrictions on insider trading—a decade ago, largely confined to the United States—are now the norm in Europe. Similar-ly, a number of European nations recently have enacted legislation banning sexual harassment. The prosecution of white-collar criminals also has increased recently in Europe. In 1989, the first Swede to be found guilty of insider trading was sentenced to five years in prison.

Not only are many American legal norms and standards of corporate conduct being adopted in other capitalist nations, but as globalization proceeds and world commerce increasingly is driven by multinational corporations, these companies may well come to adopt common ethical standards. These developments are important. But they continue to be overshadowed by the persistence of fundamental national differences in the ways in which business ethics are defined, debated, and judged.

COMPANIES CLEAN UP

Cover story **European businesses are trying to put corruption scandals behind them and adopting new codes of ethics. They hope to see virtue rewarded in the bottom line. Introduction by Jane Sasseen.**

Few subjects bring out the sceptics as much as corporate ethics. 'Business ethics . . . isn't that a contradiction in terms?' goes an old saw. Another oft-told tale has one businessman confiding to another, 'I've got an ethical dilemma; I've just shortchanged an old lady by £100. But I can't decide whether I should split it with my partner.'

The sceptics seem to have a point. Volkswagen's struggle to extricate itself from Europe's biggest industrial espionage scandal is only the latest addition to an apparently endless list of corporate misbehaviour: the collapse of fraudulent empires built by Drexel Burnham Lambert, BCCI and Robert Maxwell; British Airways' misuse of Virgin Atlantic's confidential computer records; illegal share manipulation at Guiness and County NatWest in the UK; widespread accusations that French and Spanish companies contributed to political parties in exchange for public favours and, of course, the wholesale indictment of Italy's corrupt business and political class. Whether under the 'greed-is-good' motto of the 1980s or in the cut-throat scramble to survive of the 1990s, ethics appear to rank as a low priority.

Yet despite the scandals – and to some degree because of them – European companies are gingerly stepping into the business ethics debate. Managers once dismissed the field as the preserve of academics, finding little in the ivory tower discourse to help solve the real-world conflicts thrown up by competition. Now principles and social responsibility are a live issue.

Many executives argue that the traditional 'lose your morals or you'll lose your markets' approach no longer works. 'The conflict over doing right versus doing a deal exists only in the short term,' says Olivier Lecerf, retired chairman of cement maker Lafarge Coppée and head of a study on French business ethics. 'In the long run, companies using ethical practices will win out.'

Indeed, never before have so many companies talked so openly of doing so much good. Alongside the black sheep is an equally long line of companies using ethical arguments to transform themselves, their image – and their sales. Best known is UK retailer The Body

Shop, with its less-than-subtle marketing of commitment to the environment and animal rights. But hundreds of other companies make and market environment-friendly products.

The new ethics go beyond familiar green issues, however. The Body Shop trumpets its 'non-exploitative' trade with indigenous third world peoples, the Timberland boot company runs advertisements against racism in Germany, and Italian clothier Benetton publishes a glossy magazine riddled with paeans to ethnic tolerance. The popularity of ethical investment funds – which judge companies on whether they make weapons or invest in South Africa, for example – is growing. In the UK alone, more than £15 billion (Ecu 19.6 billion) is invested in such funds, according to *Money Management* magazine. Although a small fraction of total investment, money placed with ethical unit trust funds grew by 30% over the past two years, compared with 17% growth in unit trusts overall.

The biggest change is inside companies themselves. In a trend that mirrors the environmental movement in its infancy, managers are turning to codes of conduct and 'corporate social responsibility' schemes to define their values. 'In the past, executives saw ethics as a luxury only successful companies could afford,' says Andrew Wilson, a researcher at Ashridge Management College in Hertfordshire, England, and co-author of a study on British corporate ethics. 'But repeated scandal has demonstrated how quickly a reputation can be destroyed. More and more companies believe good values make for good business, and are looking for tools that help put that belief into practice.'

For many, the starting point has been corporate social responsibility, a dressed-up version of what used to be known as philanthropy. Gone are the days when handing over a small slice of profits to charity would suffice. In the decade since it was founded, Business in the Community, a London-based organization that has emerged as a leader in the field, has convinced more than 500 of the UK's largest companies to invest time and money in educational and development projects in inner cities.

Three years ago, the non-profit making organization branched out internationally to form the Prince of Wales Business Leaders Forum; today, companies such as ABB Asea Brown Boveri, Cable & Wireless, Robert Bosch, Norsk Hydro and Grand Metropolitan have all joined US and Japanese multinationals in backing management training and environmental clean-up programmes in Asia and eastern Europe.

The arguments used to win their support have little to do with philanthropy and everything to do with the bottom line. 'Our rationale is very clear,' says Robert Davies, the Forum's chief executive. 'We believe a business case exists for getting involved in local communities. Multinational companies will be more successful globally if they act as good citizens locally.'

Companies are also looking more closely at their own ethical underpinnings. The trend is strongest in the US, but UK companies have also woken up to the issue. Written codes of ethics, once rare, are becoming common. According to London's Institute of Business Ethics, almost one-third of leading British companies boast a written code, up from 18% in 1987. Many more are considering it.

Not all codes are created equal, of course; efforts range from vague commitments to honesty and integrity to specific lists of what may and may not be done. Most outline policy on conflicts of interest, bribery and other criminal activities, and accepting entertainment. Increasingly, integrity and fairness in dealing with suppliers, employees and customers, and in marketing and sales tactics, are also stressed. Some codes commit companies to paying suppliers within 30 days, for example, or outline principles to follow in laying off staff.

The movement has been slower to catch fire in continental Europe, but there is a spark of interest. In Spain, Banco Bilbao Vizcaya has published the country's first explicit code of conduct following charges of corrupt dealings with the government. Fiat is doing the same in Italy; other companies caught in the *mani pollutti* scandal look likely to follow.

French businesspeople remain sceptical about the usefulness of written codes, but Insead professor Henri-Claude de Bettignies says they are joining the debate. 'French companies see written codes as an Anglo-Saxon gimmick,' he says, 'but are nevertheless more reflective about what practices they want to condone.'

In Germany, too, indifference is giving way as Volkswagen's troubles and the problems of recession and unification fuel a broader discussion of ethics and the use of corporate power. Companies such as Deutsche Bank, Hoechst, Siemens and Daimler-Benz may adopt codes. 'New issues with ethical dimensions – downsizing, work rules, supplier relations – are arising, while companies are being asked to defend strategies in terms of ethical and environmental values,' says Rudolf Fiege, an IBM executive who recently helped found the German Business Ethics Network. 'Companies have little choice but to react.'

Professor Henk van Luijk of the Netherlands Business School reports a similar change. While five years ago few Dutch companies even considered ethical questions, he is now frequently called by executives looking for advice on instilling codes.

Why the rush to be good? According to Martin Le Jeune, head of public policy at National Westminster Bank in London, two reasons are 'the importance of social issues to a company's image, and the glare of publicity when problems arise'. Early this year, the bank introduced a code of conduct as part of its efforts to put the Blue Arrow affair – in which executives at its County NatWest investment banking arm falsified share trading records after a failed underwriting – behind it.

Consumers' willingness to buy products that reflect their own values has led even trouble-free companies to see gain in burnishing their image. 'Buyers judge companies by their reputations,' says John Drummond, head of Integrity Works, a London-based consultancy that helps firms set ethical standards. 'If buyers are looking at whether a company is honest, whether it pollutes or is fair to staff, then it's in companies' best interests to be ethical.'

Internationalization provides another reason for companies to examine their behaviour. Having set up foreign operations, they must decide how to act when local practices differ from those allowed at home. What should they do when officals expect bribes to secure contracts, or when confronted with child labour in the third world? The scant legal framework in eastern Europe also opens a hornet's nest of ethical conflicts. And in a world of pressure groups and instant communications, the traditional response – when in Rome, do as the Romans do – will not suffice. 'Executives find themselves in situations where no clear ground rules exist,' says Andrew Wilson of Ashridge Management College. 'It is an ethical minefield that companies are only now beginning to address.'

Clear standards of behaviour have also become imperative when corporate re-engineering pushes responsibility down the hierarchy. When managers of a fast-food chain in England made a bomb scare telephone call to a competitor, sales went up temporarily, but once found out, the chain's reputation suffered nationwide. 'The flip side of downsizing is that individual managers have greater freedom to make decisions which might bring short-term advantage, but risk a company's name,' Drummond says.

If all these factors have pushed ethics up the agenda, doubt about corporate sincerity persists none the less. Critics dismiss much of the debate as a fad, with slim hopes of bringing real change. 'Most German industrialists still don't take the issue seriously,' says Martin Gruschka, business director for film production company High Definition Oberhausen. As a former consultant working with the Treuhand, he wrote about ethical conflicts in restructuring industry in the east. 'Most people were doing whatever they could get away with. The only problem was getting caught.'

Even supporters acknowledge that many companies are driven mainly by image. One European multinational criticized for years for aggressive third world sales tactics now backs socially responsible activities at home; privately, its executives admit part of the intention is to efface earlier bad publicity. 'Certainly, there are mixed motives,' says Adrian Hodges, spokesman for Business in the Community. 'But if public relations is the only reason, that will eventually show through.'

All agree that without obvious backing from the top and radical changes in performance evaluations to reflect stated values – will the salesman, for example, who relinquishes his cut-throat sales tactics be rewarded or reprimanded if orders fall? – the impact will be minimal. 'Many companies today are busy writing codes that aren't worth the paper they're written on,' says Sheena Carmichael, a London-based consultant who organized the sixth European Business Ethics Conference, held last month in Oslo. 'Ethics is about what you do, not what you say.'

Tell that to Volkswagen. The embattled carmaker ranks among Europe's biggest backers of corporate social responsibility programmes, and one of its executives is a founding board member of Germany's new Business Ethics Network – none of which prevented the company from becoming embroiled in a corporate scandal of major proportions.

ETHICS
ARE STANDARDS LOWER OVERSEAS?

The conventional wisdom
says so, but others say we are too full
of "high-toned notions."

Andrew W. Singer

ANDREW W. SINGER is editor and publisher of *Ethikos*,
a New York-based publication that examines ethical issues in business.
This is an expanded version of an article that first appeared in *Ethikos*
in March 1991.

When American business people venture abroad, a common view is that they're wandering into an ethical no-man's-land, where each encounter holds forth a fresh demand for a "gratuity," or baksheesh.

William C. Norris, who founded and for many years headed Control Data Corporation, says, "No question about it. We were constantly in the position of saying how much we were willing to pay" to have a routine service performed overseas. Norris recalls frequently facing situations such as: "The computer is on the dock, it's raining, and you have to pay $100 to get it picked up. . . ."

In South America, firms often face a "closed bidding system" when dealing with that region's large, nationalized companies, says John Swanson, a senior consultant of communications and business conduct at Dow Corning Corporation. He says that his company has been locked out of the South American market at times because it refused to pay the bribes necessary to get that business.

In Japan, bids for Government construction jobs are routinely rigged, according to one former U.S. Government official who asked to remain anonymous—a result of Japanese firms purchasing "influence" from politicians.

Donald E. Petersen, former chairman and chief executive officer of the Ford Motor Company, cites ethical challenges in much of the developing world. "Give me a military dictator with absolute power, and it doesn't matter if he's South American or African or Asian—you've got problems."

Is the United States More Ethical?

Is this common perception borne out by reality? Are business standards overseas in fact lower than those at home? In 1987, Touche Ross, the accounting firm (now Deloitte & Touche), surveyed a range of U.S. business executives, members of Congress, and business school deans. Asked to rank the top five countries in terms of ethical standards, respondents placed the United States first, followed by the United Kingdom, Canada, Switzerland, and West Germany.

Some differences were found among respondent groups. Business school deans, for instance, put Japan at the top of their list—while business executives did not rank Japan among their top five at all.

When asked about the survey, William Norris says, "I agree with the second group. Control Data tried unsuccessfully for 15 years to get into the Japanese market. They kept us out with laws and subterfuges until they could catch up [to the U.S. computer industry]. Then they opened up to U.S. firms. I think that is very unethical."

Referring to the *keiretsu*, the famed Japanese business groups, Norris says, "In our country, we call that collusion."

Many U.S. executives agree that from a business ethics standpoint, the Japanese are a special case. Take gift giving. "It is an important part of how they conduct themselves," says Donald Petersen. Often, there is little thought given to the idea: "Give me the business and I'll give you a gift."

When dealing with the Japanese, Petersen found that it was futile to try to convince them of the superiority of the

From *Across the Board*, September 1991, pp. 31-34. Reprinted by permission of the author and The Conference Board.

American approach to business, in which, for instance, the receipt of gifts of any value in the course of a business transaction is frowned upon as a potential conflict of interest. His solution when dealing with the Japanese was simply to present the policy of accepting no gifts of any value as an American idiosyncrasy.

Bruce Smart, former U.S. Undersecretary of Commerce for International Trade, says that the Japanese are very consistent in sticking to their standards. However, those standards—which accept practices such as companies buying influence from politicians—may sometimes be looked at askance by U.S. eyes. Still, if by business ethics one means consistency with standards, "then the Japanese are probably very ethical," says Smart. Probably fewer Japanese executives cheat on their business expense sheets than Americans, Smart opines.

Underdeveloped Nations: "You'll be Tested Constantly"

In general, U.S. executives see only minor differences in business ethics as practiced in the United States, Canada, and Northern Europe. But most agree that there are some departures in the practice of business ethics when it comes to Southern Europe—Italy and Spain, for instance—and a tremendous difference in the underdeveloped nations.

"Based on my 40 years at Ford, there were no more difficult problems with ethical standards in Europe than here," says Petersen. But among the underdeveloped nations—particularly those countries with autocratic governments in which power is absolute and concentrated—it is often ordinary practice to hold out a hand for a bribe, or to take a company official for a slow walk through customs, until he gets the message that a "grease" payment is required.

Petersen maintains that a company can adhere to high standards—prohibiting bribery or even grease payments—and still function. "It's difficult. You'll be tested constantly, and at times you'll think you've lost business. But if you have a service that they want, they'll come around."

A "Holier-Than-Thou" Attitude

Not all agree that the United States is justified in taking such a superior position. "We have a tendency to take a 'holier-than-thou' attitude," says John A. Seeger, management professor at Bentley College in Waltham, Massachusetts. He maintains that U.S. standards are artificial and naïve rather than too high.

"We are often prepared to pay bribes because we hear that's expected—but that's because we hear from people who want bribes," says Seeger, explaining that managers don't often speak with the people who don't pay or receive bribes. "We expect to be held up, and so we get held up. It is the classic self-fulfilling prophecy."

When discussing overseas ethical standards, there is a danger of stereotyping people. Seeger, in fact, recently wrote a prize-winning management case based on a real incident in which the owner of a Persian Gulf company, Sameer Mustafa, an Arab, refused to bribe the engineer in charge of a Gulf construction project—and suffered economically as a result. Not *only* Americans have an abhorrence of bribery, Seeger suggests.

Kent Druyvesteyn, staff vice president of ethics at General Dynamics Corporation, agrees that we should put away ideas of American superiority when discussing ethics. Too often, says Druyvesteyn, ethical discussions take the form of: "We really do things well here. But when we go abroad, they do things so badly."

William S. Lipsman, associate general counsel of the Sara Lee Corporation, recently returned from a two-year assignment in the Netherlands. He says that he found litigation ethics standards in Europe to be higher than those in the United States. Business there is conducted on a more personal basis, Lipsman explains. "The concept that you, as a business leader, would sue another business without first sitting down at a meeting, face-to-face, is unheard of."

Bruce Smart doesn't even place the United States in the top echelon when it comes to national business standards. The Canadians, British, Australians, and perhaps even the Germans rate higher, in his view. His thinking: A kind of noblesse oblige still exists among the business classes in those countries. Conversely, in the United States, where there is a less entrenched business group, the prevailing attitude is that you make it whatever way you can. This attitude reached its apotheosis in the 1980s with the insider trading scandals on Wall Street, which Smart describes as "the biggest ethical blot on U.S. business" in recent memory.

Whether U.S. standards are in fact higher than those abroad is likely to remain a moot point. But in one respect the United States stands alone: It is the only nation that has sought to legislate moral business conduct overseas.

Can We Legislate Morality?

Passed in the late '70s in the wake of Watergate and the overseas bribery scandals, the Foreign Corrupt Practices Act (FCPA) made it a felony for U.S. companies to obtain business by paying off foreign government officials. From its inception, the FCPA has been controversial. "Managers in other countries often chuckle at the United States hoping to export its morality in the form of the Foreign Corrupt Practices Act," says Gene Laczniak, management professor at Marquette University in Milwaukee.

"It's anachronistic in today's world," says William Norris, the former Control Data chief. "It's like the antitrust laws in many ways. The world has passed it by." (The antitrust laws, enacted at the turn of the century, originally embodied a strong ethical element: The Government didn't want the nation's enormous "trusts" to run roughshod over the "little guy." That worked fine as long as the U.S. economy was an isolated system, say critics. But now antitrust laws may be inhibiting large U.S. firms from competing in the international arena.) In any case, says Norris, most U.S. companies don't want to become involved in activities such as bribing foreign officials.

R. John Cooper, executive vice president and general counsel of Young & Rubicam Inc., the New York-based advertising agency, makes a similar argument. The FCPA was enacted at a time when the competitive position of U.S. companies in the world was stronger—or at least perceived to be stronger—than it is today, Cooper points out. In 1970, the United States was the source of 60 percent of the world's direct foreign investment. By 1984, according to the United Nations, that figure had dropped to 12 percent. Japanese,

The Murky Land of the FCPA

The Foreign Corrupt Practices Act (FCPA) became law in 1977, in the wake of foreign bribery scandals involving U.S. companies that shook the governments of Belgium, the Netherlands, Honduras, Italy, and Japan. One of the most notorious incidents involved an estimated $25 million in concealed payments made overseas by Lockheed Corporation in connection with sales of its Tristar L-1011 aircraft in Japan. This culminated in the resignation and subsequent criminal conviction of Japanese Prime Minister Kankuie Tanaka.

The FCPA, which makes it a crime for a U.S. corporation to bribe officials of foreign governments to obtain or increase business, is controversial, in part, because it seeks to forge a distinction between "bribes" (which it deems illegal) and "gratuities" (which the FCPA permits). The difference is murky, according to the FCPA's critics.

"The law marked the difference between gratuities paid to low-level officials and payments made to authorities," writes Duane Windsor in his book, *The Foreign Corrupt Practices Act: Anatomy of a Statute.* "In many countries a payment to a customs official is a matter of course and a matter of economic necessity. A customs official may backlog an order or hinder a shipment by elaborately checking each imported item. The detrimental effect to the shipment is obvious. In response, lawmakers sought to delineate gratuities and bribes very clearly. But in reality the definition of gratuities was so vague that some people felt it had a chilling effect [on business]." —A.W.S.

European, and East Asian firms have picked up much of the slack, launching economic forays even into America's own backyard.

The United States risks becoming economically hamstrung by statutes such as the Foreign Corrupt Practices Act, suggests Cooper. "We have to reexamine some of these high-toned notions."

In the late 1980s, Young & Rubicam and three of its executives were indicted on a conspiracy charge under the FCPA. The Government asserted that the company had "reason to know" that one of its Jamaican agents was paying off that country's Minister of Tourism to obtain advertising business. In order to avoid a lengthy trial, the company paid a $500,000 penalty, says Cooper.

One outcome of that experience is that Young & Rubicam now has a policy that forbids even facilitating payments. Facilitating (or grease) payments are considerations to secure some ordinary service in a country, such as getting a ship unloaded in a harbor, or having a telephone installed. These are permitted under the FCPA.

Shouldering an Ethical Burden

According to Cooper, Young & Rubicam's recent experience "puts us in a position in which we're very reluctant to engage in a very common practice in some foreign countries: hiring people with relationships, who have the ability to generate business from official sources." The company can't go near such people, Cooper says. With increasingly heated international competition, the act is out of date, he says. It puts too much of a burden on U.S. corporations to know everything about their foreign agents—a burden not shouldered by foreign competitors.

The FCPA might have been an "overreaction" on the part of Congress to events such as Watergate and the overseas bribery scandals, suggests John Swanson of Dow Corning. (See box on this page.) "We're competing out there with strong and vibrant economies—Japan, the Common Market. We're a player but not a dominant player. We can't have

this legislation that is clearly not understood [but which] has such an effect on the viability of trade."

The FCPA brings back bitter memories for William Norris. Some years ago, Control Data Corporation was prosecuted by the U.S. Government under the Foreign Corrupt Practices Act for making payments in Iran.

"I never felt we did anything wrong," says Norris, explaining that the company was conforming to the laws of Iran. (In 1978, Control Data Corporation pleaded guilty to three criminal charges that it made improper payments to unnamed foreign officials. It was fined $1,381,000 by the U.S. Customs Service.) Looking back on his long tenure as Control Data's chief executive, Norris says that settling—and not fighting—that case was one of the few things that he ever regretted.

But the FCPA also has its defenders. "It's a tough trade-off," admits Marquette's Laczniak, but the bottom line is that the "U.S. public doesn't want its companies to secure business by paying huge sums of money to foreign officials." The FCPA, in other words, is really just a reflection of the prevailing values of American society.

"I have sort of a hard time arguing that it should be repealed," says Bruce Smart. Bribing foreign officials tends "to run counter to the idea of democratic representative government. If we countenance bribery, we make it more difficult for those people to find a better way to do business."

As for the idea that U.S. standards have to be adjusted to reflect the new economic realities: "That's an ancient argument, morally," says General Dynamics's Druyvesteyn. "It's one that goes back to Deuteronomy, in the Bible. 'Sure, things are rough. We've had a drought, and the sheep aren't fat. We may have to add a little to the weight.'"

The Slippery Slope of Grease Payments

What about facilitating, or grease, payments, which are permitted under the FCPA as long as they are documented? Such payments are the norm for doing business in some parts of the world. Indeed, government employees are often intentionally underpaid in the expectation that they will receive such gratuities.

The issue of facilitating payments is addressed in Dow Corning's ethics code. "The company felt in the early 1980s that if it didn't put it in the code, it would be like the ostrich with its head in the ground," explains John Swanson. Because grease payments are going on in many parts of the world, they should be recognized.

If the company sends a person to Mexico, and his household possessions are locked up on the dock, and he can't get them delivered to his house without a facilitating payment, then Dow Corning will pay it, says Swanson. "We don't like it. But to get that person to work a few weeks early, we will do it."

What did William Norris do when a big computer was stuck on the dock for want of a $100 payment? "I told them to pay the $100." To fail to make the grease payment in that instance would be "carrying it too far," says Norris. In many other cases, though, Control Data refused to yield to such extortion, and the company lost sales as a result.

"It depends upon what amount of money is involved," says Gene Laczniak. "If you are paying small amounts of money to individuals just to do their jobs [and that is part of the country's culture], then that is just the cost of doing business in that part of the world. But if the money is paid to sway people to make decisions that they would not otherwise make, then that is subverting the nature of the free market system," says Laczniak. "I don't think anyone wants the system to work that way."

Joanne Ciulla, a professor at the University of Pennsylvania's Wharton School, acknowledges that facilitating payments can be somewhat problematic. In many developing countries, bureaucracies are hopelessly inefficient, she says. One is, in effect, paying for an efficient service within an inefficient system.

This presents some moral problems. If everyone uncomplainingly pays facilitating payments, a government has no incentive to be efficient. On the other hand, there is not a whole lot one company can do to change the system. Ciulla is reluctant to recommend that companies "fight windmills" by banning such payments in toto. What companies can do, she suggests, is put pressure on governments to clean up their act. Airing such concerns might have an impact in the long run.

The argument that U.S. global standards are too high, however, is "totally absurd," in Ciulla's view. People sometimes overlook the deleterious effects that bribery has on developing countries, where the widespread practice impedes the development of a free market, she says. "How do you develop if you can't open a fruit stand without paying a bribe?"

She notes that even where bribery and corruption is widely practiced, it's not condoned—at least officially. Even in the Dominican Republic—considered by many to be one of the most corrupt places on earth—no one says bribery is okay, Ciulla points out. No one bribes publicly, it's done privately.

Barbara Burns, a public relations consultant and a member of the board of directors of the International Public Relations Association, says that in some South American countries, notably Brazil, it is not unusual for public relations professionals to pay to have favorable stories for corporate clients placed in publications, often by remunerating a journalist. "But everyone knows which publications these are—so placement is not so valuable to the client," says Burns. "And if you start paying off, it undermines your credibility, and finally your business." She adds that there are also many high-quality publications in Brazil that can't be "bought."

From a company's point of view, the practice of giving grease payments can be economically hazardous—apart from possible legal sanctions. "It's very hard to figure out the expenses. How do you anticipate costs?" asks Ciulla. Governments change, and a "contact" may fall from favor. How much additional extortion might one face down the road?

Integrity has Its Rewards

Adhering to higher standards doesn't have to have negative economic consequences, suggests Dow Corning's Swanson. Some years ago, Dow Corning surveyed its top customers. These customers found the company wanting in certain areas, namely response time and certain quality issues. On the positive side, the customers said: "We know you're a company of integrity, and that you stand behind your products, people, and service." Because of the company's integrity, says Swanson, "they gave us a three-year period of grace to improve our response times and quality. Otherwise, they might have taken their business to a foreign competitor."

U.S. standards are too high, then? "I don't carry that feeling with me," says Donald Petersen. "In general, I wouldn't want to see us say it's okay to reduce our standards to those of others."

And while William Norris is opposed to legislation like the FCPA—which was badly drawn and arbitrarily enforced, in his view—he doesn't recommend that U.S. companies compromise their high standards when operating abroad, either. "I don't think it's necessary to reassess those standards," says Norris. "It's better to lose a deal now and then than to lower standards, which will demoralize the workforce." In the long run, he sees high ethical standards simply as part of a quality management approach toward business.

Ethics and Social Responsibility in the Marketplace

- Marketing Strategy and Ethics (Articles 40–43)
- Ethical Practices in the Marketplace (Articles 44–47)

From a consumer viewpoint, the marketplace is the "proof of the pudding" or the place where the "rubber meets the road" for business ethics. In other words, what the company has promulgated about the virtues of its product or service has little meaning if the company's actual marketing practices and its treatment of the consumer contradict its claims.

At its core, marketing has a very noble and moral purpose: to satisfy human needs and wants and to help people through the exchange process. Marketing involves the coordination of the variables of product, price, place, and promotion to effectively and efficiently address the needs of consumers. Unfortunately, at times the unethical marketing practices of some firms have cast a shadow of suspicion over marketing in general. Since marketing is the aspect of business that is most visible to the public, it has perhaps taken a disproportionate share of the criticism directed toward the free-enterprise system.

The generalization that all marketing practices are unethical is not supported by careful investigation of the marketplace. For example, one could contrast the marketing of Ford Pintos with Johnson & Johnson's handling of the Tylenol incident.

This section takes a careful look at the strategic process and practice of incorporating ethics into the marketplace. The first subsection, *Marketing Strategy and Ethics*, contains four articles describing how marketing strategy and ethics can be integrated in the marketplace. The first article provides a comprehensive and pragmatic conceptual base for combining social responsibility, ethics, and marketing strategy. The next article takes a critical look at some marketers' tendency to sell products by playing on consumers' fears and anxieties. The article "Strategic Green Marketing" examines the importance of companies marketing their products in ways that avoid the pitfalls of questionable environmental advertising and labeling. "Pinto Redux?" ends this subsection by scruti-

nizing how some of General Motors' problems with the "side-saddle" gas tanks in its pickup trucks compare with decisions surrounding the Ford Pinto.

The next subsection is on *Ethical Practices in the Marketplace*. "The Ethics of Bootstrapping" explores some critical ethical issues faced by a struggling start-up venture. The next article describes how ethical principles are being applied to health care marketing practices. "America's Hamburger Helper" exemplifies how McDonald's is one of America's socially responsible companies as well as being one of the nation's few truly effective social engineers. The last article reveals which companies are at the forefront of the green revolution— and which ones are lagging behind.

Looking Ahead: Challenge Questions

Does an organization have a responsibility to reveal product defects to consumers?

Given the competitiveness of the business arena, is it possible for marketing personnel to behave ethically and both survive and prosper? What are some suggestions you would make that could be incorporated into the marketing strategy for firms that want to be both ethical and successful?

In "The Ethics of Bootstrapping" article, Scott Cook makes the following comments: "What I've learned, and what all too many bootstrappers can miss, is that being truthful is good business. . . . Being ethical isn't a fairyland, Boy Scout idea, nor is it naive. I wanted to build a business for the long term. And trust is one of the most important sources of your power." Do you agree with this sentiment? Why or why not?

Which area of marketing strategy do you believe is most subject to public scrutiny in regard to ethics— product, pricing, place, or promotion? Why? What are some examples of unethical techniques or strategies involving each of these four variables?

Unit 4

Marketing By Professionals:
Some Ethical Issues and Prescriptions

Patrick E. Murphy, Ph.D. and Gene R. Laczniak, Ph.D.

Patrick E. Murphy, Ph.D., is a Professor of Marketing at The University of Notre Dame in Notre Dame, Indiana. Gene R. Laczniak, Ph.D., is a Professor of Business at Marquette University in Milwaukee, Wisconsin.

Introduction

Ethical issues facing the professions is a relatively longstanding concern. It is common practice to mention the "professional obligation" of certain practitioners to behave ethically. Examples of such professional duties are the obligations of medicine to provide health, of law to provide justice and of clergy to provide spiritual guidance. Another almost universal characteristic of the professions is the presence of a formal code of ethics and the existence of enforcement mechanisms for the code. We focus here, though, mostly on ethical questions revolving around the marketing and advertising techniques used by professionals such as accountants, dentists, lawyers and physicians.

The use of marketing and advertising techniques by professionals is an emotional and controversial topic. As Exhibit 1 recounts, the debate has raged for some time. From the Supreme Court decisions in 1976 *(Virginia State Board of Pharmacy v. Virginia Citizens Consumer Council)* and in 1977 *(Bates v. State Bar of Arizona)* that struck down prohibitions on such advertising, this issue has generated much debate in various professional communities. Feelings run deep on both sides, as exemplified by the following comment by former Chief Justice Warren Burger: "The public should never, never, never employ a lawyer or doctor who finds it necessary to advertise." His statement can be contrasted with one by a FTC official who said: "At bottom, the prejudice against advertising is that it creates pressure to compete." Related to the competition issue, is the feeling that advertising will place undue emphasis on price at the expense of the provider's quality of service. A final point of contention is that consumers seem generally much more favorably disposed to the use of advertising than many professionals.

In this article, we review the forces that have and will cause professionals to increase their marketing and advertising expenditures. We summarize the arguments for and against the use of these techniques. Then, we examine a few specific ethical issues relating to accountants, lawyers and the medical community. We conclude with **Ideas for Executive Action,** which should help advertising and marketing by professionals remain on a high ethical plane.

Exhibit 1

Legal Advertising: An Old Controversy

Over half a century ago, James F. Brennan, a California attorney, wrote a spirited argument against the prohibition, legal advertising and solicitation of clients by lawyers. Young, inexperienced, poor lawyers, he said, are forbidden to advertise or to solicit clients. But there is a sense in which this is *not* true of those attorneys who are wealthy and well established. The wealthy lawyer goes to his club and solicits the business of other wealthy persons on the golf course, at poolside, during dinner, at cocktail parties, and at other social functions. Because he has plenty of leisure, he may join philanthropic organizations and, through his activities there, may meet other persons who may be inclined, after talking to him, to retain his services.

Moreover, many lawyers work for large firms, engaged not exclusively in the practice of law but in other forms of activity closely related to law. Such firms and associations as banks, insurance companies, brokerage houses, utilities, unions, and large corporations of every kind may have one or more lawyers on their payrolls. Banks and insurance companies may advertise services related to setting up trusts and drawing up wills, all of which is the kind of work that is best done by lawyers and is likely to be done by the company's attorneys or in consultation with them. Thus, *these* attorneys benefit from the advertising done by the companies or associations with which they are affiliated; but the novice who is attempting to set up a solo practice is forbidden to advertise or to solicit.

Still others are fortunate enough to marry into the law business or to inherit one. They can afford to entertain the people who have lucrative law business to give.

All of this, Brennan said, was unfair to the impoverished young lawyer when he is denied the right to solicit business in the only way open to him. Even worse, he pointed out, was the fact that the bar associations were loaded with lawyers who worked for the big casualty insurers. It was curious, he said, that they were so eager to prevent others from soliciting business.

> Is it for the public interest or for their own interest? If the injured party has no independent legal advice as to his legal rights, these casualty insurance companies can settle with him on what they advise him his legal rights are . . . . . If (plaintiffs') attorneys file more than three personal injury cases in one year, an investigation is made in the county clerk's office and elsewhere to ascertain how they got their cases. Why not investigate attorneys for bank and trust companies, title insurance companies and casualty insurance companies to ascertain how they get their cases?

Brennan noted that an attorney may know of legal rights that a party has but of which the party himself is ignorant. Yet, if the attorney informs the party of his legal rights and offers to assist him, he violates the rule and may be disbarred.

From *Business Insights*, Spring/Summer 1990, pp. 5-9. *Business Insights,* published by the Center for Business Development and Research, College of Business Administration, The University of Southern Mississippi.

A poor man should be able to have a lawyer as well as the rich man, and he is more in need of one. The attorney who handles personal injury cases is the poor man's lawyer.

Forces Stimulating Marketing by Professionals

There are a number of developments in the last two decades that have moved professionals out of their traditional mode of operation. The ones we believe to be the most important are: emerging legal developments, growing competition and marketing's applicability to professional practice in areas such as new service development and franchising.

Legal Developments. Historically, most state and national professional organizations historically had prohibitions against advertising in their codes of conduct. The *Virginia Board of Pharmacy* case ruled "unconstitutional" a Virginia statute declaring that advertising of prescription drug prices by any pharmacist constituted unprofessional conduct. The *Bates v. State Bar of Arizona* case challenged the state bar association's ban on publicizing legal fees. The case was appealed to the Supreme Court, and it ruled in June 1977 that attorneys have First Amendment freedom of speech rights to advertise fees for routine services and that consumers have the right to receive such information. But the Court did not foresee major changes in the way that lawyers and other professionals practiced. They wrote: "We suspect that with advertising, most lawyers will behave as they always have. They will abide by their solemn oath to uphold the honor and integrity of the profession and the legal systems." The major professional associations followed the edict of the Court and relaxed advertising restrictions for dentists in 1977, and for the accounting, legal and medical professions in 1978. These decisions, then, set in motion the marketing and advertising of the professions.

Two subsequent Supreme Court cases reaffirmed the right of professionals to advertise. The first decision (the *Zauder* case in 1984) ruled that the use of illustrations or pictures in newspaper advertisements serves an important communicative function. The second case (*Shapero v. Kentucky Bar Association* in 1988) stipulated that states may not prohibit direct mail advertising aimed at specific target markets. The obvious conclusion that can be drawn is that marketing and advertising can now be legally used by professionals to promote their practice.

Growing Competition. The world of the 1990s is much more competitive for everyone, including professionals. There appears to be two reasons for this growing level of competition. First, law, architecture, dentistry and several other professions have become overcrowded with the number of new professionals entering the field. Professional schools continue to graduate large numbers of students every year. This means that the newer professionals, especially, must use marketing and advertising techniques to attract clients.

The mentality of most professionals toward promotion has also changed. They have moved from the traditional "country club" contact method of publicizing their service to a more sophisticated marketing perspective. This is not only due to the changing legal climate, but also because they see marketing as a viable mechanism to compete effectively in this changing environment. Competition probably will not diminish in the future, and most professionals (some reluctantly, however) have recognized that marketing and advertising will continue to play a major role in this competitive world.

A third competitive development is the growth in different types of professional providers. Medicine and dentistry were dominated by individual practitioners who did not view themselves as competing directly with their colleagues. Now, in medicine for example, these individual purveyors are competing with clinics, group practices, HMOs as well as hospitals. In the accounting field, the so-called Big Six (reduced from eight) is not only competing with one another, but also with smaller firms, consulting organizations and specialty companies which provide highly specialized services (e.g., auditing for health care organizations). The pressure then is on all types of professional service providers to market themselves more aggressively against the new competitive forms.

Marketing's Applicability to Professional Practice. Some professionals have found that marketing concepts such as branding, new service development, alternate delivery mechanisms and franchising can be applied to their situation. If the professional wants to meet the needs of the time conscious and mobile consumer of the 1990s, such new approaches must be explored. Just as Burger King has found consumers to be loyal to their "brand", Humana has found that its brand of medicine is preferred by some consumers. The use of brand or corporate names has made it much easier to franchise legal, dental, optical and medical clinics. Such retailing of the professions began even before the Bates decision, but has gained popularity in the 1980s. Dental World, Omnidentix Systems, Nu Vision Centers and Sterling Optical are some of the best known professional services franchises.

As mentioned, even the more traditional professional practices have expanded their product line and altered their distribution network. For instance, ambulatory surgery, alcoholic rehabilitation, psychological counseling, personal injury law and management consulting by public accounting firms are recent additions to the product portfolio of service providers. Furthermore, professionals have begun using immediate care medical centers, satellite offices and expanded hours to appeal to time conscious consumers. These developments often necessitated some type of advertising to inform consumers of the change in service distribution by the professional.

The Status of Advertising by Professionals

Though 15 years have passed since the Virginia Board and Bates decisions, the use of marketing and advertising by professionals is still a controversial topic. We now review some of the strongest arguments on both sides of the issue.

The Case for Advertising by Professionals. Several arguments can be advanced. Probably the strongest is that consumers demand such information. Individuals are in need of information about legal, medical, optical and dental services. They are used to getting information about other products and services via the newspaper and television. At minimum, consumers want to know the location of the provider and the range of services offered. Word of mouth is still the most effective information source for all products; but dissatisfied consumers, newcomers to an area and the poor may not have access to this source. Consequently, advertising offers them an easily accessible vehicle for gaining information about professionals. From an ethical standpoint, it is argued that according to the principle of distributive justice, the poor, elderly and market illiterates are more likely to be served if advertising of these services is permitted.

A second argument, and the one that legal decisions are mostly based upon, is the First Amendment right of free speech. Professionals should be able to communicate with consumers in any nondeceptive manner that they choose. Critics view advertising as "undignified", but Justice Blackmun noted in the majority opinion of Bates: "The assertion that advertising will diminish the attorney's reputation in the community is open to question. Bankers and engineers advertise, and yet these professions are not regarded as undignified."

Third, proponents contend that the costs to consumers are lower when advertising is present. This is an extension of the competition argument which states that more information in the market place will have the effect of driving down prices. In the absence of advertising, the professionals could collude and keep prices artificially high. The Federal Trade Commission has used this argument extensively and has found in one study that in cities where lawyers intensely advertised, legal fees have declined by 5%—13%. When the FTC analysis is combined with the consumer information argument, supporters suggest that advertising contributes to the efficient functioning of the market place/economy.

A final reason to support increased marketing by professionals is that it allows a new entrant to gain access to the market more easily. In the absence of advertising, it may take years for a new lawyer or accountant, or a new type of practice to make enough contacts to attain a thriving business. A specific example is Hyatt Legal Services, a legal services chain with over 200 offices nationwide employing over 600 attorneys. Hyatt spent several million dollars on T.V. ads using CEO Joel Hyatt as spokesperson to build its client base. Although this firm is one of the most successful, there are undoubtedly many more professionals who received at least modest aid from advertising.

The Case Against Advertising by Professionals. The critics of marketing and advertising by professionals articulate a number of variations on a common theme. Namely, it is "unprofessional" for individuals who consider themselves to belong to a professional community to lower themselves to use common business practices. The logical extension of this argument is that advertising undermines the relationship of trust which exists between a professional person and a client. One CPA spokesperson perceives that the best way to build a practice is to get involved in one's community. The emphasis should be on "quality control, not marketing concepts". This critic foresees a long term detrimental impact of the marketing orientation of current CPAs: "By cheapening our profession with distasteful advertising and gimmicks, will we slip undistinguished into the maze of financial service providers who also are certified, i.e., planners, life underwriters, etc.?"

A similar sentiment was expressed by a lawyer who felt that advertising contributes to the negative image of that profession. A survey conducted by a Florida bar association found that professionals are very conscious of their image with the public, and some believe that the "dignity" of the profession is compromised with the use of mass market advertising. The view that marketing by professionals has an impact on all practitioners, not just those who advertise, is well articulated by a Florida lawyer: "Advertising is a broad brush, which stains all lawyers. We tend to be perceived as greedy, self-interested people who do not care about our clients and are only interested in making a buck."

Another view expressed by critics of marketing and advertising is that the focus has shifted away from the professional's major job of healing, advising and counseling toward an emphasis on issues of lesser importance—generating a profit. They ask, do consumers want to shop for the lowest price for a heart transplant as one would for a used car? Probably not. Certainly there are some unethical professionals who do use advertising unscrupulously. Furthermore, consumers are interested in more than price. Most want a competent, knowledgeable practitioner who can solve problems; price is secondary in importance. In the final analysis, however, the Supreme Court has affirmed the right of professionals to market and to advertise their services.

Ethical Issues in Marketing by Accountants

Accountants were also reluctant to embrace marketing and advertising concepts. Times changed dramatically during the 1980s. Many accounting firms both developed advertising campaigns and employed staff people in a marketing capacity. Some of the largest ones, like Arthur Andersen, initiated consulting divisions which were engaged in extensive marketing efforts. Consequently, questions regarding the ethics of these practices became more prevalent.

The definitive position on advertising in the accounting field is contained in Section 502 (Advertising and Other Forms of Solicitation) of the AICPA Code of Professional Conduct. The emphasis in the code is on *informational,* as opposed to persuasive, advertising. Section 502 delineates what is prohibited by the code as well as what is considered ethical in advertising by accountants. For example, past experience is acceptable to mention in advertising as well as the CPA designation. However, the advertiser cannot use self-laudatory statements unless they are based on verifiable facts. Certain advertising of the largest CPA firms (Deloitte, Haskins & Sells, and Price Waterhouse) has been contested on ethical grounds. Accounting firms that are concerned about the ethical posture of their advertising need to develop guidelines that delineate what is expected. For example, Arthur Andersen has a detailed book outlining the firm's position on "Ethical Standards/Independence", which includes the complete AICPA code as an appendix.

Ethical Questions Regarding Lawyer Advertising

Some law firms have openly embraced marketing. As one CEO of a prepaid legal service commented, "We don't have attorneys that sit in the office and practice. We market law. That's all we do." The law firms that have most extensively used advertising are those specializing in personal injury, medical malpractice, immigration law or divorce. Lawyers now spend over $50 million on advertising, a ten-fold increase since 1980. The percentage of lawyers who advertise has increased from three percent to 32 percent over those years.

The American Bar Association has developed both a Model Code of Professional Responsibility and Model Rules of Professional Conduct. The state bar associations follow one of these two documents to serve as the official standard of conduct for lawyers. Several of the clauses are quite similar to those governing accountants. Alleged violations are reviewed by a state bar committee which can recommend one of several sanctions (e.g., reprimand, suspension or disbarment).

There are many potential ethical issues stemming from attorney advertising and marketing. Exhibit 2 lists some pertinent questions that could be asked about potentially unethical legal advertising. The sundry ethical issues include fear generating T.V. ads dramatized with sirens, ambulances, wrecked vehicles, or individuals being placed on stretchers, and ads that vow to help you "collect cash". An in-depth examination of law practice marketing listed over 20 categories of ethical issues including use of customer testimonials, non-informational adver-

tising and cold call solicitations. The study concluded with the following admonition:

> Inevitably, the standards which will govern all of lawyer business-getting activity will be those of honesty and fairness. Misleading and false statements and overreaching conduct will characterize prohibited marketing behavior..... The responsibility for ensuring that law practice marketing plans comply with ethical prescriptions rests squarely with the lawyers..... Lawyers who accept any marketing advice without scrutinizing its ethical propriety risk are wasting money on strategies which must be abandoned for ethical reasons. More importantly, they risk censure from the bar.

Exhibit 2

Some Ethical Questions About Lawyer Advertising

The principal difficulty, though, lies in determining just what is, for instance, misleading, or unfair, or dignified. Consider the following:

- A personal injury ad says, "No recovery—no fee". Is this misleading or deceptive for failure to mention the client may be responsible for litigation costs?
- Is a "24-Hour Legal Hotline" dignified?
- "Real People, Not a Professional Corporation or Legal Clinic". Is this misleading to the public and unfair to other lawyers?
- An ad seeking drunk driving cases shows a liquor bottle, a wrecked car, and a drunk. Is this dignified?
- "Twenty Years of Successful Criminal Practice". Is this self-laudatory; does it contain information about past performance; and does it create an unjustified expectation?
- "Low Rates". Is this sufficient fee information, or deceptive?
- In an advertising circular, "Bring this coupon in for a Free Consultation. Is this dignified or deceptive?
- "The Worst Injury of All May Be Not Being Properly Represented." Is this misleading or unfair?
- "Full Compensation for Your Injuries". Does this create unjustified expectations?
- "Everyday our lawyers are in court representing innocent people charged with crimes they didn't commit." Is this potentially fraudulent or deceptive?
- A T.V. ad for personal injury cases shows an accident, flashing lights, and injured persons being loaded into ambulances. Is this dignified or deceptive? Does it appeal to anger, fear or greed?
- "We took the fear out of legal fees." Is this deceptive? Is it telling the public to be fearful of lawyers and legal fees?
- A lawyers' referral service sells all referrals from certain counties to lawyers for a monthly fee. The service advertises an "800" phone number in the yellow pages, with a nationwide answering service based in Tennessee. The service has been approved only by a local bar association in California. Does this meet the letter and spirit of Rule 7.3?

Source: "Lawyer Advertising—Marketing, Professionalism, the Future," *Res Gestae,* August 1988, 63.

Ethical Issues Facing Medical and Dental Marketing

Of all the professions, medicine has resisted marketing and advertising most vehemently. Survey results indicate that physicians are more skeptical than other professionals toward the benefits of marketing. It may be that they perceive marketing to be primarily a selling activity and far removed from their view of the responsibilities contained in the Hypocratic Oath. Although the medical community was covered by the *Bates* decision, the American Medical Association was charged by the FTC with conspiring with state and local medical societies to suppress all forms of medical advertising. The Supreme Court handed down another decision in 1982. It affirmed the right of physicians to advertise in a truthful, nondeceptive manner.

The majority of medical advertising is undertaken by clinics, HMOs and hospitals. One of the earliest, and most controversial, hospital ads was undertaken by Sunrise Hospital of Las Vegas. There are a number of codes developed by various associations to help insure ethical advertising. The Advertising Guidelines of the Council of Medical Specialty Societies contains 13 points which stipulate that the use of incomplete information, heavy fear appeals and misleading messages are unacceptable. Many of these ethical guidelines should hold for the advertising of any product. One especially ethically charged medical area is cosmetic surgery. It is heavily advertised in some parts of the country, such as California. A number of ethical hazards of advertising cosmetic surgery has been noted by critics, including the possibility of creating oversimplified expectations. The worst case scenario is where ads manipulate individuals to demand services that are downright unhealthy (suction-assisted lipectomy, i.e., fat suction is an especially controversial procedure). Another issue pertains to promoting the professional qualifications of individuals performing cosmetic surgery. Some physicians advertise themselves as specialists without the proper training or certification—a morally, medically, and legally dubious practice. Defenders of cosmetic surgery have noted three reasons why advertising such surgery may be ethically justifiable: (1) Medicine should serve human wants, and one's appearance may improve an individual's quality of life; (2) Patients demanding this surgery are not sick and are more free to "shop around" and find the best deal; and (3) The surgical costs are voluntarily borne by the consumer.

Ideas for Executive Action

The three interested parties—professional associations, practitioners and ad agencies—must all work together to insure that advertising by the professions is on the highest ethical plane. We propose a specific suggestion for each of them.

(1) **Professional associations must continue to place emphasis on advertising issues through updated codes and guidelines, enforcement and conference sessions devoted to the topic.**

Professional societies in law, accounting, medicine and dentistry have had to change their posture toward advertising. As one practitioner aptly noted: "The question is thus not whether but how physicians shall be permitted to advertise their services." It is in this spirit that associations should look at their role to assist and guide, but **not discourage,** advertising by their professionals. For example, the Indiana State Bar Association Lawyer Advertising Committee has recommended that the association publish articles outlining changes in rules governing legal advertising and prepare a brochure to be disseminated to the public so that they can better be protected from false and misleading advertising. Professional organizations need to scrutinize the marketing programs of their members keeping ethical questions in the limelight and holding sessions that discuss such questions at association meetings. Furthermore, sanctions must be enforced so that violators know they will be prosecuted.

(2) **Professionals who employ ad agencies must hold them to high levels of integrity and continuously monitor the messages they develop.**

Professionals need to be careful in the type of agency they select to do their advertising. One recommendation would be to monitor other noncompeting professional ads and to find out what agency prepares the ads that have high integrity and credibility. Just because an agency contends that they are an "expert" in legal or medical advertising does not make them an acceptable choice. Professionals can further monitor the effect of the ad on their clientele by asking their impression of it and doing some informal research on their own.

(3) **Ad agencies and marketing consultants who wish to serve professionals should position themselves as being sensitive to the unique needs of the professional community.**

Many agencies and consultants see the growing professional advertising market as an extension of their regular business. This is possibly a mistake. Professionals are different in their orientation. Taking the high road in marketing and advertising is not just expected; it is a necessity. Therefore, marketers should develop campaigns and programs that are unquestioned in terms of integrity. Understanding the philosophical perspective of a professional is more than a semantic challenge.

References

Abbott, Andrew, "Professional Ethics," *American Journal of Sociology,* Vol. 88, 1983, 855-885.

Balzer, John E., "Attorney Advertising: Who's Really Afraid of the Big Bad Lawyer," *New England Law Review,* March 1988, 727-760.

Braun, Irwin and Marilyn Braun, "Following a Decade of Advertising: Professionals Still Face Restraints," *Marketing News,* August 14, 1987, 21.

"CMSS Develops Guidelines for Physician Advertising," *Annals of Emergency Medicine,* December 1981, 100.

Dugas, Christine, "Marketing: The Prescription for Professional Practices?" *Ad Forum,* February 1983, 42-44.

Folland, Sherman, R. Parameswaran and John Darling, "On the Nature of Physicians' Opposition to Advertising," *Journal of Advertising,* Vol. 18, 1989, 4-12.

Hite, Robert E. and Cynthia Fraser, "Meta-Analyses of Attitudes Toward Advertising by Professionals," *Journal of Marketing,* July 1988, 95-105.

"Is Dignity Important in Legal Advertising?" *ABA Journal,* August 1, 1987, A-1 and A-2.

"Lawyer Advertising—Marketing, Professionalism, the Future," *Res Gestae,* August 1988, 59-64.

Leiser, Burton M., "Professional Advertising: Price Fixing and Professional Dignity versus the Public's Right to a Free Market," *Journal of Business and Professional Ethics,* Spring/Summer 1984, 93-110.

Macklin, Ruth, "Commentary on Leiser," *Journal of Business and Professional Ethics,* Spring/Summer 1984, 114.

"Major CPA Firms Accused of Violations of Professional Conduct," *The Practical Accountant,* April 1986, 43-44.

Morreim, E. Haavi, "A Moral Examination of Medical Advertising," *Business & Society Review,* Winter 1988, 4-6.

Moss, Frederick C., "The Ethics of Law Practice Marketing," *Notre Dame Law Review,* Vol. 61, 1986, 601-696.

North, Sterling, "Lawyers in the Age of Advertising," *New England Business,* August 3, 1987, 22-25.

Stafford, David C., "Advertising in the Professions," *International Journal of Advertising,* 1988, 7, 189-220.

Stewart, Larry, "Advertising: The Need For a Strong ATLA Policy," *ATLA Advocate,* July 1989, 2 and 4.

"Suggestions for Lawyer Advertising—Avoiding Deceptive & Unprofessional Ads," *Res Gestae,* February 1989, 394-398.

Trapani, Christopher, "Advertising v. Solicitation: Shapero Ends the Controversy Over Targeted Direct-Mailings by Attorneys," *Florida Bar Journal,* February 1989, 31-33.

Walsh, William J., "CPAs and Advertising: Another Voice," *Journal of Accountancy,* November 1986, 178-180.

"What Forms of Advertising Are Permissible Under the Ethics Code?" *Journal of Accountancy,* November 1986, 98-99.

*This paper is abstracted from a chapter entitled, "The Ethics of Social, Professional and Political Marketing", which will appear in The Higher Road: A Path to Ethical Marketing Decisions, to be published by Allyn & Bacon.

Marketers Exploit People's Fears of Everything

Kathleen Deveny

Staff Reporter of THE WALL STREET JOURNAL

Flames roar through a lovely home, melting a silent smoke detector into a twisted glob. The message in the recent television commercial: One third of all smoke alarms have dead batteries. The sales pitch: The pink Energizer bunny silently thumps across the screen.

It may sound like a ghoulish satire, but the commercial from Ralston-Ralston Purina Group's Eveready Battery unit is just one of dozens that impart a frightening warning: Terrible things happen to good people. People just like you.

Marketers nowadays seem increasingly willing to sell their products by playing on consumers' anxieties, and their advertising has become scarier and more graphic. An ad for First Alert carbon monoxide detectors flashes photos of real people who died of carbon monoxide poisoning while a woman tells how her husband carried a grainy picture of their dead daughter in his wallet for 21 years. A mailing from Loving Choice Baby Products urges consumers to buy its how-to child CPR video "now . . . before it's too late." And Volvo is running print and TV ads that show real people who believe they survived terrible car crashes because they were driving Volvos.

The shrill strategy undoubtedly stems from the sense that many Americans have never been more afraid. "People today desperately want to protect themselves against the world," says Dr. Carol Moog, a psychologist and advertising consultant at Creative Focus in Bala Cynwyd, Pa.

Never mind that life expectancy is creeping upward while the incidence of home accidents—including fires, poisonings and falls—steadily declines. People are bombarded with accounts of tragedies involving everything from violent carjackings to the cancer-causing danger of electromagnetic fields.

"The level of anxiety among consumers is extraordinarily high," says Myra Stark, senior vice president and director of creative research at Saatchi & Saatchi Advertising in New York. In addition to physical threats, she says, many people are feeling vulnerable because of the economic slump and layoffs in corporate America.

Marketers of consumer products have raised the specter of bad fortune in the past, albeit more cautiously. Kellogg Co.'s All-Bran cereal ads startled people nearly a decade ago by citing links between a high-fiber diet and the prevention of cancer. Even mentioning the word cancer was considered risky because advertisers believed consumers didn't want to be reminded of death.

Andrew Langer, chief executive officer of Lowe & Partners SMS, sparked a debate in 1974 with what may have been the first "slice-of-death" ad. Tame by today's standards, the ad showed a man, played by a young John Travolta, reminiscing about his dad on his way to work in a shop. The father, it turned out, had died without amassing enough savings to put his son through college. "It was very controversial at the time, but so was the show 'All In The Family,' " Mr. Langer says. Advertising "has changed because the way we view the world has changed."

Marketers today claim their scary advertising is more a public service than a sales tactic. BRK Electronics Inc., which says it can't keep up with demand for its First Alert carbon monoxide detector, notes that it tested the ads with consumers and concluded that most wouldn't be offended. A more straightforward, educational execution of the ad just didn't catch consumers' attention, according to Richard F. Timmons, marketing director for the First Alert line. The company decided to use real people in the ads to make viewers realize that carbon monoxide poisoning could also happen to them.

To build interest in its First Alert Carbon Monoxide Detector, BRK Electronics began a public relations campaign in June pointing out that the colorless, odorless gas kills 1,500 Americans annually. The National Safety Council, however, estimates 400 Americans die each year of poisoning by gas or vapors.

Regardless of the conflicting statistics, "can you say we've gone too far if even one baby would be born without birth defects?" Mr. Timmons says. (Exposure to carbon monoxide has been associated with birth defects.)

Indeed, many marketers play on people's feelings of protectiveness about children. Loving Choice Baby Products, a unit of TransAmerica Mailings Inc. in Cleveland, contends that the benefits of the child CPR video it distributes outweigh concerns that the mailings are manipulative. "There is a really valid reason for knowing CPR—like saving your child's life," says Avvy Katz, president of TransAmerica.

Marketing experts say it's the use of real people that makes some of the ads seem so ominous. Car ads have long shown images of dual air bags and crash dummies surviving wrecks. But television ads for Volvo ads feature idyllic images of real people, including a woman and her two children and a man shooting baskets with his son. As haunting choir music plays, the date of the near-fatal accident appears superimposed over each portrait.

"The point is not to be scary," says Bob Schmetterer, a partner with Messner Vetere Berger McNamee Schmetterer, the ad agency for Volvo Cars of North Amer-

Reprinted by permission of *The Wall Street Journal,* November 15, 1993, pp. B1, B5. © 1993 by Dow Jones & Company, Inc. All rights reserved worldwide.

The View From the Couch

Dr. Carol Moog, psychologist and advertising consultant in Bala Cynwyd, Pa., analyzed some recent advertisements that use scare tactics.

ALLSTATE

Commercial shows wreckage of burned-out house and urges viewers to check their smoke detectors' batteries.

Comment: Truly frightening. Here you see all the details of a person's life destroyed. All of it is still recognizable. It's like a brilliantly shot horror-film scene. The monster has left the room, and you are looking at the blood drippings. It is as if the room had been a living organism, and you are witnessing its death.

FIRST ALERT

Television ad for its carbon monoxide detector features snapshots of real people who died from carbon monoxide poisoning, narrated by people who have lost loved ones.

Comment: We see two caring people, and only one will die. This plays on survivor guilt. He didn't protect Patti. Each of the photos clearly evokes someone who was enjoying life and then was eliminated. These are all nice people. We see a teenage boy in a football uniform that bears the team name: Angels. He was somebody's angel. Even if you realize you are being manipulated, it still works.

VOLVO

Print ad featuring pictures of people who believe they survived terrible auto accidents because they were driving a Volvo. The date of the accident appears with each portrait.

Comment: The strategy might have been to have you think that all these people died, but at the end of the ad lo and behold, you find out they have been saved by Volvo. The wording at the end— "The people on the preceding pages all share a common belief . . .—" makes it sound like Volvo is skirting around a legal issue. That doesn't cut it in psychological terms.

---

ica. Mr. Schmetterer points out that the survivors contacted Volvo, and that they aren't paid to appear in the spots. "The reality," he says, "is that every manufacturer is talking about safety in a very poignant way."

Other ads strike a chord by graphically depicting just how much viewers have to lose. A recent commercial from the Allstate Insurance unit of Allstate Corp. shows the wreckage of a recently burned-out house, as mournful cello music plays in the background. The camera lingers on melted toys and a television remote control device that is still smoldering before focusing on the real problem, a smoke detector with no batteries. Allstate says it tested the ad with consumers, and didn't receive any negative comments.

"At the end of the commercial, we wanted people to get up and check their smoke detectors," says Terre Tuzzolino, Allstate's assistant vice president of corporate relations.

But scare tactics don't always make for compelling advertising. Some marketing experts say the Energizer battery ads risk offending some consumers, and Dr. Moog of Creative Focus says the ad has other problems, as well. The interior of the house doesn't include any personal items, and the fire looks fake because it starts too quickly.

Ward Klein, vice president of marketing for Eveready, says it tested the ad with consumers, and asked specifically if people thought the spot was too threatening.

In fact, Mr. Klein says the ad scored high in ratings for "likability."

And some marketers say consumers are so interested in safety these days, they aren't put off by frightening advertising. Safety Zone, a White Plains, N.Y., company that distributes a catalog of safety products, says people even give many of its products as Christmas gifts. Among the items turning up under Christmas trees: personal alarms and smoke detectors camouflaged as tree ornaments. Melanie Lee, who co-founded the company with her husband, also believes a new product called Safe-T-Man is being purchased as a gift. Safe-T-Man is a "simulated male" who sits in the passenger-seat of a car to scare troublemakers away.

Strategic Green Marketing

Stephen W. McDaniel and David H. Rylander

Stephen W. McDaniel is Associate Professor of Marketing at Texas A&M University and David H. Rylander is Instructor of Business in the Department of Business Administration and Management at Southeastern Oklahoma State University in Durant, Oklahoma, USA.

Many have called the 1990s the "Earth Decade", or the decade when environmentalism emerges as one of the most critical issues facing consumer marketers. The term "green marketing" has been coined to describe marketers' attempts to develop strategies targeting the "environmental consumer". There is an increasingly popular notion that environmentally-based product positioning should be an important consideration in consumer marketing (Leigh *et al.*, 1988). As a result, consumer marketers should understand environmental issues and be able to incorporate this consideration into the strategic marketing management process.

CRITICAL ENVIRONMENTAL CONCERNS

The idea of including environmental concerns in strategic marketing planning is not new. Over two decades ago, questions were raised regarding whether the marketing concept leads to misplaced emphasis on customer "want" satisfaction while ignoring the long-run best interests of society and the environment (Bell and Emery, 1971; Feldman, 1971). These concerns were addressed by Kotler in his delineation of the "societal marketing concept", which called for societally responsible marketing to include four considerations in marketing decision-making: consumer wants, consumer interests, company requirements, and *societal welfare* (Kotler, 1976).

Currently, there are numerous environmental concerns that threaten societal welfare:

● landfills, which are called on to handle over 150 million tons of trash per year, are dangerously near to being full;

● the National Wildlife Federation reports that almost 40 percent of Americans experience significant health problems from the drinking water (Ottman, 1990);

● almost one-third of Americans live in areas with high levels of ozone (Ottman, 1990);

From *The Journal of Consumer Marketing*, Vol. 10, No. 3, 1993, pp. 4-10. © 1993 by MCB University Press Limited. Reprinted by permission.

- our natural resources, particularly rain forests, are being depleted at an ever-increasing rate;
- the so-called "greenhouse effect", a potential threat to our planet's long-term survival, is being given more and more serious consideration by leading world scientists.

These five environmental concerns, representative of the countless environmental issues which our world faces today, may not appear to be directly related to consumer marketing programs, but the societal marketing concept says they should be. Furthermore, there is indication that consumers are becoming increasingly concerned about these issues and are associating them with the products they buy (Adams, 1990; Allen, 1990; McKusick, 1990).

Consumer environmental consciousness is not just a passing fad. For example, environmental protection is now being called a "consensus issue" for politicians (Schwartz, 1990). A 1991 Gallup survey revealed that 90 percent of Americans consider themselves "environmentalists". A majority of consumers claim that environmental concern affects their choice of product, even if they must pay a higher price (Freeman, 1989). A Michael Peters Group poll reported that three-quarters of consumers are willing to pay more for recyclable or biodegradable packaging (Rice, 1990). The marketplace impact of this latter concern is evident in the doubling of sales of Tendercare biodegradable diapers within one year of introducing the theme "Change the world one diaper at a time" (Fisher and Graham, 1989).

MARKETING IMPLICATIONS

What does this increased environmental consciousness mean to consumer marketers? It means that they should: recognize a product's environmental implications; analyze the changing consumer and political attitudes while recognizing the role that companies can play in protecting the environment; realize that green marketing is not purely altruistic — it can be a profitable endeavor; and recognize that green marketing must be a fully integrated part of a firm's strategic marketing plan.

Businesses must first decide which environmental problems they can and should address. Every business is affected by environmental concerns in one way or another. Some businesses may have control over packaging or recycling, others may have direct control over air or water pollution. The key is deciding which concerns are feasible to address and then implementing appropriate strategies.

This approach is especially critical given the changing attitudes and perceptions of the government and consumers. A business cannot simply give lip service to the environment or make inaccurate claims. The government is reacting swiftly to false claims, as is evidenced by the crackdown on questionable degradable plastic claims. More important, consumers have developed a keen interest in the facts and are rejecting companies with insincere, inaccurate, or incomplete environmental action programs. Procter & Gamble has been especially cautious with its use of environmental symbols and degradability claims, electing to avoid public backlash at questionable green marketing ploys (Geiger, 1990).

The companies which benefit from green marketing are those which have shown a commitment to solving real problems and taking a step beyond what is required or expected. For instance, IBM, Du Pont, and Monsanto have taken significant steps to reduce the use of ozone-depleting chlorofluorocarbons. Other companies, such as Procter & Gamble, Texaco, Merck, General Electric, Amoco, 3M, and AT&T, have made environmental analysis an integral part of their corporate planning structure and process (Kirkpatrick, 1990; Smith *et al.*, 1990). McDonald's has developed information sheets, proudly pointing out its efforts toward protection of the ozone, rain forests, and other environmental concerns.

On the other hand, many other companies have failed to gain from green marketing efforts, mainly because of a lack of true commitment. They have implemented strategies prematurely and without full awareness of the real impact. Some companies have failed to realize that an environmental action plan must be fully prepared to withstand careful scrutiny by the government and the public.

Another critical point to consider is that consumers have thresholds of price and convenience. Consumers want products that are better for the environment, but not products that significantly detract from their lifestyle. The best way to meet these conflicting needs is to add value to products while making them environmentally better. A value-added approach meets consumers' qualitative needs while accommodating their desire to be environmentally conscientious (Schwartz, 1990).

APPROACHES TO GREEN MARKETING

There are two basic approaches to green marketing. The first is a defensive or reactionary approach. The second is an assertive, aggressive strategy.

Defensive

Most companies tend to take a defensive approach to green marketing. They do the minimum in order to avoid negative consequences. For example, a company might comply with minimum government environmental regulations to avoid tax or penalties. Such corporate maneuvers have been called "mostly smoke and mirrors" aimed at avoiding regulation (Smith *et*

al., 1990). A similar reactionary move is to meet minimum standards in order to avoid a consumer boycott. A third type of defensive strategy is to react to competitors' environmental moves but do no more than is needed to keep pace.

All these defensive approaches are designed to avoid negative consequences. However, a company which takes such an approach to green marketing will probably encounter no significant increase in market acceptance. Its images will not be improved relative to competitors and most customers will recognize that the effort is minimal. In general, if a company lags behind in meeting environmental standards, it will never gain a competitive advantage in this dimension and will be more susceptible to consumer or government backlash. Marc Gobe, creative director at Cato Gobe, predicts that companies not addressing the environmental issues will face declining market share (Miller, 1990).

Assertive

The alternative to a defensive strategy is an assertive approach. This strategy provides the best opportunity for a sustainable competitive advantage. The assertive approach involves being a "first mover" and also doing more than is required by government or expected by consumers. Doing this means responding to market incentives instead of to regulations. A green marketing approach which responds to the demands of the market is consumer-oriented and profit-driven (Wells, 1990).

First-mover advantage is especially critical in green marketing. The key to profiting from green marketing is the image created for the firm. The companies which follow suit will be seen as imitators, merely jumping on the bandwagon. Consumers may even be skeptical of these latecomers' true intent. On the other hand, the environmental first mover, with good strategic marketing, will be able to maintain its image as a sincere environmental activist, and this image may provide the basis for a sustainable competitive advantage. Wal-Mart is a good example of this first-mover approach. Its in-store environmental campaigns and general leadership position in environmental consciousness have paid tremendous rewards. Marketplace observers have noted that although competitors can imitate Wal-Mart programs, they will never surpass its superior image as the environmental leader (Fisher and Graham, 1989).

An assertive leadership position has other benefits as well. Aside from increased profitability, a firm may avoid scrutiny and regulation by doing more than is required. Government agencies are less likely to investigate or impose controls on a firm that is taking environmental action beyond the minimum standards. Additionally, such a company will be forcing itself into a long-term planning mode. Many firms have a myopic view of the future, but an assertive company engaging in long-term environmental planning will focus more on critical long-run concerns.

With the multiple benefits of an assertive strategy, this approach is clearly desirable for strategic green marketing. But it should be noted that this argument has omitted altruism as a motivation for green marketing. While some would consider an altruistic concern for the long-term survival of our planet reason enough to invoke an environmental action program, it is important from a business perspective to realize that this strategy is desirable on the basis of profitability alone. The consumer carries the strongest vote with the dollar, and that vote is increasingly being spent to send a message to marketers that concern for the environment is not merely a passing fad. Therefore, to get those dollar votes,

a company must take an assertive strategic position on the environment.

INCORPORATING GREEN MARKETING INTO MARKETING STRATEGY DEVELOPMENT

Incorporating green marketing into the strategic planning process has been a problem for many consumer firms, because environmental policies have been treated as sideline plans and not fully integrated into the overall planning process. It is essential to design a strategic marketing process with green marketing as an integral part. Figure 1 depicts a model for doing this.

The following is a ten-point plan designed to facilitate this process:

- *Step 1. Develop an environmental corporate policy.* This policy should state the company's mission and objectives with regard to the environment and should allow for environmental considerations to be integrated into all company decisions.

- *Step 2. Build environmental leadership at the top level of the organization.* Doing this should communicate a long-term commitment to environmental action.

- *Step 3. Hire or develop environmental advocates on the inside.* These people can concentrate on environmental

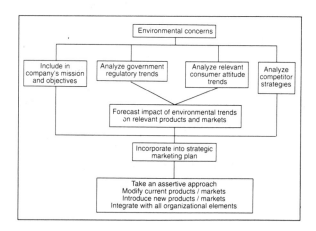

FIGURE 1.
Strategic Green Marketing Planning Model

concerns and provide a consistent environmental voice for the organization. Some companies may even create an entirely new department dedicated to environmental planning.

● *Step 4. Educate and train all employees on environmental awareness.* From the boardroom to the mailroom, an environmental consciousness must pervade the organization.

● *Step 5. Maintain active dialog with outside environmental groups and government agencies.* It is essential to stay abreast of outside needs and concerns.

● *Step 6. Develop an assertive environmental action program.* This program should be integrated into all parts of the strategic planning process.

● *Step 7. Integrate all departments to facilitate flexibility in responding to environmental needs.* Doing this may require building bridges between competing interests in the organization.

● *Step 8. Allocate adequate resources to show commitment.* This environmental commitment must be demonstrated by provision of money and personnel to implement the environmental action program effectively.

● *Step 9. Through effective advertising and publicity, communicate to customers what you are doing.* This communication will not only build customer loyalty toward your organization, but also encourage customers' co-operation in environmental efforts.

● *Step 10. Monitor consumer response with an active marketing research program.* The dynamic nature of environmental needs and demands requires constant monitoring along with flexibility to adapt.

Implementing this ten-point plan requires extensive education and communication, both internally and externally. External communication, through advertising and publicity, is most critical. Consumer marketers must be careful to follow certain guidelines to communicate correctly with their markets. Several recommendations for external communication efforts in this regard have been identified (Wells, 1990). The following guidelines are critical for successful implementation of this approach:

● Attempt to reflect a sincere commitment to the environment. It should be visible from the top level of the organization on down. This sincerity can be one of the most difficult messages to convey.

● Be prepared to withstand careful scrutiny. Environmental claims and actions must be meaningful and valid. The increasingly environmentally concerned public will accept nothing less.

● Focus on positive actions while remaining cautious of any appearance of deception. It is best to avoid direct comparisons with competitors and focus instead on what your company is doing.

● Keep claims simple and understated. Avoid general and exaggerated environmental claims. It is safer to understate than overstate, given the increasingly knowledgeable and skeptical public.

CONCLUSIONS

Findings from a recent Roper poll indicate a dramatic increase in environmental consciousness by the

American public (Garcia, 1991). The Roper Reports Service of The Roper Organization asked a sample of Americans what they thought were the "most serious" environmental problems. Destruction of the ozone, accidental oil spills, outdoor air pollution from factories, and outdoor air pollution from vehicles were all named by over one-half of the respondents. It is particularly noteworthy that the frequency of mention for these environmental concerns in 1990 was, on average, 14 percentage points higher than when the same study was done in 1988. Environmental consciousness by the American public is not only increasing, but increasing dramatically.

This article has pointed out the critical nature of environmental concerns and has provided a strategic marketing planning process for dealing with these rising concerns. In putting this process into place, consumer marketers should keep in mind the following:

● Environmentalism is not just a passing fad. It is strongly supported and here for the long run.

● "Green" consumers, a growing populace, exercise purchasing choices that reflect a preference for environment-friendly products.

● Green marketing offers increased long-run profit potential and the basis for a sustainable competitive advantage to companies that pursue it optimally.

● The most effective approach to green marketing is assertive leadership within the industry.

● Effective communication and continuous monitoring are critical processes for the long-term viability of a green marketing strategy.

● It is important to integrate green marketing carefully into the strategic planning process.

By following these guidelines, a consumer marketer can effectively plan and implement a sound strategic green marketing program. Such a program will be a necessity for corporate survival and growth in the immediate future and into the next millennium.

References

Adams, R. (1990), "The Greening of Consumerism", *Accountancy*, June, pp. 82-3.

Allen, J.E. (1990), "Single Use Packages under Direct Fire by Wastemaker Awards", *Sherman Democrat*, 15 May, p. 1A.

Bell, M.L. and Emery, C.W. (1971), "The Faltering Marketing Concept", *Journal of Marketing*, October, pp. 37-42.

Feldman, L.P. (1971), "Social Adaptation: A New Challenge for Marketing", *Journal of Marketing*, July, pp. 54-60.

Fisher, C. and Graham, J. (1989), "Wal-Mart Throws 'Green' Too", *Advertising Age*, 21 August, pp. 1, 66.

Freeman, L. (1989), "Consumers Thinking 'Green' Too", *Advertising Age*, 21 August, p. 66.

Garcia, S. (1991), "When It Comes to the Environment, It's Personal", *Adweek*, 22 July, p. 18.

Geiger, B. (1990), " 'Green' Monster", *Advertising Age*, 19 March, p. 2.

Kirkpatrick, D. (1990), "Environmentalism: The New Crusade", *Fortune*, 12 February, pp. 44-50.

Kotler, P. (1976), *Marketing Management: Analysis Planning, and Control*, 3rd ed., Prentice-Hall, Englewood Cliffs, NJ, pp. 16-18.

Leigh, J.H., Murphy, P.E. and Enis, B.M. (1988), "A New Approach to Measuring Socially

Responsible Consumption Tendencies'',
Journal of Macromarketing, Spring,
pp. 5-20.

McKusick, T. (1990), ''Third Wave
Environmentalism'', *Utne Reader*,
November/December, pp. 26-8.

Miller, C. (1990), ''Use of Environment-friendly
Packaging May Take Awhile'', *Marketing
News*, 19 March, p. 18.

Ottman, J.A. (1990), ''Environmental Concerns
Open Markets for New Products'', *Marketing
News*, 19 March, p. 21.

Rice, G. (1990), ''Being Green: US Marketers
Begin to Respond'', *Academy of Marketing
Science News*, April, p. 5.

Schwartz, J. (1990), ''Earth Day Today'',
American Demographics, April, pp. 40-1.

Smith, E.T., Cahan, V., Freundlich, N., Ellis, J.E.
and Weber, J. (1990), ''The Greening of
Corporate America'', *Business Week*,
23 April, pp. 96-103.

Wells, R.P. (1990), ''Environmental Performance
Will Count in the 1990s'', *Marketing News*,
19 March, p. 22.

Pinto Redux?

*'One of the things that baffles me about the auto companies is how they fail
to learn from earlier mistakes.'*

In the annuals of business ethics, the saga of the Ford Motor Company Pinto looms as a landmark case.

The Pinto, it may be recalled, was the subcompact automobile, first manufactured in 1970, that had been designed with its gas tank mounted between the rear bumper and the axle. This made it vulnerable to rupture during rear-end collisions. Gasoline vapor mixed with air in the passenger compartment, and a spark could explode the mixture.

Dozens of Pinto drivers and passengers were burned to death in such collisions, and many others were disfigured. (It should be added that the Pinto met all highway safety standards of the day.)

Ford apparently knew about the problem before many of the accidents occurred, but "management conducted a cost/benefit analysis of the situation and decided it was more cost effective to deal with the accidents than to institute a recall and repair the problem," as Donald P. Robin and Eric Reidenbach noted in their January 1987 article in the *Journal of Marketing.*

In retrospect, Pinto has become a metaphor for cost/benefit analysis gone askew—a morally blind and short-sighted calculus that reduced human lives to little more than dollar signs on a ledger.

A flawed pickup truck?

Now we have Pinto redux.

In early December 1992, The National Highway Traffic Safety Administration (NHTSA) opened an investigation of the pickup trucks that General Motors Corporation built from 1973 to 1987.

As with Pinto, the controversy centers on gas tanks that are said to rupture and explode in collision: the pickup tanks, in this case, are "side-saddle," outside the vehicle's steel underframe. Critics say the result is that more than 300 people have died in crashes in which there has been a fire because of fuel leakage.

As with Pinto, there is evidence that the manufacturer was aware that it had a problem. According to a former GM employee and technical expert, Ronald Elwell, test crashes at the GM proving grounds showed that the gas tanks "opened up dramatically, like a split melon" in side impact collisions, the *Wall Street Journal* reported. And pickups with over 33,000 miles were more likely to catch fire in side collisions because the gas tanks had become pitted and worn with use.

As with Pinto, GM's "side-saddle" gas tanks met federal safety standards. There was nothing illegal about putting such vehicles on the road.

'A mirror image'

"It is, in fact, a magnified mirror image of Pinto," says Clarence Ditlow, Executive Director, Center for Auto Safety, a Washington, D.C.-based advocacy group. "The events are almost one to one, except here there are more vehicles, more deaths, and more costs to the corporation."

It is emerging as one of the biggest scandals in automaking history, he suggests. "We're talking of at least 300 crash fatalities versus 27 for the Pinto. I'm convinced there will be well over $100 million in product liability settlements in this."

One recent case in Texas alone cost the company $14-$15 million, he says. GM acknowledges that it has been party to 106 lawsuits in connection with pickup truck fires. It denies that there have been 300 crash fatalities, however, suggesting that Ditlow's figures are based on incomplete statistics. Six cases have gone to trial. GM prevailed in three cases, plaintiffs in three others, the company says.

"One of the things that baffles me about the auto companies is how they fail to learn from earlier mistakes," says Ditlow.

General Motors, for its part, rejects the Pinto comparison *in toto*. "It's not the same as Pinto," Ed Lechtzin, a company spokesman, tells *ethikos*. "Pinto was an annual model vehicle, in which the company made a change because it had a problem."

Regarding the pickup trucks, "We don't have a defect. Our overall fatality rate is no different than Ford or Chrysler vehicles in the same age group. In only one area—side impact collisions where there is a fire and a fatality—are we higher. With rear impact collision, where there is a fire and a fatality, Ford is higher."

Still, the National Highway Traffic Safety Administration said it would conduct its own crash tests with the pickups, an unusual step that the agency has not taken since the 1970s, when the Pinto was called into question. The agency could recommend a recall of as many as 4.7 million vehicles sold under the GMC and Chevrolet brands.

A recall could cost the company hundreds of millions of dollars.

An infamous cost/benefit analysis

The history that GM may have ignored was dramatized in the late 1970s when a jury ordered Ford Motor Company to pay Richard Grimshaw $128.5 million for the extreme disfigurement caused by burns when the Pinto in which the then-13-year-old was riding exploded. (A judge subsequently reduced the amount to $6.5 million.)

Writes Robert Lacey in *Ford: The Men and the Machine:* "In the years that followed, Ford had to pay out many millions more in settlements of over a hundred Pinto suits, including one that involved charges of reckless homicide—the first time that Ford, or any U.S. carmaker, had ever been charged with a criminal offense.

"Ford was, finally, acquitted on this criminal charge, but the grand jury hearing in Elkhart, Indiana, and the subsequent court case at Winamac, Indiana, made headlines in 1978 and 1979. Ford's burning cars became a regular item on the nightly TV news."

It is the cost-benefit analysis conducted by Ford managers in the 1970s, however, that sticks in the collective consciousness of ethicists. "It was a cost/benefit analysis on human lives—without anyone considering the ethics of the case," says Donald Robin, now Professor of Marketing and a chaired Professor of Business Ethics at the University of Southern Mississippi.

Price of a human life: $200,725

Writes Lacey: "Cost-benefit analysis had, ironically, been something of a vogue in Washington ever since the arrival of Robert McNamara," the former Ford president and U.S. Secretary of Defense under Kennedy and Johnson. "McNamara had brought with him the cost-analysis techniques he had practiced in the USAF Statistical Control Office under Robert Lovett, and at the Ford Motor Company. Working on the same principle, the accountants at NHTSA came up with a price for a human life in the early 1970s—$200,725, the sum of twelve 'societal components.'"

Ford engineers apparently took these calculations to heart. One famous example: Fuel systems tend to leak when a car turns over. In the 1970s, Ford could have installed a fuel roll-over valve to correct the problem. Two Ford engineers, E.S. Grush and C.S. Saunby, conducted a cost/benefit analysis on just this issue in a 1972 company memorandum entitled "Fatalities Associated with Crash-Induced Fuel Leakage and Fires."

According to Lacey:

"The fuel valve, they calculated, would cost $11 per car. Add $11 in modification costs per unit to the price of 11 million cars and 1.5 million light trucks, and you get a total cost of $137 million.

"Then look at the benefits, the total value of the lives saved and the injuries avoided by the $11 per car modification. Assume, say, the avoidance of 180 burn deaths per year at a rounded-off cost of $200,000 per death. Assume the additional avoidance of 180 serious burn injuries, at $67,000 per injury, plus 2,100 burned vehicles that will not now be burned, at a saving of $700 per vehicle. If these are your figures and your assumptions, you end up with a total benefit cost of just $49.5 million—which falls short of your investment in fire prevention by some $87.5 million."

"In the final paragraph of their report, Grush and Saunby pointed out that their study concerned 'only roll-over consequences and costs.' They were not examining the expense of preventing Pinto-like rear impact fires. But, they concluded, 'similar analysis for other impact modes would be expected to yield comparable results, with the implementation costs far outweighing the expected benefits.'"

A pattern repeated?

Key Pinto decisions appeared to be driven exclusively by economics. This pattern seems to have re-emerged in the case of the GM pickup trucks.

Prior to the 1973 model year, GM, Ford, and Chrysler all designed their pickup trucks with the gas tank in the cab, above the frame, recalls Ditlow. Not only was this unsafe—there were fires and accidents—but the customers could hear the gas sloshing about beneath them, an unnerving experience.

As a result, when all three companies redesigned their pickups for the 1973 model year, they devoted some thought to placement of the gas tank.

Ford and Chrysler elected to place their pickup trucks' gasoline tanks inside the steel frame. At General Motors, by contrast, says Ditlow, the marketing division entered the fray—and argued that the company needed a 40-gallon gas tank in order to market the vehicle successfully. And such a tank could only be accommodated outside the frame.

"Economics and marketing drove the decision," recalls Ditlow, "just as marketing and economics drove the decision with the Pinto.

"And just as with the Pinto, when the crashes began, and people started burning to death, the company made settlements," often in secret. They let a few test cases go to court, to get some feel for their potential liability, and they lost those cases, suggests Ditlow. "They knew they had a hard row to hoe, as with the Pinto."

(GM's Lechtzin says the company has made settlements, but not because the company has an unsafe vehicle. It is simply cheaper to settle out of court in many cases given the vagaries of the U.S. legal system. Lechtzin notes that Ditlow's organization "is funded by trial lawyers" and one of its prime objects is "to create business for lawyers." Ditlow rejects this charge.)

What GM apparently did was to take a look at the data, and consider the cost to change the design. It elected not to redesign the gas tank until it redesigned the whole vehicle. In the meantime it would tough it out with the lawsuits, says Ditlow.

The company apparently calculated that it could save enough money by not changing the design until model year 1988 to pay for the lawsuits that were arising, the sort of hard-boiled calculation that recalls Pinto, he observes.

"To me, the concept is so alien, so irrational. Someone should have put their foot down."

Chrysler engineer: This is unacceptable

Nor would that have been so remarkable. At Chrysler, in 1966, an engineer's memo said: "It is unacceptable to put the gas tank outside the frame." The company acted on that.

It may not have been possible to learn from the Pinto fiasco when the GM, Ford and Chrysler pickup trucks were redesigned in the late sixties and early seventies, notes Ditlow, but the Pinto lesson was certainly writ in red by the late seventies. At that time, GM management could have put a plastic bladder inside its pickup gas tanks to reduce fires in the event of collisions. But senior management rejected even that option.

(General Motors put the tank inside the frame in model year 1988, but it denies that it did so for safety reasons. "Our contention is that putting it outside the frame rail doesn't make it defective," says Lechtzin. "It makes no difference in the overall family of collisions." He emphasizes that the truck's record "is no worse than Ford's or Chrysler's." The pickup trucks also meet a key Federal safety standard, i.e., they can withstand a side-impact collision at 20 miles an hour without danger of an explosion. GM also asserts that fires from high-speed collisions are a "rare occurrence."

("We feel we have a bigger public relations problem than a liability problem," says Lechtzin. Asked why the NHTSA ordered an investigation, then, he answers: "Because we gave them 70,000 pages of documents. They had no time to go through them all" without announcing that they were conducting an investigation.)

(As for the plastic bladder in the gas tank, this really wasn't a viable alternative, argues Lechtzin. "Only one car has a bladder inside, the Corvette. It [the bladder] doesn't work on anything else.")

A benchmark case

When contemplating the GM case, and its similarities to the Pinto experience, Professor Robin finds himself asking: "What is the learning curve for American business? It seems almost flat in cases like this.

"Pinto is a benchmark case," continues Robin. It has been written up extensively and entered the business ethics lore. "It illustrates what can go wrong when ethics isn't considered, when there is a lack of ethics in the organizational culture.

"Over and over again in American and foreign business the emphasis is on objectives—profits in this case—and often ethics aren't even considered.

"You have to develop core values that include ethics," he continues. "You can't give away the shop, but you can do business in an ethical manner. If we are good managers, then we run a more effective—not a less effective business—with good ethics."
—Andrew W. Singer

Scott Cook founded Intuit, maker of the check-writing-software product Quicken, in 1984 with $151,000, after being turned down by venture capitalists for the $2 million he thought he would need. The start-up cash was quickly exhausted on product development, and the Menlo Park, Calif., company scraped through three desperate years before hitting its stride. Today Intuit has 400 employees. Sales last year were $44 million, and this year's revenues are expected to reach $80 million. Despite dozens of competitors in the category, Intuit has a 70% market share.

This article is derived from conversations between Cook and associate editor Leslie Brokaw.

The Ethics of
BOOTSTRAPPING

At no time is there more pressure to cut ethical corners than when your company's survival—and your own economic well-being—is at stake

SCOTT COOK

When you're a little, struggling start-up, you're confronted by ethical questions almost every day. Your company has no visible track record, or a very limited one. Or, like us in our early years, a very shoddy one. We had a poorly selling product for several years, we had no money, and our two closest competitors were corporate subsidiaries that together spent $7 million on marketing during our launch year alone.

That's the test of your ethics, when you're staring straight at the shame of failure. Each week your ethics are challenged by the promises you make. How much do you embellish your financial condition, the resources behind you, the success of your customers? What do you tell employees? Prospects? To get the sale, do you promise things you know you can't deliver? Do you make promises to your employees that you know in your heart you can't keep? I found I couldn't do those things. I just couldn't get my enthusiasm up for it; I had to do what felt

> What I've learned, and what all too many bootstrappers can miss, is that being truthful is good business. You may solve some temporary bind by fibbing, but it will come back to haunt you. It's not just wrong; it also doesn't work.

right. Of course, no one would argue that businesspeople should do otherwise. But they *do* do otherwise, all the time. Because it's business we're talking about, and because it's cutthroat and you can rationalize almost anything, and because—especially when you're bootstrapping as we were—*it's a matter of survival.*

But what I've learned, and what all too many bootstrappers can miss, is that being truthful is good business. Apart from moral judgments, consider expediency—and expediency is what bootstrapping amounts to. Business is about doing right by the customer and by your business partners, which include vendors and employees. If you do right by them, your business will flourish. If you don't, your business won't. You may solve some temporary bind by fibbing, but it will come back to haunt you. It's not just wrong; it also doesn't work. Being ethical isn't a fairyland, Boy Scout idea, nor is it naïve. I wanted to build a business for the long term.

Reprinted by permission of *Inc.* magazine, September 1992, pp. 87, 90, 95. © 1992 by Goldhirsh Group, Inc., 38 Commercial Wharf, Boston, MA 02110.

And trust is one of the most important sources of your power.

Let me give you an example. We sell our software to retailers and dealers, who resell it to their customers, the end-users. It is common in our industry, as in a lot of industries, for salespeople to "load" the dealer with too much product. There is an old slogan, "a loaded dealer is a loyal dealer," because he won't want to push the competitor's product until he gets rid of yours first. With that in mind, some companies invent elaborate schemes to get dealers to buy more than they need; their salespeople overstate demand, exaggerating how well their product is going to sell or how big a promotion is.

Well, we don't do that. We don't think it's right to tell dealers they're going to sell 100 units a month when they're really going to sell 40—or, in our case with the major chains, 10,000 units when 4,000 is more like it.

Is this an issue of ethics or smart business? Frankly, I think the two merge. Although it means we sometimes miss higher revenues at the end of a quarter—that's why other companies load dealers, to maximize numbers so salespeople can get their commission checks or show off to the president—in the long run, being honest has served us better. For one thing, if you produce a large chunk of product and then don't get orders for three months, your manufacturing facility sits idle. That kind of boom-and-bust cycle is inefficient—it's hell on manufacturing people, who find it much easier to produce a level, constant volume of product.

We'll actually tell accounts they've ordered *too much*, that we'd like to ship them less because we think they're overbuying. And because of that, they've started to trust us in surprising ways. When we launch a new product—we've brought out three in the last year—we get into all the chain stores instantly. They don't even question it, because they know we're not going to screw them. What's more, many of the accounts now say, "We trust you, how much should we order?" Normally that would never happen. They would try to figure it out themselves, or they'd ask the salesperson and cut that recommendation in half. Instead, they're relying on our advice in ways that are very untypical for chain-store buyers and very helpful in building long-term partnerships.

What happens if you lie, and are successful? Your customers may know you lied, and employees will definitely know you've lied, and you've set up a culture in which lying's OK—or worse, in which lying is linked with success.

It's amazing how uncommon it is to think about sales that way; so many companies seem to be out to snooker dealers as much as possible. That attitude is everywhere, probably because managing a company for short-term revenue is so much easier. It's all in the numbers. If the revenues aren't there, some presidents yell a lot, and people learn to run around and get short-term sales. Those presidents tell their people, "I don't care if the demand isn't there, go and sell them." That's easy; any idiot can do that. And many idiots do.

Ethical temptations continue to come up for us. For instance, we offer a consistent price to all our major accounts; it's the best price we can afford. But some of those accounts will call and say, "Hey, if you knock 5% off your price, I'll place a big order right now." Well, more volume is better, especially for a bootstrapped company, right?

Wrong. It probably wouldn't mean any extra sales to end-users. What it *would* mean is less revenue per unit—5% less—and, more important, it would mean you lied. *All* your customers are concerned that they have the best deal, and when we say, "Nobody gets a better price than this," that's got to be true. If we trim prices for certain accounts, we're lying. It's common, but ultimately it will hurt you.

Some customers are always looking for you to bend your rules, but if you hold out, the benefits can be enormous—and not just financially. Recently we pitched a hot, exclusive promotion idea to a large wholesale distributor. We were going to offer a special version of a product if the consumer bought other software at the same time—a dealer-created bundle.

The wholesaler turned us down, so we offered it to a second wholesaler, who took it. Soon dealers started changing wholesalers to get this special product, and the first wholesaler was livid. Its reps screamed at our director of sales that we had to offer the same deal to them.

We arranged a Saturday conference call with this wholesaler's chairman, and he was *angry*. He threatened to stop promoting our products, start pushing our competitors' products—nothing illegal, but things that would hurt our business. I need to get this same promotion, he said; what are you going to do for me?

And we said, "No, we offered the promotion to you first. You turned it down. The other wholesaler bought it on the agreement that it was an exclusive for them. For us to give it to you would mean going back on our word." He said, "So don't give me the promotion. Give me a million dollars in cash and I'll simulate it." And I said we couldn't do that; it was ethically wrong. The call ended when we agreed to disagree, and we said we'd talk a few days later. We went away really nervous.

Monday morning the wholesaler's reps called and said they understood our point of view, they respected it, they knew we had come to them with other good ideas, and in fact they thought our ideas were so good they wanted to elevate us into their top rank of vendors. They'd compensate for this promotion problem in another way.

It came totally out of the blue. We thought we'd have a year of really hard sliding with that account, because once an account is pissed at you, it tends to stay pissed. But not at all; our stand enhanced our relationship.

What's clear is that if that wholesaler's management had pushed us around and succeeded, we would have lost their respect. And there was great temptation. I mean, it was *really* tempting to do something that would have been against our word.

And this is the point: while a lot of bootstrapping companies think about the *consequences of failure*—"Gee, if I don't fib about this, I'm going to fail, and if I fail, I'll lose all my money, and my wife and kids, and my self-respect"—I don't think they consider the *consequences of success*. What happens if you lie, and are successful? Your customers may know you lied, and employees will definitely know you've lied, and you've set up a culture in which lying's OK—or worse, in which lying is linked with success.

The things that help make a company successful become the elements of its foundation, the stories through which new employees learn what's right and what's expected of them, and how they can succeed. Do you want those cultural legends to be about tricking others? You've got your choice.

If you create the right culture, people will do the right thing. I remember when we were working on one ad, our graphic designer came to see me, and she seemed hesitant about it. I said, "What do your guts tell you?" She said, "I just don't think we're being straight with people." If her guts told her that, she was probably onto something. She talked to the marketing vice-president about it, and we never ran the ad.

You have to realize that as a CEO, you're a role model and an example. People learn from your actions more than you ever believe. Now, we're not perfect; there are tough judgment calls every day, by people at every level in the company, and we don't always get it right. But I know that our chances of getting it right are highest only if our culture demonstrates the right values for people. The underpinnings of how you run the company give people rules they live by, and people will really believe in them and hold them dear.

It's a rare thing, this opportunity to create a culture; there's almost no place in our world where you can do that. Normally, you take culture as a given. American culture is American culture; we lament that politicians can't lead us better, that kids don't study harder, that too many people are crooks.

But when you create a company, you *can* create a culture—not in wide variance with what surrounds you, but you can move values, subtly and not so subtly, in the direction you want. It's the most powerful thing you can do, to seed that culture the right way, because ultimately, that will become more important to the success or failure of your company than you are. The culture you establish will guide and teach all your people in all their decisions. And if you've got a choice about the culture you create, why build it on a foundation of fraud?

*P*ractical applications of healthcare marketing ethics

Robert L. Goldman, PhD

Robert L. Goldman, PhD, is senior associate, Healthcare Management Consortium, Inc., San Francisco, Calif.

ETHICS

All businesses—healthcare businesses in particular—have an absolute duty to treat their customers ethically; anything less is unacceptable. Author Goldman discusses four ethical principles that can be applied to help ensure that marketing decisions conform to the highest ethical standards.

M any healthcare professionals believe that the healthcare industry is different from other businesses, that healthcare marketing efforts, unlike those of other industries, must reflect the highest ethical standards because healthcare customers lack the knowledge needed to make truly educated choices.

A strong healthcare marketing ethics model must meet two criteria. The model must fit the realities of hospital management and must be easy to understand and follow.

For the model to have practical application, however, both consumers and providers must have balanced rights. Hospitals must be able to aggressively market their services if they are to stay in business. Consumers must have rights, too. They must be able to rely on the accuracy of a hospital's marketing claims. If consumers are forced to follow the doctrine of "Let the buyer beware," they may hesitate before obtaining qualified medical care and seek care from providers who may not take their ethical obligations as seriously.

The four ethical principles that follow can be applied to hospital marketing efforts with a minimum of expense or complicated operating procedures.

1. Put the patient's welfare first. This is the principle with which providers are most familiar. Patients must come before profits if the hospital is to profit. Patients have the right to expect care of the highest standard of quality consistent with technological and physical limitations. We accept the principle that a patient will receive all necessary care regardless of ability to pay. But, as prospective payment and forced discounts to managed care organizations cut into revenue, equivocal situations develop.

A hospital's obligation to its patients can be met while the hospital makes a profit as long the obligation is consistent with the best interests of patients as individuals and as members of a community. For example, a hospital that develops a fertility clinic as a center of excellence has an obligation to notify prospective clients of noninsured costs of $4,000 or more per treatment when multiple treatments are usually necessary.

2. Avoid unnecessary services. Marketing should not induce a patient to accept excessive, unneeded, or nonmedically indicated healthcare services, regardless of cost, risk, or source of payment. It is unethical to build demand for unneeded services. Promoting cosmetic surgery with claims of complete safety comes close to violating this principle. While much surgery in this field is justified, many patients seek cosmetic procedures with little or no knowledge of the risks involved.

3. Maintain high standards of honesty and accuracy. Healthcare marketers must do more than merely avoid false or misleading advertising. While marketing legitimately seeks to influence behavior, marketers have an obligation to provide fair and accurate information when they promote their services.

4. Be accountable to the public. Marketers should develop market-

From *Healthcare Financial Management*, March 1993, pp. 46-48. © 1993 by Healthcare Financial Management Association. Reprinted by permission.

ing plans believing that these plans will likely be revealed to the public in the future. Marketing professionals should avoid activities that they would not want their families to read about in the newspaper.

Marketers also should refuse to hide behind their duty to support their CEOs. Justifying unethical conduct by saying "I was just following orders" is obviously incorrect.

Case studies

The following true case studies illustrate some difficult ethical issues hospital marketers face on the job. When deciding on the best way to confront these "gray" ethical areas, hospitals marketers should use these questions as a guide:
▶ What are the hospital's objectives in implementing this plan?
▶ Will this marketing activity contribute to the public good, or is it merely self-serving?
▶ Are promotional efforts truthful in all aspects?
▶ Are marketing efforts not only legal but fair to the public?
▶ Do the means justify the end? That is, can results be supported based on the ethical correctness of the process?

Case 1—Marketing a new procedure. The administrator of a successful hospital is approached by an attending physician who has recently attended a seminar on a new out patient procedure that is stated to be quick and profitable.

However, the procedure is still considered experimental, and some conservative authorities regard it to be of questionable value. The physician would like to offer this new procedure and promote it with an extensive media campaign. A majority of the medical staff sees no problem. The administrator has doubts. While the administrator is not a physician and would not attempt to evaluate a clinical procedure, she is concerned about promoting a procedure such as this one. What should the administrator do?

Answer: The hospital administrator is faced with a potential violation of Principle 2: Avoid unnecessary services. In this instance, the

hospital deferred action while the physician pressed for a promotional budget. In the meantime, a freestanding surgical center approached the physician and offered to promote the procedure. The promotion was very successful.

This outcome is typical. Because of the ethical issue, the hospital lost a new revenue source and the physician's goodwill. It is up to individual hospital marketers to decide if the price is worth it. Some may fault the decision-making technique of doing nothing in the hope that the situation will go away or solve itself.

Case 2—Selecting a provider. The contract administrator for an urban medical center has several managed care contracts, including some that include capitation. The administrator now finds that a specialty gap exists in the area of cardiac surgery.

There are two groups that could be contracted with, and both have indicated that they would be willing to enter into an agreement on the medical center's terms. Group A is affiliated with Community Hospital while Group B is affiliated with Memorial Hospital.

The hospital's president has strongly urged the administrator to select Group A and Community Hospital. The president says that this choice will improve a provider network that is being developed to capture market share. Several large employers have indicated that the new organization is very attractive to them. They especially like Group A because of its excellent regional reputation.

One of the medical center's best internists has approached the administrator with reliable data that shows that Group A has a significantly higher mortality rate than Group B. What should the contract administrator do?

Answer: This is a potential violation of Principle 1: Put the patient's welfare first. In this instance, the contract manager discussed the situation with several key physicians and then with Group B, explaining to the hospital president that the difference in quality was significant. Despite the potential harm to the development of the network,

the president agreed with the contract manager and approved the decision to contract with Group B and Memorial Hospital. Shortly thereafter, the president left the medical center for reasons that had nothing to do with this decision. The contract administrator completed the negotiation process and the new contract is in place.

Case 3—Marketing in a new community. A hospital, located in a large urban area, has developed its own home health agency. The agency has been very profitable. It expects to continue operations for the next several years. In fact, the agency is considering expanding services into a new geographic area.

The new area is a nearby suburban community. While the community is an excellent target since it will protect the agency from a competing hospital's agency, there is a nonprofit agency currently providing services to the community and just breaking even because of its high percentage of Medicaid patients.

The hospital's agency does not intend to accept Medicaid patients. However, it will capture enough of the market to cause financial trouble for the nonprofit agency. The hospital's agency has determined that it will not acquire the nonprofit agency because of its reputation and management. No other agency will accept these Medicaid patients. Should the hospital's agency move forward?

Answer: The potential conflict involves Principle 4: Be accountable to the public. By entering the market, some patients will suffer (a violation of Principle 1: Put the patient's welfare first). Some hospital executives believed in moving into the market based on the need to compete successfully. However, the hospital could lose favor with the community.

In this instance, the hospital did enter the market, with some negative publicity, resulting in a compromise under which the hospital's agency agreed to buy out the local nonprofit agency and accept Medicaid patients.

Case 4—A promotional claim. A hospital marketer has decided to develop a regional promotional campaign that includes full-page advertisements in news magazines and newspapers. The marketer also has chosen to advertise on radio as part of an effort to establish the hospital as the best in the area. While the marketer feels that the hospital's physicians and employees have superior training, talent, and experience, he has no proof that can be cited in advertisements. But he thinks he has found a hook. It can definitely be stated that patients admitted to the hospital have a shorter stay than the national average. While other hospitals in the region also have a shorter stay, the absolute truth is being told. What should the hospital marketer do?

Answer: This scenario involves Principle 3: Maintain high standards of honesty and accuracy. The hospital is well known, but there is no proof that it offers services of a higher quality than any of its competitors. In this instance, the hospital went ahead with the advertising campaign. While the campaign did not seem to have a short-term effect—either positive or negative—on admissions or revenue, it could have a negative long-term effect on the hospital's credibility.

An organization's reputation for honesty is its most valuable asset. To risk damaging it is unconscionable. The hospital was later criticized in a national ethics journal for its advertising campaign. The campaign was discontinued at the end of the contract.

Conclusion

Whether a healthcare marketer is considering developing a new center of excellence, contracting with a new health plan, or promoting the hospital, he or she will face difficult ethical issues. The four ethical marketing principals presented in this article can help decision makers make the best choices.

America's Hamburger Helper

McDonald's gives new meaning to "we do it all for you" by investing in people and their neighborhoods

EDWIN M. REINGOLD LOS ANGELES

WHEN THE SMOKE CLEARED after mobs burned through South Central Los Angeles in April, hundreds of businesses, many of them black owned, had been destroyed. Yet not a single McDonald's restaurant had been torched. Within hours after the curfew was lifted, all South Central's Golden Arches were back up and running, feeding fire fighters, police and National Guard troops as well as burned-out citizens. The St. Thomas Aquinas Elementary School, with 300 hungry students and no utilities, called for lunches and got them free—with delivery to boot.

For Edward H. Rensi, president and CEO of McDonald's U.S.A., the explanation of what happened, or didn't happen, in South Central L.A. was simple: "Our businesses there are owned by African-American entrepreneurs who hired African-American managers who hired African-American employees who served everybody in the community, whether they be Korean, African American or Caucasian."

The $19-billion-a-year company has often been the target of those who disparage everything from its entry-level wage structure to the aesthetic blight of its cookie-cutter proliferation. But the Los Angeles experience was vindication of enlightened social policies begun more than three decades ago. The late Ray Kroc, a crusty but imaginative salesman who forged the chain in 1955, insisted that both franchise buyers and company executives get involved in community affairs. "If you

are going to take money out of a community, give something back," Kroc enjoined. "It's only good business."

As a result, McDonald's stands out not only as one of the more socially responsible companies in America but also as one of the nation's few truly effective social engineers. Both its franchise operators, who own 83% of all McDonald's restaurants, and company officials sit on boards of local and national minority service organizations, allowing the company to claim that its total involvement in everything from the Urban League and the N.A.A.C.P. to the U.S. Hispanic Chamber of Commerce may constitute the biggest volunteer program of any business in the nation.

Because their original prosperity came from hamburger stands in middle-class suburbs, McDonald's managers were at first reluctant to move into inner-city markets. But company executives say their first tentative steps in the '70s showed those fears to be unfounded. The policy practiced in the suburbs, which dictated that McDonald's stores reflect the communities in which they operate, was applied to the new urban markets. As a result, nearly 70% of McDonald's restaurant management and 25% of the company's executives are minorities and women, and so are about half its corporate department heads. This year McDonald's will nearly double its purchases from companies that are minority or female owned, from last year's $157 million to $300 million. Several of the biggest are owned and operated by former McDonald's managers or franchise holders.

The spawning ground for many of the new ideas and programs designed to integrate the franchises into neighborhoods in which they operate has been the company's moral and intellectual McCenter, Hamburger University, set in its own 80-acre nature preserve near Oak Brook, Ill. Since 1979 the company has held affirmative-action seminars for its executives and managers there, as well as in many of the company's 40 regional offices, on such topics as how to manage the changing work force and handle career development for women, blacks and Hispanics. Each year 3,000 employees complete affirmative-action training programs that last 1½ to 3 days. Ideas originated at headquarters and by individual franchisees have led to programs such as McJobs, which takes on mentally and physically impaired employees, and McPride, which keeps students in school and rewards them for academic achievement while they work.

Through a program devised by its store owners, the company has helped establish 153 Ronald McDonald Houses, named for the chain's trademark clown, where families of seriously ill children can stay while the child is undergoing extensive medical treatment, such as chemotherapy or bone-marrow transplants. Each house serves an average of 15 families who pay from $5 to $15 a night, if they can afford it. The local projects are supported by local fund drives, and all the money collected goes directly to the houses; McDonald's pays all administrative costs of the program, which extends to

 From *Time*, June 29, 1992, pp. 66-67. © 1992 by Time Inc. Magazine Company. Reprinted by permission.

Canada, France, Germany, Holland, Australia and New Zealand.

BUT MCDONALD'S BROADEST IMpact has been through its basic job-training system. Its 8,800 U.S. restaurants (there are an additional 3,600 overseas from Beijing to Belgrade) train American youth of every ethnic hue. "Sending a kid to the Army used to be the standard way to teach kids values, discipline, respect for authority, to be a member of a team, get to work on time, brush your teeth, comb your hair, clean your fingernails," says Ed Rensi. "Now, somehow, McDonald's has become the new entry-level job-training institution in America. We find ourselves doing things in that role that we would never imagine we would do." Among them: paying kids to study, rewarding them for staying in school, hiring physically and mentally handicapped youngsters and adults and giving sensitivity training to co-workers. In a program called McMasters, older people, usually retirees, are hired to work alongside young crew members to give the workplace a sense of family and to set an example of caring, courtesy and responsibility.

In conjunction with the vocational-rehabilitation services of several states, nearly 7,000 disabled and handicapped people have been trained to function as full McDonald's employees by job coaches drawn from within the company. Before these less fortunate employees take their places, company trainers often put young able-bodied workers in blindfolds, gloves or dark glasses to demonstrate the kind of handicaps their new colleagues have to deal with in doing the same jobs.

At Pat Newbury's McDonald's restaurant in Renton, Wash., some young employees earn an hour's pay not for flipping

"If you're going to take money out of a community, give something back."

RAY KROC,
McDonald's founder

burgers but for studying an hour before their work shift begins. In a Chicago-area restaurant, Hispanic teenagers are being tutored in English. In Tulsa, a McDonald's crew is studying algebra after work. At a Honolulu restaurant, student workers get an extra hour's pay to study for an hour after closing. In Colorado, Virginia and Massachusetts there are Stay in School programs offering bonus money for employees who receive good grades. Reading-improvement classes frequently take place at restaurants in Kansas and New Jersey.

Despite the initial skepticism of educators, McDonald's programs have managed to allay the fears of many that work and school could not mix. In February the National Association of Secondary School Principals passed a resolution commending the company for "exemplary and motivational efforts to support education, students and assistant principals."

Bob Charles, the owner of a McDonald's in Boulder, has seen some of his employed at-risk students begin to get A's af-

ter joining his McPride program, which limits them to a 14-hour workweek and pays bonuses for improvement and school attendance. Many of them have a very low level of self-esteem, says Charles. But once they come to work as part of a team and gain a sense of confidence, "you'd almost never believe the change in these kids."

Mark Brownstein's company owns 13 restaurants in Orange County, Calif., and hires elderly and handicapped workers aggressively. "They are people who need work, and we need people to work. You wonder why everybody makes a big deal about it," shrugs Brownstein. "Besides, the seniors and the special-ed kids in our stores create a sense of humanity." Owner Jonah Kaufman has 26 handicapped people, mainly with Down syndrome, on the payroll in his 12 Long Island stores. One of them, Joe King, trains new employees. Kaufman says the key to his success with the disabled is "to try not to treat them differently." McDonald's has used Braille and its own kind of sign language as aids for impaired employees. At McDonald's Oak Brook headquarters, staff workers are sought from specialized schools, such as Gallaudet University and the Rochester Institute for Technology, which has an educational center for the deaf.

Senior vice president Robert H. Beavers Jr., who gave up plans to become an electrical engineer 19 years ago to stay with McDonald's, says the company's socially minded business practices have made the company stronger: "Our energy level and our understanding of the market today are much better because of the cultural diversity we have." He points out that in the inner city, where he grew up, they say, "If you talk the talk, you better walk the walk."

In Los Angeles, they talked and they walked—and they didn't burn. So Rensi and his team intend to keep on keeping on. After all, it's only good business.

WHO SCORES BEST ON THE ENVIRONMENT

What companies are in the vanguard of the green revolution—and which are lagging behind? A FORTUNE ranking names names and shows what you can learn from the leaders.

Faye Rice

WHEN AMERICANS first demanded a cleanup of the environment during the early 1970s, corporations threw a tantrum. Their response ran the psychological gamut from denial to hostility, defiance, obstinacy, and fear. But today, when it comes to green issues, many U.S. companies have turned from rebellious underachievers to active problem solvers.

Who's in the vanguard of this revolution—and who's lagging behind? Most important, what can consumers, investors, and plain old earthlings learn from how the corporate leaders approach and tackle their environmental challenges?

To find out, FORTUNE spent three months examining the environmental records of America's biggest manufacturers—public and private companies with annual sales of $400 million or more. (Yes, service companies pollute too, but we limited our survey to manufacturers because the government collects most of its data on them.) To measure relative ranking, we scored companies from zero (worst) to ten (best) in 20 different performance categories. These included things like the percentage reductions a company achieved in emissions of toxic chemicals as well as the comprehensiveness of its written environmental policies, goals, and employee incentives. We supplemented this green index, which concentrated on the period from 1987 to spring 1993, with interviews at more than 100 companies, plus scores of discussions with government officials, environmental groups, and other experts (for more, see methodology box).

The results are displayed in the three boxes on this page. . . . Because FORTUNE chose to highlight only the leaders, the laggards, and the most improved companies, a number of the household names we examined—companies like Procter & Gamble, General Motors, and Ford—do not appear on our lists. Even so, among the blue chips that did make our cut, there are a host of surprises.

Start with this one. Dow Chemical, a company whose name was once synonymous with napalm, Agent Orange, and

---

THE 10 MOST IMPROVED

Ciba-Geigy
Hewlett-Packard
Johnson & Johnson
S.C. Johnson & Son
Minn. Mining & Mfg.
Nalco Chemical
Polaroid
Shell Oil
Sun
Union Camp

REPORTER ASSOCIATE *Jacqueline M. Graves*

THE 10 LEADERS

AT&T
Apple Computer
Church & Dwight
Clorox
Digital Equipment
Dow Chemical
H. B. Fuller
IBM
Herman Miller
Xerox

THE 10 LAGGARDS

American Cyanamid
Boeing
BP America
E.I. Du Pont de Nemours
General Electric
International Paper
Louisiana-Pacific
Maxxam
Monsanto
USX

From *Fortune*, July 26, 1993, pp. 114-116, 118. © 1993 by Time Inc. Magazine Company. All rights reserved. Reprinted by permission.

fearsome opposition to what former chairman Paul Oreffice called "nitpicking, ridiculous regulations," is now among America's top ten environmental champions. Four times a year, eight environmental advocates from around the world gather at the company's Midland, Michigan, headquarters and spend 1½ days with senior managers and board members. "This is something environmentalists have been asking for—the ear of top management," says Anthony Cortese, former dean of environmental programs at Tufts University and one of the members of Dow's Environmental Advisory Council. So far, however, Dow is the only major U.S. corporation that regularly lends its ear to such a high-level group.

At the plant level, Dow managers increasingly carry on this same kind of consultation with local environmental groups. They have an incentive to do so: Their salaries and bonuses are pegged to, among other things, how well environmental goals are met. Last year Dow added an environmental category to every employee's job appraisal form. Dow also recently put David T. Buzzelli, its senior environmental officer, on its board of directors. No other company contacted for this story has gone that far. Says Joanna Underwood, who runs Inform, an environmental research group, and is also a member of Dow's advisory council: "The message from Dow is that the environment is not a side business but an essential part of business."

In 1986, Dow launched its WRAP (Waste Reduction Always Pays) program and quickly began proving that acronym true. At a latex plant in Midland, for example, teams of workers and supervisors made a few simple changes in pipes and production equipment and improved housekeeping techniques—like making sure valves were shut. Result: They eliminated 60% of the waste that had been going to landfills, saving $310,000 in annual fees. More efficient latex production—another benefit from those changes—saved an additional $420,000 a year. Since WRAP was unwrapped, some 200 teams have discovered similar savings throughout the company.

ONE OF THE FORCES propelling corporate America's cleanup drive has been the so-called Toxic Release Inventory (TRI). Since 1986 the EPA has required that all the plants of some 10,000 U.S. manufacturers report the annual releases from their facilities into the air, ground, and water of 317 toxic chemicals (such as asbestos, freon, and PCBs) and 20 toxic chemical categories

(lead compounds, for example). Some 200 chemicals will be added to the list over the next few years. None of these releases, which are tallied by the companies themselves, necessarily violates any U.S. regulation, though other laws—the Clean Air Act, for example—may put restrictions on the same emissions. The main idea behind TRI is to provide the public with an annual environmental benchmark. As William K. Reilly, former administrator of the EPA, notes, "TRI has been a powerful tool for reducing emissions."

Dow's TRI releases per dollar of sales—a common measure used by environmental groups to avoid penalizing large companies—are now among the lowest in the U.S. chemical industry. The primary reason is that Dow wisely phased out the practice of injecting hazardous waste underground before the tally began. Meanwhile, competitor and industry sales leader Du Pont has yet to abandon underground injection. Since 1987, Du Pont's TRI releases have increased three out of five years; Dow's emissions have fallen 32% since 1988.

Dow's overseas goals are also aggressive. In 1991 the EPA asked U.S. companies to sign up for a voluntary campaign to reduce their use of 17 chemicals to 33% by 1992 and 50% by 1995, with 1988 as the base year. When Dow joined the so-called 33-50 program in 1991, its foreign businesses also took on the same goals—and even went further. Dow Europe, for example, has targeted 60 chemicals as well as the 17 on the 33-50 list.

During the past 20 years, furniture maker Herman Miller has found a way to recycle or reuse nearly all the waste left over from the manufacturing process: Fabric scraps are sold to the auto industry to reuse as lining for cars; luggage makers buy Miller's leather trim for attaché cases; stereo and auto manufacturers use vinyl for sound-deadening material. Headquarters is powered by a cogeneration facility that turns wood scraps into energy and shaves $450,000 off the gas bill. Miller even has a thriving secondhand furniture business, which buys back its old furniture and refurbishes and resells it.

That's how the company reduced solid waste 80% since 1982. How about the other 20%? Herman Miller has hired an outside consulting firm to help it meet the corporate-wide goal of zero waste to landfills by 1995. Says environmental manager Paul Murray: "There is never an acceptable level of waste at Miller. There are always new things we can learn."

To its credit, IBM has kept aggressive

environmental goals front and center despite a terrifying slide in profits, stock value, and reputation. Tops on its hit list are ozone-depleting chlorofluorocarbons (CFCs), widely used in the computer industry as solvents and cleaning agents. In 1989, when the deadline for eliminating CFCs was the year 2000 (it's now 1995), the computer giant set a worldwide goal to phase them out by the end of 1993. IBM invented various replacement technologies for the ozone depleters, such as water-based solvents. By year-end 1992, the company's CFC use had plunged 83%.

Big Blue was also one of the first major corporations to embrace industry's four-tiered approach to waste: reduce, reuse, recycle, and landfill as a last resort, which shifts the focus to generating less waste in the first place. Here's what has happened to hazardous waste at IBM from 1987 to 1991: 44% less is generated, and 72% of what is produced is recycled on-site.

"You know a company is aggressively trying to reduce waste when it has strong employee reward programs," says Inform's Underwood. Every year IBM recognizes employees for technical innovations that help the company meet its environmental goals. Among the 16 winners last year was an employee in Boca Raton, Florida, who developed an energy-efficient personal computer. His prize: $50,000.

This award-winning project demonstrates IBM's commitment to the EPA's year-old Energy Star program, which proposes to cut the energy consumption of personal computers 50% to 75%. IBM and competitors like Apple have agreed to design and manufacture at least one personal computer by 1993 that will meet this goal. The EPA estimates that converting two-thirds of all PCs to meet Energy Star standards will save 26 billion kilowatts annually by the year 2000, equivalent to the electricity consumed each year by Vermont, Maine, and New Hampshire combined.

AMERICAN Telephone & Telegraph is also steering an impressive environmental course. In 1990 the telecommunications giant established goals for reducing air emissions, CFCs, solid waste, and hazardous waste. Under the direction of David R. Chittick, AT&T's vice president of environment and safety, the company had either surpassed its goals or was ahead of schedule for meeting them by the end of last year. To engineer ozone-depleting emissions out of its operations, for instance, AT&T invested $25 million to develop an array of alternative technologies. One, called Low Solids Spray Fluxer, eliminates the need for CFC solvents that clean the excess flux from electronic circuitboards. Now AT&T is selling this technology to some 25 other companies, among them IBM.

Sometimes AT&T gives its ideas away. Last year engineers developed an alternative for 1,1,1-trichloroethane, another ozone-depleting solvent used to clean circuitboards. The company refers to the discovery as the "cantaloupe" technology because it contains a synthetic extract that appears naturally in that melon as well as other fruit. AT&T is sharing cantaloupe, which has helped reduce its 1,1,1 emissions to practically zero, with competitors for free.

In fact, AT&T managed to eliminate virtually all its ozone-depleting substances by May 15, 1993, a year and a half before the company's goal and 2 1/2 years ahead of the worldwide ban. Now AT&T doesn't have to worry about the new law that requires companies to put warning labels on all goods that contain or are manufactured with ozone-depleting substances. The company figures that the cost of tracking and labeling all the tiny components and switching systems that it once manufactured with CFCs would add up to hundreds of thousands of dollars. The early phase-out also saves AT&T $25 million annually in supply costs, since taxes on CFCs have helped send the price rocketing from about 80 cents per pound in 1986 to over $11; the substitutes average 50 cents per pound.

AT&T has embraced Total Quality Management (TQM) principles to solve the most universal office pollution problem: too much paper. First, the company established a corporate paper reduction goal of 15% by 1995; then it created a corporate TQM team to figure out how to meet it. Following classic TQM techniques, the team identified AT&T's heaviest paper users, euphemistically called fat rabbits. The fat rabbits in turn formed TQM teams to help meet the company-wide goal. The internal information management unit, fat bunny No. 2 behind copying centers, gobbled up about a quarter of AT&T's total paper use for such things as marketing and financial reports. The department's TQM teams suggested such simple ways to decrease paper consumption as eliminating cover pages and using electronic rather than printed media. Within a year the department was consuming 22% less paper.

The long-distance division compressed the

HOW THE SCORECARDS WERE DONE

FORTUNE evaluated 130 of America's largest manufacturing companies before selecting the 30 featured in the three scorecards that follow. To determine ranking, we assigned values that range from zero (worst) to ten (best) to performance in 20 key areas. Not all carried equal weight, though. Among the categories given the most importance were the amount of a company's toxic chemical releases, adjusted for sales, and its percentage reduction of those releases; the comprehensiveness of a company's environmental program (whether it has a written policy and goals, for example, or offers employee incentives); violations of environmental laws that carry large fines and penalties; and ratings by credible environmental groups.

Other important categories, carrying slightly less weight, include whether a company is potentially responsible for cleaning up an inordinately large number of Superfund sites; whether it reuses and recycles hazardous and solid waste; and whether it

participates in EPA's voluntary programs, such as 33-50 (so-called because it aims to reduce releases of 17 targeted chemicals 33% by 1992 and 50% by 1995 from a 1988 baseline).

The main data source was the reams of information gathered by the U.S. government, particularly the EPA and the Occupational Safety and Health Administration (OSHA). Also helpful were the small but growing number of investment firms that analyze environmental performance, such as Franklin's Research and Development of Boston and Covenant Investment Management of Chicago. A major source of information was the Council on Economic Priorities (CEP), a respected New York City environmental group headed by Alice Tepper Marlin. CEP's corporate reports, supervised by senior researcher Kenneth P. Scott, are often used as references by the companies themselves. Most important, we attempted to interview, in person or by phone, all 130 companies surveyed. Only a handful refused to cooperate.

spacing on some 12 million bills to major customers of its Pro Wats and CustomNet lines. The result: three million fewer sheets of paper per year and lower postal rates for a total saving of some $4 million annually.

Sun Co., parent of Sunoco, leaps onto the most improved list for being the first major company to sign the Coalition for Environmentally Responsible Economies (Ceres) principles. This corporate code of conduct on the environment was formulated in 1989 by a coalition of environmental and investor groups, including the National Wildlife Federation and the California Public Employees' Retirement System (Calpers). The code begins with the belief that "corporations must not compromise the ability of future generations to sustain themselves" and goes on to say that the signatories will "update our practices constantly in light of advances in technology ... and environmental science." Among the ten Ceres principles: protection of the biosphere, sustainable use of natural resources, environmental restoration, and management commitment to sound environmental policy. Sun completes an annual Ceres report, which the organization summarizes for the public.

Companies like Du Pont, ARCO, and General Electric have vehemently resisted shareholder resolutions to adopt the principles. "After the resolution failed at our annual meeting last year, I stuck with the Ceres people and let them know we wanted

to sign up," says Sun CEO Robert H. Campbell. The major obstacle was the wording of certain principles that, says Campbell, "gave our lawyers headaches." He fixed the problem by leaving the lawyers at home when he and his negotiating team hammered out a redraft of the original principles with slightly different wording.

Sun's TRI releases, the toxic emissions compiled annually by the EPA, are among the lowest in the petroleum industry, and Sunoco gas stations were the first outside California to install pumps for methanol, which produces lower levels of smog-forming compounds than regular gasoline. Still, Sun needs to work harder to develop solid waste reduction and recycling programs.

The computer industry led all others for having the most companies on the best and most improved lists. In the battle for the bottom, more companies from the oil and paper industries were in contention for the laggards list than from any other industry. Several aerospace companies just missed being named to the laggards list, but Boeing made it. Why? The company's written environmental policy is as weak as camomile tea and only two sentences long.

In 1988 Boeing signed up for the EPA's 33-50 program. Though this is one of the few numerical goals the aerospace company has committed to, its releases of the targeted chemicals have so far not achieved 1992 goals. Boeing's TRI emissions since 1987 have also been heading north.

DU PONT and Monsanto have comprehensive environmental principles and are working to meet aggressive goals. Both chemical companies have CEOs who are committed to environmental achievement and publish annual reports that detail progress as well as setbacks. So how did Monsanto and Du Pont wind up on the laggards list? The chemical giants could be compared to an old car that sits unused for years. Even when tires and other new parts are added, it still fails to keep pace with new models.

Du Pont sat on the opposite side of the environmental debate for years, its performance defined more by adroit lobbying efforts to kill legislation than by innovative approaches to pollution prevention. For example, Du Pont successfully delayed the phase-out of CFCs for 15 years because it was the world's largest producer of the ozone destroyers. As the inevitable deadline approached, the company stepped up its promotion of substitute HCFCs, which are less potent but still ozone depleting, instead of developing alternatives that do not harm the environment.

On the toxic release front, Du Pont dawdled during the 1970s and 1980s while other companies acted. But when the first TRI report hit the street in 1988, revealing Du Pont and Monsanto as the country's largest polluters, these two got religion. Still, their efforts have not been enough to offset the massive amount of toxic chemicals they release. In 1991, Du Pont emitted 254 million pounds of poisonous junk. As Jack Doyle, senior analyst at the nonprofit environmental group Friends of the Earth, says, "That is more than twice as much as the combined releases of Dow, BASF, Ciba-Geigy, Union Carbide, and Hoechst chemical companies."

Corporate America is finally making progress in solving the nation's pollution problems, but there is still a long way to go. A report on TRI numbers by the research group Citizens Fund notes that the chief executives of the 50 companies emitting the most pollutants live in zip codes where releases of toxic chemicals are either zero or a fraction of those in areas where their plants are located. Until CEOs no longer fear setting up residence in the same zip codes as their plants, pollution prevention should remain at the top of corporate America's agenda.

Developing the Future Ethos and Social Responsibility of Business

Business ethics should not be viewed as a short-term, "knee-jerk reaction" to recently revealed scandals and corruptions. Instead, it should be viewed as a thread woven through the fabric of the entire business culture—one that ought to be integral to its design. Businesses are built on the foundation of trust in our free-enterprise system. When there are violations of this trust between competitors, between employer and employees, or between businesses and consumers, the system ceases to run smoothly.

From a pragmatic viewpoint, the alternative to self-regulated and voluntary ethical behavior and social responsibility on the part of business may be governmental and legislative intervention. From a moral viewpoint, ethical behavior should not exist because of economic pragmatism, governmental edict, or contemporary fashionability—it should exist because it is morally appropriate and right.

This last section is composed of six articles that provide some ideas, guidelines, and principles for developing the future ethos and social responsibility of business. "The Challenge of Ethical Behavior in Organizations" begins this section by resonating some critical areas of challenge that ethical organizations are likely to face in the future. The next article points out the importance of establishing an ethical work environment and suggests steps and ingredients a company can utilize in building a business ethics program. "How to Be Ethical, and Still Come Top" describes the importance of business ethicists "getting their hands dirty" and becoming more focused on real-world ethical dilemmas that managers face. Archie Carroll's article, "The Pyramid of Corporate Social Respon-

sibility: Toward the Moral Management of Organizational Stakeholders," advocates that the total corporate responsibility of business entails simultaneously fulfilling the firm's economic, legal, ethical, and philanthropic responsibilities. The article concludes by examining the important differences between immoral, amoral, and moral management. In the next article, the author suggests a modification of the Golden Rule for a culturally diverse environment. The last article predicts trends that socially responsible businesses will pay attention to through the 1990s—and beyond.

Looking Ahead: Challenge Questions

In what areas should organizations become more ethically sensitive and socially responsible in the next 5 years?

Do you agree with the author of "Is Business Waking Up?" in regard to the prognostication of the 10 trends that socially responsible business will focus on in the 1990s? Why or why not? What other trends do you envision will be important to focus on?

Obtain codes of ethics or conduct from several different professional associations (e.g., doctors, lawyers, CPAs, etc.). What are the similarities and differences between them?

How useful do you feel codes of ethics are to organizations? Why?

The article, "The Pyramid of Corporate Social Responsibility" distinguishes between immoral, amoral, and moral management. From your perspective, which form of management is most prevalent in today's business landscape?

Unit 5

The Challenge
of Ethical Behavior
in Organizations

Ronald R. Sims

Ronald R. Sims is Associate Professor in the School of Business Administration at the College of William and Mary. His research interests include ethical behavior, experiential learning, employee and management training and development, and organizational transitions. His articles have appeared in a variety of scholarly and practitioner-oriented journals.

ABSTRACT. This paper is designed to do three things while discussing the challenge of ethical behavior in organization. First, it discusses some reasons why unethical behavior occurs in organization. Secondly, the paper highlights the importance of organizational culture in establishing an ethical climate within an organization. Finally, the paper presents some suggestions for creating and maintaining an ethically-oriented culture.

It has often been said that the only constant in life is change, and nowhere is this more true than in the workplace. As one recent survey concluded, "Over the past decade, the U.S. corporation has been battered by foreign competition, its own out-of-date technology and out-of-touch management and, more recently a flood of mergers and acquisitions. The result has been widespread streamlining of the white-collar ranks and recognition that the old way of doing business is no longer possible or desirable" (*U.S. News & World Report*, 1989, p. 42).

As the twenty-first century approaches, companies face a variety of changes and challenges that will have a profound impact on organizational dynamics and performance. In many ways, these changes will decide who will survive and prosper into the next century and who will not. Among these challenges are the following:

(1) *The challenge of international competition.*
(2) *The challenge of new technologies.*
(3) *The challenge of increased quality.*
(4) *The challenge of employee motivation and commitment.*
(5) *The challenge of managing a diverse work force.*
(6) *The challenge of ethical behavior.*

While these challenges must all be met by organizations and managers concerned about survival and competitiveness in the future, this paper will focus on the challenge of ethical behavior. More specifically, this paper will (1) discuss some reasons' unethical behavior occurs in organizations, (2) highlight the importance of organizational culture in establishing an ethical climate within the organization, and finally, (3) present some suggestions for creating and maintaining an ethically-oriented culture.

Ethics and the challenge of ethical behavior

The imperatives of day-to-day organizational performance are so compelling that there is little time or inclination to divert attention to the moral content of organizational decision-making. Morality appears to be so esoteric and qualitative in nature

Reprinted from *Journal of Business Ethics*, July 1992, pp. 505-513. © 1992 by D. Reidel Publishing Company. Reprinted by permission of Kluwer Academic Publishers.

it lacks substantive relation to objective and
titative performance. Besides, understanding
meaning of ethics and morality requires the
steful reworking of long-forgotten classroom
ies. What could Socrates, Plato, and Aristotle
h us about the world that confronts organiza-
s approaching the twenty-first century? Possibly
p in philosophical knowledge exists between
nizational executives and administrators of dif-
t generations. Yet, like it or not, there has and
continue to be a surge of interest in ethics.

The word "ethics" is often in the news these days.
Ethics is a philosophical term derived from the
Greek word "ethos" meaning character or custom.
This definition is germane to effective leadership in
organizations in that it connotes an organization
code conveying moral integrity and consistent values
in service to the public. Certain organizations will
commit themselves to a philosophy in a formal
pronouncement of a Code of Ethics or Standards of
Conduct. Having done so, the recorded idealism is
distributed or shelved, and all too often that is that.
Other organizations, however, will be concerned
with aspects of ethics of greater specificity, usefulness, and consistency.

Formally defined, *ethical behavior* is that which is
morally accepted as "good" and "right" as opposed to
"bad" or "wrong" in a particular setting. *Is it ethical*,
for example, to pay a bribe to obtain a business
contract in a foreign country? *Is it ethical* to allow
your company to withhold information that might
discourage a job candidate from joining your organization? *Is it ethical* to ask someone to take a job you
know will not be good for their career progress? *Is it
ethical* to do personal business on company time?

The list of examples could go on and on. Despite
one's initial inclinations in response to these questions, the major point of it all is to remind organizations that the public-at-large is demanding that
government officials, managers, workers in general,
and the organizations they represent all act according to high ethical and moral standards. The future
will bring a renewed concern with maintaining high
standards of ethical behavior in organizational transactions and in the workplace.

Many executives, administrators, and social scientists see unethical behavior as a cancer working on
the fabric of society in too many of today's organizations and beyond. Many are concerned that we face a
crisis of ethics in the West that is undermining our
competitive strength. This crisis involves businesspeople, government officials, customers, and employees. Especially worrisome is unethical behavior

among employees at all levels of the organization.
For example, a recent study found that employees
accounted for a higher percentage of retail thefts
than did customers (Silverstein, 1989). The study
estimated that one in every fifteen employees steals
from his or her employer.

In addition, we hear about illegal and unethical
behavior on Wall Street, pension scandals in which
disreputable executives gamble on risky business
ventures with employees' retirement funds, companies that expose their workers to hazardous working
conditions, and blatant favoritism in hiring and
promotion practices. Although such practices occur
throughout the world, their presence nonetheless
serves to remind us of the challenge facing organizations.

This challenge is especially difficult because
standards for what constitutes ethical behavior lie in
a "grey zone" where clear-cut right-versus wrong
answers may not always exist. As a result, sometimes
unethical behavior is forced on organizations by the
environment in which it exists and laws such as the
Foreign Corruption Practices Act. For example, if
you were a sales representative for an American
company abroad and your foreign competitors used
bribes to get business, what would you do? In the
United States such behavior is illegal, yet it is
perfectly acceptable in other countries. What is
ethical here? Similarly, in many countries women
are systematically discriminated against in the workplace; it is felt that their place is in the home. In the
United States, again, this practice is illegal. If you ran
an American company in one of these countries,
would you hire women in important positions? If
you did, your company might be isolated in the
larger business community, and you might lose
business. If you did not, you might be violating what
most Americans believe to be fair business practices.

The effective management of ethical issues requires that organizations ensure that their managers
and employees know how to deal with ethical issues
in their everyday work lives. Therefore, organizational members must first understand some of the
underlying reasons for the occurrence of unethical
practices.

Unethical behavior: why does it occur in organizations?

The potential for individuals and organizations to
behave unethically is limitless. Unfortunately, this
potential is too frequently realized. Consider, for

example, how greed overtook concerns about human welfare when the Manville Corporation suppressed evidence that asbestos inhalation was killing its employees, or when Ford failed to correct a known defect that made its Pinto vulnerable to gas tank explosions following low speed rear-end collisions (Bucholz, 1989). Companies that dump dangerous medical waste materials into our rivers and oceans also appear to favor their own interests over public safety and welfare. Although these examples are better known than many others, they do not appear to be unusual. In fact, the story they tell may be far more typical than we would like, as one expert estimates that about two-thirds of the 500 largest American corporations have been involved in one form of illegal behavior or another (Gellerman, 1986).

Unfortunately, unethical organizational practices are embarrassingly commonplace. It is easy to define such practices as dumping polluted chemical wastes into rivers, insider trading on Wall Street, overcharging the government for Medicaid services, and institutions like Stanford University inappropriately using taxpayer money to buy a yacht or to enlarge their President's bed in his home as morally wrong. Yet these and many other unethical practices go on almost routinely in many organizations. Why is this so? In other words, what accounts for the unethical actions of people in organizations, more specifically, why do people commit those unethical actions in which individuals knew or should have known that the organization was committing an unethical act? An example recently provided by Baucus and Near (1991) helps to illustrate this distinction.

Recently, a federal court judge found Allegheny Bottling, a Pepsi-Cola bottling franchise, guilty of price fixing. The firm had ended years of cola wars by setting prices with its major competitor, Mid-Atlantic Coca-Cola Bottling (New York Times, 1988). Since evidence showed most executives in the firm knew of the illegal price-fixing scheme, the court not only fined Allegheny $1 million but also sentenced it to three years in prison — a sentence that was suspended since a firm cannot be imprisoned. However, the unusual penalty allowed the judge to place the firm on probation and significantly restrict its operations.

In another case, Harris Corporation pleaded no contest to charges that it participated in a kickback scheme involving a defense department loan to the Philippines (Wall Street Journal, 1989). Although this plea cost the firm $500,000 in fines and civil claims, Harris's chief executive said the firm and its employees were not guilty of criminal conduct; he maintained that top managers

pleaded no contest because the costs associated with litigation would have been greater than the fines, and litigation would have diverted management attention from firm operations.

Although both cases appear to be instances of illegal corporate behavior, there is an important distinction between them. In the first case, Allegheny's executives knew or should have known the firm's activities were illegal; price fixing is a clear violation of antitrust law. Further, the courts ruled that evidence indicated the firm had engaged in the illegal act. In contrast, it is not clear that Harris Corporations' managers committed an illegal act. Some areas of the law are very ambiguous, including the area relevant to this case, the Foreign Corrupt Practices Act, and managers may not at times know what it legal or illegal; thus, a firm may inadvertently engage in behavior that is later defined as illegal or unethical (Baucus and Near, 1991).

One answer to the question of why individuals knowingly commit unethical actions is based on the idea that *organizations often reward behaviors that violate ethical standards*. Consider, for example, how many business executives are expected to deal in bribes and payoffs, despite the negative publicity and ambiguity of some laws, and how good corporate citizens who blow the whistle on organizational wrongdoing may fear being punished for their actions. Jansen and Von Glinow (1985) explain that organizations tend to develop *counternorms*, accepted organizational practices that are contrary to prevailing ethical standards. Some of these are summarized in Figure 1.

The top of Figure 1 identifies being open and honest as a prevailing ethical norm. Indeed, governmental regulations requiring full disclosure and freedom of information reinforce society's values toward openness and honesty. Within organizations, however, it is often considered not only acceptable, but desirable, to be much more secretive and deceitful. The practice of stonewalling, willingly hiding relevant information, is quite common. One reason for this is that organizations may actually punish those who are too open and honest. Look at the negative treatment experienced by many employees who are willing to blow the whistle on unethical behavior in their organizations. Also, consider for example, the disclosure that B. F. Goodrich rewarded employees who falsified data on quality aircraft brakes in order to win certification (Vandevier, 1978). Similarly, it has been reported that executives at Metropolitan Edison encouraged employees to withhold information from the press about the Three Mile Island nuclear accident (Gray and Rosen, 1982). Both incidents represent cases in which the counternorms of secrecy and deceitfulness were accepted and supported by the organization.

Figure 1 shows that there are many other organizational counternorms that promote morally and ethically questionable practices. Because these practices are commonly rewarded and accepted suggests that organizations may be operating within a world that dictates its own set of accepted rules. This reasoning suggests a second answer to the question of why organizations knowingly act unethically — namely, because *managerial values exist that undermine integrity*. In a recent analysis of executive integrity, Wolfe explains that managers have developed some ways of thinking (of which they may be quite unaware) that foster unethical behavior (Wolfe, 1988).

One culprit is referred to as the bottom-line-mentality. This line of thinking supports financial success as the only value to be considered. It promotes short-term solutions that are immediately financially sound, despite the fact that they cause problems for others within the organization or the organization as a whole. It promotes an unrealistic belief that everything boils down to a monetary

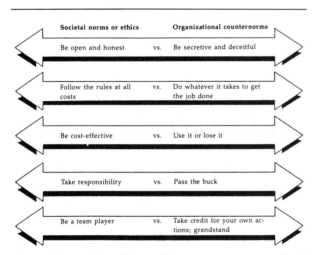

Societal norms or ethics		Organizational counternorms
Be open and honest	vs.	Be secretive and deceitful
Follow the rules at all costs	vs.	Do whatever it takes to get the job done
Be cost-effective	vs.	Use it or lose it
Take responsibility	vs.	Pass the buck
Be a team player	vs.	Take credit for your own actions; grandstand

Source: Jansen, E. and Von Glinow, M. A.: 1985, 'Ethical Ambivalence and Organizational Reward Systems', *Academy of Management Review* **10**(4), pp. 814—822.

Fig. 1. Societal norms vs. Organizational counternorms: an ethical conflict.

game. As such, rules of morality are merely obstacles, impediments along the way to bottom-line financial success.

A similar bottom-line mentality, the *"political bottom line,"* is also quite evident in the public sector.

For example, when it comes to spending money, the U.S. Congress has no equal. Although much of this expenditure is for purposes of national concern, a sizable portion is devoted to pork-barreling. Pork-barreling refers to the practice whereby a senator or representative forces Congress to allocate monies to special projects that take place in his or her home district. In many cases, the projects have little value and represent a drain on the taxpayers. They do, however, create jobs — and political support — in the home district. This practice is common, because many members of Congress believe it will help them get votes in the next election.

In some more extreme — and definitely ethically questionable — situations, such actions are designed to reward some large-scale campaign contributors in the home district. A case in point is the Maxi Cube cargo handling system. Funds for testing the Maxi Cube cargo handling system were written into the fiscal 1989 defense budget during the final Senate-House Appropriations conference at the request of Rep. John Murtha of Pennsylvania. The $10 million item was specifically targeted for a Philadelphia businessman (and contributor to Murtha's campaign) who was to manufacture the truck in Murtha's home district. The only problem was that the U.S. Army had clearly said that it had "no known requirement" for the handler. In response, Murtha was reported to be "mad as hell" at the "nitpicking" by the army. He pushed ahead anyway and used his position on the Appropriations committee to freeze a series of military budgeting requests until he got his pet project approved.

And Murtha is not alone. Rep. Les Aspin of Wisconsin got the Defense Appropriations committee to include $249 million to continue making a certain ten-ton truck (in Wisconsin, naturally) that the army was trying to phase out. It, too, was unneeded, but Aspin wanted the project for his home district. Is this legal? Yes? Is it ethical? That depends upon your point of view (Morgan, 1989). Clearly, Murtha and Aspin thought it was appropriate, given the realities of today's private and public organizations.

Wolfe also notes that managers tend to rely on an exploitative mentality — a view that encourages "using" people in a way that promotes stereotypes and undermines empathy and compassion. This is a highly selfish perspective, one that sacrifices concerns for others in favor of benefits to one's own immediate interests. In addition, there is a Madison Avenue mentality — a perspective suggesting that anything is right if the public can be convinced that it's right. The idea is that executives may be more concerned about their actions appearing ethical than by their legitimate morality — a public relations-guided morality. It is this kind of thinking that leads some companies to hide their unethical actions (by dumping their toxic wastes under cover of night, for instance) or otherwise justify them by attempting to explain them as completely acceptable.

It is not too difficult to recognize how individuals can knowingly engage in unethical practices with such mentalities. The overemphasis on short-term monetary gain and getting votes in the next election may lead to decisions and rationalizations that not only hurt individuals in the long run, but threaten the very existence of organizations themselves. Some common rationalizations used to justify unethical behavior are easily derived from Gellerman (1986):

** Pretending the behavior is not really unethical or illegal.

** Excusing the behavior by saying it's really in the organization's or your best interest.

** Assuming the behavior is okay because no one else would ever be expected to find out about it.

** Expecting your superiors to support and protect you if anything should go wrong.

Within the literature on corporate illegality, the predominant view is that pressure and need force organizational members to behave unethically and develop corresponding rationalizations; however, according to recent research this explanation only accounts for illegal acts in some cases (Baucus and Near, 1991). In their data, poor performance and low organizational slack (the excess that remains once a firm has paid its various internal and external constituencies to maintain cooperation) were not associated with illegal behavior, and wrongdoing frequently occurred in munificent environments.

According to the model developed from Baucus and Near's research (see Figure 2), illegal behavior occurs under certain conditions. For example, results from their research showed that (1) large firms are more likely to commit illegal acts than small firms; (2) although the probability of such wrongdoing increases when resources are scarce, it is greatest when resources are plentiful; (3) illegal behavior is prevalent in fairly stable environments but is more probable in dynamic environments; (4) membership in certain industries and a history of repeated wrongdoing are also associated with illegal acts; and, (5) the type of illegal activity chosen may vary

according to the particular combination of environmental and internal conditions under which a firm is operating (Baucus and Near, 1991).

Baucus and Near also suggest that conditions of opportunity and predisposition are antecedents of illegal behavior. That is, rather than tightening conditions creating pressure for illegal acts, it may be that loosening ambiguous conditions create opportunities to behave illegally. In terms of the model presented in Figure 2, large firm size provided more opportunity to engage in illegal activities than small size; the former condition may make it easy to hide illegal activities. Rules, procedures, and other control mechanisms often lag behind growth of a firm, providing organizational members with an opportunity to behave illegally because no internal rules prescribe such behavior.

Predisposition indicates a tendency or inclination to select certain activities — illegal ones — over activities because of socialization or other organizational processes. Baucus and Near (1991) avoid the assumption that a firm's managers or agents sub-

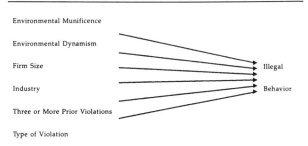

Source: 1991, Baucus, M. S. and Near, J. P.: 1991, 'Can Illegal Corporate Behavior Be Predicted? An Event History Analysis', *Academy of Management Journal* **34**(1), pp. 9–36.

Fig. 2. Modified model of the illegal corporation behavior process.

scribe to a different set of ethical standards than the rest of society. Instead, they recognize that organizations, and industries, can exert a powerful influence on their members, even those who initially have fairly strong ethical standards.

As noted above, organizations operating in certain industries tend to behave unethically. Certain industry cultures may predispose organizations to develop cultures that encourage their members to select unethical acts. If an organization's major competitors in an industry are performing well, in part as a result of unethical activities, it becomes difficult for organizational members to choose only unethical actions, and they may regard unethical actions as a standard of industry practice. Such a scenario results in an organizational culture that serves as a strong precipitant to unethical actions. The next section looks at the organizational culture-ethical behavior relationship.

Organizational culture and ethical behavior

"Do organizations vary in the '*ethical* climates' they establish for their members? The answer to the question is "yes," and it is increasingly clear that the ethical tone or climate of organizations is set at the top. What top managers do, and the culture they establish and reinforce, makes a big difference in the way lower-level employees act and in the way the organization as a whole acts when ethical dilemmas are faced. For example, there was no doubt in anyone's mind at Johnson & Johnson what to do when the infamous Tylenol poisoning took place. Company executives immediately pulled their product from the marketplace — they knew that "the J & J way" was to do the right thing regardless of its cost. What they were implicitly saying was that the ethical framework of the company required that they act in good faith in this fashion.

The ethical climate of an organization is the shared set of understandings about what is correct behavior and how ethical issues will be handled. This climate sets the tone for decision making at all levels and in all circumstances. Some of the factors that may be emphasized in different ethical climates of organizations are (Hunt, 1991; Schneider and Rentsch, 1991):

* Personal self-interest
* Company profit
* Operating efficiency
* Individual friendships
* Team interests
* Social responsibility
* Personal morality
* Rules and standard procedures
* Laws and professional codes

As suggested by the prior list, the ethical climate of different organizations can emphasize different things. In the Johnson & Johnson example just cited, the ethical climate supported doing the right thing due to social responsibility — regardless of the cost. In other organizations — perhaps too many — concerns for operating efficiency may outweigh social considerations when similarly difficult decisions are faced.

When the ethical climate is not clear and positive, ethical dilemmas will often result in unethical behavior. In such instances, an organization's culture also can predispose its members to behave unethically. For example, recent research has found a relationship between organizations with a history of violating the law and continued illegal behavior (Baucus and Near, 1991). Thus, some organizations have a culture that reinforces illegal activity. In addition, some firms are known to selectively recruit and promote employees who have personal values consistent with illegal behavior; firms also may socialize employees to engage in illegal acts as a part of their normal job duties (Conklin, 1977; Geis, 1977). For instance, in his account of cases concerning price fixing for heavy electrical equipment, Geis noted that General Electric removed a manager who refused to discuss prices with a competitor from his job and offered his successor the position with the understanding that management believed he would behave as expected and engage in price-fixing activities (Geis, 1977, p. 124; Baucus and Near, 1991).

Pressure, opportunity, and predisposition can all lead to unethical activities; however, organizations must still take a proactive stance to promote an ethical climate. The final section provides some useful suggestions available to organizations for creating a more ethical climate.

Promoting an ethical climate: Some suggestions and strategies

Recent literature has suggested several strategies for promoting ethical behavior in organizations (Adler and Bird, 1988; Burns, 1987; Harrington, 1991; Raelin, 1987; Stead *et al.*, 1990). First, chief executives should encourage ethical consciousness in their organizations from the top down — showing they support and care about ethical practices. Second, formal processes should be used to support and reinforce ethical behavior. For example, internal regulation may involve the use of codes of corporate ethics, and the availability of appeals processes. Finally, it is recommended that the philosophies of top managers as well as immediate supervisors focus on the institutionalization of ethical norms and practices that are incorporated into all organizational levels.

The philosophies of top managers as well as immediate supervisors represent a critical organizational factor influencing the ethical behavior of employees (Stead *et al.*, 1990). Research over a period

213

of more than twenty-five years clearly supports the conclusion that the ethical philosophies of management have a major impact on the ethical behavior of their followers — employees (Arlow and Ulrich, 1980; Baumhart, 1961; Brenner and Molander, 1977; Carroll, 1978; Hegarty and Sims, 1978, 1979; Posner and Schmidt, 1984; Touche Ross, 1988; Vitell and Festervand, 1987; Worrell et al., 1985).

Nielsen (1989) has stressed the importance of managerial behavior in contributing to ethical or unethical behavior. According to Nielsen, managers behaving unethically contrary to their ethical philosophies represents a serious limit to ethical reasoning in the firm. Much of the research cited in the above paragraph implicitly and explicitly states that ethical philosophies will have little impact on employees' ethical behavior unless they are supported by managerial behaviors that are consistent with these philosophies. Managers represent significant others in the organizational lives of employees and as such often have their behavior modeled by employees.

One of the most basic of management principles states that if you desire a certain behavior, reinforce it. No doubt, how ethical behavior is perceived by individuals and reinforced by an organization determines the kind of ethical behavior exhibited by employees. As a result, if business leaders want to promote ethical behavior they must accept more responsibility for establishing their organization's reinforcement system. Research in ethical behavior strongly supports the conclusion that if ethical behavior is desired, the performance measurement, appraisal and reward systems must be modified to account for ethical behavior (Hegarty and Sims, 1978, 1979; Trevino, 1986; Worrell et al., 1985). According to Nielsen (1988, p. 730):

> In many cases, mangers choose to do, go along with or ignore the unethical . . . because they want to avoid the possibility of punishments [or] to gain rewards . . .

Organizations and their managers must understand that the above recommendations are key components in the development and maintenance of an ethically-oriented organizational culture. Organizations can also enhance an ethically-oriented culture by paying particular attention to principled organizational dissent. Principled organizational dissent is an important concept linking organizational culture to ethical behavior. Principled organizational dissent is the effort by individuals in the organization to protest the status quo because of their objection on ethical grounds, to some practice or policy (Graham,

1986). Organizations committed to promoting an ethical climate should encourage principled organizational dissent instead of punishing such behavior.

Organizations should also provide more ethics training to strengthen their employees' personal ethical framework. That is, organizations must devote more resources to ethics training programs to help its members clarify their ethical frameworks and practice self-discipline when making ethical decisions in difficult circumstances. What follows is a useful seven-step checklist that organizations should use to help their employees in dealing with an ethical dilemma (Schermerhorn, 1989; Otten, 1986):

(1) Recognize and clarify the dilemma.
(2) Get all the possible facts.
(3) List your options — all of them.
(4) Test each option by asking: "Is it legal? Is it right? Is it beneficial?"
(5) Make your decision.
(6) Double check your decision by asking: "How would I feel if my family found out about this? How would I feel if my decision was printed in the local newspaper?"
(7) Take action.

An effective organizational culture should encourage ethical behavior and discourage unethical behavior. Admittedly, ethical behavior may "cost" the organization. An example might be the loss of sales when a multinational firm refuses to pay a bribe to secure business in a particular country. Certainly, individuals might be reinforced for behaving unethically (particularly if they do not get caught). In a similar fashion, an organization might seem to gain from unethical actions. For example, a purchasing agent for a large corporation might be bribed to purchase all needed office supplies from a particular supplier. However, such gains are often short-term rather than long-term in nature. In the long run, an organization cannot operate if its prevailing culture and values are not congruent with those of society. This is just as true as the observation that, in the long run, an organization cannot survive unless it produces goods and services that society wants and needs. Thus an organizational culture that promotes ethical behavior is not only more compatible with prevailing cultural values, but, in fact, makes good sense.

Although much remains to be learned about why ethical behavior occurs in organizations and creating and maintaining organizational cultures that encourage ethical behavior, organizations can benefit from the following suggestions:

** Be realistic in setting values and goals regarding employment relationships. Do not promise what the organization cannot deliver.

** Encourage input throughout the organization regarding appropriate values and practices for implementing the cultures. Choose values that represent the views of employees at all levels of the organization.

** Do not automatically opt for a "strong" culture. Explore methods to provide for diversity and dissent, such as grievance or complaint mechanisms or other internal review procedures.

** Insure that a whistle-blowing and/or ethical concerns procedure is established for internal problem-solving (Harrington, 1991).

** Provide ethics training programs for *all* employees. These programs should explain the underlying ethical and legal (Drake and Drake, 1988) principles and present practical aspects of carrying out procedural guidelines.

** Understand that not all ethical situations are clear-cut. Like many basic business situations, the organization should recognize that there are ambiguous, grey areas where ethical trade-offs may be necessary. More importantly, some situations have no simple solution (Cooke, 1991).

** Integrate ethical decision-making into the performance appraisal process.

In conclusion, even though ethical problems in organizations continue to greatly concern society, organizations, and individuals, the potential impact that organizational culture can have on ethical behavior has not really been explored (Hellreigel *et al.*, 1989). The challenge of ethical behavior must be met by organizations if they are truly concerned about survival and competitiveness. What is needed in today's complicated times is for more organizations to step forward and operate with strong, positive, and ethical cultures. Organizations have to ensure that their employees know how to deal with ethical issues in their everyday work lives. As a result, when the ethical climate is clear and positive, everyone will know what is expected of them when inevitable ethical dilemmas occur. This can give employees the confidence to be on the lookout for unethical behavior and act with the understanding

that what they are doing is considered correct and will be supported by top management and the entire organization.

References

Alder, H. J. and Bird, F. B.: 1988, 'International Dimension of Executive Integrity: Who is Responsible for the World', in S. Srivastva, ed., *Executive Integrity: The Search for Human Values in Organizational Life* (Jossey-Bass, San Francisco), pp. 243–267.

Arlow, R. and Ulrich, T. A.: 1980, 'Auditing Your Organization's Ethics', *Internal Auditor* **39**(4), pp. 26–31.

Baumhart, R.: 1961, 'How Ethical are Businessmen?', *Harvard Business Review* **39**(4), pp. 26–31.

Baucus, M. S. and Near, J. P.: 1991, 'Can Illegal Corporate Behavior Be Predicated? An Event History Analysis', *Academy of Management Journal* **34**(1), pp. 9–36.

Brenner, S. and Molander, E.: 1977, 'Is the Ethics of Business Changing?', *Harvard Business Review* **55**(1), pp. 55–71.

Bucholz, R. A.: 1989, *Fundamental Concepts and Problems in Business Ethics* (Prentice-Hall, Englewood Cliffs, NJ).

Burns, S.: 1987, 'Good Corporate Citizenship Can Pay Dividends', *Dallas Morning News* (April 15), p. C1.

Carroll, A. B.: 1978, 'Linking Business Ethics to Behavior in Organizations', *Advanced Management Journal* **43**(3), pp. 4–11.

Cooke, R. A.: 1991, 'Danger Signs of Unethical Behavior: How to Determine If Your Firm Is at Ethical Risk', *Journal of Business Ethics* **10**, pp. 249–253.

Conklin, J.: 1977, *Illegal But Not Criminal* (Prentice-Hall, Englewood Cliffs, NJ).

Drake, B. H., and Drake, E.: 1988, 'Ethical and Legal Aspects of Managing Corporate Cultures', *California Management Review* (Winter), pp. 120–121.

Geis, G.: 1977, 'The Heavy Electrical Equipment Antitrust Case of 1961', in G. Geis and R. Meier, eds., *White-Collar Crime: Offenses in Business, Politics, and the Profession* (Free Press, New York), pp. 117–132.

Gellerman, S. W.: 1986, 'Why "good" Managers Make Bad Ethical Choices', *Harvard Business Review* (July–August), pp. 85–90.

Graham, J. W.: 1986, 'Principled Organizational Dissent: A Theoretical Essay', in B. M. Staw and L. L. Cummings, eds., *Research in Organizational Behavior*, Vol. 8 (JAI Press, Greenwich, Conn.).

Gray, M. and Rosen, I.: 1982, *The Warning* (Norton, New York).

Harrington, S. J.: 1991, 'What Corporate America is Teaching About Ethics', *Academy of Management Executive* **5**(1), pp. 21–30.

Hegarty, W. and Sims, H., Jr.: 1978, 'Some Determinants of Unethical Decision Behavior: An Experiment', *Journal of Applied Psychology* **63**(4), pp. 451–457.

Hellreigel, D., Slocum, J. W., Jr., and Woodman, R. W.: 1989, *Organizational Behavior* (West Publishing, St. Paul, MN).

5. FUTURE ETHOS AND SOCIAL RESPONSIBILITY OF BUSINESS

Hunt, J. G.: 1991, *Toward A Leadership Paradigm Change* (Sage, Newbury Park, CA).

Jansen, E. and Glinow, M. A.: 1985, 'Ethical Ambivalence and Organizational Reward Systems', *Academy of Management Review* **10**(4), pp. 814–822.

Morgan, D.: 1989, 'Truck Army Does Not Want to Be Tied Up in House Turf Battle', *Washington Post* (August 12), p. A2.

New York Times: 1988, 'Corporate Prison Term for Allegheny Bottling' (September 1), p. D2.

Nielsen, R. P.: 1988, 'Limitations of Ethical Reasoning as an Action (Praxis) Strategy', *Journal of Business Ethics* **7**, pp. 725–733.

Nielsen, R. P.: 1989, 'Changing Unethical Organizational Behavior', *Academy of Management Executive* **3**(2), pp. 123–130.

Otten, A. L.: 1986, 'Ethics on the Job: Companies Alert Employees to Potential Dilemmas', *The Wall Street Journal* (July 14), p. 17.

Posner, G. and Schmidt, W.: 1984, 'Values and the American Manger: An Update', *California Management Review* **24**(3), pp. 206–216.

Raelin, J. A.: 1987, 'The Professional as the Executive's Aide-de-Camp', *Academy of Management Executive* **1**, pp. 171–182.

Schermerhorn, J. R.: 1989, *Management for Productivity* (John Wiley, New York).

Schneider, J. B. and Rentsch, J.: 1991, 'Managing Climates and Cultures: A Futures Perspective', in J. Hage, ed., *Future of Organizations* (Lexington Books, Lexington, MA).

Silverstein, S.: 1989, 'One in 15 Employees in Study Caught Stealing', *Los Angeles Times* (December 2), p. D-1.

Stead, W. E., Worrell, D. L., and Stead, J. G.: 'An Integrative Model for Understanding and Managing Ethical Behavior in Business Organizations', *Journal of Business Ethics* **9**, pp. 233–242.

Touche Ross: 1988, *Ethics in American Business: An Opinion Survey* (Touche Ross and Co.).

Trevino, L. K.: 1986, 'Ethical Decision Making in Organizations: A Person-Situation Interactionist Model', *Academy of Management Review* **11**(3), pp. 601–617.

U.S. News & World Report: 1989 (January 16), p. 42.

Vandevier, K.: 1978, 'The Aircraft Brake Scandal: A Cautionary Tale in Which the Moral is Unpleasant', in A. G. Athos and J. J. Babarro, eds., *Interpersonal Behavior: Communication and Understanding Relationships* (Prentice-Hall, Englewood Cliffs, NJ), pp. 529–540.

Vitell, S. and Festervand, T.: 1987, 'Business Ethics: Conflicts, Practices and Beliefs of Industrial Executives', *Journal of Business Ethics* **6**, pp. 111–122.

Wall Street Journal: 1989, 'Harris Corp. Is Convicted in Kickback Plan', (June 5), p. A7.

Wolfe, D.: 1988, 'Is There Integrity in the Bottomline: Managing Obstacles to Executive Integrity', in S. Srivastva, ed., *Executive Integrity: The Search For High Human Values in Organization Life* (Jossey-Bass, San Francisco), pp. 140–171.

Worrell, D. L., Stead, W. E., J. G. and Spalding, J. B.: 1985, 'Unethical Decisions: The Impact of Reinforcement Contingencies and Managerial Philosophies', *Psychological Reports* **57**, p. 355.

Creating Ethical Corporate Structures

Patrick E. Murphy
University of Notre Dame

Patrick E. Murphy is Associate Professor of Marketing at the College of Business Administration, University of Notre Dame. Dr. Murphy holds the B.B.A. degree from the University of Notre Dame, the M.B.A. degree from Bradley University, and the Ph.D. degree from the University of Houston. He is currently editor of the Journal of Public Policy and Marketing.

ETHICAL BUSINESS PRACTICES stem from ethical corporate cultures, the author writes. How does an organization go about developing that kind of culture? The most systematic approach is to build and nurture structures that emphasize the importance of ethical considerations. This paper outlines several companies' experiences with three types of ethics-enhancing structures: corporate credos, programs such as training workshops and ethics "audits," and codes tailored to the specific needs of a functional area. *Ed.*

WHAT IS AN ETHICAL COMPANY? This question is not easy to answer. For the most part, ethical problems occur because corporate managers and their subordinates are *too* devoted to the organization. In their loyalty to the company or zest to gain recognition, people sometimes ignore or overstep ethical boundaries. For example, some sales managers believe that the only way to meet ambitious sales goals is to have the sales reps "buy" business with lavish entertaining and gift giving. This overzealousness is the key source of ethical problems in most business firms.

Employees are looking for guidance in dealing with ethical problems. This guidance may come from the CEO, upper management, or immediate supervisors.[1] We know that ethical business practices stem from an ethical corporate culture. Key questions are, How can this culture be created and sustained? What structural approaches encourage ethical decision making? If the goal is to make the company ethical, managers must introduce structural components that will enhance ethical sensitivity.

In this paper, I examine three promising and workable approaches to infusing ethical principles into businesses:

• corporate credos that define and give direction to corporate values;

• ethics programs where companywide efforts focus on ethical issues; and

• ethical codes that provide specific guidance to employees in functional business areas.

Below I review the virtues and limitations of each and provide examples of companies that successfully employ these approaches.

Corporate Credos

A corporate credo delineates a company's ethical responsibility to its stakeholders; it is probably the most general approach to managing corporate

Reprinted from *Sloan Management Review*, Vol. 30, No. 2, Winter 1989, pp. 81-87. © 1989 by Sloan Management Review Association.

Table 1		The Credo of Security Pacific Corporation	

Commitment to Customer

The first commitment is to provide our customers with quality products and services which are innovative and technologically responsive to their current requirements, at appropriate prices. To perform these tasks with integrity requires that we maintain confidentiality and protect customer privacy, promote customer satisfaction, and serve customer needs. We strive to serve qualified customers and industries which are socially responsible according to broadly accepted community and company standards.

Commitment to Employee

The second commitment is to establish an environment for our employees which promotes professional growth, encourages each person to achieve his or her highest potential, and promotes individual creativity and responsibility. Security Pacific acknowledges our responsibility to employees, including providing for open and honest communication, stated expectations, fair and timely assessment of performance and equitable compensation which rewards employee contributions to company objectives within a framework of equal opportunity and affirmative action.

Commitment of Employee to Security Pacific

The third commitment is that of the employee to Security Pacific. As employees, we strive to understand and adhere to the Corporation's policies and objectives, act in a professional manner, and give our best effort to improve Security Pacific. We recognize the trust and confidence placed in us by our customers and community and act with integrity and honesty in all situations to preserve that trust and confidence. We act responsibly to avoid conflicts of interest and other situations which are potentially harmful to the Corporation.

Commitment of Employee to Employee

The fourth commitment is that of employees to their fellow employees. We must be committed to promote a climate of mutual respect, integrity, and professional relationships, characterized by open and honest communication within and across all levels of the organization. Such a climate will promote attainment of the Corporation's goals and objectives, while leaving room for individual initiative within a competitive environment.

Commitment to Communities

The fifth commitment is that of Security Pacific to the communities which we serve. We must constantly strive to improve the quality of life through our support of community organizations and projects, through encouraging service to the community by employees, and by promoting participation in community services. By the appropriate use of our resources, we work to support or further advance the interests of the community, particularly in times of crisis or social need. The Corporation and its employees are committed to complying fully with each community's laws and regulations.

Commitment to Stockholder

The sixth commitment of Security Pacific is to its stockholders. We will strive to provide consistent growth and a superior rate of return on their investment, to maintain a position and reputation as a leading financial institution, to protect stockholder investments, and to provide full and timely information. Achievement of these goals for Security Pacific is dependent upon the successful development of the five previous sets of relationships.

ethics. The credo is a succinct statement of the values permeating the firm. The experiences of Security Pacific Corporation (a Los Angeles–based national bank that devised a credo in 1987) and of Johnson & Johnson illustrate the credo approach.

Security Pacific's central document is not an ethical code per se; rather, it is six missionlike commitments to customers, employees, communities, and stockholders. The credo's objective is "to seek a set of principles and beliefs which might provide guidance and direction to our work" (see Table 1).

More than 70 high-level managers participated in formulating a first draft of the commitments. During this process, senior managers shared and analyzed examples of ethical dilemmas they had faced in balancing corporate and constituent obligations. An outside consultant, hired to manage the process, helped to draft the language. Ultimately more than 250 employees, from all levels of the bank, participated in the credo formulation process via a series of discussion groups.

Once the commitments were in final form, management reached a consensus on how to communicate these guiding principles to the Security Pacific organization. Credo coordinators developed and disseminated a leader's guide to be used at staff meetings introducing the credo; it contained instructions on the meeting's format and on showing a videotape that explained the credo and the process by which it was developed. At the meetings, managers invited reactions by posing these questions: What are your initial feelings about what you have just read? Are there any specific commitments you would like to discuss? How will the credo affect your daily work? Employees were thus encouraged to react to the credo and to consider its long-run implications.

Security Pacific's credo was recently cited as a model effort, and it serves internally both as a standard for judging existing programs and as a justification for new activities.[2] For example, the "commitment to communities" formed the basis for a

Table 2	Johnson & Johnson Credo

We believe our first responsibility is to the doctors, nurses, and patients, to mothers and all others who use our products and services. In meeting their needs everything we do must be of high quality. We must constantly strive to reduce our costs in order to maintain reasonable prices. Customers' orders must be serviced promptly and accurately. Our suppliers and distributors must have an opportunity to make a fair profit.

We are responsible to our employees, the men and women who work with us throughout the world. Everyone must be considered as an individual. We must respect their dignity and recognize their merit. They must have a sense of security in their jobs. Compensation must be fair and adequate and working conditions clean, orderly, and safe. Employees must feel free to make suggestions and complaints. There must be equal opportunity for employment, development, and advancement for those qualified. We must provide competent management, and their actions must be just and ethical.

We are responsible to the communities in which we live and work and to the world community as well. We must be good citizens—support good works and charities and bear our fair share of taxes. We must encourage civic improvements and better health and education. We must maintain in good order the property we are privileged to use, protecting the environment and natural resources.

Our final responsibility is to our stockholders. Business must make a sound profit. We must experiment with new ideas. Research must be carried on, innovative programs developed and mistakes paid for. New equipment must be purchased, new facilities provided, and new products launched. Reserves must be created to provide for adverse times. When we operate according to these principles, the stockholders should realize a fair return.

program specifically designed to serve low-income constituents in the area. However, this credo should not be considered the definitive approach to ethics management. First, the credo could be interpreted simply as an organizational mission statement, not as a document about ethics. Indeed, the examples supporting the credo and the videotape itself do stress what might just be called good business practice, without particular reference to ethical policies. And second, the credo has not been in place long enough for its impact to be fully assessed.

Any discussion of corporate credos would be incomplete without reference to Johnson & Johnson, whose credo is shown in Table 2. This document focuses on responsibilities to consumers, employees, communities, and stockholders. (The current J&J president, David Clare, explains that responsibility to the stockholder is listed last because "if we do the other jobs properly, the stockholder will always be served.") The first version of this credo, instituted in 1945, was revised in 1947. Between 1975 and 1978, chairman James Burke held a series of meetings with J&J's 1,200 top managers; they were encouraged to "challenge" the credo. What emerged from the meetings was that the document in fact functioned as it was intended to function; a slightly reworded but substantially unchanged credo was introduced in 1979.

Over the last two years, the company has begun to survey all employees about how well the company meets its responsibilities to the four principal constituencies. The survey asks employees from all fifty-three countries where J&J operates questions about every line in the credo. An office devoted to the credo survey tabulates the results, which are confidential. (Department and division managers receive only information pertaining to their units and composite numbers for the entire firm.) The interaction at meetings devoted to discussing these findings is reportedly very good.

Does J&J's credo work? Top management feels strongly that it does. The credo is often mentioned as an important contributing factor in the company's exemplary handling of the Tylenol crises several years ago. It would appear that the firm's commitment to the credo makes ethical business practice its highest priority. One might question whether the credo is adequate to deal with the multitude of ethical problems facing a multinational firm; possibly additional ethical guidelines could serve as reinforcement, especially in dealing with international business issues.

When should a company use a corporate credo to guide its ethical policies? They work best in firms with a cohesive corporate culture, where a spirit of frequent and unguarded communication exists. Generally, small, tightly knit companies find that a credo is sufficient. Among large firms, Johnson & Johnson is an exception. J&J managers consciously use the credo as an ethical guidepost; they find that the corporate culture reinforces the credo.

When is a credo insufficient? This approach does not offer enough guidance for most multinational companies facing complex ethical questions in different societies, for firms that have merged recently and are having trouble grafting disparate cultures, and for companies operating in industries with chronic ethical problems. A credo is like the Ten Commandments. Both set forth good general principles, but many people need the Bible, religious teachings, and guidelines provided by organized religion, as well. Similarly, many companies find that they need to offer more concrete guidance on ethical issues.

Ethics Programs

Ethics programs provide more specific direction for dealing with potential ethical problems than general credos do. Two companies—Chemical Bank and Dow Corning—serve as examples. Although the thrust of the two programs is different, they both illustrate the usefulness of this approach.

Chemical Bank, the nation's fourth largest bank, has an extensive ethics education program. All new employees attend an orientation session at which they read and sign off on Chemical's code of ethics. (This has been in existence for thirty years and was last revised in May 1987.) The training program features a videotaped message from the chairman emphasizing the bank's values and ethical standards. A second and more unusual aspect of the program provides in-depth training in ethical decision making for vice presidents.[3]

The "Decision Making and Corporate Values" course is a two-day seminar that occurs away from the bank. Its purpose, according to a bank official, is "to encourage Chemical's employees to weigh the ethical or value dimensions of the decisions they make and to provide them with the analytic tools to do that." This program began in 1983; more than 250 vice presidents have completed the course thus far. Each meeting is limited to twenty to twenty-five senior vice presidents from a cross-section of departments; this size makes for a seminarlike atmosphere. The bank instituted the program in response to the pressures associated with deregulation, technology, and increasing competition.

The chairman always introduces the seminar by highlighting his personal commitment to the program. Most of the two days is spent discussing case studies. The fictitious cases were developed following interviews with various Chemical managers who described ethically charged situations. The cases are really short stories about loan approval, branch closings, foreign loans, insider trading, and other issues.[4] They do not have "solutions" as such; instead, they pose questions for discussion, such

as, Do you believe the individual violated the bank's code? Or, What should X do?

Program evaluations have yielded positive results. Participants said they later encountered dilemmas similar to the cases, and that they had developed a thinking process in the seminar that helped them work through other problems. This program, while it is exemplary, only reaches a small percentage of Chemical's 30,000 employees. Ideally, such a program would be disseminated more widely and would become more than a one-time event.

Dow Corning has a longstanding—and very different—ethics program. Its general code has been revised four times since its inception in 1976 and includes a seven-point values statement. The company started using face-to-face "ethical audits" at its plants worldwide more than a decade ago. The number of participants in these four-to-six-hour audits ranges from five to forty. Auditors meet with the manager in charge the evening before to ascertain the most pressing issues. The actual questions come from relevant sections in the corporate code and are adjusted for the audit location. At sales offices, for example, the auditors concentrate on issues such as kickbacks, unusual requests from customers, and special pricing terms; at manufacturing plants, conservation and environmental issues receive more attention. An ethical audit might include the following questions.

- Are there any examples of business that Dow Corning has lost because of our refusal to provide "gifts" or other incentives to government officials at our customers' facilities?
- Do any of our employees have ownership or financial interest in any of our distributors?
- Have our sales representatives been able to undertake business conduct discussions with distributors in a way that actually strengthens our ties with them?
- Has Dow Corning been forced to terminate any distributors because of their business conduct practices?
- Do you believe that our distributors are in regular contact with their competitors? If so, why?
- Which specific Dow Corning policies conflict with local practices?

John Swanson, manager of Corporate Internal and Management Communications, heads this effort; he believes the audit approach makes it "virtually impossible for employees to consciously make an unethical decision." According to Swanson, twenty to twenty-three meetings occur every year. The Business Conduct Committee members, who act as session leaders, then prepare a report for the

Developing a structure is not sufficient by itself. The structure will not be useful unless it is supported by institutionalized managerial processes.

Audit Committee of the board. He stresses the fact that there are no shortcuts to implementing this program—it requires time and extensive interaction with the people involved. Recently the audit was expanded; it now examines internal as well as external activities. (One audit found that some salespeople believed manufacturing personnel needed to be more honest when developing production schedules.) One might ask whether the commitment to ethics is constant over time or peaks during the audit sessions; Dow Corning may want to conduct surprise audits, or develop other monitoring mechanisms or a more detailed code.

When should a company consider developing an ethics program? Such programs are often appropriate when firms have far-flung operations that need periodic guidance, as is the case at Dow Corning. This type of program can deal specifically with international ethical issues and with peculiarities at various plant locations. Second, an ethics program is useful when managers confront similar ethical problems on a regular basis, as Chemical Bank executives do. Third, these programs are useful in organizations that use outside consultants or advertising agencies. If an independent contractor does not subscribe to a corporate credo, the firm may want to use an ethical audit or checklist to heighten the outside agency's sensitivity to ethical issues.

When do ethics programs come up lacking? If they are too issue centered, ethics programs may miss other, equally important problems. (Dow's program, for example, depends on the questions raised by the audit.) In addition, the scope of the program may limit its impact to only certain parts of the organization (e.g., Chemical Bank). Managers who want to permanently inculcate ethical considerations may be concerned that such programs are not perceived by some employees as being long term or ongoing. If the credo can be compared with the Ten Commandments, then ethics programs can be likened to weekly church services. Both can be uplifting, but once the session (service) is over, individuals may believe they can go back to business as usual.

Tailored Corporate Codes

Codes of conduct, or ethical codes, are another structural mechanism companies use to signal their commitment to ethical principles. Ninety percent of Fortune 500 firms, and almost half of all other firms, have ethical codes. According to a recent survey, this mechanism is perceived as the most effective way to encourage ethical business behavior.[5] Codes commonly address issues such as conflict of interest, competitors, privacy, gift giving and receiving, and political contributions. However, many observers continue to believe that codes are really public relations documents, or motherhood and apple pie statements; these critics claim that codes belittle employees and fail to address practical managerial issues.[6]

Simply developing a code is not enough. It must be tailored to the firm's functional areas (e.g., marketing, finance, personnel) or to the major line of business in which the firm operates. The rationale for tailored codes is simple. Functional areas or divisions have differing cultures and needs. A consumer products division, for example, has a relatively distant relationship with customers, because it relies heavily on advertising to sell its products. A division producing industrial products, on the other hand, has fewer customers and uses a personal, sales-oriented approach. A code needs to reflect these differences. Unfortunately, very few ethics codes do so.

Several companies have exemplary codes tailored to functional or major business areas. I describe two of these below—the St. Paul Companies (specializing in commercial and personal insurance and related products) and International Business Machines (IBM).

The St. Paul Companies revised their extensive corporate code, entitled "In Good Conscience," in 1986. All new employees get introduced to the code when they join the company, and management devotes biannual meetings to discussing the code's impact on day-to-day activities. In each of the five sections, the code offers specific guidance and examples for employees to follow. The statements below illustrate the kinds of issues, and the level of specificity, contained in the code.

• Insider Information. For example, if you know that the company is about to announce a rise in quarterly profits, or anything else that would affect the price of the company's stock, you cannot buy or sell the stock until the announcement has been made and published.

• Gifts and Entertainment. An inexpensive ball-point pen, or an appointment diary, is a common gift and generally acceptable. But liquor, lavish entertainment, clothing, or travel should not be accepted.

• Contact with Legislators. If you are contacted by legislators on matters relating to the St. Paul, you should refer them to your governmental affairs or law department.

The "Employee Related Issues" section of the code is the most detailed; it directly addresses the company's relationship to the individual, and vice versa. This section spells out what employees can expect in terms of compensation (it should be based on job performance and administered fairly), advancement (promotion is from within, where possible), assistance (this consists of training, job experience, or counseling) and communications (there should be regular feedback; concerns can be expressed without fear of recrimination). It also articulates the St. Paul Companies' expectation of employees regarding speaking up (when you know something that could be a problem), avoiding certain actions (where the public's confidence could be weakened), and charting your career course.

The company also delineates employee privacy issues. The code outlines how work-related information needed for hiring and promotion is collected. (Only information needed to make the particular decision is gathered; it is collected from the applicant/employee where possible. Polygraphs are not used.) The St. Paul informs employees about what types of information are maintained. Finally, information in an individual's file is open to the employee's review.

The code covers other important personnel issues in depth, as well. It touches on equal opportunity by mentioning discrimination laws, but the emphasis is on the company recognition of past discrimination and its commitments to "make an affirmative effort to address this situation in all of its programs and practices." Data acquired from the St. Paul supports this point. Between 1981 and 1986, hiring and promotion increased 60 percent for minorities in supervisory positions and 49 percent for women in management—even though overall employment rose only about 3 percent during this time. In addition, the code informs employees that the company will reimburse all documented business expenses. And it covers nepotism by stating that officers' and directors' relatives will not be hired; other employees' relatives

can be employed, so long as they are placed in different departments.

Being an ethical company requires providing clear guidelines for employees. The St. Paul Companies' extensive discussion of personnel policies does just that. Employees may strongly disapprove of certain policies, but they are fully informed. The termination policy, for example, states that employment is voluntary and that individuals are free to resign at any time; the company, too, can terminate employees "at any time, with or without cause." Some people may consider that policy unfair or punitive, but at least the rules of the game are clear. One limitation of the code is that all sections are not uniformly strong. For example, the marketing section is only one paragraph long and contains few specifics.

The second illustration is of a code tailored to the company's major line of business. IBM's "Business Conduct Guidelines" were instituted in the 1960s and revised most recently in 1983. New employees receive a copy and certify annually that they abide by the code. It has four parts; the most extensive section is entitled "Conducting IBM's Business." Since IBM is, at its core, a marketing and sales organization, this section pertains primarily to these issues.

Six subsections detail the type of activities IBM expects of its sales representatives. First, "Some General Standards" include the following directives, with commentaries: do not make misrepresentations to anyone, do not take advantage of IBM's size, treat everyone fairly (do not extend preferential treatment), and do not practice reciprocal dealing. Second, "Fairness in the Field" pertains to disparagement (sell IBM products on their merits, not by disparaging competitors' products or services). In addition, it prohibits premature disclosure of product information and of selling if a competitor already has a signed order. Third, "Relations with Other Organizations" cautions employees about firms that have multiple relationships with IBM (deal with only one relationship at a time, and do not collaborate with these firms).

The fourth and fifth sections address "Acquiring and Using Information for or about Others." The code spells out the limits to acquiring information (industrial espionage is wrong) and to using information (adverse information should not be retained). Employees must determine the confidentiality of information gathered from others. The final section outlines IBM's policy on "Bribes, Gifts, and Entertainment." The company allows customary business amenities but prohibits giving presents that are intended to "unduly influence" or "obligate" the recipient, as well as receiving gifts worth more than a nominal amount.

One might contend that it is easy for a large, profitable company like IBM to have an exemplary code. On the other hand, one could also argue that a real reason for the company's continued success is that its sales representatives do subscribe to these principles. Is this a perfect code? No. The gifts area could use more specificity and, even though the company spends millions of dollars a year on advertising, that subject is not addressed in any section of the code. Further, IBM's legal department administers the code, which may mean that problems are resolved more by legal than ethical interpretation.

When should a company use a tailored code of ethics? If a company has one dominant functional unit (like IBM), or if there is diversity among functional areas, divisions, or subsidiaries, then a tailored code might be advisable. It allows the firm to promulgate specific and appropriate standards. Tailored codes are especially useful to complex organizations because they represent permanent guidelines for managers and employees to consult.

When should they be avoided? If a firm's leaders believe specific guidelines may be too restrictive for their employees, then a tailored code is an unsatisfactory choice. Codes are not necessary in most small firms or in ones where a culture includes firmly entrenched ethical policies. If a credo is similar to the Ten Commandments, and programs are similar to religious services, then tailored credos can be considered similar to the Bible or to other formal religious teachings. They provide the most guidance, but many people do not take the time to read or reflect on them.

Conclusion

My research on ethics in management suggests several conclusions that the corporate manager may wish to keep in mind.

• **There Is No Single Ideal Approach to Corporate Ethics.** I would recommend that a small firm start with a credo, but that a larger firm consider a program or a tailored code. It is also possible to integrate these programs and produce a hybrid: in dealing with insider trading, for example, a firm could develop a training program, then follow it up with a strongly enforced tailored code.[7]

• **Top Management Must Be Committed.** Senior managers must champion the highest ethical postures for their companies, as James Burke of J&J does. This commitment was evident in all the companies described here; it came through loud and clear in the CEOs' letters, reports, and public statements.

• **Developing a Structure Is Not Sufficient by Itself.** The structure will not be useful unless it is supported by institutionalized managerial processes. The credo meetings at Security Pacific and the seminars at Chemical Bank are examples of processes that support structures.

• **Raising the Ethical Consciousness of an Organization Is Not Easy.** All the companies mentioned here have spent countless hours—and substantial amounts of money—developing, discussing, revising, and communicating the ethical principles of the firm. And in fact there are no guarantees that it will work. McDonnell Douglas has an extensive ethics program, but some of its executives were implicated in a recent defense contractor scandal.

In conclusion, let me add that managers in firms with active ethics structures—credos, programs, and tailored codes—are genuinely enthusiastic about them. They believe that ethics pay off. Their conviction should provide others with an encouraging example.

References

The author would like to thank Bernard Avishai, Gene Laczniak, Michael Mokwa, Lee Tavis, and Oliver Williams, C.S.C., for their helpful comments on an earlier version of this article.

1
P.E. Murphy and M.G. Dunn, "Corporate Culture and Marketing Management Ethics" (Notre Dame, IN: University of Notre Dame, working paper, 1988).

2
R.E. Berenbeim, *Corporate Ethics* (New York: The Conference Board, research report no. 900, 1987), p. 15, pp. 20–22.

3
A more detailed discussion of Chemical's comprehensive program, and of Johnson & Johnson's, appears in *Corporate Ethics: A Prime Business Asset* (New York: Business Roundtable, February 1988).

4
One of the case studies appears in "Would You Blow Whistle on Wayward Colleague?" *American Banker*, 17 June 1988, p. 16.

5
Touche Ross, *Ethics in American Business* (New York: Touche Ross & Co., January 1988).

6
Berenbeim (1987), p. 17.

7
G.L. Tidwell, "Here's a Tip—Know the Rules of Insider Trading," *Sloan Management Review*, Summer 1987, pp. 93–99.

How to be ethical, and still come top

The study of business ethics is one of the more enduring management fads of the past decade. So why do many managers consider it irrelevant?

ALTHOUGH the first course in business ethics was offered by Harvard Business School back in 1915, it is only since the mid-1980s that business schools have truly taken the subject to their hearts. Blame this renewed interest on a string of business scandals: Drexel Burnham Lambert, Guinness, Salomon Brothers, Robert Maxwell and Recruit, not forgetting Olivetti, Fiat and a big chunk of the rest of corporate Italy; the list can seem endless.

Market-driven as ever, business schools have risen to the challenge. In America alone, on one estimate, more than 500 courses on business ethics are on offer; 90% of the country's business schools now teach the subject. Globally, more than 20 dedicated research units now study the topic, and business-ethics journals abound. Appropriately, Europe's first such publication, *Etica Degli Affari*, was Italian.

While courses in business ethics are now among the most popular on business-school curriculums, many academics admit in private that the influence of their teaching is minimal. Managers, it seems, find the topic too arcane and inaccessible. Worse, they feel it has little relevance to everyday business decisions, where right and wrong are by no means always clear-cut. So where are the business ethicists going wrong?

An article* by Andrew Stark, a professor of management at the University of Toronto, attempts to answer that question. The fundamental difficulty with business ethics, thinks Mr Stark, lies in the way business schools have chosen to tackle it. Most of the leading academics in business ethics have a grounding in moral philosophy, a discipline that takes the concept of altruism—doing good simply because it is right—rather seriously.

As a result, most of the advice on business ethics offered by academic papers (and by much business-school teaching) tends towards moral absolutism. If ethics and the interests of the business conflict, managers and employees are invariably told that they must always do the right

thing—for no other reason than that it is right. As one recent treatise on business ethics put it, "If in some instance it turns out that what is ethical leads to a company's demise, so be it."

Back in the real world, however, no businessman is going to sacrifice his company on the altar of such altruistic extremism. What most managers want to know is how they should juggle what Mr Stark calls the "confusing mix of self-interest, altruism and other influences" that make their businesses tick. Yet on the subject of mixed motives, business ethicists have for the most part been unhelpfully silent.

A second, related problem is that business ethics has mostly concerned itself with grand theorising, trying to answer questions such as "Is capitalism ethically justifiable?" and "Can a profitable business ever be ethical?". Weighty as they are, these questions have little relevance to a manager struggling to run a business as ethically as possible.

Business ethicists have not helped their case by couching their arguments in language that is foreign to managers schooled in the lexicon of finance and economics. Mr Stark cites one (depressingly typical) paper on business ethics which argued that "utilitarian and situation ethics, not deontological or Kantian ethics ... should be used in a regional code of conduct for multinational companies." Small wonder that few managers read on, or that most mainstream management academics see business ethics as a "soft" subject.

All this leaves business ethics in a state of unhelpful flux. Increased interest in the topic has undoubtedly concentrated managers' minds on the need for mechanisms to help resolve ethical dilemmas in the workplace. To that end, many firms (including, last month, Fiat) have implemented ethical codes of conduct and set up ethics ombudsmen, ethics committees and the like. But once these new mechanisms are in place, managers are left with little guidance from business ethicists about how, precisely, they might best make use of them. If their discipline is to survive, business ethicists must start getting their hands dirty.

Mr Stark reckons that an emerging generation of academics, disillusioned by the arcane teachings of their forebears, is starting to do just that by tackling many of the dilemmas managers face each day—those which business ethicists have previously side-stepped. And at the heart of what Mr Stark calls "the new business ethics" is a willingness to tackle head-on the vexed question of mixed motives.

At first sight, the work of Robert Solomon, of the University of Texas, looks dauntingly arcane: he claims to base his theory of ethical management on Aristotle's concept of "virtue". In practice, however, Mr Solomon's ideas are accessible to any businessman. Managers, he notes, are taught to be tough, which can mean they sometimes take a decision regardless of its ethical consequences. But temper such toughness with a set of easy-to-understand managerial virtues—Mr Solomon cites sensitivity, courage, persistence and honesty—and managers will find they can combine "a willingness to do what is necessary" with an "insistence on doing it humanely." This may sound an obvious sort of compromise, but it is the kind of ethical advice many managers have been looking for.

Laura Nash, of the Boston University Graduate School of Management, takes the argument a stage further. For managers to be able to resolve ethical dilemmas, says Ms Nash, they should think of their business in terms of covenants—with employees, customers, suppliers and so on. A manager's primary obligation is therefore to ensure his covenants with each of these mean that "all parties in a commercial endeavour should prosper on the basis of created value and the *voluntary* exchange of resources." In other words, a compromise: management can never be wholly altruistic or spotlessly ethical, but the harm done to others can be minimised.

Such moderate pragmatism is a world away from the moral absolutism usually preached by business ethicists. If it is the start of a trend, it may bring the theory of business ethics and the reality of doing business much closer together. Whether it will prevent even a single business scandal is another matter.

---

* "What's the Matter with Business Ethics?" By Andrew Stark. Harvard Business Review, May-June 1993.

From *The Economist*, June 5, 1993, p. 71. © 1993 by The Economist, Ltd. Distributed by The New York Times Special Features.

The Pyramid of Corporate Social Responsibility: Toward the Moral Management of Organizational Stakeholders

Archie B. Carroll

Archie B. Carroll is Robert W. Scherer Professor of Management and Corporate Public Affairs at the College of Business Administration, University of Georgia, Athens.

F or the better part of 30 years now, corporate executives have struggled with the issue of the firm's responsibility to its society. Early on it was argued by some that the corporation's sole responsibility was to provide a maximum financial return to shareholders. It became quickly apparent to everyone, however, that this pursuit of financial gain had to take place within the laws of the land. Though social activist groups and others throughout the 1960s advocated a broader notion of corporate responsibility, it was not until the significant social legislation of the early 1970s that this message became indelibly clear as a result of the creation of the Environmental Protection Agency (EPA), the Equal Employment Opportunity Commission (EEOC), the Occupational Safety and Health Administration (OSHA), and the Consumer Product Safety Commission (CPSC).

These new governmental bodies established that national public policy now officially recognized the environment, employees, and consumers to be significant and legitimate stakeholders of business. From that time on, corporate executives have had to wrestle with how they balance their commitments to the corporation's owners with their obligations to an ever-broadening group of stakeholders who claim both legal and ethical rights.

This article will explore the nature of corporate social responsibility (CSR) with an eye toward understanding its component parts. The intention will be to characterize the firm's CSR in ways that might be useful to executives who wish to reconcile their obligations to their share-

> *Social responsibility can only become reality if more managers become moral instead of amoral or immoral.*

holders with those to other competing groups claiming legitimacy. This discussion will be framed by a pyramid of corporate social responsibility. Next, we plan to relate this concept to the idea of stakeholders. Finally, our goal will be to isolate the ethical or moral component of CSR and relate it to perspectives that reflect three major ethical approaches to management—immoral, amoral, and moral. The principal goal in this final section will be to flesh out what it means to manage stakeholders in an ethical or moral fashion.

EVOLUTION OF CORPORATE SOCIAL RESPONSIBILITY

W hat does it mean for a corporation to be socially responsible? Academics and practitioners have been striving to establish an agreed-upon definition of this concept for 30 years. In 1960, Keith Davis suggested that social responsibility refers to businesses' "decisions and actions taken for reasons at least partially beyond the firm's direct economic or technical interest." At about the same time, Eells and Walton (1961) argued that CSR refers to the

Figure 1
Economic and Legal Components of Corporate Social Responsibility

Economic Components (Responsibilities)	Legal Components (Responsibilities)
1. It is important to perform in a manner consistent with maximizing earnings per share.	1. It is important to perform in a manner consistent with expectations of government and law.
2. It is important to be committed to being as profitable as possible.	2. It is important to comply with various federal, state, and local regulations.
3. It is important to maintain a strong competitive position.	3. It is important to be a law-abiding corporate citizen.
4. It is important to maintain a high level of operating efficiency.	4. It is important that a successful firm be defined as one that fulfills its legal obligations.
5. It is important that a successful firm be defined as one that is consistently profitable.	5. It is important to provide goods and services that at least meet minimal legal requirements.

"problems that arise when corporate enterprise casts its shadow on the social scene, and the ethical principles that ought to govern the relationship between the corporation and society."

In 1971 the Committee for Economic Development used a "three concentric circles" approach to depicting CSR. The inner circle included basic economic functions—growth, products, jobs. The intermediate circle suggested that the economic functions must be exercised with a sensitive awareness of changing social values and priorities. The outer circle outlined newly emerging and still amorphous responsibilities that business should assume to become more actively involved in improving the social environment.

The attention was shifted from social responsibility to social responsiveness by several other writers. Their basic argument was that the emphasis on responsibility focused exclusively on the notion of business obligation and motivation and that action or performance were being overlooked. The social responsiveness movement, therefore, emphasized corporate action, proaction, and implementation of a social role. This was indeed a necessary reorientation.

The question still remained, however, of reconciling the firm's economic orientation with its social orientation. A step in this direction was taken when a comprehensive definition of CSR was set forth. In this view, a four-part conceptualization of CSR included the idea that the corporation has not only economic and legal obliga-

tions, but ethical and discretionary (philanthropic) responsibilities as well (Carroll 1979). The point here was that CSR, to be accepted as legitimate, had to address the entire spectrum of obligations business has to society, including the most fundamental—economic. It is upon this four-part perspective that our pyramid is based.

In recent years, the term corporate social performance (CSP) has emerged as an inclusive and global concept to embrace corporate social responsibility, responsiveness, and the entire spectrum of socially beneficial activities of businesses. The focus on social performance emphasizes the concern for corporate action and accomplishment in the social sphere. With a performance perspective, it is clear that firms must formulate and implement social goals and programs as well as integrate ethical sensitivity into all decision making, policies, and actions. With a results focus, CSP suggests an all-encompassing orientation towards normal criteria by which we assess business performance to include quantity, quality, effectiveness, and efficiency. While we recognize the vitality of the performance concept, we have chosen to adhere to the CSR terminology for our present discussion. With just a slight change of focus, however, we could easily be discussing a CSP rather than a CSR pyramid. In any event, our long-term concern is what managers do with these ideas in terms of implementation.

Figure 2
Ethical and Philanthropic Components of
Corporate Social Responsibility

Ethical Components (Responsibilities)	Philanthropic Components (Responsibilities)
1. It is important to perform in a manner consistent with expectations of societal mores and ethical norms.	1. It is important to perform in a manner consistent with the philanthropic and charitable expectations of society.
2. It is important to recognize and respect new or evolving ethical/moral norms adopted by society.	2. It is important to assist the fine and performing arts.
3. It is important to prevent ethical norms from being compromised in order to achieve corporate goals.	3. It is important that managers and employees participate in voluntary and charitable activities within their local communities.
4. It is important that good corporate citizenship be defined as doing what is expected morally or ethically.	4. It is important to provide assistance to private and public educational institutions.
5. It is important to recognize that corporate integrity and ethical behavior go beyond mere compliance with laws and regulations.	5. It is important to assist voluntarily those projects that enhance a community's "quality of life."

THE PYRAMID OF CORPORATE SOCIAL RESPONSIBILITY

For CSR to be accepted by a conscientious business person, it should be framed in such a way that the entire range of business responsibilities are embraced. It is suggested here that four kinds of social responsibilities constitute total CSR: economic, legal, ethical, and philanthropic. Furthermore, these four categories or components of CSR might be depicted as a pyramid. To be sure, all of these kinds of responsibilities have always existed to some extent, but it has only been in recent years that ethical and philanthropic functions have taken a significant place. Each of these four categories deserves closer consideration.

Economic Responsibilities

Historically, business organizations were created as economic entities designed to provide goods and services to societal members. The profit motive was established as the primary incentive for entrepreneurship. Before it was anything else, the business organization was the basic economic unit in our society. As such, its principal role was to produce goods and services that consumers needed and wanted and to make an acceptable profit in the process. At some point the idea of the profit motive got transformed into a notion of maximum profits, and this has been an enduring value ever since. All other business responsibilities are predicated upon the economic responsibility of the firm, because without it the others become moot considerations. **Figure 1** summarizes some important statements characterizing economic responsibilities. Legal responsibilities are also depicted in Figure 1, and we will consider them next.

Legal Responsibilities

Society has not only sanctioned business to operate according to the profit motive; at the same time business is expected to comply with the laws and regulations promulgated by federal, state, and local governments as the ground rules under which business must operate. As a partial fulfillment of the "social contract" between business and society, firms are expected to pursue their economic missions within the framework of the law. Legal responsibilities reflect a view of "codified ethics" in the sense that they embody basic notions of fair operations as established by our lawmakers. They are depicted as the next layer on the pyramid to portray their historical development, but they are appropriately seen as coexisting with economic responsibilities as fundamental precepts of the free enterprise system.

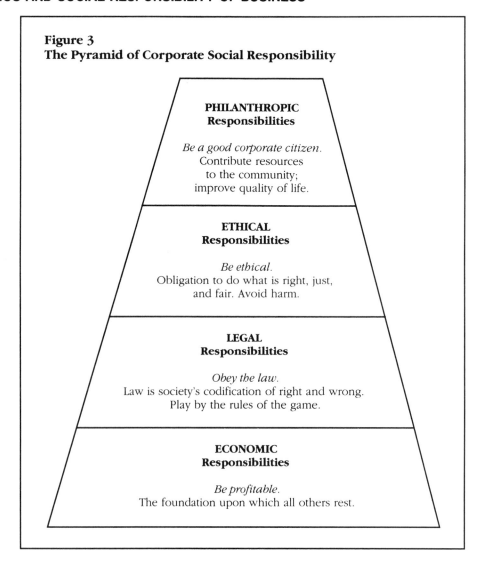

Figure 3
The Pyramid of Corporate Social Responsibility

PHILANTHROPIC
Responsibilities

Be a good corporate citizen.
Contribute resources
to the community;
improve quality of life.

ETHICAL
Responsibilities

Be ethical.
Obligation to do what is right, just,
and fair. Avoid harm.

LEGAL
Responsibilities

Obey the law.
Law is society's codification of right and wrong.
Play by the rules of the game.

ECONOMIC
Responsibilities

Be profitable.
The foundation upon which all others rest.

Ethical Responsibilities

Although economic and legal responsibilities embody ethical norms about fairness and justice, ethical responsibilities embrace those activities and practices that are expected or prohibited by societal members even though they are not codified by law. Ethical responsibilities embody those standards, norms, or expectations that reflect a concern for what consumers, employees, shareholders, and the community regard as fair, just, or in keeping with the respect or protection of stakeholders' moral rights.

In one sense, changing ethics or values precede the establishment of law because they become the driving force behind the very creation of laws or regulations. For example, the environmental, civil rights, and consumer movements reflected basic alterations in societal values and thus may be seen as ethical bellwethers foreshadowing and resulting in the later legislation. In another sense, ethical re-

sponsibilities may be seen as embracing newly emerging values and norms society expects business to meet, even though such values and norms may reflect a higher standard of performance than that currently required by law. Ethical responsibilities in this sense are often ill-defined or continually under public debate as to their legitimacy, and thus are frequently difficult for business to deal with.

Superimposed on these ethical expectations emanating from societal groups are the implied levels of ethical performance suggested by a consideration of the great ethical principles of moral philosophy. This would include such principles as justice, rights, and utilitarianism.

The business ethics movement of the past decade has firmly established an ethical responsibility as a legitimate CSR component. Though it is depicted as the next layer of the CSR pyramid, it must be constantly recognized that it is in dynamic interplay with the legal responsibility category. That is, it is constantly pushing the legal responsibility category to broaden or expand while at the same time placing ever higher expectations on businesspersons to operate at levels above that required by law. **Figure 2** depicts statements that help characterize ethical responsibilities. The figure also summarizes philanthropic responsibilities, discussed next.

Philanthropic Responsibilities

Philanthropy encompasses those corporate actions that are in response to society's expectation that businesses be good corporate citizens. This includes actively engaging in acts or programs to promote human welfare or goodwill. Examples of philanthropy include business contributions of financial resources or executive time, such as contributions to the arts, education, or the community. A loaned-executive program that provides leadership for a community's United Way campaign is one illustration of philanthropy.

The distinguishing feature between philanthropic and ethical responsibilities is that the former are not expected in an ethical or moral sense. Communities desire firms to contribute their money, facilities, and employee time to humanitarian programs or purposes, but they do not regard the firms as unethical if they do not provide the desired level. Therefore, philanthropy is more discretionary or voluntary on the part of businesses even though there is always the societal expectation that businesses provide it.

One notable reason for making the distinction between philanthropic and ethical responsibilities is that some firms feel they are being socially responsible if they are just good citizens in the community. This distinction brings home the vital point that CSR includes philanthropic contributions but is not limited to them. In fact, it would be argued here that philanthropy is highly desired and prized but actually less important than the other three categories of social responsibility. In a sense, philanthropy is icing on the cake—or on the pyramid, using our metaphor.

The pyramid of corporate social responsibility is depicted in **Figure 3**. It portrays the four components of CSR, beginning with the basic building block notion that economic performance undergirds all else. At the same time, business is expected to obey the law because the law is society's codification of acceptable and unacceptable behavior. Next is business's responsibility to be ethical. At its most fundamental level, this is the obligation to do what is right, just, and fair, and to avoid or minimize harm to stakeholders (employees, consumers, the environment, and others). Finally, business is expected to be a good corporate citizen. This is captured in the philanthropic responsibility, wherein business is expected to contribute financial and human resources to the community and to improve the quality of life.

No metaphor is perfect, and the CSR pyramid is no exception. It is intended to portray that the total CSR of business comprises distinct components that, taken together, constitute the whole. Though the components have been treated as separate concepts for discussion purposes, they are not mutually exclusive and are not intended to juxtapose a firm's economic responsibilities with its other responsibilities. At the same time, a consideration of the separate components helps the manager see that the different types of obligations are in a constant but dynamic tension with one another. The most critical tensions, of course, would be between economic and legal, economic and ethical, and economic and philanthropic. The traditionalist might see this as a conflict between a firm's "concern for profits" versus its "concern for society," but it is suggested here that this is an oversimplification. A CSR or stakeholder perspective would recognize these tensions as organizational realities, but focus on the total pyramid as a unified whole and how the firm might engage in decisions, actions, and programs that simultaneously fulfill all its component parts.

In summary, the total corporate social responsibility of business entails the simultaneous fulfillment of the firm's economic, legal, ethical, and philanthropic responsibilities. Stated in more pragmatic and managerial terms, the CSR firm should strive to make a profit, obey the law, be ethical, and be a good corporate citizen.

Upon first glance, this array of responsibilities may seem broad. They seem to be in striking contrast to the classical economic argument that management has one responsibility: to maximize the profits of its owners or shareholders. Economist Milton Friedman, the most outspoken proponent of this view, has argued that social matters are not the concern of business people and that these problems should be resolved by the unfettered workings of the free market system. Friedman's argument loses some of its punch, however, when you consider his assertion in its totality. Friedman posited that management is "to make as much money as possible while conforming to the basic rules of society, both those embodied in the law and those embodied in ethical custom" (Friedman 1970). Most people focus on the first part of Friedman's quote but not the second part. It seems clear from this statement that profits, conformity to the law, and ethical custom embrace three components of the CSR pyramid—economic, legal, and ethical. That only leaves the philanthropic component for Friedman to reject. Although it may be appropriate for an economist to take this view, one would not encounter many business executives today who exclude philanthropic programs from their firms' range of activities. It seems the role of corporate

Figure 4
Stakeholder/Responsibility Matrix

Stakeholders	Economic	Legal	Ethical	Philanthropic
		Types of CSR		
Owners				
Customers				
Employees				
Community				
Competitors				
Suppliers				
Social Activist Groups				
Public at Large				
Others				

citizenship is one that business has no significant problem embracing. Undoubtedly this perspective is rationalized under the rubric of enlightened self interest.

We next propose a conceptual framework to assist the manager in integrating the four CSR components with organizational stakeholders.

CSR AND ORGANIZATIONAL STAKEHOLDERS

There is a natural fit between the idea of corporate social responsibility and an organization's stakeholders. The word "social" in CSR has always been vague and lacking in specific direction as to whom the corporation is responsible. The concept of stakeholder personalizes social or societal responsibilities by delineating the specific groups or persons business should consider in its CSR orientation. Thus, the stakeholder nomenclature puts "names and faces" on the societal members who are most urgent to business, and to whom it must be responsive.

By now most executives understand that the term "stakeholder" constitutes a play on the word stockholder and is intended to more appropriately describe those groups or persons who have a stake, a claim, or an interest in the operations and decisions of the firm. Sometimes the stake might represent a legal claim, such as that which might be held by an owner, an employee, or a customer who has an explicit or implicit contract. Other times it might be represented by a moral claim, such as when these groups assert a right to be treated fairly or with due process, or to have

their opinions taken into consideration in an important business decision.

Management's challenge is to decide which stakeholders merit and receive consideration in the decision-making process. In any given instance, there may be numerous stakeholder groups (shareholders, consumers, employees, suppliers, community, social activist groups) clamoring for management's attention. How do managers sort out the urgency or importance of the various stakeholder claims? Two vital criteria include the stakeholders' legitimacy and their power. From a CSR perspective their legitimacy may be most important. From a management efficiency perspective, their power might be of central influence. Legitimacy refers to the extent to which a group has a justifiable right to be making its claim. For example, a group of 300 employees about to be laid off by a plant-closing decision has a more legitimate claim on management's attention than the local chamber of commerce, which is worried about losing the firm as one of its dues-paying members. The stakeholder's power is another factor. Here we may witness significant differences. Thousands of small, individual investors, for example, wield very little power unless they can find a way to get organized. By contrast, institutional investors and large mutual fund groups have significant power over management because of the sheer magnitude of their investments and the fact that they are organized.

With these perspectives in mind, let us think of stakeholder management as a process by which managers reconcile their own objectives with the claims and expectations being made on them by various stakeholder groups. The challenge of stakeholder management is to ensure that the firm's primary stakeholders achieve their objectives while other stakeholders are also satisfied. Even though this "win-win" outcome is not always possible, it does represent a legitimate and desirable goal for management to pursue to protect its long-term interests.

The important functions of stakeholder management are to describe, understand, analyze, and finally, manage. Thus, five major questions might be posed to capture the essential ingredients we need for stakeholder management:

1. Who are our stakeholders?
2. What are their stakes?
3. What opportunities and challenges are presented by our stakeholders?
4. What corporate social responsibilities (economic, legal, ethical, and philanthropic) do we have to our stakeholders?
5. What strategies, actions, or decisions should we take to best deal with these responsibilities?

Whereas much could be discussed about each of these questions, let us direct our attention here to question four—what kinds of social responsibilities do we have to our stakeholders? Our objective here is to present a conceptual approach for examining these issues. This conceptual approach or framework is presented as the stakeholder/responsibility matrix in **Figure 4**.

This matrix is intended to be used as an analytical tool or template to organize a manager's thoughts and ideas about what the firm ought to be doing in an economic, legal, ethical, and philanthropic sense with respect to its identified stakeholder groups. By carefully and deliberately moving through the various cells of the matrix, the manager may develop a significant descriptive and analytical data base that can then be used for purposes of stakeholder management. The information resulting from this stakeholder/responsibility analysis should be useful when developing priorities and making both long-term and short-term decisions involving multiple stakeholder's interests.

To be sure, thinking in stakeholder-responsibility terms increases the complexity of decision making and may be extremely time consuming and taxing, especially at first. Despite its complexity, however, this approach is one methodology management can use to integrate values—what it stands for—with the traditional economic mission of the organization. In the final analysis, such an integration could be of significant usefulness to management. This is because the stakeholder/responsibility perspective is most consistent with the pluralistic environment faced by business today. As such, it provides the opportunity for an in-depth corporate appraisal of financial

as well as social and economic concerns. Thus, the stakeholder/responsibility perspective would be an invaluable foundation for responding to the fifth stakeholder management question about strategies, actions, or decisions that should be pursued to effectively respond to the environment business faces.

MORAL MANAGEMENT AND STAKEHOLDERS

At this juncture we would like to expound upon the link between the firm's ethical responsibilities or perspectives and its major stakeholder groups. Here we are isolating the ethical component of our CSR pyramid and discussing it more thoroughly in the context of stakeholders. One way to do this would be to use major ethical principles such as those of justice, rights, and utilitarianism to identify and describe our ethical responsibilities. We will take another alternative, however, and discuss stakeholders within the context of three major ethical approaches—immoral management, amoral management, and moral management. These three ethical approaches were defined and discussed in an earlier *Business Horizons* article (Carroll 1987). We will briefly describe and review these three ethical types and then suggest how they might be oriented toward the major stakeholder groups. Our goal is to profile the likely orientation of the three ethical types with a special emphasis upon moral management, our preferred ethical approach.

Three Moral Types

If we accept that the terms ethics and morality are essentially synonymous in the organizational context, we may speak of immoral, amoral, and moral management as descriptive categories of three different kinds of managers. Immoral management is characterized by those managers whose decisions, actions, and behavior suggest an active opposition to what is deemed right or ethical. Decisions by immoral managers are discordant with accepted ethical principles and, indeed, imply an active negation of what is moral. These managers care only about their or their organization's profitability and success. They see legal standards as barriers or impediments management must overcome to accomplish what it wants. Their strategy is to exploit opportunities for personal or corporate gain.

An example might be helpful. Many observers would argue that Charles Keating could be described as an immoral manager. According to the federal government, Keating recklessly and fraudulently ran California's Lincoln Savings into the ground, reaping $34 million for himself and his family. A major accounting firm said about Keating: "Seldom in our experience as accountants have we experienced a more egregious

Figure 5
Three Moral Types and Orientation Toward
Stakeholder Groups: Owners and Employees

Type of Management	*Orientation Toward Owner/Shareholder Stakeholders*
Immoral Management	Shareholders are minimally treated and given short shrift. Focus is on maximizing positions of executive groups—maximizing executive compensation, perks, benefits. Golden parachutes are more important than returns to shareholders. Managers maximize their positions without shareholders being made aware. Concealment from shareholders is the operating procedure. Self-interest of management group is the order of the day.
Amoral Management	No special thought is given to shareholders; they are there and must be minimally accommodated. Profit focus of the business is their reward. No thought is given to ethical consequences of decisions for any stakeholder group, including owners. Communication is limited to that required by law.
Moral Management	Shareholders' interest (short- and long-term) is a central factor. The best way to be ethical to shareholders is to treat all stakeholder claimants in a fair and ethical manner. To protect shareholders, an ethics committee of the board is created. Code of ethics is established, promulgated, and made a living document to protect shareholders' and others' interests.

Type of Management	*Orientation Toward Employee Stakeholders*
Immoral Management	Employees are viewed as factors of production to be used, exploited, manipulated for gain of individual manager or company. No concern is shown for employees' needs/rights/expectations. Short-term focus. Coercive, controlling, alienating.
Amoral Management	Employees are treated as law requires. Attempts to motivate focus on increasing productivity rather than satisfying employees' growing maturity needs. Employees still seen as factors of production but remunerative approach used. Organization sees self-interest in treating employees with minimal respect. Organization structure, pay incentives, rewards all geared toward short- and medium-term productivity.
Moral Management	Employees are a human resource that must be treated with dignity and respect. Goal is to use a leadership style such as consultative/participative that will result in mutual confidence and trust. Commitment is a recurring theme. Employees' rights to due process, privacy, freedom of speech, and safety are maximally considered in all decisions. Management seeks out fair dealings with employees.

example of the misapplication of generally accepted accounting principles" ("Good Timing, Charlie" 1989).

The second major type of management ethics is amoral management. Amoral managers are neither immoral nor moral but are not sensitive to the fact that their everyday business decisions may have deleterious effects on others. These managers lack ethical perception or awareness. That is, they go through their organizational lives not thinking that their actions have an ethical dimension. Or they may just be careless or inattentive to the implications of their actions on stakeholders. These managers may be well intentioned, but do not see that their business decisions and actions may be hurting those with whom they transact business or interact. Typically their orientation is towards the letter of the law as their ethical guide. We have been describing a sub-category of amorality known as unintentional amoral managers. There is also another group we may call intentional amoral managers. These managers simply think that ethical considerations are for our private lives, not for business. They believe that business activity resides outside the sphere to which moral judgments apply. Though most amoral managers today are unintentional, there may still exist a few who just do not see a role for ethics in business.

Examples of unintentional amorality abound.

Figure 6
Three Moral Types and Orientation Toward
Stakeholder Groups: Customers and Local Community

Type of Management	Orientation Toward Customer Stakeholders
Immoral Management	Customers are viewed as opportunities to be exploited for personal or organizational gain. Ethical standards in dealings do not prevail; indeed, an active intent to cheat, deceive, and/or mislead is present. In all marketing decisions—advertising, pricing, packaging, distribution—customer is taken advantage of to the fullest extent.
Amoral Management	Management does not think through the ethical consequences of its decisions and actions. It simply makes decisions with profitability within the letter of the law as a guide. Management is not focused on what is fair from perspective of customer. Focus is on management's rights. No consideration is given to ethical implications of interactions with customers.
Moral Management	Customer is viewed as equal partner in transaction. Customer brings needs/expectations to the exchange transaction and is treated fairly. Managerial focus is on giving customer fair value, full information, fair guarantee, and satisfaction. Consumer rights are liberally interpreted and honored.

Type of Management	Orientation Toward Local Community Stakeholders
Immoral Management	Exploits community to fullest extent; pollutes the environment. Plant or business closings take fullest advantage of community. Actively disregards community needs. Takes fullest advantage of community resources without giving anything in return. Violates zoning and other ordinances whenever it can for its own advantage.
Amoral Management	Does not take community or its resources into account in management decision making. Community factors are assumed to be irrelevant to business decisions. Community, like employees, is a factor of production. Legal considerations are followed, but nothing more. Deals minimally with community, its people, community activity, local government.
Moral Management	Sees vital community as a goal to be actively pursued. Seeks to be a leading citizen and to motivate others to do likewise. Gets actively involved and helps institutions that need help—schools, recreational groups, philanthropic groups. Leadership position in environment, education, culture/arts, volunteerism, and general community affairs. Firm engages in strategic philanthropy. Management sees community goals and company goals as mutually interdependent.

When police departments stipulated that applicants must be 5'10" and weigh 180 pounds to qualify for positions, they just did not think about the adverse impact their policy would have on women and some ethnic groups who, on average, do not attain that height and weight. The liquor, beer, and cigarette industries provide other examples. They did not anticipate that their products would create serious moral issues: alcoholism, drunk driving deaths, lung cancer, deteriorating health, and offensive secondary smoke. Finally, when McDonald's initially decided to use polystyrene containers for food packaging it just did not adequately consider the environmental impact that would be caused. McDonald's surely does not intentionally create a solid waste disposal problem, but one major consequence of its business is just that. Fortunately, the company has responded to complaints by replacing the polystyrene packaging with paper products.

Moral management is our third ethical approach, one that should provide a striking contrast. In moral management, ethical norms that adhere to a high standard of right behavior are employed. Moral managers not only conform to accepted and high levels of professional conduct, they also commonly exemplify leadership on ethical issues. Moral managers want to be profitable, but only within the confines of sound legal and ethical precepts, such as fairness, justice, and due process. Under this approach, the orientation is toward both the letter and the spirit of the law.

Law is seen as minimal ethical behavior and the preference and goal is to operate well above what the law mandates. Moral managers seek out and use sound ethical principles such as justice, rights, utilitarianism, and the Golden Rule to guide their decisions. When ethical dilemmas arise, moral managers assume a leadership position for their companies and industries.

There are numerous examples of moral management. When IBM took the lead and developed its Open Door policy to provide a mechanism through which employees might pursue their due process rights, this could be considered moral management. Similarly, when IBM initiated its Four Principles of Privacy to protect privacy rights of employees, this was moral management. When McCullough Corporation withdrew from the Chain Saw Manufacturers Association because the association fought mandatory safety standards for the industry, this was moral management. McCullough knew its product was potentially dangerous and had used chain brakes on its own saws for years, even though it was not required by law to do so. Another example of moral management was when Maguire Thomas Partners, a Los Angeles commercial developer, helped solve urban problems by saving and refurbishing historic sites, putting up structures that matched old ones, limiting building heights to less than the law allowed, and using only two-thirds of the allowable building density so that open spaces could be provided.

Orientation Toward Stakeholders

Now that we have a basic understanding of the three ethical types or approaches, we will propose profiles of what the likely stakeholder orientation might be toward the major stakeholder groups using each of the three ethical approaches. Our goal is to accentuate the moral management approach by contrasting it with the other two types.

Basically, there are five major stakeholder groups that are recognized as priorities by most firms, across industry lines and in spite of size or location: owners (shareholders), employees, customers, local communities, and the society-at-large. Although the general ethical obligation to each of these groups is essentially identical (protect their rights, treat them with respect and fairness), specific behaviors and orientations arise because of the differing nature of the groups. In an attempt to flesh out the character and salient features of the three ethical types and their stakeholder orientations, **Figures 5** and **6** summarize the orientations these three types might assume with respect to four of the major stakeholder groups. Because of space constraints and the general nature of the society-at-large category, it has been omitted.

By carefully considering the described stakeholder orientations under each of the three ethical types, a richer appreciation of the moral management approach should be possible. Our goal here is to gain a fuller understanding of what it means to engage in moral management and what this implies for interacting with stakeholders. To be sure, there are other stakeholder groups to which moral management should be directed, but again, space precludes their discussion here. This might include thinking of managers and non-managers as distinct categories of employees and would also embrace such groups as suppliers, competitors, special interest groups, government, and the media.

Though the concept of corporate social responsibility may from time to time be supplanted by various other focuses such as social responsiveness, social performance, public policy, ethics, or stakeholder management, an underlying challenge for all is to define the kinds of responsibilities management and businesses have to the constituency groups with which they transact and interact most frequently. The pyramid of corporate social responsibility gives us a framework for understanding the evolving nature of the firm's economic, legal, ethical, and philanthropic performance. The implementation of these responsibilities may vary depending upon the firm's size, management's philosophy, corporate strategy, industry characteristics, the state of the economy, and other such mitigating conditions, but the four component parts provide management with a skeletal outline of the nature and kinds of their CSR. In frank, action-oriented terms, business is called upon to: be profitable, obey the law, be ethical, and be a good corporate citizen.

The stakeholder management perspective provides not only a language and way to personalize relationships with names and faces, but also some useful conceptual and analytical concepts for diagnosing, analyzing, and prioritizing an organization's relationships and strategies. Effective organizations will progress beyond stakeholder identification and question what opportunities and threats are posed by stakeholders; what economic, legal, ethical, and philanthropic responsibilities they have; and what strategies, actions or decisions should be pursued to most effectively address these responsibilities. The stakeholder/responsibility matrix provides a template management might use to organize its analysis and decision making.

Throughout the article we have been building toward the notion of an improved ethical organizational climate as manifested by moral management. Moral management was defined and described through a contrast with immoral and amoral management. Because the business landscape is replete with immoral and amoral managers, moral managers may sometimes be hard to find. Regardless, their characteristics have been identified and, most important, their perspective or orientation towards the major stakeholder groups has been profiled. These stakeholder orientation profiles give managers a conceptual but practical touchstone for sorting out the different categories or types of ethical (or not-so-ethical) behavior that may be found in business and other organizations.

It has often been said that leadership by example is the most effective way to improve business ethics. If that is true, moral management provides a model leadership perspective or orientation that managers may wish to emulate. One great fear is that managers may think they are providing ethical leadership just by rejecting immoral management. However, amoral management, particularly the unintentional variety, may unconsciously prevail if managers are not aware of what it is and of its dangers. At best, amorality represents ethical neutrality, and this notion is not tenable in the society of the 1990s. The standard must be set high, and moral management provides the best exemplar of what that lofty standard might embrace. Further, moral management, to be fully appreciated, needs to be seen within the context of organization-stakeholder relationships. It is toward this singular goal that our entire discussion has focused. If the "good society" is to become a realization, such a high expectation only naturally becomes the aspiration and preoccupation of management.

References

R.W. Ackerman and R.A. Bauer, *Corporate Social Responsiveness* (Reston, Va.: Reston Publishing Co, 1976).

A.B. Carroll, "A Three-Dimensional Conceptual Model of Corporate Social Performance," *Academy of Management Review*, 4, 4 (1979): 497-505.

A.B. Carroll, "In Search of the Moral Manager," *Business Horizons*, March-April 1987, pp. 7-15.

Committee for Economic Development, *Social Responsibilities of Business Corporations* (New York: CED, 1971).

K. Davis, "Can Business Afford to Ignore its Social Responsibilities?" *California Management Review*, 2, 3 (1960): 70-76.

R. Eells and C. Walton, *Conceptual Foundations of Business* (Homewood, Ill.: Richard D. Irwin, 1961).

"Good Timing, Charlie," *Forbes*, November 27, 1989, pp. 140-144.

W.C. Frederick, "From CSR_1 to CSR_2: The Maturing of Business and Society Thought," University of Pittsburgh Working Paper No. 279, 1978.

M. Friedman, "The Social Responsibility of Business Is to Increase its Profits," *New York Times*, September 13, 1970, pp. 122-126.

S.P. Sethi, "Dimensions of Corporate Social Responsibility," *California Management Review*, 17, 3 (1975): 58-64.

Another View of the Golden Rule

Joseph L. Mancusi

Joseph L. Mancusi, Ph.D., is president of the Center for Organizational Excellence located in Alexandria, Va.

As a psychologist and motivational speaker, I try to draw the audience into the emotional side of issues quickly. To do this, at the start of a talk I often imitate one of 30 different accents I have perfected over the years. They are not accents of groups but accents of individuals who have taught me something and individuals I respect.

Strange things happen. Whether I use a southern accent in Southern California or a Pakistani accent in Pittsburgh, the audience rejects the introduction they have just heard. Their faces reveal their thoughts, "Something is wrong. We didn't pay to hear this."

The audience discounts what I have to say because the accent doesn't fit their concept of a psychologist. We all do this every day. When faced with information that does not agree with our expectations or biases, we quickly explain away the accomplishments of the individual as a special case. We lose the individual in the stereotype of the group.

Cultural diversity can be a terrible concept the way it is often applied to the work force. The terms Hispanic, Asian and African-American are legal, political terms; but they are often detrimental to meeting the needs and opportunities that individuals provide. There are more differences between three Asians from Thailand, Taiwan

> T he audience discounts what I have to say because the accent doesn't fit.
>
> ■

and Korea; or three Hispanics from Cuba, Puerto Rico and Mexico; or three African-Americans from rural Mississippi, Los Angeles and Haiti than there are between a Caucasian, an African-American and an Oriental all born in New York's Little Italy.

In managing a group of individuals, with the best of intentions we apply the Golden Rule: Do Unto Others As You Would Have Them Do Unto You. In a culturally diverse organization, this is a shortsighted, sometimes insensitive, mistake. We need the Mancusi Platinum Rule: Do Unto Others As They Would Like To Have It Done Unto Themselves. When we put the individual first, we communicate with the cultural nuances needed to understand each employee.

The Golden Rule gets us into trouble in culturally diverse organizations; several examples come to mind. The Edsel was designed by people using the Golden Rule. A radical, large car that guzzles gas and needs constant

repair is useful if you have a large garage, plenty of money and a "stay-at-home-wife" who can take it in to be fixed. This was true of Ford executives, not American consumers.

To improve reading skills among the African-American work force, a hospital financed a speed reading course for employees. Of the 12 people who showed up, only one was an African-American. Moreover, the average educational level of the students was six years of college! The real problem was that many of the employees, regardless of race, were functionally illiterate. Many were unmotivated or did not know the benefits of a reading course. The hospital supervisors failed to provide the needed coaching and counseling to get them to attend the reading course. The supervisors were uncomfortable approaching employees of a different race. As a result, the speed reading course was essentially useless for the target audience.

An insurance company looked into the effectiveness of its Equal Employment Opportunity (EEO) programs. They discovered that new Asian agents sold the most insurance, followed by white agents, then Black agents. Management's erroneous conclusion was that the Asians didn't need any help because they out sold every other agent group. Wrong.

In the same company, however, actuaries were in short supply; and it was very costly—up to $30,000—to recruit each mid-range to high-level actuary. Asian actuaries were often very effective at the lower-level jobs. Most of the Asian applicants had superior math skills. However, Asian

Reprinted with permission from *HRMagazine* (formerly *Personnel Administrator*), Vol. 36, No. 4, April 1991, pp. 104, 102. *HRMagazine,* published by The Society for Human Resource Management, Alexandria, VA.

employees soon hit a glass ceiling. Many had poor communication skills and subsequently, did not instill confidence in customers over the phone, a needed skill in higher-level jobs.

The solution seemed simple: provide language and speech courses to help the Asian actuaries become "accent free" on the telephone. This would certainly be a cheaper, more sensible program, rather than paying $30,000-plus to recruit from outside the company. But, the company refused to suggest it because they were afraid of being labled unfair, prejudiced or culturally insensitive by members of the Asian community.

Another problem with cultural diversity is that we allow the behaviors and desires of some individuals to speak for an entire community of people. Sensitivity must be to individuals—not to groups—because groups are far too diverse. Group leaders should not be the judges of what is right for each of us, or they become dictators to all of us.

The real issues of cultural diversity are fairness, equity, opportunity and enrichment. The workplace is the repository of many good and bad aspects of society. To be successful companies must meet individual needs in the work force where society in general has failed.

But, should we divide the work force into men and women, white and blacks, Asians and disabled and others? A better way to handle cultural diversity issues is to assume that everyone in your organization is in a cultural group of one.

Needs assessments, training programs, motivation, communication and advancement should be tailored to each individual. Not blindly applied in some across the board attempt at fairness. This means that supervisors and managers must be rewarded on the basis of how well they develop all people and how well they meet individual needs, not by how well they meet goals and quotas. And, it means that sensitivities and communication must flow both ways.

The advantage of an effective culturally-diverse company is that multiple talents can be used to solve complex problems. Customer sensitivities and needs can be met. New sources of recruitment located. World markets opened. Relationships and respect strengthened. Satisfaction and loyalty to the company encouraged.

In the process, all of us are uplifted. True fairness flows from meeting the individual's needs and from creating a corporate vision that looks for excellence in relationships and teamwork, not only in service and product.

Some important advantages of doing business in the United States are that women can and do compete successfully, that people from other countries make their contributions, that people of color can achieve positions of leadership based on talent and accomplishment. For all of our diversity and even division, we are still freer and more open than countries where people of different religions, different ethnic groups and different languages literally take arms against each other and must be separated by troops.

Organizations must become culturally diverse. We do not have the luxury of eliminating half the work force from the problems we need to solve.

In truth, we are all people of color, sex and accent. What we do to others can hurt each of us, unless we follow the Mancusi Platinum Rule: Do Unto Others As They Would Like It Done Unto Themselves.

Is Business Waking Up?

CRAIG COX

10 Trends Toward Social Responsibility for the Nineties

IF THE TERMS life-cycle analysis, giraffes, stakeholder management, and the vigilante consumer sound new to you, 1992 promises to expand your vocabulary—and perhaps change the way you do business. For behind these words lies a collection of trends that are reshaping American business.

Some of these developments have been inspired by political events, others by market forces and demographic changes. All signal a change in the way we think about jobs, government, ethics, and the role business should play in our society.

Will each of these trends pan out the way we think they will? Our powers of prognostication are formidable, especially considering the piles of clips, books, notes, and interviews from which they were generated. But ultimately, American business will go where businesspeople like you steer it. And if these trends are any indication, you've got a pretty good idea where you want to go: toward a more responsive, responsible, humane, and environmentally sensitive workplace.

1.

THE PURSUIT OF HAPPINESS

TWENTY-FIVE YEARS after young baby boomers were first called on to drop out of society in the sixties, a significant portion of them have in fact decided to leave the rat race behind. We're not seeing a bunch of Timothy Leary wannabes, however. We're seeing well-educated, talented individuals "cashing out"—taking their hard-earned dollars and climbing down from the corporate ladder for a more satisfying existence.

Money is still important, of course, but time (especially for family life) and freedom are dominating this new lifestyle. Fully 25 million Americans now work at home part-time or full-time, according to one survey, and entrepreneurial activity by these seekers of the good life is at an all-time high. "The wave of new entrepreneurs that appeared in the United States during the 1970s and 1980s is just the leading edge of a much broader trend," futurists Marvin Cetron and Owen Davies tell us.

To avoid losing this valuable talent, companies are offering more flexible schedules, telecommuting opportunities, and other ways for employees to recharge their batteries when energy reserves run low. For example, sabbaticals are increasingly popular elements of company benefit packages. At Convergent Technologies, five-year veterans can get thirteen weeks of Personal Growth Leave with full pay and benefits. Both Wells Fargo and Xerox offer Social Service Leave Programs (with full pay and benefits, for six months to a year) to selected employees who have put in more than three years of service. We at *Business Ethics* believe the trend toward the Pursuit of Happiness is so significant, we've added a column of the same name, beginning this issue.

2.

THE GREENING OF THE CORPORATION

IN THE WAKE OF BHOPAL, the Exxon Valdez oil spill, and Earth Day 1990, it's not surprising to find business becoming more sensitive to environmental concerns. It's also

Reprinted by permission of *Business Ethics*, January/February 1992, pp. 20-22. *Business Ethics*, The Magazine of Socially Responsible Business.

not surprising to find more than a smidgen of skepticism greeting this new corporate posture. And, while we readily acknowledge that much of this new sensitivity is little more than a public relations ploy, there are reasons to applaud. The Responsible Care Initiative launched by the Chemical Manufacturer's Association—an environmental program endorsed by all 185 members—shows great promise, as does the famous Monsanto Pledge to cut toxic air emissions by 90 percent by 1992. The Valdez Principles have also gone a long way toward forcing companies to rethink their priorities. And Green Cross's life-cycle assessments are helping businesses rethink not simply their manufacturing byproducts, but the waste management consequences of their products as well.

Large and small corporations like Exxon, Union Carbide, Walt Disney, and Patagonia have created a new position—vice president of the environment—to help keep ecological issues on the corporate agenda. And Bell Atlantic, General Electric, Dow Chemical, and others have taken it a step further, creating community advisory panels at many facilities, designed to maintain a dialogue between companies and their neighbors. What's great about the green trend is that any company can get involved—and can start small. Recycling paper and office supplies, printing letterhead on recycled paper, and using energy-efficient light bulbs are great first steps. Every little bit helps.

3.
THE "GIRAFFE" STANDS UP

INDIVIDUALS CAN MAKE A DIFFERENCE simply by sticking their necks out for the common good, as The Giraffe Project says. This notion is being played out all over the country by executives, entrepreneurs, managers, and assembly-line workers who are donating their time and skills to help the underprivileged. Say what you will about President Bush's "Thousand Points of Light," volunteerism is at an all-time high, and trendwatcher extraordinaire Faith Popcorn reports in her new book, *The Popcorn Report,* that there is a new surge of altruism afoot nationwide.

Take one example: After industrialist Eugene Lang "adopted" an entire sixth-grade class in Harlem—promising to pay college tuition for those who stayed in school—literally dozens of executives followed suit, stepping forward to personally mentor classes of underprivileged youth. Lang's I Have A Dream Foundation today has more than 140 projects nationwide, not to mention the Midnight Basketball Leagues springing up in Atlanta, Baltimore, and Chicago, where business leaders sponsor teams that get gang members off streets. Or hundreds of adopt-a-school programs run by business leaders.

Individuals want to make a difference. And companies that encourage this through mentoring programs, educational initiatives, and other community connections not only reap goodwill from employees and the public, they also help build a saner society within which to do business. The giraffes win too, of course, by being a part of something bigger than themselves.

4.
SWORDS INTO PLOWSHARES

WITH THE RATHER DRAMATIC exception of that little geopolitical tussle in the Persian Gulf last year, and, yeah, civil war in Yugoslavia, and what they like to call "ethnic strife" in various parts around the globe, uh, you might say that peace has broken out all over. At least the Cold War is over, and whether or not we get a peace dividend, the break-up of the Soviet Union and the Warsaw Pact will surely change the way the mammoth defense industry does business. President Bush's announcement last September that he wanted to cut $20 billion from the defense budget sent shock waves through an already ailing industry and signaled the beginning of a major shakeout among weapons manufacturers.

We're not going to see wholesale peace conversion any time soon, but there is some evidence that defense contractors are trying to dump their more unprofitable divisions. The question is whether anyone will want to pick them up. Unisys reported not long ago that it was unable to find a buyer for its Paramax unit and was undertaking a $500 million public offering instead. Then, in late November, CEO James Unruh withdrew the offering altogether to avoid having to sell, as he put it, "at 'fire sale' prices." Analysts say we shouldn't be surprised to see some mergers in the near future, as times get tougher. And Wall Street is increasingly finding defense stocks out of favor. The defense industry isn't going to go away, but the message that government is sending should be fairly clear: diversify.

5.
MARKETING THE GOOD CAUSE

SMALL, ALTERNATIVE-MINDED companies first started crowing about their political correctness in the sixties, but only now has cause-related marketing reached the mainstream. Environmental packaging is one pretty obvious example, with trash bag companies falling over one another in recent years to proclaim their product the most biodegradably correct. Now we've got Burger King putting their burgers in brown bags made from recycled paper, and letting people

know they're doing everything they can to save the rainforests. Avis sells us rental car service by telling us it's better to do business with an owner (the company is worker-owned). Ashland Oil gives us charming TV vignettes about its scholarship programs. McDonald's lets us know they don't mind hiring mentally retarded workers. And everybody seems to be a sponsor of the Olympics.

One of the most sincere examples of cause-related marketing, though, is the Body Shop, a British cosmetic company whose socially responsible practices (environmentally sound packaging, natural ingredients, no animal testing) have turned the cosmetics industry on its well-powdered ear. In response to the Body Shop's great performance ($378 million in sales in 1990), the venerable Esteé Lauder has introduced its own socially responsible product line, Origins Natural Resources, complete with minimal packaging, natural ingredients, and a plan to donate part of the profits to charity. Good practices are catching on.

6.
IT'S A FAMILY AFFAIR

IT HAS TAKEN AWHILE, but American business has begun to figure out that the old nuclear family is about as common these days as a five-cent cigar. And to their credit, many companies have responded with family-friendly policies, such as flextime, on-site child care centers, elder care arrangements, parental leave, and telecommuting. Kodak and Bausch & Lomb last summer even opened a day camp for employees' kids.

The reasons should be abundantly clear. Women now make up more than half of the country's workforce, and with the baby boomlet of the eighties still in diapers, companies need to adapt—or suffer lagging productivity from the moms (and sometimes even dads) in their workforce. Child care remains the biggest issue for young families, so look for caring companies to put together joint ventures, such as the one IBM, American Express, Allstate, and two smaller companies are pursuing in Charlotte, North Carolina. The $2 million, 194-child facility exceeds state standards and can be used by employees as well as the public. "As long as (the center) supports an increase in the quality of care, we're willing to support it," an IBM official told *The Wall Street Journal.* Watch for the sentiment to spread.

7.
BUSINESS AS THE CONSUMER'S KEEPER

THE AGE OF REAGANOMICS is over. Just ask George Bush. Or read the newspapers. What you'll find is Congress and legislatures and the courts moving quickly to fill the regulatory vacuum left by a decade of unbridled capitalism. The new Clean Air Act, the Americans with Disabilities Act, the 1990 Nutritional Labeling and Education Act, new rules on TV advertising to kids, as well as precedent-setting product liability cases clogging up the courts tell us that deregulation is a thing of the past.

Businesses are already responding by creating visible, and (mostly) accountable codes of conduct. The Valdez Principles, the Responsible Care Initiative, and the BENS Principles for weapons exporters are the first of what promises to be a long line of conduct codes drafted to beat the regulators to the punch. Expect to see much closer cooperation between industry and government in the years to come, as well. The old adversarial relationships didn't work before, and they won't work now.

8.
THE COOPERATIVE WORKPLACE

WITH AMERICAN BUSINESS likely to face a skilled-labor shortage in the next decade, and with new generations of workers less inclined to be old-style "organization men," the trend toward more open-minded management is here to stay. Companies are finding it's much cheaper (not to mention more pleasant) to keep workers happy than to hire and train replacements. They're also finding that to really succeed with "quality" programs, management and labor need to cooperate more closely than ever before to achieve their mutual goal: Customer satisfaction. At more and more companies, participatory management today is flattening the hierarchy, and many companies are expanding opportunities for employee ownership and "stakeholder" (everyone with a stake in the company) management.

Diversity is another watchword for the nineties, as companies cope with the challenges of a workforce that is not only multicultural, but features more women, and a more visible gay and lesbian population. A handful of innovative employers, the most recent of which was Lotus, have extended spousal benefits to partners of gay and lesbian employees. And companies like Digital are taking the lead on "valuing differences" of all sorts among employees. Such programs, said Lotus officials, are only fair. In the coming years, progressive policies like these will be more than fair, they'll be fairly common.

9.
IN US YOU CAN TRUST

WE ARE ENTERING the age of what Faith Popcorn calls the "vigilante consumer," an era in which doing business will have more to do with building relationships than marketing products. At the core of this relationship-building is trust. The public wants to know what's in a product, how it was tested, who produced it, and under what working conditions. They even want to know where the package will go once it's been discarded. If the savings-and-loan bailout is teaching American consumers anything, it is that trustworthiness can no longer be assumed.

As one gesture of good faith, more and more companies are folding up the Golden Parachutes that enabled laid-off executives to walk away with millions. Other companies are introducing service guarantees to match the product guarantees that have long been standard. In the financial services industry, look for banks to start paying attention to their local communities and marketing themselves as "back to the basics" institutions. Toll-free consumer information lines (already a staple on most products) will also become a vital connection between consumers and companies in the years ahead.

10.
HUMANIZING THE MACHINE

THE EXPLOSION OF TECHNOLOGY is well documented, but less explored are the ways in which technology can work toward socially responsible goals. Computer bulletin boards are helping to democratize large corporations by allowing any employee to send a message to the CEO. New telephone technology will help consumers block access to unwanted callers. And, in a recent *Wall Street Journal* article, George Melloan argues that "the communications revolution soon will spread to millions more people, making them richer, freer, and better informed."

Cellular phone systems, for instance, can be set up in much less time than landline systems, he notes. And the cost of an earth-to-satellite connection has dropped in the last five years from $500,000 to only $150,000. That means wider access to the global marketplace and expanded opportunities for responsible trade. It also promises to have political implications. Soviet dissidents reportedly employed faxes and modems to maintain contact during the darker days of resistance.

Here at home, technology has already given workers more freedom by allowing telecommuting arrangements, and has made them more efficient by increasing access to computers and fax machines. The most innovative companies are riding the crest of this wave of technological advances, keeping an eye toward humanizing the workplace—and the marketplace.

"I CAN NEVER THINK of the future," Albert Einstein once said. "It comes soon enough." Most businesspeople would agree about the speed at which tomorrow approaches, but unfortunately few have the luxury to put it out of their minds. The trends we've described above should give you a sense both of what's here today and what will be arriving tomorrow. Some, we hope, may even provide a path toward appropriate responses.

The rest is up to you.

Index

accountants, advertising by, 177, 178–179, 180
acquisitions, 32
Addams, Jane, 140
Adler, Nancy, 19
advertising, 11, 114; by professionals, 176–181; "slice of death," 182
Aetna Life & Casualty, 134, 135, 137; sexual harassment and, 71–72
affirmative action, 222
African Americans: business and, 43; McDonald's and, 200
AIDS, 53, 155–159; privacy rights scenario and, 56–58
alcoholism, employee assistance programs and, 41–42, 148, 149, 150, 152, 153, 154
Allegheny Bottling, 210
Allied Tech, 93–94
Allstate Insurance, 183
Alltel Mobile Communications, 30
Americans with Disabilities Act of 1990 (ADA), 75–78; workplace privacy and, 53
amoral management, 232, 233, 234–235
anxieties, exploitation of, by marketers, 182–183
Apple Computer, 52
Archer Corporation, 41–42
Aristotle, 19
Asian Americans, in insurance industry, 236–237
Aspin, Les, 211
assertive leadership, green marketing and, 186–187
AT&T, 9, 46, 57, 58, 91–92, 133, 145, 203–204

background check, ethics and, of employees, 48
Backlash: The Undeclared War Against American Women (Faludi), 140
bait-and-switch sales techniques, 33
balanced protection policies, 46–50
Bates v. State Bar of Arizona, 176–181
Bell Telephone, 145
bid rigging, 97, 100
Bird, Frederick, 19
blacks. *See* African Americans
Body Shop, The, 167–168
Boeing, 204
Boesky, Ivan, 32, 33
Boisjoly, Roger, 98–99, 101
bootstrapping, 194–196
bottom-line-mentality, 211
bribery, 26, 33, 96, 111, 112, 165, 171, 222–223
BRK Electronics, 182, 183
Burke, James, 219, 223
Bush, Norm, 149, 150, 151, 152, 153, 154
business schools, study of business ethics by, 224

Call Interactive, 46
"cantaloupe" technology, 204
carbon monoxide detectors, 182
Carpenter, Michelle M., 134, 135
case study method, of ethical education, 7–8, 152–153
categorical imperative, 7, 14–15, 17, 63
cellular phone systems, 240
Challenger disaster, 96, 98–99, 101
Champion International Corporation, 147
Charles Schwab, 61

Chrysler Corporation, 192, 193
Citicorp, 74, 132
Clipper Chip, 52
Coalition for Environmentally Responsible Economies (Ceres) principles, 204
Coca-Cola Inc., 145
codes of ethics, 12, 26, 32, 34, 35, 40–43, 109, 110, 114–115, 116, 220, 221–223
Commonwealth Electric Company, 97, 100
competitive pressures, 33
comprehensive planning for change, layoffs and, 84–90
computers, employee theft and, 59–61
consensus building, in Japanese business, 100
consequences, teleological theory and, 64
consumers, 239–240
Continental Corporation, 133, 134, 136
Control Data Corporation, 172
Corning Inc., 135
corporate ethics codes, 12, 26, 32, 34, 35, 40–43, 109, 110, 114–115, 116, 220, 221–223
corporate ethics test, 40–43
cost/benefit analysis, Ford Pinto and, 191, 192
Cox, Claude, 138
credit bureaus, privacy and, 46
credos, corporate, 217–220, 221, 223
cultural diversity: differences in ethical values and, 42, 170–173; golden rule and, 236–237
Cummins Engine Co., 12, 111

decentralization, ethical consequences of, 25, 27
Decker, Sharon Allred, 134, 137
defamation lawsuits, 91–92
DeGeorge, Richard, 37
Degler, C., 141
Denny's Restaurants, discrimination and, 79–80
dental advertising, 177, 179–180
deontological theory, 63–64
disciplinary policies, written, 47, 48
Disclosure Rule, 14, 15, 16
discrimination: Americans with Disabilities Act and, 75–78; Denny's and racial, 79–80; sex, 82
distributive justice, 12
diversity, work force, 41, 240
Dow Chemical, 202–203
Dow Corning, 111–112, 130, 173
downsizing, 26, 46
Drexel Burnham Lambert, 32
drug testing, of employees, 46, 48, 49, 53, 148–154
Dry Creek Vineyard, 146
Du Pont, 205
due process, right of employee to, 46, 49
Duke Power Co., 134, 137
Dynamic Disposal Inc. (DDI), 128–129

E. F. Hutton, 33, 112
Eells, Richard, 225–226
egoism, 64
electronic mail systems, workplace privacy and, 55
electronic surveillance, of employees, 46, 48, 49
embezzlement, 9, 81–82
Emerson, Ralph Waldo, 25, 26
employee assistance programs (EAPs), 41–42, 148, 149, 150, 152, 153, 154

employee incentive plan scenario, 122–123
employees: computer scan and, 59–61; privacy rights of, 46, 47, 48, 49, 50, 51–55, 56–58, 148, 156, 221, 234; theft by, 9, 46, 49, 59–61, 62–65, 81–82
employment at will, 46, 49, 50; whistleblowing and, 104–105
Energy Star program, of IBM, 203
Engelhard, 137
entertainment, business, 222
environment, 233, 238–239; corporate environmental policies and, 202–205; corporate recycling efforts and, 144–147; green marketing and, 184–190
environmental packaging, 239
Equal Employment Opportunity Commission (EEOC), 73, 236
Equal Pay Act, 73–74
Equifax, 46
Equity Group Inc., 146
espionage, corporate, 33, 222
ethical audit, 109, 110, 111–112, 220
ethical behavior, 208–216
ethical education, case study method of, 7–8, 152–153
ethical relativism, 62–63
Europe, business ethics and, 163, 164, 165, 166, 167–169
Ewing, David, 95, 100

Faludi, S., 140
family-oriented programs, 133–138
fears, exploitation of, by marketers, 182–183
Federal Trade Commission (FTC), 176, 178, 180
Fel-Pro Inc., 133–134, 136, 138
Fidelity Investments, 52
firings. *See* layoffs
First Alert, 182, 183
Foman, Robert, 33
Ford Motor Company, 111, 191, 192, 193
Foreign Corrupt Practices Act (FCPA), 171–173
fraud, 33

G. D. Searle, 97
Gates, William, 52, 134–135
gender bias, 82
gender gap, Equal Pay Act and, in wages, 73–74
General Dynamics, 59, 60, 112
General Electric, 33, 74, 96, 109–110, 132
General Motors, 111, 191, 192–193
gifts: ethical issues in accepting, 11, 111, 220, 221, 222–223; exchange, 170–171
Ginental, Shelley, 148, 149, 150, 151, 152, 153, 154
Giraffe Project, 239
glass ceiling, 141–142
Glidden, David, 38, 39
global management, ethics and, 40
golden rule, 7, 9–10, 14, 15–16, 63–64, 234, 236–237
Golden Turnkey Systems Inc., 146
Gonzalez, Tammy, 60–61
government contract issues, 96, 97, 99–100
green marketing, 184–190
grievance committees, 150
GTE Corporation, 92

H & H Music, 53
Halfin, Mark, 19
Hanna Anderson, 29
Harris v. Forklift Systems, 72
Harris Corporation, 210
health care insurance, 112; employees with AIDS and, 156; workplace privacy and, 53–54
health maintenance organizations (HMOs), 149
health screening, 48
Herman Miller, 203
Hewlett Packard, 112
HIV, 53, 155–159; privacy rights scenario and, 56–58
Hoffman, W. Michael, 37
Hunter v. Allis-Chalmers, 72
Hydraulic Parts and Components Inc., 99–100

Iacocca, Lee, 33, 112
IBM, 34, 114, 203, 221, 222, 223, 234
immoral management, 231, 232, 234–235
"implied employment" contracts, 48, 49
insider trading, 32, 33, 34, 109, 220, 221–222
insurance industry, Asian Americans and, 236–237
integrity, 18–22
intimacy, among co-workers, 82
Intuit, 194
Intuition Ethic, 14–15, 16

J. C. Penney, 9–10
Jackson, Rick, 123
James, William, 24, 101
Japan, 100–101, 170–172; business ethics in, vs. Europe and United States, 163–166
Johnson & Johnson, 31, 112, 126, 133, 218, 223
Johnson, Paul, 57
Josephson, Michael, 36, 37–38, 39
justice, 228, 234; distributive, 12

Kant, Immanuel, 7, 17, 19
Karp, Hank, 37, 38
Keating, Charles, 231–232
Kelley, Jim, 149, 150, 151, 152, 153, 154
kickbacks, 99–100

Lang, Eugene, 239
Lauffenburger, Michael, 60
law, business ethics and, 7
layoffs, 112; comprehensive planning for, 84–90; defamation lawsuits and, 91–92
legal advertising, 176–177, 179, 180
legal components, of corporate social responsibility, 226, 227, 228, 231
legitimacy, 230
Levin, Michael, 36, 37
Levine, Dennis, 32, 33, 34
lie detector tests, for employees, 48, 49, 222
Lockheed Corporation, 172
Loving Choice Baby Products, 182

Madaras, Laura, 146
Mancusi Platinum Rule, 236–237
marketing, 176–181; exploitation of fears in, 182–183; green, 184–190; social responsibility and, 239
Mascotte, John, 133, 134, 136
Masi, Dale, 149, 150, 151, 152, 153, 154

Massachusetts General Hospital, 137–138
MCA, 103
McDonald's Inc., 200–201, 233
McDonnell Douglas, 109, 114–115, 223
McNamara, Robert, 192
ME International, 30
medical advertising, 177, 179–180
mellowing factor, in managers, 10
mergers, 32, 34, 46
Mickens, Ed, 57
microinequalities, 142
Microsoft Corporation, 134–135
Milgram, Stanley, 38
Miller, Edward, 123
minority women, unequal wages of, 73
"mommy track," 141
Monsanto, 205
Monsanto Pledge, 239
moral audit, 126–129
moral management, 231–235
moral reasoning, 114–115
Morton, Thiokol, 98, 101

NASA, 99, 101
Nash, Laura, 224
National Association for the Advancement of Colored People (NAACP), Denny's and, 79–80
National Highway Traffic Safety Administration (NHTSA), 191, 192
NCR Corporation, 134
nepotism, 112, 222
Newton, Lisa, 37, 38, 39
NIBCO Inc., 146
Nissan Motors, 55
non-competition agreement, 48, 49

ombudsman, 12, 47, 48
opportunity pressures, 34
organizational ethics, 12, 47, 48
organizational pressures, ethics and, 33–34
Ortbal, John, 145

PepsiCo Inc., handling of syringe scare by, 120–121
personal values, vs. corporate values, 32–33
Peterson and Sons Winery, 147
philanthropic components, of corporate social responsibility, 227, 228, 229, 231
Picard, Sara, 93–94
Pinkerton Security & Investigation Services, 60–61
Pinto, Ford, 191, 192
place determination, 113
Platinum Rule, Mancusi's, 236–237
Polaroid Corporation, 111, 116
political action committees (PACs), 221
polygraph tests, for employees, 48, 49, 222
Pragmatism (James), 101
preferential treatment, 222
price fixing, 26, 210
price negotiation, 113
Privacy for Consumers and Workers Act, 55
privacy rights, 46, 47, 48, 49, 50, 51–55, 148, 221, 234; HIV and, 56–58, 156
Procter & Gamble, 91, 92, 185
professional ethics, 7, 15, 17
promotion presentation, 113–114
promotions, 82–83

protestant work ethic, business ethics in United States and, 164
PSE&G, 30
psychological egoism, 64
Public Service Co. of Colorado, 92

rationalization, 62–63
Raytheon Corporation, 132
recession, effect of, on ethical behavior, 130–132
reciprocal dealing, 222
recycyling, 144–147
"right to know" laws, 48
Ritz-Carlton Hotels, 30
Rivera, Sam, 136, 138
Roosevelt, Eleanor, 141
Rowe, Mary, 142
rules, deontological theory and, 63–64

sabotage, employee, 59–61
Saturn, 30, 31
Schlafly, Phyllis, 140
Schmidt, David, 38–39
Schwartzkopf, William, 97, 100
Securities and Exchange Commission (SEC), 34, 109
Security Pacific Corporation, 218, 223
self-interest, egoism and, 64
sexism, 82
sexual harassment, 70–72, 96; myths of, 66–97
Shapero v. Kentucky Bar Association, 177
"slide of death" advertising, exploitation of fears by marketers and, 182
smoking, workplace privacy and, 54
soapbox factor, in business ethics, 6
soft factor, in business ethics, 6
Solomon, Robert, 224
Sommers, Christina Hoff, 36
South Africa, divestment from, 8
speech, freedom of: advertising and, 178; employee's right to, 46, 47, 48
Sprint, 145
Stark, Andrew, 224
Stead, Jerre L., 134
Steelcase Inc., 145–146
Steinreich, Joseph, 137
Sun Co., 204
Swanson, John, 220–221
syringe scare, handling of, by PepsiCo Inc., 120–121

tampering: handling of syringe scare by PepsiCo Inc. and, 120–121; handling of Tylenol poisoning scare by Johnson & Johnson and, 112, 126, 219
Tanklow, Karen, 137–138
Tannen, Deborah, 74
teleological theory, 64
Tenneco Gas Co., 138
termination-at-will doctrine, 46, 48
theft, employee, 9, 46, 49, 59–61, 62–65, 81–82
Tillich, Paul, 95–102
total quality management (TQM), 41, 204
TransAmerica Mailing Inc., 182
Trans-Union Credit Information, 46
TRW, Inc., 46
TS Print Center, 147
TV test, 7
TW Services Inc., 79–80
Tylenol poisoning scare, Johnson & Johnson's handling of, 112, 126, 219

United Telephone of Florida (UTF), 145
unintentional moral managers, 232–233
unions, 49, 150
United States, business ethics in, vs.
  Europe and Japan, 163–167
utilitarian principle, 7, 12, 15, 17, 64, 228,
  234

Valdez Principles, 239
values: corporate, statements, 29–31;
  culture and, 170–173
*Virginia State Board of Pharmacy v. Virginia
  Citizens Consumer Council,* 176–181

Vitti, Bernie, 94
Vocational Rehabilitation Act of 1973, 151
volunteerism, 239
Volvo Cars of North America, 182–183

wage gap, Equal Pay Act and, 73–74
Wallace, Doug, 57–58, 94, 123
Wal-Mart, 54
waste management, 111
"Whistleblower's Protection Act," 104
whistleblowing, 11, 47, 95–96, 97, 99,
  103–108, 164–165

white-collar crime, 32
Winer, Michael, 146
WITT Company, 144–145
women: Equal Pay Act and, 73–74; sexual
  harassment and, 66–69, 70–72, 96; in
  workplace, 139–143
WRAP (Waste Reduction Always Pays)
  program, of Dow Chemical, 203
wrongful discharge, 49
Wydman, Marcy R., 144–145

Zeitler, Eddie L., 52

Credits/
Acknowledgments

Cover design by Charles Vitelli

1. Ethics, Values, and Social Responsibility in Business
Facing overview—Alcoa photo.

**2. Employees and the Workplace: Ethical Issues and
Dilemmas**
Facing overview—Buick Motor Division photo.

3. Business and Society
Facing overview—United Nations photo by Rick Grunbaum.

4. Ethics and Social Responsibility in the Marketplace
Facing overview—General Motors photo.

**5. Developing the Future Ethos and Social Responsibility of
Business**
Facing overview—United States Steel Corporation photo.

PHOTOCOPY THIS PAGE!!!*

ANNUAL EDITIONS ARTICLE REVIEW FORM

■ NAME: _____ DATE: _____

■ TITLE AND NUMBER OF ARTICLE: _____

■ BRIEFLY STATE THE MAIN IDEA OF THIS ARTICLE: _____
_____
_____
_____
_____

■ LIST THREE IMPORTANT FACTS THAT THE AUTHOR USES TO SUPPORT THE MAIN IDEA:
_____
_____
_____
_____
_____

■ WHAT INFORMATION OR IDEAS DISCUSSED IN THIS ARTICLE ARE ALSO DISCUSSED IN YOUR TEXTBOOK OR OTHER READING YOU HAVE DONE? LIST THE TEXTBOOK CHAPTERS AND PAGE NUMBERS:
_____
_____
_____
_____
_____

■ LIST ANY EXAMPLES OF BIAS OR FAULTY REASONING THAT YOU FOUND IN THE ARTICLE:
_____
_____
_____
_____

■ LIST ANY NEW TERMS/CONCEPTS THAT WERE DISCUSSED IN THE ARTICLE AND WRITE A SHORT DEFINITION:
_____
_____
_____
_____

*Your instructor may require you to use this Annual Editions Article Review Form in any number of ways: for articles that are assigned, for extra credit, as a tool to assist in developing assigned papers, or simply for your own reference. Even if it is not required, we encourage you to photocopy and use this page; you'll find that reflecting on the articles will greatly enhance the information from your text.

ANNUAL EDITIONS:
BUSINESS ETHICS 94/95
Article Rating Form

We Want Your Advice

Here is an opportunity for you to have direct input into the next revision of this volume. We would like you to rate each of the 53 articles listed below, using the following scale:

1. **Excellent: should definitely be retained**
2. **Above average: should probably be retained**
3. **Below average: should probably be deleted**
4. **Poor: should definitely be deleted**

Your ratings will play a vital part in the next revision. So please mail this prepaid form to us just as soon as you complete it.
Thanks for your help!

Annual Editions revisions depend on two major opinion sources: one is our Advisory Board, listed in the front of this volume, which works with us in scanning the thousands of articles published in the public press each year; the other is you—the person actually using the book. Please help us and the users of the next edition by completing the prepaid article rating form on this page and returning it to us. Thank you.

Rating	Article	Rating	Article
	1. Business Ethics: A Manager's Primer		28. Promises to Keep
	2. Principles of Business Ethics: Their Role in Decision Making and an Initial Consensus		29. The Moral Audit
			30. The New Crisis in Business Ethics
			31. Work and Family
	3. Integrity: An Essential Executive Quality		32. The (R)Evolution of the American Woman
	4. Ethics in Practice		33. Business Rethinks, Refines, Recycles, and Recoups
	5. State Your Values, Hold the Hot Air		
	6. Understanding Pressures That Cause Unethical Behavior in Business		34. Combating Drugs in the Workplace
			35. AIDS in the Workplace: The Pandemic Firms Want to Ignore
	7. To Pose a Question of Ethics		
	8. The Corporate Ethics Test		36. Social Responsibility and Need for Low Cost Clash at Stride Rite
	9. Balanced Protection Policies		
	10. What the Boss Knows about You		37. Is U.S. Business Obsessed with Ethics?
	11. A Reluctant Invasion		38. Companies Clean Up
	12. In-House Hackers: Rigging Computers for Fraud or Malice Is Often an Inside Job		39. Ethics: Are Standards Lower Overseas?
			40. Marketing by Professionals: Some Ethical Issues and Prescriptions
	13. Ethics and Employee Theft		
	14. Six Myths of Sexual Harassment		41. Marketers Exploit People's Fears of Everything
	15. Sexual Harassment: What to Do		
	16. Three Decades after the Equal Pay Act, Women's Wages Remain Far from Parity		42. Strategic Green Marketing
			43. Pinto Redux?
	17. The Americans with Disabilities Act: The Cutting Edge of Managing Diversity		44. The Ethics of Bootstrapping
			45. Practical Applications of Healthcare Marketing Ethics
	18. Denny's: The Stain That Isn't Coming Out		
			46. America's Hamburger Helper
	19. Torn between Halo and Horns		47. Who Scores Best on the Environment
	20. After the Layoff: Closing the Barn Door before All the Horses Are Gone		48. The Challenge of Ethical Behavior in Organizations
	21. Companies Discover That Some Firings Backfire into Costly Defamation Suits		49. Creating Ethical Corporate Structures
			50. How to Be Ethical, and Still Come Top
	22. "You're Fired"		51. The Pyramid of Corporate Social Responsibility: Toward the Moral Management of Organizational Stakeholders
	23. Changing Unethical Organizational Behavior		
	24. Why *Your* Company Should Have a Whistle-blowing Policy		
			52. Another View of the Golden Rule
	25. Implementing Business Ethics		53. Is Business Waking Up?
	26. Ethical Judgment		
	27. Pepsi Faces Problem in Trying to Contain Syringe Scare		

(Continued on next page)

ABOUT YOU

Name_____ Date_____

Are you a teacher? ☐ Or student? ☐

Your School Name _____

Department _____

Address _____

City _____ State _____ Zip _____

School Telephone # _____

YOUR COMMENTS ARE IMPORTANT TO US!

Please fill in the following information:

For which course did you use this book? _____

Did you use a text with this Annual Edition? ☐ yes ☐ no

The title of the text? _____

What are your general reactions to the Annual Editions concept?

Have you read any particular articles recently that you think should be included in the next edition?

Are there any articles you feel should be replaced in the next edition? Why?

Are there other areas that you feel would utilize an Annual Edition?

May we contact you for editorial input?

May we quote you from above?

No Postage
Necessary
if Mailed
in the
United States

ANNUAL EDITIONS: BUSINESS ETHICS 94/95

BUSINESS REPLY MAIL

First Class   Permit No. 84   Guilford, CT

Postage will be paid by addressee

The Dushkin Publishing Group, Inc.
Sluice Dock
DPG **Guilford, Connecticut 06437**